Conyngham Crawford Taylor

The Queen's Jubilee and Toronto

Conyngham Crawford Taylor

The Queen's Jubilee and Toronto

ISBN/EAN: 9783743318496

Manufactured in Europe, USA, Canada, Australia, Japa

Cover: Foto ©ninafisch / pixelio.de

Manufactured and distributed by brebook publishing software (www.brebook.com)

Conyngham Crawford Taylor

The Queen's Jubilee and Toronto

THE

QUEEN'S JUBILEE

AND

TORONTO "CALLED BACK"

FROM 1887 TO 1847.

ITS WONDERFUL GROWTH AND PROGRESS, ESPECIALLY AS AN IMPORTING CENTRE,
WITH THE DEVELOPMENT OF ITS MANUFACTURING INDUSTRIES;
AND REMINISCENCES EXTENDING OVER THE FOUR DECENNIAL PERIODS,
FROM 1847 TO 1887, INCLUDING
THE INTRODUCTION OF THE BONDING SYSTEM THROUGH THE UNITED STATES.

THIS REVISED EDITION

CONTAINS THE PROGRESS OF THE CITY FROM 1886 TO 1887, THE OPENING AND
CLOSING OF THE LONDON AND COLONIAL EXHIBITION, WITH A FULL
ACCOUNT OF THE CELEBRATION OF THE QUEEN'S JUBILEE
IN LONDON, TORONTO AND OTHER PLACES
THROUGHOUT THE WORLD.

With Illustrations.

ALSO A VIEW OF THE PROPOSED ESPLANADE WITH BRIDGES, BY KIVAS TULLY,
ESQ., IN 1850, VIEWS OF THE CITY IN 1817 AND 1880, AND A
MAP OF TORONTO.

BY

CONYNGHAM CRAWFORD TAYLOR,
Of Her Majesty's Customs.

TORONTO:
PUBLISHED FOR THE AUTHOR BY
WILLIAM BRIGGS, 78 & 80 KING STREET EAST.
1887.

HON. JOHN BEVERLEY ROBINSON, LIEUTENANT-GOVERNOR OF ONTARIO.

TO

The Hon. John Beverley Robinson,

LIEUTENANT-GOVERNOR OF ONTARIO,

(SON OF THE LATE HON. SIR JOHN BEVERLEY ROBINSON, BARONET, CHIEF JUSTICE OF UPPER CANADA),

WHO,

As Private Citizen, Mayor, Member of Parliament, or, as at Present, the Representative of

HER MAJESTY, QUEEN VICTORIA,

In the Premier Province of the Dominion, has always Exhibited the Warmest Interest in all that has tended to Promote the Growth and Progress of Toronto, whether in

Arts, Sciences, Literature, Religion, Trade, Commerce, or Manufactures,

These Pages are Respectfully Dedicated by

THE AUTHOR.

PREFACE TO THE REVISED EDITION.

In the Chapter of Introduction I stated that "nothing would appear of which the writer was not an eye-witness," and that statement has been verified. In the present edition it is necessary to explain that the eighty additional pages contain, chiefly, accounts of the Indian and Colonial Exhibition and the celebration of the Queen's Jubilee, and I had hoped to have been present in England at either one or the other. Circumstances, however, over which I had no control, prevented me from seeing them, but what is given has been carefully selected from the most authentic sources, which are, however, so various as well as numerous, that it would be both tedious and unprofitable to credit them to their authors, especially as in weaving the web the original threads have in some instances changed their texture, though it is hoped without losing either their substance or their brilliancy. Being chiefly facts, however, and many, if not all, of a valuable character, the success of the first edition leads me to hope the present will be found still more useful and interesting. Many of the incidents related previously are now even more appropriate, having much in relation to the life and history of Her Majesty the Queen, from personal knowledge, although at the time not written with any view to the present Jubilee celebration.

The progress of Toronto during the past year has had a full share of attention, and the statistics as to its growth and prosperity as a Commercial and Manufacturing Centre which are given, cannot fail to interest everyone who is loyal to the fair City of Toronto.

C. C. TAYLOR.

TORONTO, *July, 1887.*

Page 74, for George Sherwood, read Samuel Sherwood.
" 118, for H. C. Dwight, read H. P. Dwight.
" 164, for cook's gallery, read cook's galley.
" 263, for Morgan Baldwin, read Henry G. Baldwin.
" 323, for H. B. Chaffin, read H. B. Claflin.
" 387, for deprive, read deprives.

———

A reader should sit down to a book, especially of the miscellaneous kind, as a well-behaved visitor does to a banquet. The master of the feast exerts himself to satisfy all his guests, but if, after all his care, there should be something or other put on the table that does not suit this or that person's taste, they politely pass it over without noticing the circumstance, and commend other dishes, that they may not distress their host or throw any damp on his spirits.—*Erasmus.*

CONTENTS.

PAGE

CHAPTER OF INTRODUCTION—Not an Autobiography, nor a Book of Travels, nor a Romance, nor yet a Political Dissertation of Free Trade or Protection, but a Narrative of Facts from Personal Knowledge and Observation—Early Days—Todd, Burns & Co. and Pim Bros. & Co., Dublin—Incidents from 1841 to 1847—Daniel O'Connell—Something like Fenianism—Father Matthew—Evangelical Alliance—Dublin Castle—Lord-Lieutenants—Reviews in Phœnix Park—Holiday Excursions—Donnybrook Fair—St. Patrick's Cathedral—Emigration—Departure for New York—First Impressions of New York—From New York to Toronto—Arrival.   9–46

1847 TO 1857.

First Impressions of Toronto—Shopping—Appearance of Toronto in 1847—Gossip—Incidents in 1847—Richmond Street Wesleyan Church—Rev. James Caughey—A. & S. Nordheimer—Toronto Post Office—Toronto Gas and Water Works—The Circulating Medium—Store Pay—Retail Importing—Wholesale Trade in 1847—Prominent Men in 1847—Lord Elgin—Toronto Police Force—First Strike in Toronto—Immigrant Fever—Bathing—Great Fire on King Street in 1848—Establishment of Celebration of Queen's Birthday—First Retail Dry Goods Store on Yonge Street—Selling on the Sterling Cost—Business Houses in Toronto 1847-1850—Prominent Men in 1850—A Tour of Observation—First Return Visit to Europe—Windsor Castle and Queen Victoria—Commencement of Commercial Travelling in Canada—Public Institutions—Financial Affairs in 1850—Toronto in 1850—Bonding System via United States—First Great World's Fair in 1851—Turning the First Sod of the Northern Railway—Mayor Bowes—Lady Elgin—Tariff in 1850-1851—The Industrial Crystal Palace—The Esplanade—Rossin House—Mercantile Agencies—Erastus Wiman—Paris in 1855—Passports—Queen Victoria and Prince Albert in Paris—Procession on the Boulevards—The Queen at Versailles—Departure from Paris—Incidents During the Queen's Visit—The Imperial Cent Gardes—Paris Universal Exhibition—The Queen Opening Parliament—Great Peace Rejoicings in London—Fireworks in Green Park—Great Naval Review at Portsmouth—The Queen's Arrival Fleet—Close of the First Decade   47–144

1857 TO 1867.

Financial Crisis in 1857—Desjardins Canal Accident—Art Treasures Exhibition in Manchester—Queen's Reception in the Building—Royal Mail Cunard Steamer "Persia"—Visit of the Prince of Wales to Canada, 1860—Death of Prince Albert—Buying in Europe, its Pleasures and Responsibilities—Fenian Raid, 1866—Decimal Currency and American Silver 145-176

1867 TO 1877.

Confederation—Paris Universal Exposition, 1867—Fenianism in Manchester—Assassination of Thomas D'Arcy McGee, M.P.—Tariffs of England, United States and Canada from 1860 to 1876—Metropolitan Church—Toronto in 1870, 1871—Return of Rev. Dr. Punshon to England—St. James' Cathedral Clock 177-194

1877 TO 1886.

Protection versus a Revenue Tariff—Exhibition Buildings—Marquis of Lorne and H.R.H. the Princess Louise—Farewell Visit of the Vice-regal Party—Arrival of the Marquis of Lansdowne—First Visit to Toronto—The Semi-Centennial Celebration—Captain Joseph Dutton, R.N.—Population of British Cities—Comparative Population of Seven Canadian Cities—Climate of Toronto—Snow—The Toboggan—Departure of Toronto Troops for the North-West—Return of the Toronto Contingent—Arrival at North Toronto—How to see Toronto in 1886—Toronto the Centre of the Dominion—Population and Assessment Returns—Toronto Street—Population of Toronto at Different Periods—Value of Buildings Erected During the Years 1882-1885—Commercial Travellers' Association—Toronto Custom House—Civil Service Examinations—Total Imports to Toronto since 1849—Coal Imported to Toronto in 1885—Coal Produced at Nanaimo, B.C.—The Imports of Toronto Compared with Cities in the United States—Exports from Toronto in 1885.. 195-238

1886.

Introductory—Ontario Assembly in 1886—State Dinner at Government House—Toronto Board of Trade—Banks in Toronto—Public Companies—Assets of Banks in Canada—Toronto Gas Works—Toronto Water Works—Meat Markets and Horses of Toronto—Toronto a Manufacturing City—Toronto Manufactures—Percentage of Growth of Manufactures in 50 Years—J. & J. Taylor, Toronto Safe Works—Taylor Bros.—Brown Bros. & Co.—Rolph

Contents.

1886—Continued.

PAGE.

Smith & Co.—Heating of Buildings in Toronto E. & C. Gurney Co. (Limited)—The Grand "Trunk" House of the Dominion—H. E. Clarke & Co.—The Queen's Hotel 239-259

Toronto's Natural Advantages—A City of Churches—Ministers Since 1847—The Salvation Temple and Army—An Educational Centre—Great North-Western Telegraph Co. 260-268

Toronto a Musical City—F. H. Torrington—Chamber Music—Jenny Lind—Mrs. John Beverley Robinson and Mrs. J. G. Beard—The Musical Festival—Vocal Society—Choral Society—Philharmonic Society—St. Michael's and St. Basil's—The Manufacture of Pianos in Toronto—Heintzman & Co. Mason & Risch—Octavius Newcombe & Co. Lansdowne Piano Co. 271-294

Benevolent Institutions—The Lakeside Home—Toronto a Literary City—The *Globe* and *Mail*—The *World* and *News*—The *Evening Telegram*—The *Christian Guardian* and Methodist Book and Publishing House—The Free Library King Street in 1886—Messrs. R. Walker & Sons—W. A. Murray & Co.—The Art of Pottery—Mr. Glover Harrison—New Buildings Approaching Completion—Buildings Proposed to be Erected this Year—The Manning Arcade—New Bank of Montreal 295-314

Toronto Post Office in 1886—A Place of Residence—Governors-General of Canada since 1847—Lieutenant-Governors of Ontario—Mayors of Toronto—Extent of City—Toronto Street Railway Company.... 315-319

Street Traffic—The Model Wholesale Dry Goods Warehouse of the Dominion—Corsets—The Telfer & Harold Manufacturing Co.—The Lace and Embroidery Trade—White, Joselin & Co.—Yonge Street in 1886—Messrs. T. Eaton & Co—Great Increase in Imports—The Arcade—Summer Resorts—Queen's Park—Exhibition Park—Lorne Park—Canadian Pacific Railway—Dominion Day, 1886—Toronto Zoological Gardens 320-336

The Indian and Colonial Exhibition—Opening Ceremonies—International Exhibitions—Rebellion of 1837—Toronto's Loyalty—The Princess Victoria—Queen Victoria's Accession—The Coronation—The Queen's Crown—The Coronation Chair—Regalia—The Coronation Medal—The Queen and Her Family—The Heir Apparent—The Royal Household—Civil List—The Queen's Dominions 337-369

1887.
THE QUEEN'S JUBILEE.

The Queen's Jubilee—India—Fifty Years' Progress—Jubilee Exhibitions, Manchester, Liverpool, Saltaire and Newcastle—Opening of the People's Palace—London—Various Countries—Canada—Toronto—Dominion Day, Jubilee Celebrations—Toronto in 1887—Wyld, Grasett & Darling—Rossin House—St. Alban's Cathedral—Importers—Manufacturers—Exhibition of Manufactures 370-409

Sherbourne Street Methodist Church—Proposed Drives Round the City Trans-Pacific Steamers—New Buildings in Toronto—Precious Metals in the World—New Lieutenant-Governor—Statistics of Toronto—Steamers, a Comparison—British and Canadian Railways—Remarkable Features in the Jubilee Procession—The Children's *Fete* in Hyde Park—Jubilee Choral Concert 409-420

LIST OF ILLUSTRATIONS.

	PAGE
Victoria, Queen and Empress .... *Frontispiece*	
Hon. John Beverley Robinson, Ex-Lieut.-Governor of Ontario	4
Map of Toronto	8
View of Toronto, C.W., in 1847........................	47
Knox Church in 1848	79
Windsor Castle	89
Crystal Palace	102
St. James' Cathedral	105
Toronto Esplanade	110
Place de la Concorde, Paris........................	121
Notre Dame Cathedral, Paris	130
Former Post Office (Present Office of Receiver-General)	143
Government House and St. Andrew's Church	158
Metropolitan Church	187
Exhibition Building....	197
The Marquis of Lansdowne	202
Rossin House	221
Knox College....	222
Normal School	225
Toronto Custom House	231
View of Toronto, 1886	239
Osgoode Hall..........................	240
The Queen's Hotel	259
St. Andrew's Church, King Street West	262
The Salvation Army Temple	265
University of Toronto	267
Canadian Institute, Richmond Street West..............	269
F. H. Torrington, Esq........... ....;	277
The Lakeside Home.........................	296
The *Globe* Building	301
The *Mail* Building	302
The *Telegram* Building	304
Rev. Egerton Ryerson, D.D....	307
Toronto Post Office..	317
John Macdonald & Co.'s Warehouse.....	322
Yonge Street Arcade	331
His Royal Highness the Prince of Wales..............	342
Hon. Sir Charles Tupper, G.C.M.G., C.B	354
New Warehouse of Wyld, Grasett & Darling	394
Cathedral of St. Alban the Martyr......................	398
Permanent Exhibition of Manufactures..................	408
Sherbourne Street Methodist Church...............	410
Bank of Montreal, Toronto	413

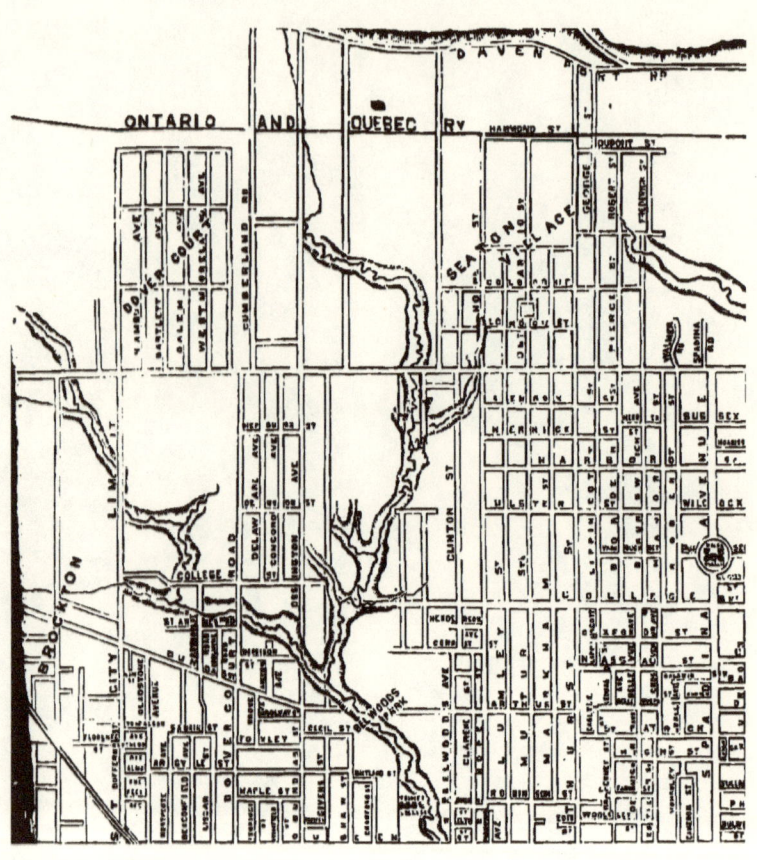

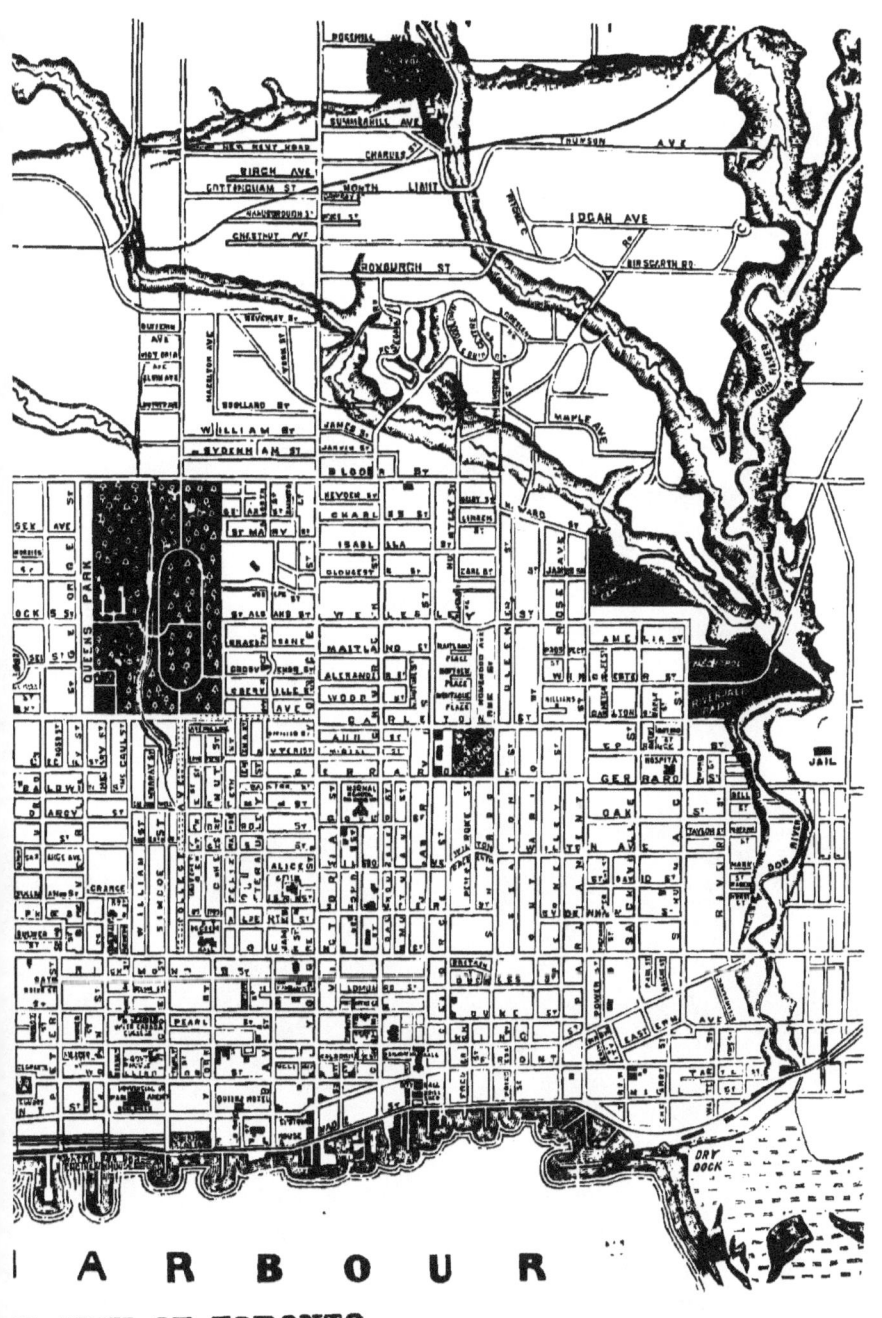

TORONTO "CALLED BACK."

CHAPTER OF INTRODUCTION.

I do not intend to write an autobiography. In "calling back" from memory the facts and incidents to be related, there was no intention of their ever meeting the public eye, but they were written partly for recreation and partly for personal and family gratification.

As, however, nothing will appear of which the writer was not an eye-witness, it may be that in narrating scenes of life in Dublin, or in describing grand sights witnessed in London, or Paris, or the great Naval Review at Portsmouth, the interest of some reader may be so awakened, on either side of the Atlantic, as to lead him to turn to an account of the growth and progress of Toronto.

Since the writer's first trip to Europe from this city he has influenced a number of families to make it their home, and they in turn have influenced others; and should in the future any capitalist, manufacturer, or any other desirable citizen of any other city or country, be induced to adopt Canada, and especially Toronto, as his future place of residence, and contribute in any way to its wealth and population, his object will be attained.

Nor do I intend to write a book of travels. There are gifted individuals who, having made a trip across the Atlantic, and "run through" from Liverpool to London, then over the

Continent, and perhaps gone round the world in 90 days, have the faculty of writing so easily, that on their return home they write a book; but the present writer makes no pretensions to such literary ability, although, from an average of travels of 10,000 miles a year, by sea and land, for many years, materials might be furnished for such a purpose.

One could tell of passages made in nearly all the old Cunard Royal Mail steamers,—the *Asia, Africa, Arabia, America, Europa, Niagara,* and *Persia,* the last of the ocean paddle-wheel steamers crossing the Atlantic (the *Scotia* only excepted); with recollections of the celebrated Commanders, who had the proud boast of never having lost a life,—Lott, Stone, Leitch, Harrison, Shannon, and Commodore Judkins; also of the splendid steamers of the Inman Line, then of our own Allan Line, and occasional trips in the "White Star;" of hairbreadth 'scapes from rocks and icebergs, of storms and winds, from the gentle zephyr through all the gradations of ships' "log" record,—light and strong breezes, half gales and whole gales, thunder storms, hurricanes, and tremendous hurricanes, with an occasional cyclone, described by a writer as "a magnificent scene. The whole ocean, from the central speck on which he stood to the vast vanishing circle of the horizon, as one boundless, boiling cauldron.

"Millions of waves simultaneously leaping in thunder from the abyss and rearing themselves into blue mountain peaks, capped with white foam and sparkling in the sunlight for a moment, to be swallowed up in the darkness of the roaring deep the next. A lashing, tossing, heaving, falling, foaming, glancing rise and fall of liquid mountains and valleys, awful but ravishing to look upon."

And then might turn to beautiful, calm weather, pleasant company, music, games, mock trials; splendid bills of fare—four meals a day, with every delicacy that money could procure; refined society, comprising distinguished statesmen, ambassadors with their suites, celebrated divines and historians, poets and men of leisure, merchant princes and buyers, representing all the large mercantile houses, some of the best patrons of the

Chapter of Introduction.

ocean steamers; also of people of all nationalities, English, Irish, Scotch, American, French, German, Italian, Portuguese, Turks, Spaniards, Russians, and Japanese; of the hardships of the steerage as well as the luxury of the saloon; all of which might make a readable volume.

In the hands of the distinguished novelist, Wilkie Collins, whom I have heard read from his own works in this city, the facts with which I could furnish him might be woven into a romance equal in interest to the "Woman in White."

The inimitable Dickens, whom I have also heard and by whose tombstone—which, amongst the numberless monuments in the Poets' Corner, Westminster Abbey, in memory of the great poets, essayists, novelists and dramatists in past centuries, is most remarkable for its plainness, and without any epitaph but "Dickens"—I afterwards stood, could have produced out of the materials a book quite as true to life as "Martin Chuzzlewit."

Or the lamented Hugh Conway might have given to the world another volume quite as popular as "Called Back;" but simple facts and "a plain, unvarnished tale" are all that are offered in these pages.

A residence for several years in Lancashire, with an opportunity of seeing the working of the principle of Free Trade; afterwards six years travelling through the United States, and sending large orders to be shipped from England to the principal cities, from Baltimore to St. Louis, in the face of a tariff which averaged 60 per cent., and watching the growth of the manufacturing industries during that time; and, in addition to all this, the experience of an importer to Toronto, with a tariff gradually increasing from 12½ per cent. to 25 per cent., ought to furnish some valuable information.

But in writing on the growth and progress of Toronto, it is best to allow every person to draw his own conclusions as to whether our city has been benefited by the multiplication of manufacturing establishments, as well as to the question of how far she is indebted to the present policy for their success.

To go over the ground taken by those who so ably and

beautifully described the progress of Toronto in its civic and political phases during the

SEMI-CENTENNIAL

from 1834 to 1884, would be quite superfluous. The programme of the celebration itself forms a splendid record of the events which transpired during that period.

The grand tableaux in the daily processions, illustrating the progress of the city, from the rude and uncivilized to the high state of refinement at the present time, were most striking and impressive.

If, however, the growth and progress of Toronto as an importing centre has been given, the writer has never seen it, and yet, in this respect, there are distinct marks of contrast between the present and the past which are not only striking but marvellous.

Perhaps, with the exception of London and Chicago, no other city in the world has made such rapid strides in the march of progress, and this it will be my endeavor to show to the best of my ability.

Early Days.

"I have observed, that a reader seldom peruses a book with pleasure till he knows whether the writer of it be a black or a fair man."—*Addison.*

My uncle, Dr. Conyngham Crawford, having refused to accept a commission in the British Army offered by the Marquis of Conyngham, on account of religious scruples on the part of his parents, adopted the medical profession, and came to the United States, where he became a celebrated physician and lecturer in one of the medical colleges in Philadelphia. Having no prospect of a family, he expressed the wish that my parents should call me after him, partly from a wish to perpetuate the name in our branch of the family, and with the intention of leaving me his property should I survive him.

When school days came I was, at his request, educated with a view of qualifying for the same profession. Having mastered the course of classics required for the examination at Apothe-

Chapter of Introduction.

caries' Hall, Dublin, which was necessary as preparatory for the studies for the degree of Medical Doctor, I was about to enter for examination, when, in my thirteenth year, news came of my uncle's death.

The letters from the executors contained a copy of his will, in which all his property, real and personal, was left to me.

Glad to find that I should not be compelled to continue the study of medicine, which I never fancied, I decided to enter into a mercantile life, and through the introduction of a personal and intimate friend of Mr. Todd's, soon entered the celebrated house of Todd, Burns & Co., the youngest lad who had ever entered on a salary.

As I may describe another of these splendid establishments, for which Dublin has since become so famous, I shall only give a general idea of this house, so well known to all travellers from America.

When I entered there, in 1840, it was the largest house in Great Britain; the house of Shoolbred & Co., of Tottenham-Court Road, London, being its only equal as to the number of employees, while inferior in amount of trade done.

Including fifty well-educated lads from Scotland, there were 400 living on the premises, and for comfort of domestic arrangements, strict system, and thorough discipline, the house could not be excelled in the world at the time.

There being an opinion in America that apprentices to the dry goods trade in the Old Country are badly paid, I shall just state the terms on which these boys were engaged and kept for five years. In addition to first-class board, with comfortable bed-rooms, use of reading-rooms and magnificent library, each boy was paid £5 the first year, and £5 advance the succeeding four years, when they were at liberty to remain or leave for a better situation.

The oversight of their moral and commercial training was particularly attended to, and a schoolmaster kept in the house for their general education. This was attended to every evening in a splendid school-room devoted to the purpose, with every school requisite.

Todd, Burns & Co.

The house of Todd, Burns & Co. is situated at the corner of Mary and Jervis Streets, and within sight of Nelson's Pillar in Sackville Street and the General Post Office at the corner.

Along this street any fine day might be seen a long line of carriages, representing the wealth, beauty and fashion of the city, only surpassed by the brilliant display of equipages on the occasion of a levee, drawing-room, or ball at the Castle.

A walk to the Post Office, at the corner of Sackville and Mary Streets, at nine o'clock any night, afforded a most enjoyable sight, especially in summer when it was clear daylight. Nine Royal Mail coaches stood in the Post Office yard to receive the mails, each with coachman and guard in scarlet and gold. A gunsmith was always in attendance to examine the cavalry pistols and blunderbus of each guard to see they were in perfect order, and while the clock was striking the hour the thoroughbreds, four-in-hand, prancing and rearing, emerged from the yard into Sackville Street, while the guards vied with each other in their performances on their key bugles. In Sackville Street the horses were let go to do their ten miles an hour, a beautiful sight to behold.

While a large wholesale trade was done, the chief feature of the establishment was the extensive retail branch, conducted strictly on the departmental system, each department managed by a buyer.

The system of introducing customers to the different departments was managed by Messrs. Todd and Burns personally, assisted by a large staff of superintendents, the principals giving special attention to the humbler classes, while the more aristocratic were looked after by the superintendents.

The domestic arrangements for the accommodation of so many young men were very complete, and the diet excellent; whether the moral tone was improved or not by the use of beer, a barrel of that beverage was made to disappear every day.

The house of Todd, Burns & Co. still maintains its high rank amongst the great establishments of Britain.

Chapter of Introduction. 15

I left on account of greater inducements to assist in the establishment of the house of

Pim Bros. & Co.

This firm, composed of three brothers, Jonathan, William, and Thomas, a leading family of the Society of Friends, had been in an exclusively wholesale business in William Street up to the year 1841.

At this time an old military barracks in South Great St. George's Street, off Dame Street, and in the vicinity of Stephens' Green, Merrion Square, and other fashionable localities, was guarded by sentries, when Messrs. Pim Bros.—thinking an establishment on the south side of the Liffey, similar to that of Todd Burns & Co. on the north, would be equally successful—conceived the idea of buying the property, which was about to be abandoned by the Government. They were not long in putting their ideas into practice. Having turned the premises into a warehouse, they set about to engage competent young men to conduct the business, and as even a year's experience in the house of Todd, Burns & Co. was a great recommendation, I had only to make application to get an engagement; and in this way twenty-five were engaged, the writer being the youngest. With this staff, from which the buyers and managers were selected, we commenced to lay the foundation of what in seven years became the model house of Great Britain, and has continued to grow ever since, till at the present time it has attained to the same position there that the house of A. T. Stewart & Co. occupied for so many years in America.

The principle on which this great house was founded was to throw the whole responsibility on the heads of the departments, the firm not interfering in any way except to supply unlimited capital, and allow the results of each stock-taking to show the merits or demerits of the managers.

When fully organized there were twenty-two regular departments, the business of each being kept as distinct as if in different buildings, and as this was the first house in which this system was discovered and applied, a brief description of its workings may be interesting and useful to some who have not yet adopted it.

The difficulty always had been, that where a salesman went from one department to another he got the credit of the sale, while the department in which the goods were sold had nothing to show for it. This defect still existed in Todd, Burns & Co. and the large London houses.

To cure this defect, a system of furnishing to each department bill-heads, with the name of department printed at top, was introduced. To each of these bill-heads a cheque at the bottom was attached with name of department to correspond. When a sale was made, no matter to what department the salesman belonged, these cheques were filed in the cashier's desk during the day, and the next morning a lot of boys set to work, with large sheets prepared for the purpose, entering every amount to credit of each of these twenty-two departments; thus showing daily, weekly, monthly, and at stock-taking—semi-annually—an exact return of each department's business, and of each salesman's work during that period. Of course, the goods had been previously charged to each department in the counting-house.

To complete this system, when one salesman went through a number of departments, which was sometimes allowed, as in the case of a friend, bill-heads were provided, with "general" cheques, on which the amount sold in each department was distinctly stated, the entry boys being careful to separate these amounts and distribute them under their proper headings; and further, each department had a locked till for coppers, of which one man had the sole charge, and who, every day, emptied the contents into linen bags, all stamped with name of department and credited to each accordingly. As no bill was given for less than sixpence, and the giving a bill over that amount was compulsory, change was got at the desk, and the amount of sale dropped into these tills, so that the returns were exact.

It was the duty of each manager—or, in his absence, of the second in charge—every morning, to examine the bill-heads, after distribution by the porters, to see that they did not get mixed in being taken from the lockers.

As the buying is at the foundation of every mercantile business, buying the best goods from the best houses was the great object, and proved to be an extraordinary success in this house.

As the wholesale and retail branches were under the same buyer's management, his responsibility was so much the greater; and when a buyer decided to visit his particular market he had no one to consult, having a *carte blanche* to go when he thought proper, and buy just what he considered right.

Buyers were supposed to spend a guinea a day while on their trip, with the price of a pint of wine extra, which was invariably charged at all the commercial hotels, whether they used it or not. It being the prerogative of the president at the dinner-table to order for each guest, it would be entirely *infra dig.* for any house to attempt to violate so time-honored a custom, even when the principals happened, as in our case, to be the very leading "Friends" in the country. The custom still prevails in all commercial rooms at hotels in England.

These commercial dinners are always supposed to be enjoyed after the business of the day is over, and if goods were opened that appeared to have had less than the usual care in selection, or were a little inferior in value to the buyer's usual purchases, it was a sort of standing joke that Mr. So-and-so had bought such a lot of goods "after dinner."

The inducements held out to buyers by interested manufacturers required a firm resolution to refuse all sorts of presents which were offered, and which, if accepted, placed him under an obligation, greater or less, to purchase.

The writer has had most liberal offers, sometimes so far as to pay all his expenses visiting celebrated castles in Warwickshire, etc., all of which he felt it his duty most positively to decline.

The system of "shopping" as practised in America was positively unknown to us.

The rule was that no customer should be allowed to leave the house without being served. This bore heavily on young lads just leaving home, having the fear of dismissal before their eyes; and yet it was almost invariably enforced, the only exception being by reference to a superintendent.

It was assumed that, as there was no restriction imposed on the buyers, they were supposed to be constantly supplied with every line of goods in their department, and every line complete in widths, shades, prices and variety, and in this particular alone was there ever a question put to the buyers.

If a salesman was asked why he had not sold any particular article and he said it was not in stock, while this was no excuse for him, as he was expected to sell something else, the buyer was generally asked why he had not the article in stock; and, having full scope to order or personally select at all times, no excuse was accepted, but it was looked upon simply as to that extent neglectful on his part.

As to the control of his assistants, it might be said to be almost absolute. The orders were, if they did not suit in every respect not to continue their services. For years the writer felt this a delicate position to be placed in, as all his assistants were older than himself; and it being the custom to redu the number at the dull season—and the heads were expected to name the one or two that must go—he had the satisfaction of never having one in his department discharged during six years, always managing to have them changed to another department.

To explain the absence of the shopping system it is necessary to state that, the rules of these houses being known, no person appeared to enter the house except with the intention of buying. The ladies of the higher classes came with their lists all prepared, and were shown from department to department till all was selected; so, through all classes, there was no time for bantering, as there was no idea of anything but a fixed price. So, with this throng of customers from morning till night, the business moved like a piece of machinery or clockwork. No person was allowed to remain in the business who violated any rule, and no allowance was made for even the slightest delinquency, the system of fines being the slightest punishment for such delinquency—after these, dismissal.

Chapter of Introduction.   19

The rule of serving every customer being enforced led to wonderful expedients to accomplish the object.

Frequently ladies declining to buy an article at the counter, yet purchasing the exact duplicate when brought from the wholesale department, salesmen have often been heard to boast that they could sell black for white, which they often did. No person was allowed to stand idle for a moment, and no "buzzing" or "clubbing" was allowed. Every head of a department was expected to see every man constantly employed. The writer's wholesale department upstairs occupied a position from which a view of over one hundred young men could be obtained at any time, and this was a favorite spot of the governor's, where he could observe all without been seen. In chatting he would sometimes say, "Who is that young man counting the flies on the ceiling?" if the young man happened to show an indolent manner.

The number of salesmen was so great, and the changes so frequent, the heads of the firm scarcely knew even their names, except those of the managers.

The system of daily business was strictly regular, commencing exactly at 8 o'clock, and ending at 7 in summer and 6 in winter. During these hours a continuous line of carriages might be seen extending nearly half the length of the street, a watchman in livery always in attendance outside to take messages and parcels.

For six years the house was never without workmen constantly employed in carrying out extensions and improvements, as number after number on the street was added, and continued to go on during all my subsequent visits to the city up till a comparatively recent period; and only a few days ago I heard the enlargement was still going on.

The average sales in the retail department alone, all for cash, were £1,000 sterling per day in 1847.

In addition to the inside business of the house were the manufacturing departments: the celebrated poplins employed several hundred hands; the grey calicos, at Greenmount Spinning Works, owned by the firm, and the manufacture of upholstery, trimmings, and paper and leather branches employed several hundreds more ; and such was the enterprise of the firm that a time of depression was unknown. Even during the potato famine, in 1846, there was no falling off in the business, although this might have been expected in some of the departments, such as jewellery and silks, yet the sales showed no diminution.

ROUTINE OF DAILY BUSINESS.

The first bell rang at 7.30, when the junior hands and porters went down to sweep and dust—the former inside the counters, the latter outside. At 8 o'clock the second bell rang for all others to be in their departments. At the same time a porter stood at the main entrance, watching the clock opposite, over the main stairway, and precisely to the minute the doors were opened, when a large number of customers, who waited for the time to arrive, would be admitted. The arrangements for meals were posted up in the library every Monday morning, showing a division into three classes, which changed alternately every week, giving all an equal privilege as to time.

At 8.30 the first bell for breakfast was the signal for the first class, at 9 for the second, and at 9.30 for the third, no one being allowed to leave his place till his reliever returned. Dinner and tea were arranged on the same principle.

The weather was the only thing that affected our daily business, the complaint of hard times or falling off in trade being quite foreign to us.

The short hours of business, especially on the long summer days—part of the time being clear daylight till 10 o'clock—gave us all a fine opportunity for enjoyment and recreation.

Those who preferred to remain at home had the advantage of a magnificent library, which, although established by a monthly contribution from each young man (which was compulsory), had become the property of the firm. This, with the news room, containing all the leading magazines, periodicals, and latest newspapers, was an inestimable boon, and highly appreciated by the lovers of literature.

At 11 o'clock precisely the door was locked ; and so strict

was the rule, I have seen the porter refuse to turn back the key in the lock to admit a late-comer, the transgressor of the rule being obliged to seek lodgings elsewhere, with the certainty of a reproof in the morning, and, if repeated, of dismissal.

At 11.30 a superintendent went round every room with a dark lantern to see that every one was in his proper bed, and all lights put out.

Every morning the house doctor went round the rooms, and if any were sick, or shamming, a sick diet was immediately prescribed; and on Sundays, if any remained in their rooms, whether to carry on a flirtation with the good-looking chambermaids or from a fit of laziness, the same sick diet was prescribed.

The cooking arrangements were perfect. Twenty legs of mutton could be roasted at one time, while the stewing, steaming, and boiling in the same range all went on at the same time; one hundred loaves of Manders' celebrated bread were cut by a machine daily.

The domestic arrangements of the house generally would well repay a visit from travellers.

The magnificent plate-glass front of the house, comprising from 74 to 88 in consecutive numbers in the street, was on a fine day lined with carriages, while this line sometimes extended beyond. We select one out of many of the equipages for description. Look at this

EQUIPAGE

and its appointments. Mark the exquisite balance of that claret-bodied chariot upon its springs; the fine sway of the sumptuous hammer-cloth in which the smiling coachman sits buried to the middle; the exact fit of the saddles sitting into the curve of the horses' backs, so as not to break to the most careless eye the fine lines which exhibit action and grace. See, when they stand together, alert, fiery, yet obedient to the weight of a silken thread; and as the coachman sees you studying his turnout, observe the perceptible feel of the reins, and the just visible motion of his lips, conveying to the quick ear of his horses the premonitory, and to us inaudible, sound, while, without drawing a hair-breadth upon the traces, they paw their fine hoofs and expand their nostrils impatiently. Come nearer, and observe not a speck or a raised hair on those glossy coats. Observe the nice fit of the dead black harness, the modest crest upon the panel, the delicate picking out of white upon the panels, and if you would venture upon a freedom of manners, look in through the window of rose-tinted glass and see the luxurious cushions, and the costly and splendid adaptation of the interior.

One of the twin-mated footmen waits upon my lady as she completes her purchases, and as she, with a charming smile, says good-bye to the salesman—who had recognized a carriage customer before she had spoken ten words, was certain of it as soon as she took off her glove, and had enjoyed a *tête-a-tête* for which a Prince Royal might sigh and an ambassador might negotiate in vain—hands the parcel to the footman, who with silver-headed stick attends her ladyship to the door.

The twin footman flies to the carriage door, the small foot presses on the carpeted step, the airy vehicle yields lightly and recovers from the slight weight of the descending form, the coachman inclines his ear for the half-suppressed order from the footman, and off whirls the admirable structure as if horses, footmen, and chariot were but the parts of some complicated centaur—some swift-moving monster upon legs and wheels.

Mr. Thomas Pim combined business with pleasure. He owned a yacht, and was the only member of the Bristol Yacht Club who was not by birth a nobleman. In the winter the skipper was appointed to work in the warehouse. Mr. Pim always kept a saddle-horse in the city, and had daily rides in the Phœnix Park. His residence was Monkstown Castle, near Kingstown.

In 1846, the potato crop having failed, we never saw one for six months. This increased the consumption of bread in the house to an enormous extent.

The bakers' attempt to raise the price of bread was checked by Mr. Pim's threat to open large public bakeries, and sell at a small profit, adding, that if the people would not buy his bread he would put a slice of bacon in every loaf.

As an instance of the generosity of this firm, Mr. John West, for many years head superintendent, having taken a trip to America, speculated largely in lands near Chicago. After spending a few years in Paris as agent for their celebrated poplins, for which thirteen prize medals have been obtained, he determined to return to America and settle on his property. Before leaving he was invited to a supper given by the firm, when on turning up his plate he found a cheque for £1,000 sterling placed there as a parting gift.

And this firm, with its princely revenues, army of assistants, thousands of dependents, its several branch establishments and numerous agents, all working with a clockwork regularity incomprehensible to the muddling proceedings of Ordnance, Horse Guards, Admiralty, Woods and Forests and Public Works, is a model of the firms which organize the labor of the staple trade of Great Britain. Neither are the principals money-grabbing drudges. They can afford time, as we have seen, for healthful recreation; neither do any of their dependents appear to be overworked. Such is the establishment of which the writer had the honor of being one of the founders.

INCIDENTS FROM 1841 TO 1847.

Daniel O'Connell.

No name will remain more prominently on the pages of Irish history than that of Daniel O'Connell. His persuasive oratory, his brilliant wit, and laughter-provoking humor, attracted great crowds to listen to his speeches in Conciliation Hall. While his persevering efforts in the House of Commons were the best proof of his patriotism, it may be, that had he confined his ambition to the attainment of a "Home Rule" for Ireland, he might have succeeded at the time in seeing his object accomplished. In 1843 he confidently stated that the great repeal year had arrived, the repeal of the union being avowedly the object he had in view.

As history appears to be repeating itself in Ireland, when a Lord Mayor refused to hoist the city flag on the occasion of the visit of the Prince of Wales in 1885, and, while I write, the new Lord Mayor is said, in a despatch from Dublin, to join in a movement to erect a monument to the three Fenians who were executed in Manchester for the murder of Policeman Brett, one is reminded that, nearly forty years ago, the celebrated Daniel O'Connell, having been elected Lord Mayor amidst scenes of terror and riot, was said to have displayed his feelings by having the statue of King William III. in College Green painted bronze with as much green as possible.

This celebrated equestrian statue, said to be the finest in Europe, had a short time before been overturned by an explosion of gunpowder, and, after its re-erection, was painted orange and blue—the Trinity College students, close by, taking great pains on the 12th of July to add decorations of ribbons and flowers of the same color.

The agitation for the repeal of the union was prosecuted with systematic vigor by its advocates. The city was divided into districts, and house-to-house visitation carried on by the collectors of the "repeal rent," and as some of the contributors showed considerable ignorance of the nature of the object, they sometimes innocently stated their belief that the repeal would be over next week "for sure," and the knowing ones, to help the joke, would tell them it was coming over from England "in three ships." The climax of the excitement on this question was reached by Mr. O'Connell issuing a proclamation calling a mass-meeting to be held upon the Strand of Clontarf, a suburb of the city, near the Hill of Howth. All went well for the cause until the afternoon of the day before the meeting.

In the meantime the guards on the Bank of Ireland, the Castle, and all the barracks, were doubled, and orders issued for supplies of rations for the men and provender for the horses as in the time of siege.

Chapter of Introduction. 25

O'Connell promised that half a million of men would meet next day to show the British Government their strength, but not being an advocate of "physical force," like Smith O'Brien and the Young Ireland party, he warned them against any display beyond that of numbers. However, the Government, regarding these meetings as an attempt at intimidation, determined to stop the proceedings, and a counter proclamation was issued that afternoon forbidding the meeting. This led to O'Connell's advising its postponement *sine die*. Nevertheless, the Government, to effectually prevent any further demonstration, marched the troops through the city the next day. Fully 15,000 of all arms marched with fixed bayonets and drawn swords, while artillery and cavalry, with nets of hay attached to the saddles and every arrangement for battle, made the streets echo with their warlike tread.

In the midst of this scene appeared Tom Steele, the "head pacificator," waving a green branch under the immediate direction of O'Connell himself, driving through the dense masses of people and advising them to retire peaceably to their homes. The subsequent arrest and conviction of O'Connell, after a long trial in the four courts, on a charge of high treason, is a matter of history. The punishment was reduced to six months' imprisonment in Richmond Bridewell, and here on any Sunday during that time might be seen thousands of people all round the grounds, eager to catch a glimpse of his jolly face through the bars. Provisions, delicacies of all kinds, and a variety of presents, with every manifestation of sympathy, were given him to the fullest extent.

At the expiration of the time he made his triumphal procession through the city, seated on a large car drawn by four horses, with a white-bearded Irish harpist and some of his most intimate friends around him. The procession, which was about six miles in length, halted at the Bank of Ireland, where the last Irish Parliament had met, and round after round of cheers were given, after which they passed on through the city.

By this step on the part of the Government peace was secured, but from that time O'Connell's sovereignty ceased to exist. He had led the peasantry in sight of the promised land, but failed to enter.

The hot-headed Young Ireland party supplanted him, and a farcical rebellion followed under Smith O'Brien. The abortive O'Connell agitation resulted in nothing more than the uprising at Balgarry. The Liberator was essentially a man of peace, opposed to secret societies and everything resembling physical force.

After a lapse of many years a statue has been erected to his memory, at the foot of Sackville Street. A monument representing one of the round towers of Ireland stands close to the vault in which the body (except the heart, which was left in Rome, where he died,) is deposited.

The writer, a few years ago, visited the beautiful cemetery of Glasnevin and entered the vault. The coffin was covered with fresh flowers gathered close by, the cemetery being a perfect flower garden. The Botanical Gardens, almost adjoining, are only excelled by Kew Gardens, in London, and contain every specimen in botany, from the lily of the valley to the cedars of Lebanon.

Something Like Fenianism.

The establishment of Pim Bros. & Co. was so situated that it ran back to the wall of the Lower Castle yard. From our bedroom windows we could see the guard of cavalry parade, and had a view of the Chapel Royal connecting with the Castle itself.

Whether it was the favorable position which the house occupied for an attack on the Castle, or not, a plot was discovered in which a large number of the young men were implicated.

The police, having had private information, prepared for a descent on the establishment.

A large number of us usually went down to the Pigeon House Fort on Dublin Bay, as here there was deep water for a swim, and one morning, having gone as usual about 5 o'clock, on our return we found the police had been through the bedrooms, expecting to find their prey. In their trunks papers containing their commissions to various rank were found. Quite a number of arrests were made, and some who had been out for a swim, whose friends had been out on the watch to warn them, thinking discretion the better part of valor, made tracks for the land of liberty. Amongst the number was one who at present is doing a large business in Louisville, Kentucky.

One of those who were arrested, and who held the commission of captain, as his papers showed, was, up to a late date, a corset manufacturer in New York. The Government did not prosecute any of those who were arrested, so they were allowed to get out of the country, possibly for their country's good.

Father Matthew.

During this time the Rev. Theobald Matthew, familiarly known as Father Matthew, was busily engaged in his good work of temperance and total abstinence. His influence over the masses, especially of his own Church, was something remarkable.

On Sunday afternoons he was to be seen in the open square at the back of the Custom House, administering the pledge to the thousands who knelt on the pavement while he passed from rank to rank placing his hand on the head of each person. This was considered equivalent to taking a pledge, and each of these received a medal, which no doubt was carefully preserved.

Dr. Cuyler, of New York, said lately in a speech at Exeter Hall, London, that in 1842 he made his first speech by the side of Father Matthew in the City Hall, Glasgow. The doctor stated he was then but a youth, and Father Matthew gave him a warm kiss, which he felt to be a kind of consecration to temperance work.

The writer has a pleasing recollection of attending one of Father Matthew's addresses, in front of a Roman Catholic chapel at Donnybrook, when also a youth, and also of the kind-hearted, benevolent-looking father taking him by the hand, which he warmly shook, and drawing him from the crowd to a position near himself, where he stood to the close of the address.

Evangelical Alliance.

At this time the Evangelical Alliance was formed in London, and shortly after the formation of the Irish branch followed, in Dublin. Ministers of all Evangelical denominations united cordially on the seven fundamental points which constituted the basis, the English Church clergymen alone keeping aloof.

Archbishop Whately, being opposed to the movement, issued a manifesto forbidding ministers under his jurisdiction to unite with the dissenters or nonconformists.

One curate refused to submit to his orders, and was deposed from his position. Being an old man with a family, and having no other means of support, great sympathy was shown in his case. A public meeting was held in the Rotunda, and resolutions passed sympathising with him and condemning the action of the Archbishop.

At the same time meetings were held at which the action of the Alliance in London, in refusing to admit representatives of the Methodist Episcopal Church South into the Alliance, on the ground of the slavery then existing, was discussed.

Bishop Soule, and his colleague, Rev. Mr. Sargent, came over as the Southern deputation to ask for admission, and were refused, it being proved that the Bishop himself held slaves at the time.

The feeling at these meetings was very strong, and intensified by the presence, a short time before, of Frederick Douglas, who denounced the whole system of American slavery, and from personal experience of the horrors of the lash, the gag, and the thumbscrew, had depicted the evil in such a way as to carry the feelings of his audiences completely away; and with true British feeling in favor of freedom, the American representatives were allowed to return home to relate the failure of their mission.

Having had the pleasure of being present at the great Evangelical Conference held in New York about ten years ago, when representatives from every part of the civilized world were present, including a converted Brahmin in his native costume,

I could not help contrasting the circumstances with the feeble commencement—the growth and spread of this organization being truly wonderful.

During the month of January, this year, the present Archbishop of Dublin assisted in the services of the Evangelical Alliance.

Dublin Castle.

The balls at the Castle were the occasion of great excitement, their splendor equalling any given at Buckingham Palace, and causing a large amount of money to be circulated amongst all classes.

Having had the *entrée* to the gallery of St. Patrick's Hall, through a friendly official, I had an opportunity of witnessing these brilliant gatherings. The feathers and diamonds on some of the most beautiful women in the world, mingling with the brilliant military uniforms of the gentlemen, shown to the best advantage by about 2,000 wax-lights, was a scene not soon to be forgotten.

The House of Commons, thirty years ago, voted the abolition of the Vice-Royalty by a majority of three to one. The measure was dropped solely in deference to Irish opposition, particularly the opposition of the citizens of Dublin, who liked the pageant, the entertainment and the expenditure.

The glory of Dublin would depart with its Viceroy, and this the citizens knew full well.

Lord-Lieutenants.

Earl de Grey, during his term of office, gained the reputation of being stingy.

It was customary for every Lord-Lieutenant to send beef for a Christmas Dinner to the Mendicity Institution. It was reported that Earl de Grey had sent cheap and inferior meat.

On the occasion of his departure from the Castle the usual military arrangements were carried out. The streets, all the way from the Castle along Dame Street, College Green, and down to the Westland Row Station, were lined on both sides with troops, through which the Vice-Regal carriages passed amidst dense throngs of people.

Suddenly an addition to the crowd was made, by the appearance of four men carrying on their shoulders the carcase of an ox, minus the meat, and marching close to the carriage of the Lord-Lieutenant, and so amidst the cries of "shins of beef," the Vice-Regal party made their ignoble exit.

Such is the temper of a certain class in that city as to make the popularity of any high official to a great extent dependent on imaginary as well as real grievances. And yet, while this state of feeling exists, the city is so overrun with "purveyors" of every kind "to His Excellency," that were the Castle a whole town in itself there are as many bakers, butchers, grocers, Italian warehousemen, hatters, furriers, boot and shoe makers, wine and spirit merchants, dairymen, and even chimney-sweepers, "to Their Excellencies," as indicated by their own sign-boards, as would amply supply all the demands of Dublin Castle.

The Earls of Carlisle and Eglinton were very popular as Lord-Lieutenants during their term of office.

A despatch from Dublin, January 28th, 1886, says:—"Lord Carnarvon, ex-Viceroy of Ireland, left Dublin Castle to-day, accompanied by his wife, for their home in England. The retiring Viceroy was followed to the railway station by enormous crowds, and his route all the way to Kingstown, where he took the ferry for Holyhead, was lined with people anxious to witness his departure. He was cheered al t continuously from the time he left Dublin Castle until he ted from the Irish coast. The enthusiasm of the populace enomenal."

Reviews in Phœnix Park.

Up to the time of Louis Napoleon being proclaimed Emperor of France, the Battle of Waterloo was commemorated on the 18th of June by a sham fight.

The Duke of Wellington, from regard for the feelings of the Emperor, ordered these reviews to be discontinued.

On the open ground near the Vice-Regal Lodge, commonly called the "Fifteen Acres," but really of much larger extent, these grand military displays took place. The flower of the British Army, stationed at the various barracks, including lancers, dragoons, hussars, infantry and artillery, generally numbering from 10,000 to 15,000 men, took part in these manœuvres.

Here for several years Lord Cardigan, the future hero of the charge of the Light Brigade, could be seen on his Arabian charger, at the head of the 11th Hussars, or Prince Albert's Own, of which he was colonel.

This regiment, wearing the loose jacket worn in commemoration of their having won a battle when only partially dressed, and with crimson trousers over the new saddle cloths lately presented by Prince Albert, made a splendid appearance. The sight attracted immense crowds, and was very imposing.

Holiday Excursions.

Where there were so many points of interest, the difficulty was to decide on some particular place to resort to in these delightful outings.

There was Maynooth, with its College and beautiful grounds, and a magnificent library always open to visitors, and close by was the splendid seat of the Duke of Leinster; Clontarf Castle and the Hill of Howth were other attractive points for a holiday excursion. There were Kingstown and Bray, and Killiney Hill, from which a magnificent view, on the land side, could be had away back to the city, with the intervening bathing villages; and on the other side the Bay of Dublin, said to rival that of Naples, and the Irish Channel studded with ships from every clime; but the County Wicklow seemed to offer the greatest inducements for a day of real pleasure.

At 5 o'clock on a fine summer's morning, with a splendid four-in-hand before a car holding ten on each side, and the "well" in the centre well filled with cold fowl and hams, and all the necessary appendages, and generally with one or two musical instruments, the twenty mile drive over a road without an uneven spot in the whole distance—over hill and down dale, amid ever-changing scenes of beauty and romantic grandeur, with the perfume of the hawthorn in the fresh morning air—was as exhilarating as delightful, and for pleasure could not be exceeded in the world.

The supply of provisions being reserved for a later period of the day, breakfast was served at the first stopping place, Roundtown.

The way in which the first supply of beefsteak and ham-and-eggs disappeared always astonished the good-looking girls who waited at the table, and while a second edition was being prepared the most boisterous merriment went on.

The seat of Lord Monck, formerly Governor-General of Canada, was passed, as also that of Lord Powerscourt. Mountains and glens, lakes and waterfalls succeeding each other, the "seven churches" at Glendalough, the most attractive spot, is reached.

Here is the lake of which Tom Moore has written:

> "By that lake whose gloomy shore
> Skylark never warbled o'er."

The water is said to possess some peculiar quality which has the effect of driving away the warblers.

From this lake rises a precipitous rock several hundred feet in height, and in the face about midway up is a cave, called St. Kevin's bed, having, at the bottom, the appearance of the form of a man in the solid rock, giving rise to the legend that here St. Kevin took refuge from the wiles of a fascinating young lady who pursued him, and at length, having made her way to the mouth of the cave where he lay, feet outward, he pushed her into the lake below.

On the stone are carved the names of nearly all celebrated Irish travellers, including Sir Walter Scott, Rev. Cæsar Otway, Mr. and Mrs. S. C. Hall, and others.

The guide who "coins" legends always assists visitors to enter this cave, which is a very dangerous operation, and more especially so in getting out, as this is done feet foremost. Not being able to see where you are going, and the deep lake immediately below, you are entirely at the mercy of the guide, who places your feet in certain niches known only to herself—the guide at that time being a woman called Kathleen, said to be the name of the victim of St. Kevin's determined celibacy.

The scenery in this neighborhood is unsurpassed, and continues to be very fine till the destination of the day's excursion is reached, at the Vale of Avoca, of which Tom Moore says:

"There's not in this wide world a valley so sweet."

Donnybrook Fair.

"Who has not heard of sweet Donnybrook Fair?
An Irishman, all in his glory, was there,
With his sprig of shillolah, and shamrock so green."

During the time of the writer's residence in Dublin this celebrated gathering was in full blast, once a year.

Whether there was a sale of merchandise, as at Leipsic, or a grand bazaar, such as is seen in the grounds of the nobility in England, for some benevolent or charitable object, or a cattle fair, during the day, I do not profess to know, but in the evenings and at night, when the crowds poured into the grounds, it had peculiar features in which it differed from all other fairs.

It must be admitted that nothing so bad was seen as what, when a boy, I had witnessed at fairs in other parts of Ireland.

At some of these the "who'll-tread-on-the-tail-of-my-coat" challenge was literally given, and promptly accepted by opposite factions, and the battle commenced. Those who had no cudgels were supplied with pokers, tongs, and other weapons, taken without permission from the neighboring houses by the women, who also supplied ammunition in the shape of paving stones; and soon heads were broken and the blood flowed copiously. This generally continued till either the priest appeared on horseback, and by the free use of a long whip, or the constabulary with fixed bayonets, dispersed the rioters.

Sometimes when the constables were attacked they fired on the mob, wounding some and killing others.

The rush to Donnybrook was very great, although the general character of the crowds differed from those to be seen on the road to the Derby. There was an entire absence of the aristocratic four-in-hand and other carriages of a stylish character, and none of the "dust veils" worn by the gentlemen in dry weather. The usual mode of conveyance was by the outside cars, and if one of these happened to be disengaged, the driver made the tempting offer to parties on the road to "rowl" six of them out for a shilling.

The first sight of the grounds, if not imposing, was certainly very surprising. Like a vast military camp the tents were spread all over, interspersed with, and surrounded by, a miscellaneous collection of shows of all kinds from every part of Great Britain and Ireland.

There were menageries and theatres, peep shows and Punch and Judys, giants, dwarfs, fat women and living skeletons, monstrosities of all kinds, acrobats, jugglers, clowns, mountebanks, gypsies, nigger minstrels, organ grinders, hurdy-gurdy men, and thimble-riggers, all inviting customers with a din that is utterly indescribable. In the tents were fiddlers and pipers, and the dance went on merrily, while the free use of whiskey contributed to make matters still more lively.

Occasionally a batch of Trinity College students, bent on fun, would appear rushing through the crowd, and from one show to another, up on the platforms, and down again, then through the tents, much to the astonishment of proprietors and the great amusement of visitors.

The whole business has been entirely abolished by law as a public evil.

The memory of years spent in Dublin is pleasant. As a place of residence it possesses many attractions. Its squares and parks, especially Phœnix Park, with the Zoological Gardens close by; the Botanical Gardens at Glasnevin; the beauty of its suburbs, and its historical associations, all combine to make it the pride of its citizens.

Chapter of Introduction.

To lovers of first-class music, especially cathedral and choral, Dublin is unsurpassed in all that can delight the ear.

To be privileged to hear the choir of Trinity College Chapel at early matins, then the Chapel Royal choir at ten o'clock, from which, if we choose, to go to Christ Church at twelve, and St. Patrick's at three, would be to enjoy the very greatest treat in this class of music.

Trinity College Chapel on a Sunday morning is a moving sight.

Five hundred young men in college gowns, thronging the chapel from end to end—the very flower of British youth, in manly beauty, in strength, in race, in courage, in mind—all kneeling side by side, bound together in a common bond of union by the grand historic associations of that noble place; all mingling their voices together with the trebles (all well-trained boys) of the choir and the thunder music of the organ.

This is a spectacle not often equalled, and to take a share in it a privilege not to be forgotten.

In the beautiful grounds of Trinity College the writer was accustomed to take his morning walk, frequently meeting the celebrated Archbishop Whately, with whom it was a favorite resort.

St. Patrick's Cathedral.

The choral music of St. Patrick's Cathedral is almost unrivalled in its combined powers of voice, organ and scientific skill. The majestic harmony of effect thus produced is not a little deepened by the character of the church itself, which with its dark rich fretwork, knightly helmets and banners, and old monumental effigies, seems all filled and overshadowed by the spirit of valorous antiquity.

Mrs. Hemans, who after residing in Dublin for several years, died there, and was buried in St. Anne's Churchyard, speaks of the exquisite music of St. Patrick's, the effect of which is such as once heard can never be forgotten. "If earthly music can ever be satisfying it must be such as this, bringing home to our bosoms the solemn beauty of the Liturgy, with all its endeared associations, in tones that make the heart swell with ecstacy and the eyes often flow with unbidden tears."

There was one anthem frequently heard within these walls which Mrs. Hemans used to speak of with peculiar enthusiasm— that from the 3rd Psalm, "Lord, how are they increased that trouble me!" The consummate skill exhibited in the adaptation of sound to sense in the noble composition is, in truth, most admirable. The symphony in the fifth verse—"I laid me down and slept,"—with its soft, dreamy vibrations, gentle as the hovering of an angel's wing, the utter *abandon*, the melting away into slumber implied by the half-whispered words that come breathing as from a world of spirits, almost "steep" the senses in forgetfulness, when a sudden outbreak, as it were, of light and life bursts forth with the glad announcement—"I awaked, for the Lord sustained me"—and then the old sombre arches ring with an almost overpowering peal of triumph, bearing to heaven's gate in the exalting chorus which follows.

The leading singers in the cathedrals were David Weyman, Vicar-Choral of St. Patrick's; Dr. John Smith, composer to the Chapel Royal, and R. W. Beatty, Professor of Music to Christ Church, with the celebrated Robinson Brothers leading tenor and bass.

Dr. Smith, although a very corpulent man, was said to be the only true counter-tenor singer of the day, taking the highest notes with his natural voice as pure as the warbling of a bird. The first named three gentlemen were eminent composers, whose works appear in every complete Church Psalmody.

Emigration.

Who should emigrate? This is a question much more easily asked than answered. The best answer appears to be, "those who are obliged to do so."

If this be so, and America has been peopled with those who have come from every country in Europe, how does it happen that there is on every hand such an accumulation of wealth?

Chapter of Introduction. 37

Was all this acquired by people who came here, not from choice, but of necessity?

If so, the possession and use of brain and muscle must have stood in good stead in the absence of other capital.

And yet the rule is that few, if any, do leave the Old Country from choice; and none who are really doing well at home should emigrate with the expectation of doing better, no matter what their occupation or profession may be.

But those who are not doing well, who find it difficult, with an increasing family, to keep up appearances, and find it necessary to make a change, may safely emigrate with a fair prospect of improving their condition.

If these pages should meet the eye of any young man wishing to know about Canada, and Toronto in particular, he may be able to form a pretty correct opinion of the chances of success from the facts stated.

No doubt that in proportion to the population the failures in business in America are more numerous than in Great Britain, especially if the figures of mercantile agencies can be relied on.

But if a city can grow in wealth and prosperity like Toronto, in a comparatively short time, as no city in the Old Country (London always excepted) is doing, *it is clear that some must become rich* where on the whole so much has been accumulated.

There are exceptions to the rule as to emigration. Some do leave home who are well to do, but have some ulterior object in the future as to the settlement of their families.

The hope of doing better for one's self in a new country, the dreams of youth, and correspondence with friends, with the love of novelty and, perhaps, adventure, influence many young men.

Having gained an excellent position by remaining in the house from its establishment, while about 2,000 young men had come and gone, and being one of the two who alone remained of the original founders, when we had decided to leave for America the heads of the firm were incredulous at first, but finding our decision was made, the leading partner used all his persuasion to induce us to remain, telling us we would "cry salt tears" when we found ourselves in America.

But all to no purpose, we had determined to find out for ourselves what America was like.

In the meantime addresses of regret and good wishes were prepared and signed by hundreds of our companions in the business, and arrangements made for a presentation supper at considerable expense.

The writer, having conscientious objections to these festive occasions, which generally ended in over-indulgence, with much regret at offending his friends, declined the intended honor, and all his subsequent experience has confirmed his opinion that he acted rightly in his decision.

A volume could be written on this subject. Having heard all the celebrated temperance lecturers in England and America, including Mr. John B. Gough and Hon. Neal Dow, also Cardinal Manning, Sir Wilfred Lawson, Wm. Lloyd Garrison, Dr. Rees, and a host of others, I can say, I never heard a statement of the evil effects of intemperance exaggerated, but have seen instances as terrible as any they have related in actual life.

Where are the 2,000 young men with whom I associated in one house alone ? The history of many I know, but cannot enter more fully into the subject. When the question of temperance is growing to be of such intense interest in Canada and in Toronto, and the future merchants, manufacturers, and bankers of the city are to take part in the movement, the writer, who can safely say he has come into actual contact with more business young men in Great Britain and America than any other man in Toronto, gives it as his deliberate opinion, that nothing short of total abstinence is a safeguard against evil consequences, whether travelling or at home.

The reception of various addresses from societies and friends, in a quiet way, wound up my connection with the beautiful city, which I have never missed an opportunity of visiting, when time has permitted, on my business journeys to Britain.

Departure for New York.

"Isle of Beauty, fare thee well."

On the 17th of March, 1847, our party of five, and a man-servant who accompanied one of our friends, sailed from Liverpool in the ship *Sheridan*, Captain Cornish, of the "Dramatic" Line — the other three being called respectively the *Garrick*, *Roscius*, and *Siddons*.

Not being pressed for time, we had decided to come by a sailing vessel, and as far as the writer is concerned it was the first and last experience in that line.

When time becomes money it does not pay to roll on the deep from side to side, in the most beautiful weather, in a dead calm for days together.

The voyage was devoid of interest and very unlike any of my after passages in steamers. The cabin passengers were few, and those of the steerage had a hard time. The Captain, being a harsh man, thought nothing of kicking them should they trespass on the after part of the deck, where they would sometimes lie down to get away from the surroundings of the forecastle.

On the other hand, we who liked a change would fain get out on the bow, or the jib-boom, and watch the figure-head of the gallant ship, as she alternately rose high on the crest of a wave and then plunged into the deep abyss.

Our first adventure in this way taught us a lesson. Standing on the forecastle we scanned the horizon for the sight of a sail, when quietly a ring was made with chalk around our feet, and out of this we were expected not to move till we had "paid our footing," and of course we could not refuse the jolly tars their usual *douceur*.

Had we been in a hurry the passage would have been a terrible tax on our patience. Now terrific storms, with thunder's roll and lightning's flash — and so vivid was the lightning, that from pitch darkness the sea, as far as the eye could reach, was suddenly lit up so as to appear like an ocean of flame. Again followed a dead calm, with a ground-swell so heavy that in the roll the mainyards would dip in the water; the rolling so violent that standing was impossible, and many a fearful pitch took place.

When sea-sickness had done its work amongst the steerage passengers, the natural passion for a fight soon showed itself amongst our Hibernian friends.

The Munster and Connaught men soon got up a good old-fashioned faction fight, perhaps to illustrate the beauties of "Home Rule" on the "rolling deep."

So at it they went, hammer, tongs, and shillelahs, pitching each other down the hatchways, head over heels. Matters having become serious, the sailors thought it time to spoil the sport. Handspikes, from "heaving" the capstan were heaved to some purpose, and the Irishmen soon beat a retreat.

The most remarkable incident of the voyage was having spoken a vessel one hundred days out from Ireland, short of provisions, which were libe·   v supplied from our ship.

And so twenty-six day: ed, and the land appearing in sight we soon arrived in New York.

First Impressions of New York.

"Hail! Columbia."

Our youthful dreams of this city represented it metaphorically as having its streets lined with orange trees and paved with gold, but this illusion was soon dispelled.

From Liverpool docks—five miles in length and having twenty miles of dockage, with massive gates set in everlasting granite—to the wooden wharves of New York, must strike the eye of every one arriving there as a wonderful contrast.

On reaching the dock over piles of merchandise and emigrants' baggage, we found ourselves in a sea of mud. One of our party, on taking "soundings," reported a depth of twelve inches in the middle of the street.

On our way to the hotel we were struck with the melancholy appearance of the private streets,—long lines of houses, having green outside shutters all closed, without the appearance of a flower-pot, or the face of a chambermaid airing curtains or looking out, presented a striking contrast to scenes so familiar just left behind, when wall flowers and crocuses were blooming, and where windows were opened every morning all the year round.

It being now the middle of April, we expected spring weather, and feeling hearty after the sea voyage, enjoyed the fresh air. Our astonishment on reaching a hotel was very great to find the guests crowded round a stove, nearly red hot, all very grave, ruminant, expectorant and whittling. Our appearance soon attracted attention, and remarks were made as to the freshness of our complexion (a compliment we could not truthfully return), and we were informed that they "guessed" (the first time we had heard the word so applied) we would not be long in the country before we should lose all that high color. Not at all anxious to adopt the sallow shade, we were by no means encouraged, and having made necessary arrangements, and feeling uncomfortable with the sickening heat, rushed out of doors to get relief; and never for the week we remained in the city did we venture again near one of those health-destroying inventions.

The stoves of the present time are entirely different, and in every way adapted to the climate.

We soon found that to see Broadway, including A. T. Stewart's marble store and Barnum's Museum, was to see New York.

A. T. Stewart's was very fine in marble, and the inside arrangements were very superior, but the system of doing business did not appear to us as perfect as that we had just left.

We were struck with the signs of "Dry Goods Store," "Flour and Feed," "Help Wanted," etc., none of which we had seen before, and had to enquire what they meant. We found that "helps" meant servants, and as there were no masters, the term "boss," which we have never yet known the meaning of, was used to distinguish what in the Old Country is known by the other familiar term.

On enquiring as to the police, none of that class appearing

to us on the streets, we were told they might be known by the wearing of a small metal badge fastened to the collar of the coat, with the stars and stripes and "*E pluribus unum*" inscribed upon it, and further, that no man in the country could be found to wear a uniform.

This accounted for the entire absence of anything in the shape of livery on the coachmen.

To wear a livery button or cockade would be derogatory to the dignity of men who were all equal.

The ladies on the streets were invisible as to their faces, each having a green woollen barege veil tightly drawn over the face.

The appearance of Astor House illuminated, on the night of our arrival, as seen from the Park opposite, was very fine. This was effected by a candle being placed in every pane of glass in the whole building, and the name "Taylor" in gas over the principal entrance. This we found was in celebration of one of General Taylor's victories in Mexico.

The experience of our first morning at the hotel did not alter the unfavorable impression of the previous day.

According to our usual custom, our boots were left outside our doors, pretty well coated with mud, and on taking them in found them just in the same condition. In reply to our enquiries why they were not cleaned, we were told, if we required that labor performed we must make a special contract with a person that they would send; the arrangement was made accordingly.

The cheery voice of the English chambermaid, as she knocked at the door and called "hot water, sir," with boots which might serve as a mirror, by the application of "Day and Martin's" blacking, were all sadly missed.

Breakfast was announced by the ringing of a bell, when we found what was to us a novel bill of fare. The selections by the guests were chiefly in the shape of mush, buckwheat cakes, pickles and green tea, while we were satisfied with old-fashioned ham-and-eggs and coffee. The solemnity of the proceedings was quite remarkable; so far we had not seen the shadow of a smile on any one's countenance. Having got through we found all the other guests had long since disappeared, and then, with-

Chapter of Introduction.

out giving offence, we gave full vent to our feelings by hearty bursts of laughter, and the mutual exclamation, "And this is America!" How different from all our expectations!

On Sunday we observed in the churches notices that gentlemen were "not to spit in the pews," and the clergymen during the service made free use of the "cuspadores."

But "*tempora mutantur nos et mutamur in illis*." We have lived to see the millionaires and aristocrats of New York vie with the "*crème de la crème*" of London society, and the Central Park equipages, including crests and mottoes, with livery of every hue, rivalling Rotten Row and the carriage drives in Hyde Park; while a four-in-hand coaching club copies the style, as far as the roads will admit, of the Brighton Club of noblemen in London.

Touching crests and mottoes, a story is told of the celebrated Lundy Foot, manufacturer of the snuffs known all over the world as "Irish Blackguard" and other remarkable brands, known only to the writer by enjoying many a good sneeze in passing the mill near Essex Bridge.

When Mr. Foot first got a carriage, he adopted as a motto beneath the family crest, the Latin words, "*Quid rides?*"—why do you laugh? On his first appearance, the Dublin street boys, quick to catch a new idea and enjoy a joke, taking the words in their English orthography, set up the cheer, "Quid rides! Quid rides!"

The upper ten of New York, no doubt, are more careful in the selection of their mottoes.

To see New York to-day is to see an almost entirely new city. Some of the old buildings, as the Astor House and City Hall, remain, but the magnificent warehouses on Broadway and adjacents streets are unsurpassed in the world, and nearly all have been built since that time.

A. T. Stewart's fine store was latterly turned into a wholesale warehouse, and the magnificent new marble block, bounded by 10th and 11th Streets and Broadway and the Bowery, a perfect palace, was opened as the great retail house of America, and altogether the finest in the world.

The hotels, for magnificence, are of world-wide fame, while Central Park, Brooklyn Bridge, the great reservoirs at 42nd and 150th Streets, the Grand Central Depot, all so often described, are now striking objects of interest.

The splendid private residences, of 5th Avenue especially, are magnificent in style and finish.

From New York to Toronto.

By night steamer on the Hudson River the travelling was very fine and comfortable. The steamer *Isaac Newton*, then called a floating palace, landed us at Albany. The New York Central to Rochester and Buffalo was then taken. The rails consisted of a plain plate of iron fastened to the sleepers with iron spikes. We were informed, that for one of these plates to start at one end and obtrude itself into the car, to the danger of life and limb, was a matter of common occurrence.

We escaped this danger and arrived safely at Rochester, where, for the first time, we noticed frame houses and plank sidewalks, with both of which we soon became familiar. Arriving, via Buffalo, at the Falls,—the station at Buffalo consisting of the open firmament above and the street below,—we took up our abode at the American Hotel, from which we were to make our first visit to Canada.

The ice was coming down from Lake Erie in great masses, and the only means of crossing was a small ferry-boat, which took passengers across to the landing below the Clifton House. On enquiry we found that this boat had not crossed for several days, and it was quite uncertain when any attempt would be made. The ice became more and more massed, forming the usual bridge.

Having waited for several days the ice at length began to move, when the ferryman asking us if we would risk the crossing, we consented. The ice at this time was floating in large packs; so off we started, with two oarsmen, and with one foot on the ice and one in the boat they pushed the boat by main force through. To have been carried a hundred yards below the landing would have sealed our doom, but having worked our way through we placed our feet for the first time on Canadian soil. Having executed this dangerous navigation we soon tasted the pleasures of land travelling.

The stage for St. Catharines was soon ready, and we shortly found ourselves "at sea" on dry land.

Having driven a long distance on what we thought was a field or common, there being no sign of hedge or fence visible, we enquired when we should reach a road. With a smile of self-complacency and a look of pity for our *freshness* or verdancy, the driver informed us we had been on the main road all the time. It so happened that the year before, being the year of the memorable potato famine in Ireland, the Government had spent immense sums in making and repairing roads, to give employment to the people, the consequence of which was the greatest perfection in road-making; and without exaggeration, the worst road you could find was infinitely better than any we saw for years afterwards, not excepting the city macadamized streets. We soon found, however, that to mention this to our driver only subjected us to his contempt.

Our driver appeared to think "the lines" had fallen to him in pleasant places, and was quite satisfied with the state of things; while the writer, years after, on handling "the lines" (as Americans say for reins) over mud, slush, old planks and corduroy, found it incumbent to drive from his memory the smooth roads, hawthorn hedges, and the beauties of highly cultivated landscapes left behind, and think only of farms without rent, and the real necessaries of life enjoyed so abundantly, in this land where the inhabitants possess truly a "goodly heritage."

ST. CATHARINES

was reached at length, and here we rested for the night, and the next afternoon started with four good horses in the Mail Stage for Hamilton.

To attempt a description of this journey as it appeared to us at the time would only result in failure.

With both hands we grasped the seat to save our heads from bumping against the top of the conveyance, and many times when we got into a deep rut we had to use rails from the fence to pry the wheels out. And so at 2 o'clock on Sunday morning, covered with mud and thoroughly exhausted, we reached Weekes' Hotel, the clerk at the time being Mr. Riley, so long and well known afterwards in Toronto in connection with the firm of Riley & May, of the Revere House.

Having been regular church-goers, we were in our places in the red brick Wesleyan Church on John Street, at 11 o'clock, and soon found we were on British soil and amongst our own countrymen under the same Queen and flag. Here we soon found friends, and myself relatives, the first day, and with the natural longing for old familiar faces when far away from home, we walked ten miles to Copetown to see a family with whom we had been acquainted in Dublin, and were amply repaid for our visit. Again taking the regular Mail Stage, we arrived in Toronto, after a tedious ride, and put up at Macdonald's Hotel, King Street, then the best in the city.

VIEW OF TORONTO, C.W. 1847.

TORONTO FROM 1847 TO 1857.

First Impressions of Toronto.

Our first view from the door of Macdonald's Hotel, which stood on the site of the present Romain buildings, did not give us a favorable impression of the town. From near Bay Street to the corner of York was an immense vacant space filled with rubbish, and at the back a dirty lane with a few of what we for the first time heard of by the name of "shanties."

Walking eastward as far as the Market, and, returning to Yonge Street, proceeding as far north as Queen, we found we had, so far as business was concerned, seen Toronto, with the exception of a few wholesale warehouses to the south of King.

Having never seen a view of Toronto, except one which appeared a short time before in the London *Illustrated News*, our expectations were not of a very sanguine character,—that view representing the "City" of Toronto something like what a view of Oakville might be at the present time. Why it should be called a city was something we could not quite understand, as even towns in Canada lately honored with that appellation are far superior in architecture to what Toronto was at that time,—such cities as Guelph, Brantford and London having kept pace with the improvements which have taken place in the intervening years.

Everything appeared flat, dull, uninteresting, and especially unfinished. Not a single point of attractiveness could we discover in or about the place, although we were quite taken with the people.

The contrast between the city we had left and Toronto was most depres'ing, and grew more marked as we viewed the outskirts. Having letters from friends we soon found a cordial welcome to several homes, which went a great way to reconcile us to the place.

On enquiry we found, rather to our surprise, that there were two churches having organs, something we had not expected to find: one was in the old Cathedral and the other in the Richmond Street Wesleyan Church.

On being introduced to Rev. Messrs. Cooney and Harvard by letters, the former took us with pride to see the new church on Richmond Street. It then stood on an almost vacant lot, there being no building between it and Bay Street.

On entering he pointed with a good deal of satisfaction to the fine organ, which stood behind the pulpit at the time. We attended divine service on the following Sunday, when Mr. Cooney preached, and were much interested. The musical portion of the service was very pleasing and effective. A well-known alderman of the city at the present time was leader of the tenors, and the writer has a distinct recollection of his flexible voice as he glided from tenor to counter-tenor, and occasionally appeared imperceptibly to run into a falsetto, which added much to the harmony and contributed very greatly to the general effect.

We were equally pleased in the old Cathedral. The beautifully composed and impressively delivered sermons of the Rev. Mr. Grassett were such as should never be forgotten, while the music was of a very high order.

During the week we had an opportunity of visiting some of the retail stores, the principal of which were Betley & Kay's, corner of King and Yonge Streets; Walker and Hutchinson's, P. Patterson's, and Walter McFarlane's.

My friend and companion of seven years, dropping into Betley & Kay's, was immediately offered a situation, which he accepted, much to my surprise, as we had not decided to remain in Toronto at the time; and here my loneliness commenced.

My destination was Brockville, where I intended to go, having a letter from my grand-uncle (and his uncle) to the Hon. George Crawford, who was to advise me as to my future movements.

The unwillingness to part with my friend, and the unsolicited offer of a situation, also on King Street, with the desire to have a rest after so much travelling, led to my acceptance of the offer, and so we entered on our new career.

To compare the business of King Street in 1886 with what it was in 1847 could give no conception of the difference which it may be imagined we found after leaving the business already described.

The prospect of its being only temporary alone made it at all endurable, while it gave time to arrange plans for the future and get some knowledge of the mode of doing business before deciding where to choose as a future field of operation. The want of system in showing goods, the bantering about price, and the lack of customers, made it tiresome beyond description.

Here we first became acquainted with the habit of

"SHOPPING,"

either for amusement or for comparison of prices before purchasing. The custom was almost universal to go from Yonge Street to the Market before deciding on what or where to buy. The common expression was: "We will look around, and return if not better suited elsewhere." At the same time the anxiety to press sales was painfully apparent, the offer of a reduction in price being the principal inducement held out.

This of course led to exaggeration, and often misrepresentation, and was altogether demoralizing to both seller and buyer. The few houses named were, I believe, exceptional in this respect, and were the first to introduce the "one price" system.

In consideration of my previous experience, the principal of the business in which I had made a temporary engagement immediately took charge of a customer where any deviation from the marked price was asked, well knowing that on no account would I condescend to such a practice.

The arguments of friends to induce us to settle in Toronto were drawn more from the absence of the rudeness and inconvenience that existed before we were born, or the wonderful future that lay before the city, than from any especially attractive features the present afforded.

Amusements or entertainments there were scarcely any. There was the old Mechanics' Institute, where the present Police Court now stands—then a dirty lane,—where a subscriber could read books or papers. This, and the auction room of William Wakefield, who, by his genial humor and English physiognomy, did all in his power to entertain his customers, were about the only places of resort of an evening.

And so summer came on, and recollections of botanical and private gardens, parks, squares, delightful suburbs, music, lectures, literary entertainments, all crowded on one's memory to make the contrast painful.

Suburbs there were none, except Yorkville, then an embryo village with a few scattered houses, the best being the residence of Mr. Bloor, which still remains. As no resident of Toronto went there except on business, the journey was not often undertaken.

Toronto business men lived either over their stores, or on some street south of Queen.

Our first tour of exploration in the outskirts was along Carlton Street from Yonge, then a clay road without houses or sidewalks. Having got as far as the present Homewood Avenue, we found a small gate-house, and on entering the wicket discovered a natural pathway through a thick pine grove. Proceeding north we reached the house now occupied by Homer Dixon, Esq., and finding further progress that way, or egress, impossible, retraced our steps.

Our next adventure was along Bloor Street east to the present cemetery fence, and thence backwards again; and these for a time constituted our only recreation grounds, except the College Avenue.

In taking a morning or an afternoon walk, there was the absence of many pleasing objects so familiar in former every-day life. The "wee crimson-tippit" flowers that covered the pasture fields like a carpet; the banks of primroses, buttercups and violets, abounding by every roadside; the double line of hawthorns whose blossoms perfumed the air with their delicious fragrance, and the honeysuckle and wall-flowers in every lane; the meadows, thick with May flowers, all were missed during this first summer in Toronto. For the hedgerows we found the unsightly snake fence, and for the evergreens of holly, laurel, and ivy, the everlasting, monotonous pines, good for use but not very ornamental.

The study of this class of "flora" no doubt might be interesting to those who studied the subject from a utilitarian point of view, and the smaller species might have been discovered by an adventurous descent down the ravine to where the river Don flowed in its native beauty; and some ferns and beautiful wild flowers might have been discovered, very interesting to students in botany; but to the casual observer these beautiful objects were at that time conspicuous by their absence.

Along Church Street, any summer's afternoon, especially in a swamp at the south-east corner of the present beautiful Normal School grounds, could be heard the music of a frogs' concert, accompanied at a short distance with the tintinabulation of the bells on the necks of the cows which roamed through the browny-green pastures and amongst the thick bush which prevailed east of Church and north of Queen Streets. These sounds were further augmented by the cackling of flocks of geese, which, in their amphibious character, had their choice of both native elements.

The song of the lark, the thrush, the blackbird, and goldfinch, so familiar before, was no more heard; the buzz of the bumblebee, and the whirr of the numerous insects that abounded in the bush, being the only substitute.

Apart from its political history, which has been given so repeatedly, Toronto possessed no points of interest beyond what any town on the shore of Lake Ontario possesses at the present time, except that she had made a step in advance and outgrown them in population and trade.

The young friends with whom we became acquainted, and whose ideas were circumscribed by the visible horizon, would not admit of the superiority of any other place in any respect. If you spoke of London, Dublin, or New York as great places, you were immediately met with the question, "Was not Toronto also a city?" And the statement that she had one street forty miles long extinguished all your arguments and left them masters of the situation.

When it is borne in mind that at that time Toronto, as far as intercourse with the outer world was concerned, was far more isolated than is Regina to-day, it will be admitted that these young people had a pretty good conceit of the place.

A correspondence was soon opened with friends in Great Britain with a view to importing goods, either to Toronto or Montreal, and at the same time I had an opportunity of writing to my uncle's executors in Philadelphia, as to the property already referred to. The reply was to the effect that the climate of Mississippi was bad, and if I went there I could not find an honest lawyer in the State. The American war coming on prevented further efforts for several years. Under these circumstances I allowed the matter to rest until I visited that city, when no trace of the executors could be found, and only at the Centennial, in 1876, did I discover my uncle's tomb in "Macpelah" Cemetery, where a handsome marble monument is erected to his memory. It may be that, like the Lawrence-Townley estate, the property may turn out to be of fabulous value.

Toronto in 1847.

To give an idea of the general appearance of Toronto at this time, it may assist the imagination to conceive of all its present attractions being removed, and all the improvements that have taken place still unanticipated.

To do this it will be necessary, commencing with the Island, to remove every building there at present, leaving the lighthouse, Privat's Hotel, which then stood near the present gap, and two or three fishermen's huts at the West Point.

Crossing the Bay, the whole Esplanade must be taken away, leaving two or three wharfs with a ragged edge of stagnant water between.

The whole of the railway tracks, with all buildings and stations, must next disappear.

Coming north, all the block, stone and wood pavements; all the street railway tracks; all telegraph poles and wires, except a single line to Hamilton and Montreal; all the gas lamps except about a hundred; all the water hydrants except about twelve; all that are called "modern conveniences," which are now considered indispensable in every house; the suburbs of Brockton, Parkdale, Seaton Village, Riverside, Leslieville; all the streets north of Queen and west of John—leaving some scattered houses outside these limits—except Yonge and Church Streets.

As it is supposed there are at present 30,000 houses in the city and suburbs, you must imagine 26,500 of these taken away, leaving 3,500 as composing the entire city at that time. From these 3,500 you may deduct 2,500 of frame and rough-cast houses, leaving 1,000 of a better class; from which again, if you take 500 two-storey red brick, you have 500 which comprised all the best buildings, including churches, banks and private residences, the best of the latter being those at present on Bay Street, and a few detached mansions scattered over the city.

To complete the picture must be added the absence of every shade tree—except those on College Avenue—which now adorns and beautifies the city; every flower-bed and conservatory, and in stores all plate-glass windows.

In addition to all this you have to conceive of 90,000 of the population being left out, and some idea may be formed of Toronto in 1847.

At this time only four of the present churches were in existence: the Richmond Street Wesleyan, Power Street Roman Catholic, St. George's Episcopalian, and Little Trinity. The others that were then built have either been burned down, or removed to give place to present structures, amongst which are the St. James' Cathedral, which has taken the place of the old one burned in 1849, and Knox Church, on the site of the old one burned in 1847.

Not one of the banks or large insurance buildings; none of the wholesale houses as they now appear; none of the benevolent institutions, then existed; and none of the public schools or colleges except Upper Canada College.

Front Street occupied the same relative position to the Bay as the Esplanade does at present.

There were no buildings on the south side except the Custom House, and only a few scattered along on the north side, leaving the view of the Bay uninterrupted.

There was a skating-rink near where the Custom House now stands.

Going westward from Yonge Street, on the north side of Front, where the warehouse of Messrs. McMaster, Darling & Co. now stands, was the residence of Judge Macauley; next that of Judge Jones; further west the residence of Mr. Joseph Rogers, and at the corner of Bay Street was the Baldwin mansion.

Where the Queen's Hotel now stands Capt. Thomas Dick had four dwellings; these afterwards were used as Knox College, and subsequently were turned into a hotel kept by Mr. Swords.

Holland House, in the rear, on Wellington Street, lately the residence of ex-Mayor Manning, and at present the Reform Club, and which was built in 1832 by Hon. Henry John Boulton, and from its peculiar style of architecture sometimes called "The Castle," was occupied by Mr. Boulton at this time.

At York Street corner, a picturesque cottage was the residence of Capt. Strachan, son of the Bishop of Toronto, whose palace adjoined with the entrance on Front Street. This building is now a boarding-house.

Turning up Simcoe to corner of Wellington you saw the Hagerman mansion, and returning eastward on Wellington, the little white house lately occupied by Mr. Mercer, standing by itself at the corner of Bay.

When Toronto was first settled most of the buildings were

erected at the upper end of the Bay, towards the river Don, and it was generally supposed that the east end would become the principal part of the city. As the buildings were extended, however, they began to creep westward and northward.

The town in its young days was much scattered, the roads were bad, and communication between distant portions of the town, at least in certain seasons of the year, was difficult; in consequence, houses of business were started at each extremity, which, in some cases, realized to their owners handsome profits.

As the town increased the footpaths were improved, business became more concentrated, and at this time was almost confined to the space between York Street and the Market, and it was doubtful whether, if the best store was removed to either extremity, it would do a paying business. The necessary consequence of this state of things was that the value of property and rents within the limits mentioned had risen enormously.

In the absence of street railways the few travellers who had occasion to reach the steamboats in summer (in winter the stages called for passengers at their houses) were limited for accommodation to a few old-fashioned one-horse cabs, owned by well-known drivers, and the number of horses and vehicles of all kinds was so small as to make it an easy matter for any inquisitive person to know the owner of every particular turn-out in the town.

The only city omnibus at this time was one that ran to Yorkville every hour, and a ride in this was not very exhilarating at certain seasons, especially when the frost was breaking up. The jolting was terrific, but as few or none of the Toronto people lived in Yorkville, there was not much travel up or down.

An hourly omnibus started from the Market to Parliament Street, but it did not pay and was soon discontinued.

The question of meat being an important one, it may be stated, from actual experience, that after repeated endeavors to masticate the beefsteaks, my young friend and myself came to the conclusion that, having heard that oxen were employed in the country for ploughing and other purposes, the Toronto market was supplied with beef from their carcases after their usefulness as living animals had departed. The supply of vegetables was excellent.

Gossip.

The extent to which regard for local boundaries, customs, and every-day chit-chat is sometimes carried, can only be realized in a small town.

At home, in this nook, all life is lived under minute inspection of neighbors, and perhaps the unavoidable supervision of parson and squire.

The fierce light that beats upon the throne is not clearer than that which exhibits the young man "sowing his wild oats." He sins under a microscope, and the professional gossip finds rich material for the next social or tea-party by placing him under the instrument for the general entertainment of the company, and so the engagement of lovers is discussed as earnestly as if each person were personally or directly interested in the result of every matrimonial arrangement.

In 1847 Toronto had not outgrown the habits which characterize the country town. The gossip which prevails where every person knows all about the business and social life of his neighbors, was still noticeable, and the absence of all foreign news, oftener than once a fortnight, gave a local character to the general topics of conversation.

Every birth, marriage and death furnished material for discussion in every family circle, and very much as it is on board ship, out at sea, the most trivial matters were invested with exaggerated importance.

On Sundays, generally, three carriages could be seen at St. James' Cathedral, and as a good deal of rivalry existed between the owners of two out of three, in the style of the appointments, the coachmen's livery, and horses and harness, their appearance on driving from church was a standing topic at almost every dinner-table; the dresses of the ladies coming in for a full share of the criticism, of course of a good-natured character.

The arrival of the English mail, once a fortnight, created a pleasing diversion for a time from the monotony of daily life. The news telegraphed from New York ahead of the mails was given in a condensed form, in printed "extras," which were issued by the newspaper people; there being no second edition of papers as at present.

Incidents.

Amongst the incidents of the summer of 1847 a strange one occurred, which afforded matter for town-talk for some time, although at the present time it would probably be confined to the daily police reports.

A gentlemanly-looking person was observed for several evenings to promenade a portion of King Street—between Yonge and Church—fashionably dressed, and when nearly opposite the present *Globe* office, stand near a lamp post and read what appeared to be letters, then, using a white handkerchief, make signals of a mysterious character, and repeat the same time after time and evening after evening. At length a plan was laid to discover the identity of the individual by a number of young men approaching in a body. Apparently afraid of detection the "gentleman" took to his heels, making for the darkness which prevailed beyond Simcoe Street, where the gas lamps ended. A policeman joining in the chase an arrest was made, and the prisoner taken to the police station to account for "his" conduct. On being brought to the light, and the hat, which was a handsome silk one, removed, behold a maiden stood "revealed in all her charms," which was clearly seen by her long flowing tresses falling over her shoulders.

On being brought before the magistrate the next day, wearing the same clothing, she was discharged with a reprimand, but the motive which led to such an extraordinary adventure was never fully explained.

During the summer a young minister, to whom the writer was introduced, was engaged to be married, and asked me to be his best man on the occasion, to which I consented.

On the Sunday following my first interview he was appointed

to preach somewhere on the Dundas Road, and requested me to accompany him, stating that he would call for me with a horse and buggy. Feeling curious to know what description of vehicle that might be, never having heard the name before, and at the same time thinking it very repulsive, and also wishing to have a specimen of Canadian driving horses, besides being assured that a drive on Sunday on a mission of piety, necessity, or mercy, was perfectly justifiable, the arrangement was made.

Arriving at the place in good time, my friend preached an excellent sermon, apparently to the edification of the congregation.

On our return to the city he appeared to be in excellent spirits, and showed off the trotting qualities of the horse to good advantage. When near Queen Street we espied a pig lying in the middle of the road. He said to me that if the animal did not get out of his way he would drive over it. No sooner said than done. The squealing of the pig being likely to set the owner in pursuit the horse got a loose rein, and in a short time we were out of sight, never pulling up till I found we were in the old barrack square. This was my first experience of buggy riding and fast trotting in Canada.

I attended to assist my clerical friend in the matrimonial affair, some fifty miles west of Toronto, the following October.

So much has been written on the condition of the streets of Toronto that the subject has become monotonous, and as in 1886 it still continues to engage a large amount of public attention, nothing will be said in this connection from personal observation, the writer preferring to quote the descriptions of a few other parties, some of which were written prior to 1847.

The first is that of a lady, ten years previously, Mrs. Jamieson, wife of Vice-Chancellor Jamieson.

This lady, whose name is pleasantly familiar to lovers of art and literature, was for some time a resident of Toronto. She reached the city by way of New York, Albany and Queenston, towards the end of 1836.

Her husband, then Attorney-General, had been a resident for several years, but she arrived unexpectedly and he was not there to meet her.

When she stepped from the boat her foot sank ankle deep in the mud, and there being no conveyance at hand she was compelled to walk through the muddy, uninviting streets to her husband's residence near the foot of Brock Street.

It was during her abode here that she wrote her "Winter Studies" and "Summer Rambles." She describes the city as it appeared in the winter:

"What Toronto may be in summer I cannot tell; they say it is a pretty place. At present its appearance to me, a stranger, is most strangely mean and melancholy. A little ill-built town, on low land at the bottom of a frozen bay, with one very ugly church without tower or steeple, some government offices, built of staring red brick, in the most tasteless and vulgar style imaginable; three feet of snow all around, and the grey, sullen wintry lake, with the dark gloom of the pine forest bounding the prospect,—such seems Toronto to me now."

As a set-off to this desponding account, she admits that some of the shop fronts on King Street are rather imposing, and declares, in a patronizing kind of way, that the front of Beckett's apothecary shop is worthy of Regent Street in appearance.

A few words from Sir H. R. Bonnycastle, in 1845, may be given. He "was greatly surprised and pleased to see the alterations since 1837, then not one-third of its present size. Now it is a city in earnest, with upwards of 20,000 inhabitants, gas lit, with good plank sidewalks, and macadamized streets, vast sewers and houses of brick or stone. The main street, King Street, is two miles in length. St. George's church was built in 1844."

Another writer says: "Few who now stroll down the well-boarded sidewalks of King Street reflect upon the inconveniences attending this recreation to their sires and grandsires and granddames, who were compelled to tuck up their garments and pick their way from tuft to tuft and from stone to stone.

"It was no unusual sight to behold the heavy lumber waggon sticking fast in the mud, up to the axle, in the very middle of King Street, opposite to what is now McConkey's refectory.

"The party-going portion of the citizens were content either to trudge it, or to be shaken in a cart drawn by two sturdy oxen. The fashionable cry then was 'Mrs. McTavish's cart is here,' and the 'gee up' resounded as clearly among the pines and elms as the glib 'all right' of the modern footman along the gas lit street.

Since those days the art of photography has been discovered, and it is not probable that Mr. Eli Palmer—the only artist of which Toronto could boast in 1847—could have brought his camera with the Daguerrean process to bear on Mrs. McTavish's cart to get a good picture in a conveniently short space of time.

A late number of London *Fun* thus describes a scene in the studio of a photographer in that city:

MR. JUGGINS—"Look here, Mr. Photygrapher, 'ow much d'yer want to take me and the missus and the kids altogether?"

PHOTOGRAPHER—"Well, I could take a carte of you for five shillings."

MR. JUGGINS—"Cart, be blowed! Stick us in a waggonette."

No doubt Mrs. McTavish would have preferred a waggonette also, and had the art attained its present state of perfection an instantaneous photograph could have been taken that would have been quite interesting.

"A little nonsense now and then
Is relished by the wisest men."

Mr. Wm. Osborne—who had left Dublin, in consequence of the failure of the silk trade, when French goods were first admitted free of duty—was a good specimen of a Dublin gentleman, and amongst other stories about the state of Toronto streets in former years, related the following, without in any way vouching for its accuracy:

A gentleman, walking on the loose planks forming a sidewalk on King Street, espied a good-looking hat in the middle of the street. Curious to see and pick up the hat, he managed to reach it, and on removing it, discovered to his surprise the head of a living man underneath.

This individual at once appealed for help and deliverance, urging, as a special plea, that if prompt assistance was not rendered, his horse, which was underneath, would certainly perish.

The usual mode of extrication by the use of shovels and oxen was soon applied, and man and horse excavated.

This being the climax of exaggeration on this muddy question, it must now be dismissed.

Apart from the social enjoyments among friends—and of those we had a full share—there was nothing, either in the business or surroundings, to lead to a preference of Toronto to any other place, when the world was before us where to choose.

In business, the farmers were always complaining about something. Prices of produce were too low or too high; the former from too good crops, and consequent low prices, and the latter because they had not enough to sell.

The roads were a constant source of complaint, which appeared to be natural from our little experience of mud and ruts, and when winter came on they generally had either too much snow or too little.

Those leaving home in sleighs, fifty or sixty miles back, found bare streets, and had a hard time to get back to sleighing again.

As my friend and myself had never heard complaints of roads before, this topic became terribly monotonous, and the same remark applies to the prices of produce, although in Toronto a trade of the greatest importance.

There was the prospect of trade increasing by the growth of towns and villages outside, and the facilities for transport by water navigation in summer; but as railroads were not thought of, and there was neither steam nor water power, except what could be got in the Don river for the latter, and by importing coal for the former, little was said of manufactures, and the prospect of their establishment was exceedingly dull.

The prospect of the growth of Toronto—from the two facts of the great agricultural country at its back, and the harbor and water communication in the front—led to a decision, and within a few months of arriving in the country the writer was in communication with friends in England with a view to importing a stock of goods, which was successfully accomplished the next year.

Information as to Toronto in England was not very flattering. A gentleman had a servant-maid whose brother had enlisted in a regiment which was subsequently ordered to Canada. While quartered in Toronto, the young man took to himself a helpmate, an Anglo-Canadian, who afterwards returned with him to England. On his arrival at home his sister paid him a visit. On her return her mistress asked her if she had seen her new sister; she replied in the affirmative, adding, "But Lor', mammy, she's not very dark. I thought she'd be black."

As an example of the accuracy of description, Mr. R. Montgomery Martin wrote about this time :—" The country bordering Lake Ontario is well wooded; through the numerous openings the prospect is enlivened by flourishing settlements, the view being extremely picturesque along the White Cliffs of Toronto, (?) heightened on the north by the remarkably high land over Presque Isle, called the Devil's Nose."

Richmond Street Wesleyan Church,

around which so many hallowed memories will ever cluster, is one of the four which remain of those existing in 1847.

Thinking it may interest many who have been associated with it in years gone by, and some since its erection in 1845, a copy of the inscription on the brass plate at present in the corner stone is given on the opposite page.

This *fac simile* was obtained by the writer twenty-five years ago, in England, from the Rev. J. P. Hetherington, who was one of the resident ministers at the time it was built.

It will be seen that it was called a chapel, after the English custom, and was a representative British institution, as we were told the next day after our arrival in the city.

This church, like City Road in London, which it resembles in the plainness of its architecture, may be regarded as the cathedral of Methodism in Toronto.

In 1847, the congregation worshipping here was styled the

IN THE NAME OF THE
EVER BLESSED TRINITY
THIS CORNER STONE WAS LAID BY
THE REV^D MATTHEW RICHEY, A.M.,
CHAIRMAN OF THE WESTERN CANADA DISTRICT,
AND THE REV^D E. EVANS, SECRETARY IN CONNEXION
WITH THE BRITISH WESLEYAN CONFERENCE, ON THE
20TH DAY OF AUGUST, IN THE 8TH YEAR OF THE REIGN OF
VICTORIA, A.D., 1844.

THE REV^D J. P. HETHERINGTON, AND THE REV^D J. B. SELLEY, BEING RESIDENT MINISTERS.

MESS^{RS}

JOS^H WILSON	ALEX^R HAMILTON
J. G. BOWES	R^D WOODSWORTH
THO^S STORM	SAM^L SHAW
W^M OSBORNE	JN^O STERLING
THO^S WHEELER	C. & W. WALKER

TRUSTEES FOR THIS CHAPEL.

R^D WOODSWORTH, BUILDER.

T. WHEELER,
ENGRAVER.

loyal British Wesleyan body, while the Adelaide Street people were said to be more of the American type, and not quite so loyal.

However that may have been, the union which took place in 1840 settled the matter and made both one, which event was celebrated by a union tea-meeting in Richmond Street Church.

Dr. Alder, who had been sent out by the British Conference, had been the means of effecting this consummation; but so strong was the feeling against it that several of the British ministers would not remain in Canada, and went to the Lower Provinces, amongst whom were Dr. Richey, father of the present Lieutenant-Governor of Nova Scotia, and Rev. Ephraim Evans, while shortly after Rev. Enoch Wood and Rev. S. D. Rice came up to supply their places.

This church had the peculiarity of having, till the late improvements, the entrance door at the same end as the pulpit, which appeared to cause a good deal of annoyance to some ministers while conducting the service.

Rev. Dr. Dixon, from England, on one occasion remarked in the course of the service, that he wished they had put the pulpit at the other end. It had one good effect, however, on those who were a little bashful, by inducing them to come in good time, and so be spared the gaze of those whom they had to face on entering the doors.

Rev. James Caughey.

In the fall of 1853—while waiting in Kingston for the Toronto boat, the last of the season—I met, at the British American Hotel, the Rev. James Caughey, the celebrated revivalist, on his way to Toronto. Having frequently heard him when in Dublin, he seemed pleased when I reminded him of the fact.

The night was very stormy, and after some conversation in the saloon about mutual friends, we retired for the night to the same stateroom. I noticed that he did not undress, and on enquiry as to his reason he replied he thought better to be prepared for anything that might happen during the night.

This may have been a wise precaution, but it did not appear to me to be conducive to comfort.

On arriving at Toronto, I escorted him to the house of Mr. Richard Yates, whose guest he was during the following six months. The excitement he created was not confined to the Richmond Street Church and congregation, but extended to every church. People of all denominations flocked in crowds every night, Saturday excepted, during six months, with unabated interest. The effect was marvellous; numbers who thought he addressed them individually, when describing particular characters, waiting at the close of the service to enquire who had told him of their case. There were many remarkable cases of restitution and conscience-money paid to the customs. On one occasion, at night, when the house was crowded to the doors, and the writer occupied a pew almost in the centre of the church, the preacher, in the middle of his sermon, in making a point by way of illustration, referred to some remarkable case which had occurred in Dublin (of which, however, I had not heard), and, supposing that I must have known of the case, stated that his friend—mentioning my name—was cognizant of the facts; as every eye was immediately turned to where I sat, my situation was rather embarrassing.

As his visit was so intimately associated with Richmond Street Church, it will not be considered out of place to refer to it in connection with other reminiscences, that church being one of the few land marks remaining of Toronto, in 1847, and many remarkable men having, from time to time, occupied its pulpit.

A. & S. Nordheimer.

In 1847 this firm occupied premises on the north side of King Street, nearly opposite their present establishment.

The senior partner, Mr. Abraham Nordheimer, was an accomplished musician, and it was quite a treat to witness the enthusiasm he displayed when exhibiting the fine points of the instruments to intending purchasers.

Mr. Samuel Nordheimer undertook the outside work, travelling a great deal, and to this firm is due to a great extent the credit of having educated the taste of the people of Canada up to its present high musical standard.

Prior to this time, if an Old Country family had brought out a piano, although not of the most modern style, they were supposed to have belonged to the better class of society at home; but even these instruments were few and far between.

It was on Mr. S. Nordheimer's journeys, between Toronto and Montreal, that the writer first became acquainted with him, and soon found that by his universal courtesy, polished manners and pleasing address, he was winning golden opinions, not only in the towns and cities, but amongst the better class of farmers; and the firm being sole agents for the Chickering & Stodart and Dunham pianos, soon succeeded in placing a large number of these instruments in the hands of the better class of people, all over Canada. The fame of the firm is now as extensive as the Dominion, and their success has been as great as their highest ambition could have desired.

In the chapter on "Toronto as a Musical City," reference will be made to their successful efforts to induce the first-class musicians and vocalists of the world to visit Toronto, when it was little known, and had few attractions for these great artists; but the influence of Messrs. Nordheimer—through their connections in Europe and the United States—overcame all difficulties, and to them is due, from the citizens of Toronto, a debt of gratitude for many a musical treat during the past thirty-five years.

The Toronto Post Office.

In 1847, and up till 1852, the whole business of the Toronto Post Office was transacted in a small building on Wellington Street, where the present Exchange now stands. The delivery office was a room about 20 x 40 feet, and the distributing room was an old cellar-kitchen some 20 feet square.

The staff up to 1850 consisted of a postmaster, three clerks, and a letter carrier. The postmaster was Mr. Charles Berczy, and the clerks, John Armstrong, Christopher Walsh, and W. H. Pearson (now secretary of the Consumers' Gas Co.), who succeeded Geo. H. Wilson, the present accountant of the Bank of Montreal, in 1847.

John McCloskey was letter carrier, and a charge of one "copper" was made on each letter delivered by him.

At this time, and up till 1850, the English mails were only delivered fortnightly—by stage from Halifax in winter, and partly by steamboats in sum   . The rate of postage on English letters was 1s. 2½d. sterling, or 1s. 4d. Halifax currency (about 27 cents); the postage to Halifax was 2s. 9d.; Quebec 1s. 6d.; Montreal, 1s. 2d.; Kingston, 9d.; Windsor, 10½d; the lowest rate being 4½d.

In 1850 there were only about 400 boxes in the Post Office.

Postage stamps were at this time unknown, and the postage on paid letters was written in red ink, and on unpaid in black.

The only visible representative of Her Majesty on ordinary occasions was either Mr. Walsh or Mr. Armstrong, who for the time being combined in themselves the offices of receiving, delivery and inquiry clerks; and as every letter must be taken to the Post Office, these gentlemen were known to every man, woman and child in Toronto and Yorkville who ever posted a letter.

The arrival of the English mail, once a fortnight, broke in on the usual monotony and brought a rush to the wicket from which the delivery, both general and particular, took place.

Up to 1852 the Post Office Department was under the control of the Imperial Government, which was represented by Mr. Stayner, but at this time, almost simultaneously with the introduction of the bonding system through the United States, the business was transferred to the Canadian Government, and the mails began to arrive once a week, via Boston and New York, alternately. These mails were conveyed in charge of conductors, of whom there were three—Messrs. McNamee, Malone and Magillivray—two taking the mails to above ports respectively, and one extra to supply in case of need. The conductor taking the outgoing mails waited at his port for those coming in, and this system continued for many years. During Mr. Malone's time of conducting the mails a circumstance occurred, illustrating the economy of the Government at that day.

The writer, in company with Mr. John Kay, Mr. Patrick Hughes and three others, on our way from England, accompanied the mails from Boston, arriving at Suspension Bridge on Saturday night too late to connect with the train for Toronto. Feeling anxious to get home, instead of staying over Sunday at the Bridge we telegraphed for a special train to meet us at Hamilton; the charge to be forty dollars.

On arriving at Hamilton we found an engine and one car all ready, and took on board Mr. Malone and the English mails, with a Roman Catholic clergyman who wished to get to Toronto with us. To this gentleman we offered a free passage, but hoped to receive from the Post Office authorities a share of the cost of the special train. The trip was made within an hour, perhaps then the "fastest time on record." On the following Monday one of our party waited on Hon. Mr. Foley, Postmaster-General, stating the case, and asking for the proportion of the expense for carrying the mails; his reply was, that the letters would have been in quite time enough for the merchants on Monday morning by first regular train. He did not even consider that Mr. Malone would have had to pay his expenses at a hotel over Sunday, and so we had to pay the whole bill.

Toronto Gas and Water Works.

In 1841 Mr. James Crapper had been brought out from London by Mr. Furness, and in the same ship were imported the gas and water pipes to commence the supplying of the city with these two great requisites.

In 1847 there may have been altogether about 100 gas lamps, and at this time the Consumers' Gas Co. was established, on the principle that the consumers, by taking up the stock, would themselves get all the benefit. Mr. Henry Thompson sold all the shares, the writer being one of the first to subscribe. Since that time the success of the Company is well known.

The water supply was very imperfect, especially in case of fire, and even up to 1850 no arrangement had been made to keep the city furnished with a constant and adequate supply.

The licensed carters were compelled under a penalty to attend all fires, for the purpose of conveying water from the Bay in casks.

As the first who arrived was entitled to two dollars' reward, these men were in the habit of filling their casks at night, and carting them to their own houses so as to be ready for a race at the first sound of the fire alarm.

It was very remarkable, that about this time scarcely a Saturday or Sunday night passed without a fire taking place.

Some said they occurred opportunely on these nights, because everybody was at liberty, and the firemen being volunteers, their occupations were not interfered with; while others went so far as to say that the very love of excitement, in some way to relieve the monotony that prevailed over everything, had led to the wilful acts of incendiarism, which undoubtedly took place, but which were all overruled for the growth and general improvement of the city.

The fire brigade in 1850 consisted of four engine companies, two hook and ladder and one hose company; Mr. Ashfield being then the chief engineer.

The old hand-engines were not very powerful, and when the firemen grew tired at the pumping, the law compelled any bystanders to "lend a hand;" while many were willing, many more could be seen taking their departure when there was a prospect of a "draft" for active service.

There were some remarkable instances of destruction of property, one of which the writer distinctly remembers.

A fire took place in a frame building on King Street, one door from the corner of Yonge, then occupied by Messrs. Betley & Kay. The flames from the wooden building were driven by an easterly wind into the millinery and mantle room over the store of Betley & Kay. On the arrival of the firemen the fine windows were immediately smashed in with axes, when the door might have served as well, and when the fire was extinguished it was found that a number of fine silk velvet mantles had been placed at the door of the room to prevent the water from spreading to other parts of the building.

The Circulating Medium.

In the house I had just left the daily cash sales averaged £1,000 sterling. This amount was taken in five cashiers' desks, by boys under sixteen years of age, and the rapidity with which the change had to be given may be judged from the number of cheques handed in from about four hundred salesmen.

The coins were farthings, half-pence, pence, sixpences, shillings, half-crowns, crowns, half-sovereigns and sovereigns.

Farthings were strictly charged on all amounts to 2s. 6d., and no salesman could omit them at 2s. 5¾d. The desks have frequently been swept out to find a missing half-penny, as everything must balance. There being no Canadian Silver Currency at this time, the process of making change out of what was technically called "specie" was a perfect study. There were Mexican and United States dollars and half-dollars; United States 6¼, 12½, and 25-cent pieces; English sixpences, shillings half-crowns, with a miscellaneous assortment from every other country.

Coin and bank note detectors were used in every place to ascertain the value of the coin and the genuineness of bank notes, especially those from the United States.

As each had to make his own change in the absence of a cashier, this was found to be a work of great difficulty, to know when a York shilling ceased to possess that value by reason of abrasion or defacement and became a 10-cent piece, and involved many a dispute; and the same with all the other coins. In payment of a debt the Mexican dollar would go for 5s. 1d., or $1.02, but in independent trading it was just $1.

Anyone visiting New York at this time, and buying a newspaper, if he gave a good 25-cent piece would generally lose in change, through the manipulation of the boys, from one to four cents, just as the boy happened to have more or less of the small coins. Toronto had no newsboys at this time. As for coppers, I have no doubt a great many brass buttons found circulation just by flattening the shanks. This state of things continued more or less for years, till the Decimal System was introduced by Act of Parliament, and the present silver coinage issued.

Previous to this all wholesale or importing accounts were kept in sterling for French and English accounts, Halifax currency, or $4 to the pound, for Canadian, and in dollars and cents for the United States.

Store Pay.

This kind of business was on the whole more agreeable to salesmen than the system of cash sales.

Every builder or contractor made an arrangement with the various trades and stores for a line of credit, by which they could pay their workmen as much of their wages as possible with the smallest amount of cash.

Orders were given on the stores, and mechanics' wives went to make their purchases, carefully concealing their written "orders" as long as the knowing salesman failed to draw out the fact of their existence; the object of the caution on the part of the frugal housewives being to ascertain the "cash" price of the goods. If the "cat was let out of the bag" the salesman at once "stood at ease," knowing well that the customer had no alternative but to take out the value of the order. A few immigrants, in perfect innocence, would present these orders at once, much to the satisfaction of the salesman.

The block of buildings known as Ritchey's Terrace, and other large buildings, including churches, St. Lawrence Buildings, etc., were largely paid for in this way.

The time of "strikes" had not then arrived, the supply of labor always being fully equal to the demand.

Retail Importing.

The only retail importers of dry goods at this time were Mr. Peter Patterson, who occupied a portion of the present premises of Messrs. R. Walker & Sons, and was supplied direct by Messrs. Heron & Dickson, of Glasgow, who had arrangements to supply not more than one house in each principal town in Canada; and Messrs. Walker & Hutchinson, who also had arrangements for getting their goods direct from Great Britain. Nearly every dry goods firm, as well as hardware and others, called themselves importers, and had the term on their signs.

This importing, however, was not direct, but was carried on through the wholesale houses to whom they gave their orders, which were sometimes delivered in the original packages. In this way, in after years, we imported almost every class of goods to order, including jewellery and fancy goods for one of the present leading jewellery houses on King Street, raw furs for manufacturing, oil paintings, fire-arms, fancy stationery, and, in fact, any class of goods for which an order was given.

Wholesale Trade in 1847.

In 1847 the wholesale dry goods trade was entirely confined to Yonge Street, south of King.

First came Mr. William McMaster, where the Dominion Bank now stands; next was Mr. John Robertson's warehouse. At the corner of Melinda Street, where the splendid warehouse of Messrs. Hughes Bros. now stands, was the old red brick store of Messrs. Ross, Mitchell & Co.; a door or two further south Mr. W. L. Perrin occupied a plain brick building, and below Wellington Street were Messrs. Moffat & Murray, and Messrs. Bryce, McMurrich & Co. On the east side, north of Wellington, was the warehouse of Messrs. Bowes & Hall, and these comprised the whole of the dry goods warehouses at that time. There being no houses exclusively in the millinery trade, that was done by the same houses.

The wholesale grocery trade was represented by Messrs. F. & G. Perkins, Mr. A. V. Brown, and Whittemore, Rutherford & Co.

There were no exclusively wholesale houses in the hardware trade, nor in earthenware, jewellery, hats, caps or furs. The oldest house in the latter trade is that of Mr. James H. Rogers; the business having been established by his father in 1815.

The large block at the corner of King and Toronto Streets was, in 1847, the finest wholesale house in the city, and was occupied by Messrs. Whittemore, Rutherford & Co. as a wholesale grocery warehouse, and afterwards they added dry goods, being the only house in which both classes of goods were combined. This building is at present being demolished to make room for the new Quebec Bank, thereby removing one of the most prominent of the old landmarks of the city.

Prominent Men in 1847.

Amongst the prominent men to be seen on King Street in 1847 was the Right Reverend John Strachan, Lord Bishop of Toronto. Although small in stature, his lordship was dignified in manner and commanded universal respect.

Mr. Peter Brown—father of Messrs. George and Gordon Brown—was a gentleman of venerable appearance and much respected.

The Messrs. Ridout Brothers, hardware merchants, Mr. Rice Lewis, Mr. John Harrington, and Mr. T. D. Harris, all in the same business, occupied prominent positions as business men.

Mr. E. F. Whittemore, of the firm of Whittemore, Rutherford & Co., took an active part in every benevolent and philanthropic enterprise, and was distinguished for his temperance principles

Mr. Hugh Scobie, proprietor of the *British Colonist*, was a man of commanding presence and universally respected.

Lord Elgin.

In January, 1847, Lord Elgin—two months after his second marriage, to Lady Mary Louise Lambton, daughter of Lord Durham—sailed for America in the Cunard steamer *Hibernia*, and encountered unusually rough weather, the voyage being most uncomfortable. They arrived at Halifax on the 20th, intending to proceed to Montreal by way of Fredericton, but the condition of the roads was not suited to such an undertaking, so they re-embarked for Boston, arriving on the 25th. They set out for Montreal the following morning, and reached their destination on the 29th, three days' journey, and took up their abode at Monklands.

He was young and healthy, and could work eighteen hours a day; possessed an amiable temper, and always a pleasant demeanor, and did not consider it derogatory to his dignity to walk to church.

In 1849 the Rebellion Losses Bill was assented to, and riots occurred in consequence in Montreal. After this the seat of Government was removed to Toronto, in 1850.

Lord Elgin was very popular in Toronto, and his levees were always well attended. During the summer of that year he gave a *fête champêtre* at his residence, near where the Central Presbyterian Church now stands, and as the view as far as Queen Street was almost uninterrupted, the entertainment was as pleasant as the name was appropriate. The writer has a pleasant recollection of a cordial greeting and a hearty shake of his hand on that occasion.

The garden party given by the present Lieutenant-Governor on the occasion of the visit of the members of the British Association last year, showed by the surroundings the vast improvement that has taken place since that time.

The beauty of the grounds which surround the present Government House, with its luxurious furniture, and conservatory, fragrant with the perfume of rare exotics, contrasts in a striking manner with former times.

Toronto Police Force.

There were about a dozen of policemen, having as a Chief Mr. George Sherwood. The Chief being a quiet, good-natured man, did not insist on any strict regulations as to the dress or discipline of the men.

They wore a sort of uniform, but without uniformity, except in one respect—they were uniformly slovenly. Day & Martin's blacking and white gloves were not considered at all necessary; the latter had not come into fashion, and as to the former, the men might say as to their boots what was generally said as to waggons and carriages, that if the mud was taken off they would be just as dirty in a short time again.

It could not be wondered at, that in a city so celebrated for mud as Toronto, the buggies were allowed to remain for months in a dirty condition, when only a short time ago London *Punch* gives a conversation between a tourist in the Highlands of Scotland and his hostler. The tourist says, " Why haven't you cleaned my carriage, as I told you last night ?" Hostler—" Hech, sir, what for would it need washing ? It will be just the same when you be using it again."

There was not much improvement in the Police Force till the appointment of Captain Prince, who, by the introduction of a semi-military system of discipline, brought about a complete revolution in every respect; not only in the dress and discipline of the men, but in the selection of a superior class, both as regards physique and intelligence, forming in a short time a body of police equal to that of any city in the world.

The best men selected were from the Irish Constabulary, who had been drilled at the barracks in Phœnix Park, Dublin.

First Strike in Toronto.

In 1847 the first sewing machine was introduced by Messrs. Walker & Hutchinson. The tailors in their employment, regarding this innovation as contrary to all their time-honored ideas of the manufacture of clothing, at once rebelled.

Had not the old needle been used by hand since the fig-leaves were made into garments in the Garden of Eden ? Then, why should a new-fangled machine be invented to supersede the ancient system ?

The machine was only in use a few days when Messrs. Walker & Hutchinson, finding it so objectionable, agreed to discontinue its use, and handed it over to their men to use it as they thought proper.

A day was appointed for the display of their triumph over machinery, and the discarded machine was exhibited on King Street, in the centre of a procession of the workmen, after which it was returned to the manufacturers in New York.

The firm, in order to remove every trace of dissatisfaction, treated the men to a banquet, given the same evening.

Immigrant Fever.

The effects of the potato famine in Ireland were painfully visible in the appearance of the immigrants arriving by Quebec during the summer. It was estimated that 240,000 had died from starvation in Ireland. It was not that the people who had the means failed to stretch out the hand of charity. Wonderful acts of liberality and self-denial occurred, but the whole means of Ireland were inadequate to support her destitute poor.

The British ships were too few to carry over the provisions necessary to save human life. Then every English heart, while looking with terror at the future, throbbed with sympathy for their dying brethren, and the relief distributed was received with the liveliest gratitude—the writer's brother being one of the "relief" agents appointed by the Government, related many instances of a most touching character in his district and towards himself personally.

Enormous sums were subscribed to relieve the distressed. Noble and fearless men ventured into the haunts of famine and distress, and examined the evil before trying to remedy it.

In the hour of calamity all differences of creed were laid aside, and the Roman and English priests met at the bed of the dying, joining in administering temporal and spiritual aid to the sufferers; and, by a kind Providence, a fine summer and better crops gradually brought about a better state of things.

The late Hon. W. E. Forster, when a young man, represented the Society of Friends in Ireland during the terrible famine, and his services as a distributer of relief earned for him the love and gratitude of many a suffering soul, though it was his strange fortune forty years later to be regarded as the worst enemy of Ireland.

When the world was horrified by the Phœnix Park murders, it came out on the trial of the assassins that Mr. Forster had been selected as another victim, so that, notwithstanding the respect and veneration with which the young Quaker had been regarded by the peasantry while engaged in the merciful work of relieving hunger and soothing the pillow of death in 1846, yet the same peasantry held the kind-hearted, though firm and bluff Chief Secretary in utter execration, and taught their children to curse him as the representative of blood-and-iron tyranny.

As the result of imperfect nourishment, and other causes, the emigrants who left for America were decimated by ship fever, and hundreds were buried at Grosse Isle, below Quebec, who died on board the ships or at the quarantine station.

There were many cases in Toronto, and in attending these, Bishop Power and Dr. Grassett contracted the disease, from which they both died while faithfully and fearlessly discharging their duties.

Bathing.

Before the Esplanade was formed, a favorite place for a swim was off Rees' wharf, nearly opposite the Parliament Buildings and other quiet spots along the shore of the Bay.

Here, on a fine summer's morning, many of the leading merchants and clerks from King Street might be seen indulging in the healthy exercise. The only restriction was as to time, there being none as to dress. No person was allowed to bathe after seven o'clock, before which time it was perfectly legal.

By those of us who had been accustomed to "disport beneath the crested wave" on the Atlantic Coast, *in puris naturalibus*, the privilege was highly appreciated and enjoyed.

One morning the writer chose a spot in front of the Commissariat Depot, which was always guarded by a sentry, who, with fixed bayonet, "walked his lonely round" in front of his box. These sentries appeared to be authorized to enforce the rule as to time.

Not knowing it was past seven o'clock, I had quite prepared for a dip, when the sentry advanced a few paces, and, in a very decided tone, said if I went into the water he "would do his duty." Not liking the look of the cold steel, and thinking that in this case discretion was the better part of valor, I quickly dressed, and apologizing for having mistaken the hour, beat a retreat.

Great Fire on King Street in 1848.

This fire originated eastward of the Cathedral, and spread rapidly as far as Jarvis Street, and northward to Adelaide, then across to the old City Hall and Market, all of which were speedily consumed. The Rectory of St. James escaped, but the Cathedral, taking fire from some sparks which lodged on the spire, was entirely consumed. One bucket of water would have extinguished it, when first discovered, but there was no way of reaching it, the fire hose being quite inadequate for the purpose. The writer distinctly recollects the falling of the spire. When the fire had done its work, and the crash became inevitable, it was supposed the spire would fall outwards, and the spectators kept a long way off, when, to the surprise of every one, it fell almost perpendicularly, top foremost, the vane on the top striking the flag at the front door. The buildings on the opposite side were badly scorched, but escaped destruction.

Establishment of Celebration of Queen's Birthday.

To Toronto belongs the honor of having first inaugurated this celebration.

In the year when every throne in Europe was shaken, when Louis Philippe and his illustrious Queen were driven by the mob from the Tuilleries, and every vestige of Royalty on which the latter could lay their ruthless hands was destroyed, and when in disguise the Royal pair escaped to England as a haven of refuge, never did our noble Queen sit more firmly on her throne; and the feeling of loyalty appeared to be intensified by the surrounding contrast.

At that time it was proposed to celebrate her birthday in Toronto, but it was not till the following year that it was fully kept, and shortly afterwards it was made a legal holiday, other cities having taken the matter up and followed the example set by Toronto.

In 1850 Monsieur Napheygi, Secretary to the celebrated Louis Kossuth, the Hungarian patriot and orator, who had

KNOX CHURCH IN 1848.

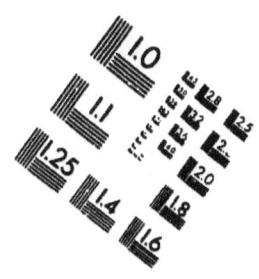

**IMAGE EVALUATION
TEST TARGET (MT-3)**

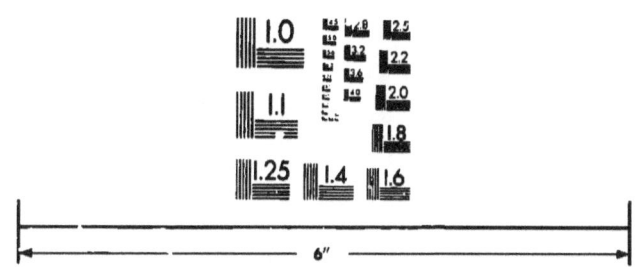

Photographic
Sciences
Corporation

23 WEST MAIN STREET
WEBSTER, N.Y. 14580
(716) 872-4503

visited Toronto, assisted in the celebration of Her Majesty's birthday by a grand display of fireworks in front of the Parliament Buildings.

First Retail Dry Goods Store on Yonge Street.

Up to 1849 the retail dry goods trade was confined to King Street, and to a very limited portion of that street.

The only dry goods sold on Yonge Street were in connection with groceries, in a store kept by Mr. James Leask, one door south of Queen Street.

Mr. John Macdonald having decided to start a store, with the enterprise and pluck which has characterized all his movements, decided to try the experiment of an exclusively dry goods business, and in a short time was doing a thriving trade, one door south of Richmond Street, then known as the "Large 103," that being the number on the street at that time, and the figures conspicuously painted in front of the building.

The result of this venture is referred to in the chapter on the Model Wholesale Dry Goods Warehouse of the Dominion.

SELLING ON THE STERLING COST.

The system of selling at an advance on the sterling cost gave buyers the privilege of inspecting the invoice books before the arrival of the goods, and if the buyer knew of special cheap lines, and wished to favor a particular customer, these lots were selected beforehand and laid aside as soon as opened. In this way Mr. Macdonald secured many a lot which, by judicious advertising, he brought before the attention of the public and soon acquired the reputation of selling cheap goods.

The population of Toronto in 1847 was 21,050.

Total assessment, £122,981, or $591,924; total expenditure, £7,288, or $29,152.

The total importations to Toronto in 1848 were £197,225 5s. 3d., equal to $788,901.05. The same year Montreal imported goods valued at £1,003,027 17s. 9d., or $6,452,111.55, or nearly eight times as large as Toronto.

In 1849 Toronto showed value imported to be £326,863 17s. 9d., or $1,307,455.55, and Montreal £1,236,533 6s. 3d., or $4,946,133.25, Toronto having within the year brought the proportion as compared with Montreal from one-eighth to about one-fourth.

Business Houses in Toronto, 1847-1850.

WHOLESALE DRY GOODS.

Bowes & Hall.
Bryce, McMurrich & Co.
John Ewart, jun. & Co.
Henry Fowler.
Gilmour & Coulson.
William McMaster.
Moffatt, Murray & Co.
P. J. O'Neill.
W. L. Perrin & Co.
John Robertson.
Ross, Mitchell & Co.
Taylor & Stevenson.
Shaw, Turnbull & Co.
Topping & Brown.
R. Wightman & Co.

RETAIL DRY GOODS.

John Macdonald.
P. Paterson.
Betley & Kay.
J. Carmichael.
Edward Cooper.
William Creighton.
John Eastwood.
Arthur Lepper.
Walker & Hutchinson.
Robert Sargant & Co.
George Bilton.
Richard Hastings.
Walter Macfarlane.
Scott & Laidlaw.
Hughes & Co.
Thomas Lailey.
Charles Robertson.
John Ritchey, jun.

RETAIL DRY GOODS—Continued.

J. R. Mountjoy.
G. B. Wylie.
J. Charlesworth.

WHOLESALE GROCERS.

A. V. Brown.
Thomas Brunskill.
Fitch & Matthews.
B. Torrance & Co.
F. & G. Perkins.
George Munro.
Whittemore, Rutherford & Co.

RETAIL GROCERS.

Alexander Ogilvy & Co.
A. M. Smith.
K. M. Sutherland.
Richard Yates.

HARDWARE MERCHANTS.

John Harrington.
Rice Lewis.
T. Haworth.
T. D. Harris.
Ridout Brothers.
Darling Brothers.
Hayes Brothers.
P. Paterson & Son.

DRUGGISTS.

Neil C. Love.
Joseph Beckett & Co.
Lyman Bros. & Co.
W. H. Doel.
Hugh Miller.
J. C. Lattridge.

JEWELLERS.
Rossin Brothers.
E. M. Morphy.
George Savage.
J. G. Joseph.
Henry Jackson.

FURRIERS.
Joseph Rogers.
John Salt.
J. G. Joseph.
J. Bastedo.

CHINA AND EARTHENWARE.
Patton & Co.
H. F. Norris.

HIDES AND LEATHER.
James Beaty.

MERCHANT TAILORS.
C. & W. Walker.

MUSICAL INSTRUMENTS.
A. & S. Nordheimer.

BOOKSELLERS AND STATIONERS.
Brewer, McPhail & Co.
Thomas Maclear.
Henry Rowsell.
Hugh Scobie.
A. H. Armour & Co.

BOOTS AND SHOES.
Thomas Thompson.
Edward Dack.
Brown & Childs.

WATCHMAKERS.
J. E. Ellis.
William Bell.

CLOTHIERS AND OUTFITTERS.
Evans & Hamilton.

FANCY GOODS.
James Skelton.

SADDLERY HARDWARE.
Alexander Dixon.

MANUFACTURERS.

STOVES.
J. R. Armstrong.
G. H. Cheney & Co.

PAPER.
John Taylor & Brother.

FURNITURE.
Jacques & Hay.

IRONFOUNDER.
James Good.

STEAM MILLS.
Gooderham & Worts.

SOAP AND CANDLES.
P. & R. Coate.
Peter Freeland.

STARCH.
J. A. Cull.

PIANOS
John Thomas.

GLUE.
Peter R. Lamb.

AXES.
Samuel Shaw.

Prominent Men in 1850.

ALPHABETICALLY ENUMERATED.

Dr. W. T. Aikens.
Hon. R. Baldwin.
F. W. Barron, *Principal U. C. Co'lege.*
M. Barrett, *First English Master, U. C. College.*
Charles Berczy, *Postmaster.*
Hon. W. H. Blake, *Chancellor.*
W. H. Boulton, M.P.P.
Hon. Col. Bruce, *Secy. and A.D.C. to Earl of Elgin.*
Hon. R. E. Burns, *Judge.*
John Cameron, *Cashier Commercial Bank.*
Hon. R. E. Caron, *Speaker Legislative Council.*
W. G. Cassels, *Manager Bank of B.N. America.*
H. H. Croft, *Prof. of Chemistry and Vice-Chancellor of University.*
R. G. Dalton, *Barrister.*
Lieut.-Colonel DeSalaberry, *Deputy Adjutant-General.*
Hon. W. H. Draper, *Judge Queen's Bench.*
J. C. P. Esten, *Vice-Chancellor.*
George Gurnett, *Clerk of the Peace.*
Rev. Anson Green, *Wesleyan Book Steward.*
Hon. Francis Hincks, *Inspector-General.*
J. G. Hodgins, *Secretary of Education Department.*
J. G. Howard, *Architect.*
W. B. Jarvis, *Sheriff.*
Hon. L. H. Lafontaine, *Attorney-General*
Hon. Jas. Leslie, *Provincial Secretary.*
Hon. J. B. Macauley, *Chief Justice.*

W. F. Meudell, *Collector of Customs.*
Rev. John McCaul, LL.D., *President University.*
A. T. McCord, *City Chamberlain.*
Hon. Archibald McLean, *Judge.*
E. J. Palmer, *Daguerrean Artist.*
Rev. Bishop Power.
Hon. J. H. Price, *Commissioner Crown Lands.*
William Proudfoot, *President Bank of Upper Canada.*
T. G. Ridout, *Cashier Bank of Upper Canada.*
Hon. J. B. Robinson, *Chief Justice.*
Dr. John Rolph.
Rev. Egerton Ryerson, *Chief Supt. of Education.*
Rev. Henry Scadding, *First Classical Master U. C. College.*
Hon. Henry Sherwood, *Barrister.*
J. G. Spragge, *Vice-Chancellor.*
Hon. and Right Rev. John Strachan, *Lord Bishop of Toronto.*
G. W. Strathy, *Professor of Music.*
Hon E. P. Tache, *Receiver-General.*
John F. Taylor, *Clerk and Master in Chancery.*
Kivas Tully, *Architect and Civil Engineer.*
Wm. Wedd, *Third Classical Master U. C. College.*
Hon. C. Widmer, *Surgeon.*
Rev. M. Willis, D.D., *Prof. Divinity, Knox College.*
William Wilson, *Cashier Bank of Montreal.*

It is worthy of note that the residences of all the leading men whose names are given were all south of Queen Street, except one or two who lived on that street. This will give a good idea of the improvement that has taken place in this respect.

The upper stratum of society was decidedly refined and intellectual, and not by any means as exclusive as some have represented it. Nothing so invidious in class distinctions existed as was found in Montreal up to a late period, when the line was distinctly drawn between wholesale and retail merchants, and in other ways the "upper ten" principle strictly carried out.

The number of churches in Toronto at this time was 27, divided as follows:—4 Episcopal; 1 Presbyterian Church of Scotland; 4 Wesleyan; 1 Presbyterian Church of Canada; 2 Congregational; 1 United Presbyterian; 1 Methodist New Connexion; 1 Catholic Apostolic; 1 Primitive Methodist; 2 Baptist; 1 Disciples; 2 Roman Catholic.

A Tour of Observation.

Before deciding on settling in Toronto, the writer took a trip to New York to consult with his friend and companion of the previous seven years, Mr. Edward Martin, who had preceded him, and had, like Mr. A. T. Stewart, brought out a stock of Irish embroideries, then giving employment to thousands of girls all over Ireland, and sold all over the world. My friend continued in the same trade, adding lace goods when the embroidery business fell off, and retired quite recently with a large fortune.

It was thought best that I should make a tour of several of the states as far west as Ohio, then the most rising and prosperous state in the west. Returning by the New York Central, all the large towns were visited up to Buffalo, and then Erie and Cleveland were reached by steamer. From the latter place, down to Cincinnati, the only mode of travelling was either by the stages or canal boats drawn by horses. There appeared to be nothing, either in the manners of the people met with or the mode of doing business, to induce me to settle on that side of the line.

Being invariably taken for an Englishman, and addressed as "stranger," I found that an Englishman was more of a foreigner than one of any other nationality.

There were whole villages in Ohio owned by Germans or Dutch, on the communistic principle, and no English spoken.

Apropos of speaking languages I may mention that having an uncle, who was an elder in the Methodist Episcopal Church, stationed near Syracuse, on my way through I called to see him. Having two daughters at a large school in the centre of the state of New York, he wished me to go and see them. The distance to drive being about twenty miles, we stopped to rest with one of my uncle's parishioners, and in conversation with the lady of the house she asked me whether I had spoken the English language before I came to America.

At once perceiving that her question was put on account of my being a native Irishman, I answered her accordingly.

Having seen persons from different parts of Europe in that country, and all speaking their own language, she naturally thought I should know mine.

We found my cousins boarding with the family of the sheriff of the county, and the lady herself busy with a broom, after using which to good purpose she was soon ready to entertain us in her drawing-room. "Helps" being hard to find, most of the ladies were obliged to help themselves.

Being everywhere reminded that I was now in a free country, I have frequently regretted not having crossed the Ohio River into Kentucky, where slavery was in full vigor, and human chattels were bought and sold every day; and never having experienced any particular oppression in the country from which I had recently come, I failed to appreciate the advantages of the freedom of which I was so constantly reminded as existing in the United States.

Describing the gaiety going on in Washington while slavery existed there at this time, Whittier writes:

> Pitying God! Is that a woman
> On whose wrists the shackles clash?
> Is that shriek she utters human,
> Underneath the stinging lash?
> Are they men whose eyes of madness
> From that sad procession flash?

> Still the dance goes gaily onward—
> What is it to wealth and pride
> That without the stars are looking
> On a scene which earth should hide;
> That the slave ship lies in waiting,
> Rocking on Potamac's tide?

This being the year in which Louis Philippe and his accomplished consort were driven from the Tuilleries, and every vestige of royalty ruthlessly destroyed, and Lamartine & Co. had established the Republic of "*Liberté, egalité, et fraternité*" in France, additional favor seemed to have been given to these principles.

While there was much to admire in the apparent absence of poverty, and a good degree of prosperity which seemed to exist, and an appearance of greater equality amongst all classes the further west I went, it was plainly seen that distinctions still existed, and society was divided into classes, as in every other community. There were some illiterate and others educated, some rude and rough in manners, others more refined and cultured.

To judge of the manners of the people at the *table d'hôte* of the best hotel in Cleveland at the time, and compare them with these seen at present, the decision must be, that a marvellous improvement has taken place, as well as in all other western cities.

This being the place where a stranger has the best opportunity of remarking the habits of people, my first impression was one of surprise that so little time should be devoted to table enjoyment. When the gong sounded there was a perfect rush, and a grab at everything that could be reached. Vegetables of all kinds, with pickles, were mixed up, and made to disappear before the waiters had time to present the bill of fare, and then fish, flesh and fowl were taken on the same plate, with a variety of puddings and pies; all of which were conveyed to the mouth with the knife, the fork only doing duty while the meat was being cut; and by the time a person not in a hurry got through with his soup, and was discussing the bill of fare, the table was half empty, and almost entirely so by the time the substantials were reached.

The most surprising thing was to find these people afterwards quietly sitting round, apparently having abundance of time on their hands.

On returning to Canada a trip was taken to Quebec, including a short stay at the principal towns and cities *en route*.

Were it possible for a large proportion of the persons leaving the British Islands to postpone their decision as to their destination till they had travelled through the principal States of the Union, and over a portion of this Dominion, it can scarcely be doubted that by far a larger number would prefer Canada. But as, either through correspondence with friends, or the representations of interested agents, nearly all decide as to the place of their future settlement, they lose the advantage to be gained by actual observation.

This delightful trip, entirely by water on the lake and river steamers, could not fail to make a favorable impression. No longer addressed as "stranger," I everywhere found friends, and a thorough "home" feeling was constantly experienced, till on my return to Toronto there was no hesitation as to making it my future home.

First Return Visit to Europe.

The passage to England, on the Cunard steamer *Niagara*, in the winter of 1849-50 was a most perilous one. When on the Banks of Newfoundland we found ourselves suddenly surrounded by immense fields of ice, which increased so rapidly that in a few hours the man at the mast-head sung out, "Nothing but ice all around!" Having Her Majesty's mails on board, Capt. Leitch was not to be kept long in such a position, and having consulted with his officers, determined to push through. Orders were given to go ahead at half-speed, and after several hours of bumping and grinding, that was terrible to witness, the cry came from aloft, "Clear water ahead!" and on getting out of the ice we found the grand vessel almost as helpless as a log on the water. Every float on both paddle-wheels had been literally torn to pieces, except six, and these vessels not being rigged for sailing, like the modern screw steamers, there was no prospect of progress from that quarter.

With the foresight which has characterized the Cunard Line from the commencement, duplicate floats were on board, and the carpenter's crew, in spite of the rolling of the vessel, in a comparatively short time had all the floats replaced, and we were soon again under full steam for Liverpool.

Shortly after arriving in London a partnership was formed with Mr. James Stevenson, with whom I had lived for several years in Dublin, and who was then residing in London, as buyer and manager with Munt, Brown & Co., Wood Street, London, Luton and Dunstable. Mr. Stevenson came to Toronto in the following spring.

Windsor Castle.

"Imperial dome of Edward, wise and brave!
Where warlike Honor's brightest banners wave,
Thy royal piles that rise elate,
With many an antique tower in massy state."

Never having seen Her Majesty the Queen, I expressed a wish to visit Windsor with that object, and accompanied by my brother, who was buyer for the house of Brown, Davis & Halse, of Gresham Street, and afterwards for Cook Sons & Co., St. Paul's Church Yard, went down to that historical town.

We knew by the Royal Standard floating from the Castle tower that Her Majesty was at home, and after inspecting the portions of the Castle accessible to visitors during the Queen's residence there, and St. George's Chapel, and getting a splendid view of the surrounding country from the top of the tower, we had not yet seen any indication of the Queen's appearance, and were returning to the railway station to take the first train for London, when, while walking in a private street, without a single person in sight, we heard the noise of horses' feet, and presently an equerry in royal livery came in view, and immediately afterwards the Queen and Prince Albert, in an open carriage and pair, enjoying a quiet drive. We, of course, un-

WINDSOR CASTLE.

covered our heads, and in return had a most gracious bow and smile from Her Majesty, Prince Albert at the same time raising his hat in response to our salutation.

This was an opportunity seldom enjoyed, even by residents of London, and often earnestly desired by Americans, and although having seen Her Majesty frequently afterwards, no sight on state occasions was so gratifying as this one.

Commencement of Commercial Travelling in Canada.

In 1850 the firm of Taylor & Stevenson was established, and their business was carried on at the corner of Yonge and Colborne Streets, in the building now occupied by Messrs. Buntin, Reid & Co. It was then newly built, and was one of the finest warehouses in the city.

Mr. Stevenson having had extensive connections with all the straw goods manufacturers in London and Bedfordshire, that trade was made a leading branch. The first importations of these goods, in the spring of 1851, were the largest that had ever been made into Canada, and having sent out circulars, we had buyers from Windsor in the west to Brockville in the east. The whole importations were closed out in a few weeks, and such was the quantity to be entered and packed that all hands were obliged to work for several weeks every night, except Saturday, till 2 or 3 o'clock, so as to get the goods forwarded within a reasonable time. To obviate this in future, the idea of taking the orders beforehand and shipping the goods direct soon took shape, and in the fall of that year samples were got out from the leading manufacturers, and the writer undertook to travel for orders.

After the close of navigation there was only one regular mode of travelling. Weller's line of Mail Stages left daily for Montreal and Quebec, and in this way the writer, who was the first commercial traveller in Canada, started from Toronto.

In these days of Pullman cars and commercial hotels, to hear travellers complain of the discomforts and annoyances is rather amusing to those who have ploughed through mud and slush, sometimes carrying rails off the fences to "pry" the wheels of the stages out of the ruts, and, again, in snow, carrying shovels to dig out the horses when large drifts were encountered; all which is known to the writer by actual experience.

The accommodation for baggage for nine or ten passengers consisted of a "rack" at the back of the stage, so that baggage trunks and 300 lbs. weight of samples were never even thought of up to the time of the opening of the railroads.

To meet this difficulty the writer had his samples sent out in miniature models, so small that samples representing *thousands of dozens*, for which he actually took orders, could all be carried in a small valise.

The experiment was a great success; the goods were all packed in England to the various marks, and in the spring of 1852 were shipped in bulk to the various merchants, from Quebec to Windsor, or sent to Toronto for distribution.

During that fall not a single traveller was met on the whole road, but the following season a gentleman appeared as a competitor from a New York house, and one or two others, amongst them Mr. Darling, of Montreal, in the hardware trade, and Mr. D. B. Macdonald, in fancy dry goods.

The summer trips by steamers were very pleasant, but in the winter there was nothing but hardships, and in crossing the ice at different points very great danger. My rule was, that wherever the mail driver would venture I would go.

On one occasion, in crossing from Belleville to Picton, the ice had melted, and in the whole distance across the Bay of Quinte no ice could be seen—the horses being almost knee deep in water. Again, in crossing from Kingston to Cape Vincent with four horses in the Mail Stage, and a heavy mail with a large number of passengers, where the ice was cracking, the horses had to "jump the cracks." Many rivers and canals were crossed in this way.

One adventure on the road will give an idea of snow drifts.

The town of Brockville was always to me, whether in summer or winter, a delightful resting-place, a sort of oasis in my travels from east to west, or *vice versa*. Young men away from home in a new country will appreciate my feelings when I say, that to find a sort of Canadian home, when a young traveller, was indeed a delightful feeling. Here I always rested for a few days amongst my friends—the Hon. George and Messrs. John and James Crawford and their connections, and especially Mr. Sheriff Sherwood, and the late Hon. John Ross, whom I had the pleasure of meeting there frequently.

In the winter of 1853 I arrived there from the East in a heavy snow storm; it was the 23rd of December, and I wished to get to Toronto by Christmas Day.

On the 24th the Mail Stage came along, and having supplied ourselves with wooden shovels, we started for Kingston. Having got on a few miles we found the drifts getting worse, and after repeated efforts in literally digging the horses out, we were compelled to put up at a small tavern on the road side, and here, with bitter regrets at my folly in not remaining at Brockville, where I might have spent a pleasant Christmas, we were compelled to remain all Christmas Day.

In the meantime the pathmasters had been notified by messengers that the track must be opened at their peril to allow Her Majesty's Mails to proceed.

On the 26th we again started, having much the same shovelling as before, when, having got on a few miles, we heard the sound of the down stage's horn, and knew the track had been broken, and arrived in Kingston in a reasonable time.

The formation of the Commercial Travellers' Association followed soon after the opening of the railroads, and has grown to immense proportions, as the annual reports of the various associations now existing abundantly show.

In the last year (1874) in which the writer travelled in connection with the Toronto Association, his orders taken, in the United States and Canada, with some assistance, represented close on half-a-million dollars, and during the year scarcely a day was lost. With the comforts and facilities afforded by the Pullman and Wagner cars, enabling travellers to work all day and travel at night, and the best hotels on the Continent competing for the patronage of the commercial travellers, the occupation has become, from being a drudgery, quite a pleasant life.

Having served a good apprenticeship, and then given a son to succeed me in the Association, anything connected with commercial travelling is still a matter of great interest.

The following newspapers were published: *British Colonist, Christian Guardian, Daily Patriot and Express, Globe, North American, Canada Gazette, Church, Examiner, Mirror, Watchman*.

It will be seen that of all the papers published in 1850 only two continue, the *Globe* and *Christian Guardian*, the latter being the oldest established weekly paper in Upper Canada.

W. H. Smith says of Toronto in 1850:—"Let a traveller, starting from Montreal on a summer trip, proceed westward till he arrives at Toronto. He sees a city, which he is told fifty years ago was a swamp, with street beyond street and building after building. He sees town lots selling for £10,000 an acre where thirty or forty years ago flourished a garden; a magnificent church being erected where an old settler told him he once shot wild ducks."

In connection with the old Mechanics' Institute it should be recorded that Mr. Robert Edwards was the polite and obliging Secretary for many years, and it is also due to the memory of Mr. John Harrington to state that it was chiefly through his exertions and the liberality of the citizens that the present Free Library building was erected. The Music Hall in the upper part was, for years, the principal place for concerts, lectures and various exhibitions, and many celebrated men appeared from time to time on its platform, including Wilkie Collins, Proctor, Pepper, Punshon, and many others.

Important public meetings were held, and public balls and banquets took place in this Hall, for any of which its capacity would be insufficient at the present time.

The office of the Express Company, styled the European, United States and Canadian Express Company, was on Front Street, and James Burns was agent.

Public Institutions.

Athenæum and Commercial News Room.
Mechanics' Institute.
Post Office.
Telegraph Office.

University (old building).
Upper Canada College.
Osgoode Hall.
Parliament Buildings.

Financial Affairs 1850.

REVENUE.	£	s.	d.	EXPENDITURE.	£	s.	d.
Assessment	8,540	0	0	Interest	4,800	0	0
Rental	3,417	5	0	Salaries	2,875	0	0
Fees	1,325	0	0	Roads	1,355	0	0
Licenses	994	0	0	Gas	1,277	7	4
Drainage	150	0	0	Fire	1,600	0	0
Fees & Arrears of Taxes	2,366	4	0	Redemption of City Notes	850	0	0
Cash on hand	530	5	0	Use of County Jail	600	0	0
				Ward Appropriation	500	0	0
				Incidental Police Expenditure	110	0	0
				Printing and Stationery	280	0	0
				Coroner's Expenses	115	0	0
				Miscellaneous	2,094	0	0
				Estimated Revenue over Expenditure	16	6	8
	£17,322	14	0		£17,322	14	0
	or $69,290	80			or $69,290	00	

CITY DEBT.	£	s.	d.	ASSETS.	£	s.	d.
Debentures	67,372	15	6	Outstanding Rents, Fees, Debts, Taxes, and Cash on hand	2,436	9	0
Corporation Notes	17,346	15	0	Leaving to be paid	84,727	16	2
Sundries	2,444	14	8				
	£87,184	5	2		£87,184	5	2
	or $348,737	04			or $348,737	04	

Toronto in 1850.

In 1850 the principal streets running east and west were Front, King, Richmond, Adelaide and Queen; running north and south were Yonge, Church, Bay and York. These were the most thickly settled and best business portions of the city.

The two principal thoroughfares, and the streets containing the largest number of shops, were King and Yonge.

A little eastward of the centre of the city were situated the Market Building and City Hall. The old City Hall was a decent, old-fashioned pile of red brick, the front of which was on King Street. Beneath and behind was the Market, walled in, and enclosed with gates.

After the fire the new City Hall, the present one, was erected of white brick, opposite the Market Square, and running down towards the Bay.

This is a very strange looking building, and it was unfortunate for the reputation of the architect employed that he had not left the Province before he completed the building, instead of afterwards.

The old City Buildings having been destroyed in the great fire, a magnificent pile of buildings was erected in their place, called the St. Lawrence Hall and St. Lawrence Buildings.

At this time the St. James' Cathedral was in the course of erection; Knox Church, Holy Trinity, and St. Michael's had been built.

Bonding System via United States.

In the spring of 1848 there were no new spring goods shown in Toronto till the middle of May, on the opening of navigation. The arrival of sailing vessels, which then conveyed all freight to Quebec, was looked for with great anxiety. The ladies, in the meantime, were compelled to wear their last spring bonnets, dresses and mantles, and the retail dry goods men had a chance of selling off their old stock from the previous season. The effect of this was that when the goods arrived in Toronto the country storekeepers, who awaited the event, came in a body to the city, and at seven o'clock in the morning it was no unusual sight to see as many as thirty or forty on the street, awaiting the opening of the warehouses, and ready to grab at the first lot of goods they could get their hands on—styles and prices being considered a matter of no importance: they wanted British and foreign dry goods, and were determined to have them. There was no time for making prices; that was to follow after the rush, and each man filled his locker or bunk with an indiscriminate collection, subject to revision on the first opportunity. When, perhaps, his neighbor's back was turned, to make a fair exchange was considered no robbery, should he happen to spy a chance lot of something he coveted in his neighbor's bunk. As the goods were sold at sterling prices, with a certain advance added, the invoice book was then called into requisition, and goods entered accordingly. In this way the whole importations were generally pretty well cleared out in a few weeks, and as the country merchants were supposed to have laid in their whole season's stock, the wholesale houses had a quiet time in the warehouse after this, however it might be in the counting house, the financing following such a system requiring much tact and ingenuity. This state of things could not continue, with the increasing demand for early spring goods, and something must be done in the way of improvement.

While British and foreign goods were arriving at Boston or New York weekly, Canadian merchants were debarred from getting any of their importations from these ports via the American railroads, there being no law to permit it.

The firm of Hill, Sears & Co., of Boston, a branch of the London firm of Alfred Hill & Co., seeing a prospect of getting hold of the Canadian business, supported by the Montreal and Toronto wholesale houses, undertook to make arrangements for a bonding system, and after some negotiations with the Government at Washington, were successful in their object. In the spring of 1852 permission was given to allow goods for Canada to pass through on the bonding system at present in operation. The writer, with representatives of two other wholesale houses, spent a week in New York with brokers at the Custom House, completing the arrangements for the despatch of the first goods by that route, and after many days' delay on the road, a large lot of goods, comprising the bulk of the spring imports, arrived at Oswego.

Toronto Bay was then frozen solid, and as merchants east, west and north were anxiously awaiting the arrival of the goods, there was no other course but to make a channel for the steamer *Admiral* to get out. This was accomplished by sawing the ice from Yonge Street to the Queen's wharf, and in this way the spring goods arrived comparatively early.

First Great World's Fair.

The year 1851 was remarkable for the grand project of Prince Albert to assemble a display of the industrial resources of the world. Subscriptions were raised, men of science were chosen to form a committee, and a colossal palace of glass was erected from a design suggested by Mr. (afterwards Sir) Joseph Paxton, head gardener to the Duke of Devonshire, at Chatsworth. The building from which the design was taken was the smallest of the conservatories of the "Palace of the Peak," and contained the celebrated Victoria Regia lily. When the great palace was built in Hyde Park, a mighty bazaar of nations was summoned.

Nor was the summons unavailing. Before the opening London was crowded with foreigners and native visitors, all anxious to enter the wonderful dome. Even immense London could not afford accommodation for the throngs that poured in; people walked the streets through the night or slept in cabs, unable to procure a bed.

And who that witnessed it can ever forget the opening scene? Her Majesty, in the pride of beauty and glory and domestic happiness, looking around on the representatives of all nations, while the Venerable Archbishop of Canterbury pronounced his benediction on that meeting of the nations in peace and prosperity.

Then day by day poured into that fancy palace the strangely mingled crowd of voluble Frenchmen, grave Germans, sharp

Americans, active, monkey-like Chinamen, and sensual-looking Turks; while the rustics, who had never travelled beyond their native village, gazed with astonishment, and even with awe, as they entered the lofty transept, which actually enclosed tall elm trees, and where the tropical plants, the fountains, the statuary, and the rich fabrics of India realized the tales of the "Arabian Nights," and seemed the work of enchantment.

The building was afterwards removed to Sydenham, and was greatly enlarged so as to form the now celebrated Crystal Palace.

At this exhibition Canada was well represented, and obtained a large number of prizes and medals.

Turning the First Sod of the Northern Railway.

On October 15th, 1851, the first sod of the Northern Railway was turned by Lady Elgin, assisted by Mayor Bowes, nearly opposite the Parliament Buildings.

Mayor Bowes was in full official costume—cocked hat and sword, knee breeches, silk stockings, and shoes with steel buckles.

The earth dug by her ladyship, with a beautiful silver spade, was taken by His Worship a short distance in an oak wheelbarrow, the whole ceremony creating great interest.

Mr. F. C. Capreol had so far seen his much ridiculed scheme carried into effect.

No longer laughed at and spoken of as "Mad Capreol," as the writer has often heard him called, he had shown great method in his madness. Having been a fellow-passenger with him when crossing on his visit to England to raise the necessary capital—at first by a kind of lottery scheme, and afterwards in the legitimate way—I saw his determination to carry out his plans, and the clear prospect he had of the future of the undertaking.

Had his energies been spared, the Huron and Ontario Ship Canal might soon be an accomplished fact, not at all more improbable than the Manchester Ship Canal was fifteen or twenty years ago.

Tariff in 1850-51.

Mr. W. H. Smith, writing at this time on the tariff, says: "We are a queer people. While we are writing a public meeting is being held in the St. Lawrence Hall, Toronto, for the purpose, as the requisition says, of addressing a petition to Her Most Gracious Majesty, Queen Victoria, and the British Legislature, for the purpose of obtaining a more favorable home market for the staple productions of the country than we at present enjoy, and for the adoption of such a course of commercial policy towards the Colonies generally as may prove beneficial to them and to the Mother Country.

"Do not these gentlemen fear that the British Prime Minister, in glancing over the Canadian tariff, will be apt to tell the signers of the petition that 'Jupiter helps those who help themselves.'

"In our legislative wisdom we charge on sugar, tea and coffee, articles which we cannot produce ourselves, a duty of $12\frac{1}{2}$ per cent.; while on tobacco, which we can grow, we charge the same.

"On wine, rum and brandy, which we do not make, we charge 25 per cent.; while whiskey, which we do make, we admit at $12\frac{1}{2}$ per cent.

"On spices, fruits, etc., which we cannot produce, we charge 30 per cent.; while hemp, flax and tow, undressed lard, charcoal, broom corn, and wool are admitted at $2\frac{1}{2}$ per cent.; and still further, as if this were not sufficient, we extend our liberality and admit pot and pearl ash, wheat and Indian corn duty free."

All dry goods, hardware, etc. at this time paid a duty of $12\frac{1}{2}$ per cent. *ad valorem*.

In the fall of 1852 the locomotive *Lady Elgin* was tried, on the 6th October, on the Northern Railroad, by order of the Engineer, under whose direction the engine was erected. This was the first locomotive run in Upper Canada.

A considerable number of persons congregated near the Queen's wharf to witness the trial, and appeared much pleased with the "iron horse" as he snorted along the track. The rails were laid for about fourteen miles.

The contract for the railroad from Toronto to Guelph was given at this time to Messrs. C. S. Gzowski & Co., for £7,408 currency per mile—£355,600 for the whole distance.

It was also in 1852 that the contract for the establishment of a line of steamers between Liverpool and the St. Lawrence was completed, the contracting parties being Mr. J. Young, then late Commissioner of Public Works, and Messrs. Kean & McCarthy, the ship owners.

The conditions were that Messrs. Kean & McCarthy should keep up a regular line of large and powerful screw steamers to leave Liverpool for the St. Lawrence monthly or fortnightly, while navigation was open, and monthly during the winter to Portland; the maximum passage rates to be £21 sterling, first-class; £12 12s, second-class; and £6 6s., third-class. These steamers began to run the following spring.

Two years later the contract was annulled, and an arrangement made with the firm of Edmonstone, Allan & Co., of Montreal. The small fleet of the last named company has since developed into the line well known as the Allan Line of Trans-Atlantic Steamships.

At this time Toronto had begun to display a rapidity of growth and stability, produced by wholesome enterprise, both encouraging and remarkable. In describing its appearance in 1852 it was said that such strides had been taken in improvement that the effect produced on the mind of a stranger, when entering the bay and viewing the city from the deck of a steamer, was very pleasing and striking. In the evening the spires and domes, lighted up with the parting rays of the setting sun, the dark woods at the back, and the numerous handsome villas which flanked the bay, combined in creating an effective *coup d'œil.*

A most prominent object at the eastern end was the jail, by no means a picturesque or prepossessing one, but still might be taken as an indication of the generally substantial and appropriate character of the buildings, being a solid symmetrical mass of gray lime-stone, sufficiently significant of its purpose—perhaps in the same sense as that in which the traveller stated that he always knew he was in a civilized country when he saw a gibbet!

Be this as it may, the writer has a distinct recollection of seeing two men hung off a platform erected on the west side of the wall which surrounded the building and which still remains.

The lighthouse on the point of the peninsula, the Lunatic Asylum, Government Wharf, Parliament Buildings, City Hall, and Trinity Church, all attracted the eye.

The sites of the St. James' Cathedral and St. Michael's, could also be seen.

The Industrial Crystal Palace.

Exhibitions of the Provincial Agricultural Association of Canada West, incorporated in July, 1847, were held irregularly till 1852.

At the close of the Exhibition in Toronto in 1852, it was resolved to memorialize the Government to appropriate a certain sum of money to purchase land whereon to erect permanent buildings for the holding of their annual exhibitions.

To this resolution is due the structure then erected, for in granting to the Corporation of the City of Toronto the fee simple of that portion of the garrison reserve lying immediately south of the Lunatic Asylum, for a public park, the Government made it a condition that not less than twenty acres should be appropriated for the holding of the Provincial Association's annual exhibitions whenever it might be required for that purpose.

This condition was accepted by the Council with a liberality which did them honor, at once appropriating £5,000 for the purpose of erecting permanent buildings thereon.

On the 15th July, 1852, the corner stone was laid by W. H. Boulton, Mayor, in the presence of a large number of citizens. The band of the Royal Canadian Rifles performed at intervals during the ceremony.

This building was afterwards used as a military barracks, and was occupied by the 13th Hussars, the band of which regi-

INDUSTRIAL CRYSTAL PALACE

ment for several years contributed so much to the pleasure of the people of Toronto; and here, in 1860, His Royal Highness the Prince of Wales was entertained at a public ball.

The *Anglo-American Magazine* says:—" Dwelling in a city whose every stone and brick has been placed in its present position under the eyes of many who remember the locality as the sight of primeval woods the region of swamp; of some who have seen the lonely wigwam of the Mississauqua give place to the log house of the earlier settler, and this in its turn disappear to be replaced by the substantial and elegant structures of modern art,—we find we are justified in yielding to the pardonable if vain desire to tell the wonderful metamorphosis of forty years.

" It is meet that we should rejoice over the triumphs of civilization, the onward progress of our race, the extension of our language, institutions, taste, manners, customs and feelings.

" In no spot within British territory could we find aggregated, in so striking a manner, the evidences of this startling change. In none should we trace, so strongly marked, the imprint of national emigration. In few discover such ripened fruits of successful colonization.

"The genius of Britain presides over the destiny of her offspring. The glory of the empire enshrouds the prosperity of the colony, the noble courage and strength of the lion inspires and protects the industry of the [beaver. The oak and the maple unite their shadows over the breasts that beat in unison for the common weal.

" We boast not superior intelligence, we claim not greater or even an equal share of local advantages over the sister cities of our country; but we assert, in sincerity of belief and in justice to ourselves, a rapidity of growth and a stability produced by wholesome enterprise as encouraging as it is remarkable.

" The fine bay in front of the city is formed by the remarkable peninsula (this was before the gap was formed) which, commencing at the river Don, stretches away westward, with a singular bend or curve at its western extremity, until it approaches the mainland opposite the garrison. Here a very narrow channel, marked by buoys, admits vessels of almost any tonnage to shelter and safe anchorage.

"Over this extended sheet of water may be seen, in summer, many a graceful and tidy little craft, gliding along under the skilful management of the amateur crew—yachting being a favorite amusement and source of recreation to the inhabitants after the toils of the day and the confinement of their occupations. A considerable number of steamers, both British and American, arriving and departing almost hourly, and numerous sailing vessels, laden with the produce of the back country or freighted with valuable imports from other lands, impart animation and bustle to the scene, which truly indicates the commercial activity of a thriving population; while the wharves which skirt the bay, with their large warehouses and busy throng of stevedores, porters, carts and cabs, confirm this impression."

The assessed value of the property in the Corporation was $12,465,600. The value of dutiable and free goods imported was $2,778,388; the exports, $1,636,824.

In the past year the beauty of the principal streets had increased very greatly. St. James' Cathedral had been completed, except the spire. This church, built of white brick (for which Toronto had become famous), in the restored style of architecture, was then decidedly the most beautiful and appropriate religious structure to be found in Canada. In the order of civil architecture, the Court House, then in course of erection, was considered to be as fine a structure of its own kind as the church.

But public buildings may sometimes proceed rapidly, while general distress prevents improvements in domestic architecture. This, however, was not the case in Toronto.

A correspondent of the Montreal *Herald* writes at this time: "Upon King Street we noticed the builders at work in five or six places, besides observing several new and handsome brick houses, where a year ago wooden ones stood. Our readers who are acquainted with Toronto will remember the corner of Bay and King Streets, which used to be disfigured by some wooden

ST. JAMES' CATHEDRAL.

the
prin
Esp
squ
offe
A
prop
it m

shanties; these have been completely swept away, to make room for elegant brick houses. While the retailers have been improving their places of business, the wholesale houses have also continued to augment in number and beauty."

The present Bank of Commerce was then newly built, and was by far the finest wholesale warehouse in the city, and was about to be occupied by Messrs. Ross, Mitchell & Co., wholesale dry goods merchants.

During the times the Parliament remained in Toronto, between 1850 and 1857, many men celebrated in history could be heard to speak. Papineau, W. L. Mackenzie, Cauchon, Cartier, Prince, Merritt, Gugy, Drummond, Dorion, Hincks, D'Arcy McGee, Baldwin, John Sandfield Macdonald, and others.

When Mr. McGee rose to speak, the most profound attention prevailed, all admitting the superior charm of his eloquence. No matter what the subject of debate might be, it was invested with new interest, and having at command art, science, poetry, and history, his ideas were clothed in most beautiful language, and were full of originality, and given with such a sprinkling of wit and humor as never failed to delight his listeners.

In 1852 Mr. George Brown made his maiden Parliamentary speech, which occupied two hours.

On the 28th of December, 1853, Lord Elgin left Toronto, and was succeeded by Sir Edmund Head, in 1854.

The Esplanade.

It is said that when the Grand Trunk Railway was being built, the Company offered to build stone wharves or quays along the front of the city, with iron bridges across the tracks at the principal crossings, and at less than the cost of the present Esplanade, but through the obstructiveness of some, and the squabbling and procrastination of others, of the Corporation, the offer was withdrawn.

At present, when so much public attention is directed to the proposed new street and general improvement of the city front, it may be interesting to refer to the various schemes proposed from 1850 to 1854, and for this purpose we extract a few items from Maclear's *Anglo-American Magazine.*

The "Editor's Shanty" was supposed to be the resort of representative characters, under the *sobriquets* of the "Doctor," the "Laird," and the "Major."

These gentlemen met to discuss the current events, and to review the literature of the week.

The question of the proposed Esplanade having come up for discussion, the Laird begins:

"But, Major, what was ye gaun to say aboot the Toronto Esplanade at our last meetin', when Mrs. Grundy telt us the supper was ready? I see the newspapers are makin' a great fuss about it now. One day we have a long report from Cumberland to the Northern Railway directors, another day a letter from the City Surveyor about it, in another it is announced that Gzowski and the Grand Trunk contractors are gaun to make the thing at once. Did ye hear onything mair aboot it?"

MAJOR—"I was then going to draw your attention to a long letter which appeared in the May number of the *Canadian Journal*, prior to any of these you have just mentioned, the author of which signs himself "A Member of the Canadian Institute," and advocates strongly the importance of making provision for public walks, baths, wash-houses, etc., and sets forth a new plan for the Esplanade, by which the railways can be brought into the very heart of the city without the necessity of level crossings. I thought at the time that the plan, although probably too costly, and on too grand a scale, was a feasible one, and deserving of more attention than it seems to have received. Since then I am glad to see that the Chief Engineer of the Northern Railway has taken it up, and strongly recommended its adoption, with slight modifications."

LAIRD—"Before we gang any further, I would like to ken the correct meaning of level crossings, for there were nae railroads when I was at schule, maist saxty years syne, and I'm rather particularly concerned in this matter—one of my friends has a water lot near Yonge Street."

MAJOR--"When one railway crosses another on the same

horizontal plane, or where a railway crosses a street in the same manner, that is to say, without either being bridged, it is termed a level crossing, and they are the cause of a great many accidents."

Doctor—"You will recollect, Laird, of that serious collision, only a few months ago, near Detroit, when one passenger train ran into another on a level crossing, to the great destruction of life and property. Level crossings have always been a source of danger, and should, at any cost, be avoided, if possible, in crowded thoroughfares."

Laird—"I understand it noo. Indeed I thocht it was that, yet I aye like to mak sure; but I dinna see why the needna gang slower through a town; there's nn use to biss through as if the deil was at their heels."

Doctor—"Yes, my good Laird, but there are innumerable chances of danger, however slow the trains may travel,—the locomotives themselves have been known to become unmanageable and run away. Horses are apt to get frightened, women and children may be overtaken while crossing the tracks, or old gentlemen, like yourself and the Major, who do not hear quite so well as in your younger years, may make even as narrow escapes as *he* did at Waterloo."

Laird—"Toot, mon, I can hear yon whussle half a mile awa'. I'm no sae deaf as a' that, and maybe there are some older and deafer than me (joking). I'll tell ye, Doctor, gin there be as muckle danger as you say, gentlemen in your profession should keep a *calm sough*. A broken leg noo and then would aye be mair grist to your mill. I think we'd better cry quits noo, as we're gettin' aff the thread, and I'm anxious to hear aboot this plan of the Major's. It's strange I didna see the letter he spoke of."

Major—"Indeed, Laird, it's altogether my fault. I lent the *Journal* for May to a friend of mine, who only returned it a few days ago, but here it is; and, although the letter is rather long, it refers to various other matters, which we may discuss at another time. With your permission I will read the letter."

Doctor and Laird—"Do. Go on, go on."

MAJOR—"There was a lithographed plan which accompanied the letter, and you will have some trouble to understand the letter without it. However, here goes."

[Major reads the letter]:

"To the Editor *Canadian Journal*,—The water frontage of Toronto, extending over a length of from two to three miles, and up to the present time almost unoccupied, is now about to be used for railway purposes.

"Adjoining thereto, and extending about three-fourths of a mile along the south side of Front Street, immediately to the east of the old fort, a tract of land, averaging in width about 100 feet, was some years ago reserved for the public as a promenade or pleasure ground, which reserve is also being appropriated by the railway companies for their own use.

"Much has lately been written, and far more has been said, regarding the occupation of the water frontage by the railway companies. One party advocates the conversion of every foot of ground now lying waste, into track, brick and mortar Another party, with more concern for the healthful recreation of future generations than the convenience of the present, insists on these reserves for pleasure grounds being retained for the purpose they were originally intended to serve. All must admit that the interests of the public and the railway companies are one in the most important particulars, and that every facility should be afforded them in endeavoring to establish their work; but, if in so doing it be found expedient that these public grounds should be surrendered for the purposes of business—the life and soul of all commercial cities—it ought not to be forgotten that posterity has some claim on the representatives of the public at the present day, and some effort should be made to provide breathing space for those who come after us.

"It will indeed be a reproach if, within the limits of the City of Toronto, comprising an area of six square miles, and which, half a century ago, was just emerging from the wilderness, a few acres be not set apart and held inviolate for these purposes."

TORONTO ESPLANADE.
THE DESIGN OF KIVAS TULLY, C.E.
(BIRD'S EYE VIEW FROM THE NORTH AMERICAN HOTEL)

pu
cro
und
Loo
and
tap
n' th
brid
thin
M.
You
as th
want
roads
[M
"It
entire
nine r
only l
and fc
"Fr
of and
and p
trees t
"Th
the wl
The br

Doctor—"I quite agree with the writer in many respects. It will indeed be a great reproach if space be not left for a few parks and public walks. She has now, exclusive of the proposed Esplanade and Terrace, only one lung for the airing of 40,000 human beings, with almost a certainty of that number reaching 100,000 in ten years. I refer to the College Avenue, a strip of land about half a mile long by 130 feet wide, and if that be insufficient now for the recreation of the inhabitants, what will it be in ten years hence?"

Laird—"Onybody will admit that the arguments in favor of public works are guid, an' that it's better to hae nae "level crossings" if ye can arrange so as no to hae them, yet if I understand your plan, Major, I dinna think it'll work weel. Look at the number of bridges required to cross the railways, and the trouble it wad be to climb up a slope as high as the tap of a locomotive, just to come doun the other side again, and a' the gudes frae the wharves wad hae to be drawn up to the bridge and doun again to the street, in the same way. I rather think the carters wad gie up work a'thegither."

Major—"Ah, Laird, I see you are laboring under a mistake. You have forgotten that Front Street is already about as high as the bridges would require to be, and that slopes would be wanted only from the wharves upward, similar to the present roads from the wharves up to the level of Front Street."

[Major continues to read]:

"It is proposed to set apart a strip of land throughout the entire length of the city, of a width sufficient to accommodate nine railway tracks, to be level with the wharves, to be crossed only by bridges, and to be used solely as a railway approach and for railway connections.

"Front Street to be converted into a Terrace above the level of and separate from the railway approach, by a retaining wall and parapet, to be 120 feet wide, and planted with rows of trees throughout the entire length.

"The entire area south of the Front Street Terrace to be on the wharfage level, and reached by slopes from the bridges. The bridges may be of iron of a simple ornamental character.

"It is also proposed to reserve certain portions for the landing of steamboats, for private forwarders, for baths and washhouses, or for general public service. The places allotted for this purpose on the plans are situated at the foot of York and Yonge Streets, and at the rear of the St. Lawrence Hall, and are named, respectively, the Niagara, the City, and St. Lawrence Basins; while contemplating improvements on so grand a scale, the selecting of a site to be dedicated to a great public building should not be lost sight of. I refer to one of which even now the want is felt, viz.: The Canadian Museum, for the formation of which the Canadian Institute is making strenuous exertions, and also a permanent home for that Society.

"The very best situation would doubtless be in the vacant space at the intersection of Yonge Street with the grand Terrace (where the Custom House and Soap Factory now stand), or south of the railway tracks facing the bridges from Yonge Street, as shown on the plan.

"There can be no good reason why the building should not be sufficiently extensive to include a Merchants' Hall and Exchange under the same roof, or offices for telegraph companies, brokers, etc., in its basement, or why it should not be as ornamental and imposing as its central position would require, or the purpose of its erection demand."

Mr. Cumberland's report is then read, when the Major proceeds.

MAJOR—" After these two documents we come to the last that has appeared on this subject—a letter from Mr. Thomas, City Surveyor. I feel rather fatigued, Doctor, perhaps you will read the extract marked. You will see that the leading feature of Mr. Thomas' plan is to build a street or Esplanade over the railway tracks on stone piers and brick arches, extending the whole length from Simcoe to Parliament Streets, with flights of stone steps leading up thereto at intervals. I can scarcely yet venture an opinion, but it seems to be rather an extravagant idea of the value of space, to put one street over another on arches, when the same object can be attained at much less cost by taking in sixty or seventy feet more of the bay."

DOCTOR reads: "I purpose, therefore, to make Front Street, from Simcoe to Parliament, a business street, and of such a width as not to destroy the Custom House, or the valuable wholesale and other stores already built and now in course of erection on the south side of Front Street to the Esplanade, securing the frontage of these valuable water lots.

"I would then leave from Front Street a depth of from one hundred to one hundred and fifty feet, for the building lots, whereon to erect, as may be required, the railway stations, the proposed large hotel, wholesale stores and goods warehouses, with other principal frontages to the railroads on the wharfage level on the south; also to an Esplanade on the south of Front Street, constructed on piers and arches over the lines of railway, sixty-six feet in width, on the Front Street level, with an open space of twenty feet area for light and ventilation to the lower storey of the buildings in front of the tracks. The buildings would have their north frontage on Front Street; passengers would enter the respective stations as the goods would be received on Front Street. The Esplanade, by this arrangement across the most central part of the city, would be in the proper place on the Front Street level, with the railroad cars running underneath, having arched openings on the north side of the railroad to the buildings, and on the south side to the wharfage, being in appearance like a continued station. The passengers would be protected from heat and dust in summer, and the trains from snow accumulations in winter.

"The buildings being erected with handsome stone frontings to the Esplanade and Bay, would give the city a magnificent appearance, with the arched frontage of the Esplanade as a basement to the whole.

"Trees may be planted for shade opposite the piers on the lower level, which would form an avenue for the raised Esplanade, along the entire distance, which might be limited at the outset, from Simcoe Street to George Street. From that point east and west the railroad may be open. The raised Esplanade over the railroad to have five lines of rails, with five arches in brickwork turned over them, continuous on stone piers, backed up with brickwork."

LAIRD —" Ah, doctor, I canna say I like yere plan either. Nane o' them are equal to the ane I had many a chat about wi' my auld friend, Sir R. Bonnycastle, now dead, poor man, an' wi' Mr. Howard, the architect. Keep awa' yere new-fangled plans frae me; what wi' yere bridges, an' brick arches, an' tree-plantin', and level crossin's, and so on, its enough to dumbfounder a body. Na, na, gentlemen, the auld plan is a plan ye can all understan', it's a simple one, an' the simplest way is often found the best way."

DOCTOR—" I confess I feel quite taken aback, not having thought of the subject before. It appears to me, however, that there are many good things in all of them, which, if combined together, might form a better plan than any one of them."

This ends the "sederunt" of these gentlemen in 1850, and it may be remarked in 1886, that if we cannot have a work as solid and grand as the Thames embankment in London, we can have one which in point of situation and beauty of prospect may form a more delightful promenade, and now appears to be the time for prompt action to secure its establishment.

Rossin House.

With the prospect of railroads being built, and the consequent increase of travel, the want of a first-class hotel was much felt, and Messrs. Rossin Bros., very popular and enterprising gentlemen, then doing the principal watch and jewellery business, undertook to canvass the wholesale merchants and others interested in the growth and prosperity of the city, for subscriptions towards building an hotel worthy of the Queen City. The stock was soon taken up, and debentures of £100 or $400 each were issued, one of which the writer willingly took in behalf of the firm, just as all others did, not with a view of making profit but to promote the enterprise. The ground was secured and the first hotel built and finished, and was placed in the hands of Mr. A. C. Joslin as proprietor. It being found that it did not pay, Messrs. Rossin Bros. bought up the debentures at 50 per cent. discount, which the holders were willing to lose to keep the concern afloat, and in this way it was continued till it was burned down. It was soon re-built on a much grander scale, and has gone on increasing in size and splendor ever since.

In June of 1853 the Grand Trunk Railway was opened to Portland, and at the close of the year the Great Western was opened from the Suspension Bridge to Hamilton and London, and within a month was completed to Windsor.

The contract for the road from Toronto to Montreal was signed by Mr. Jackson and his associates on the arrival in London of the Hon. John Ross. The line from Toronto to Hamilton was undertaken by another contractor, at £1,000 more per mile than the Grand Trunk.

The writer travelled in the old leather-swung stage from Hamilton to London the night before the opening of the road, and in anticipation of their occupation being about to go the following day, the hotel-keepers at the different places where the horses were changed were especially grumpy.

The St. James' Cathedral organ, built by Messrs. Warren Bros., of Montreal, was put in its place on 17th May, and was worthy of the reputation of that firm. The choir at this time was composed of effective and well-trained singers, and the whole musical service gave great satisfaction.

Mercantile Agencies.

The system of reporting the standing of business men by regular subscription rates was commenced in Toronto in 1855. Previous to that time there had been private correspondence with New York, but no regular agency had been opened, nor was the arrangement publicly known.

A Mr. Hart was sent to Toronto by the firm of R. G. Dun & Co. at this time, to obtain subscribers, and the firm of Taylor & Stevenson was among the first to give their names. Having received a sufficient number to warrant them in opening an office, Mr. Kimball arrived shortly afterwards from New York, and commenced his agency in the Exchange Buildings, Wellington Street.

The principle of giving information as to every man in business was not well received by a portion of the press. Several severe articles appeared, denouncing the introduction of such a system of espionage. The agents were called pimps, detectives, spies, informers, and eaves-droppers, and the business community was called upon to denounce the whole business, and stamp it out, as a blot on the respectability of the city. Lawsuits for defamation of character were threatened, and although the agent and his assistants were well received personally, the system was looked upon as wholly disreputable.

To think that a man's private business was to be exposed by strangers who had no legitimate means of knowing the circumstances, was said to be an outrage on public decency, and only a system of black-mail for the purpose of extorting money and compelling business houses to subscribe to the agency in self-defence.

Notwithstanding all this opposition, the business grew in strength from day to day, and merchants found that the information received was, on the whole, of a more reliable character, because more disinterested and independent, than could be obtained by references from one house to another. It had been known that merchants' references were more or less unreliable, on account of the interest they had in keeping up the credit of their customers, who, if in the books of a house to any great extent, would not be likely to receive an unfavorable character, and in this way other houses would be led to give them credit on the strength of these interested statements, often resulting in a loss to the new creditors, while the old had an opportunity of reducing their line of credit, and saving themselves either partially or entirely from loss.

In this appeared to be the secret of success of the mercantile agencies, the information given being alike to all subscribers, and recorded in their books for constant reference, with changes in rating given from time to time, and all preferences or securities regularly registered and reported.

The style of R. G. Dun & Co. was shortly afterwards changed

to Dun, Wiman & Co., by the introduction of Mr. Erastus Wiman into the firm. The name of

MR. ERASTUS WIMAN

is so intimately connected with Toronto as to deserve more than a passing notice. Although a resident of the United States, he is still a British subject, a Canadian and a Torontonian, and owes his present high position more to Canada than to the United States. In Toronto he commenced his career as a printer boy at $1.50 per week, which at twenty he was proud to have advanced to $4.50 per week. From this he became a market reporter, then commercial reporter on the staff of the *Globe*, and Superintendent of the Toronto Exchange, and in 1860 became connected with the mercantile agency of R. G. Dun & Co. He was subsequently promoted to the position of travelling reporter, and in 1862 became manager of the Toronto office, succeeding Mr. Kimball. In 1863 he was transferred to the Montreal office—both the Toronto and Montreal districts being placed under his administration. This continued till 1866, when he was transferred to the New York office, and admitted as a partner in the firm. Owing to the war the business had run down, and was sustained chiefly by the amount of money made in Canada. This success, with his knowledge of printing, gave Mr. Wiman great advantages, and firmly established his position. The business has grown to vast proportions. The books of the firm are published quarterly, and contain one million names. They employ forty printers, and have standing in type twenty tons agate, costing one dollar per pound.

There are one hundred and six branch establishments throughout the country—forty of the managers being Canadians, with salaries ranging from fifteen hundred to twelve thousand dollars per annum. There are about one thousand Canadians employed in the business.

On the death of Mr. Barlow, the interest of that gentleman passed into the hands of Mr. Wiman, and he became virtually the working-head of the entire agency. The consolidation of the two Canadian Telegraph Companies is due, to a great extent, to his assistance, placing the whole system on a paying basis, Mr. H. C. Dwight being made general superintendent.

Mr. Wiman has shown his liberality to this city in the free gift of the baths which are called after his name, and which cost about fifteen thousand dollars.

On returning from Europe after making spring purchases in February, 1855, on board the Cunard Steamer *Canada*, a terrible hurricane was encountered. One tremendous sea broke over the forward part of the ship, carrying an immense hawser, weighing several tons, off the forecastle, and rushing along, stove in all the doors on the main deck, throwing the sailors down and breaking one man's leg. The water rushed into the intermediate cabin, and when the passengers jumped out of their berths, they found themselves up to the middle in water. On being removed to the saloon, where they lay wrapped in blankets waiting for dry clothing, one of them, a gentleman at present in Toronto, who had supposed the ship was sinking, asked amidst the raging of the storm, and much to the amusement of those who had similar experience before, whether "she was nearly full yet." The storm soon abated and Boston was reached in safety.

In June of the same year, when great numbers were going to the Paris Exhibition, a delightful passage was made in one of the Allan Line steamers from Quebec. Amongst the passengers were the late Col. R. L. Denison, of Toronto, and Messrs. Kirchkoffer, Meredith, and Fraser, of Port Hope, who proved to be most agreeable '*compagnons de voyage*." The two former never having seen the Old Country, and the two latter having been away from boyhood, described their sensations as very peculiar on approaching the Irish coast, and every they saw in Liverpool proved to be intensely interesting to the.

Paris in 1855.

Having completed my purchases in Britain, I went to Paris and got through my business there. In anticipation of a matrimonial arrangement in England, and a return to Paris in a few days, apartments were secured at my usual stopping place, the

Hotel de Tours, in the Place la Bourse; and through the kindness of our commissionaires, a stand in the balcony of a fan manufactory in the Boulevard des Italians was promised, from which a view of the great processions would be had.

Leaving England on the 16th of August, by the Great Western Railway from Birmingham, and stopping at Oxford, the unique classical and historical city of colleges, libraries, parks, gardens, meadows, and "academic groves," of indescribable beauty, so familiar to the greatest scholars of Great Britain for many centuries; then through Reading and Windsor to London, and thence, *via* Dover and Calais, Paris was reached; and here was spent the week during which the Queen's stay continued. While during the summer the great Exposition was the attraction, the grand sights connected with the Queen's visit caused quite a diversion to every point where the Royal party appeared.

Passports.

The system of passports being then strictly enforced, with the crowds that were then flocking into Paris the delay and annoyance was very great.

These passports were procured from the French Consul-General in London, and bore the Imperial Seal of France. They described minutely the bearer's height, measurement, color of eyes and hair, complexion, expression, shape of countenance, nationality, religion and destination, and, having passed all the inspections, must be deposited with the proprietor of your hotel, so that the police could have access to them at all times during your stay.

While the clash of arms and deeds of heroism on the fields of Balaclava, Inkerman and at Alma were still fresh, and the thunder of the artillery of the allied armies of Great Britain, France and Turkey was still booming at Sebastopol, Queen Victoria and Prince Albert, amidst scenes of unparalleled splendor, made their grand entry into Paris, to visit the International Exhibition in the Palais de l'Industrie.

By special order of the Emperor, great preparations were

made for this visit. Every house was cleaned or renovated, and the most lavish decorations were to be displayed, especially where the procession was to pass.

The success of the allied armies in the Crimea, the recent demonstration by the allied fleets at Sveaborg, and the commencement of another bombardment of the Russian lines south of Sebastopol, were circumstances of such happy augury, that the Queen seemed to carry victory and good fortune in her train, while the glorious weather gave unbounded hope and joy to the royal progress.

On the evening of the 18th of August, Her Majesty arrived at the Strasbourg railway station from Boulogne. Here a military band struck up the National Anthem, thrilling many a heart. At the close of the performance, Her Majesty, leaning on the arm of the Emperor, trod the soil of the bright Capital of France amid intense applause.

The Emperor was in full costume, and wore the riband of the Garter; Prince Albert, the Prince of Wales, and the Princess Royal came next with their suite; then Prince Napoleon, accompanied by a host of high officers of State. The illustrious party entered the open carriages, six in number, drawn by four horses, prepared to convey them to St. Cloud.

The Procession on the Boulevards.

It was curious to observe the intense desire displayed by all classes to make this wonderful city look its best and fairest before the eyes of the Island Queen, and to inspire Her Majesty with a due appreciation of the claims which Paris had to be considered the gayest and most brilliant capital in the world; and these claims were overpoweringly displayed.

The great width of the Boulevards and the asphalt sidewalks afforded a splendid opportunity for displaying the decorations. The arch on the Rue Lapelletiere was very magnificent, while trophies, including sculpture of great merit, chains of streamers, hung with flags, evergreens and flowers, extended throughout the route. This was especially observable in that

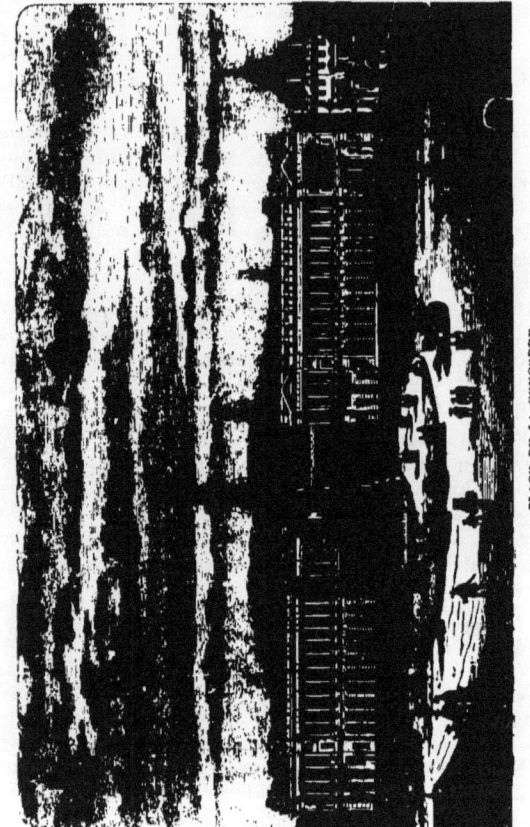

PLACE DE LA CONCORDE.

noble street, the Rue de la Paix, near the Madeleine, the whole street being brilliantly ornamented.

Those who do not know Paris will have some difficulty in realizing the splendid aspect of the line of Boulevards, with the bright sunlight pouring down, without a cloud; the pavements and carriage ways swarming with people; the lofty houses with their jalousied windows thrown open and filled with spectators; the extensive range of balconies all occupied, and in every direction that indescribable air of excitement which marks a great event.

The route of the procession lay along the Boulevard de Strasbourg, the Port St. Denis, the Boulevards Bonne Nouvelle, Poissonniere, Montmartre, des Italiens, des Capucines, and the Madeleine, down the Rue Royal, across the Place de la Concorde, and by the Champs Elysees, the new Avenue de l'Emperatrice, and the Bois de Boulogne to St. Cloud.

About four o'clock, the troops, numbering fully 100,000 men —half of the line and half of the Imperial Guard—began to take up their position on this immense and splendid route, while penned in behind them the myriads of spectators settled into their places, to await the arrival of the illustrious visitors.

The Prefect of Police put the numbers down at 800,000. It is worthy of note that, during the whole week, not a single disorderly or intoxicated person was observed amongst these vast multitudes.

The sight of the military alone was magnificent in the extreme. The gay uniforms of the various regiments produced a marvellous effect—Chasseurs d'Afrique, Zouaves, Garde Mobile, Imperial Guard, Voltigeurs and Cent Gardes, all in the most picturesque costumes, and in great variety, formed a military spectacle unsurpassed in modern times, and seemed to impress the Royal party, and to be enjoyed with great admiration.

The Queen at Versailles.

The party entered the Palace by the central gateway in the grand front. The Grand Court, 380 feet in width, is separated from the Place D'Armes by stone parapets flanking an iron railing richly charged with gilded ornaments, and the central gateway is surmounted by the ancient Crown Shield of France, charged with three *fleur-de-lis*. At the extremity of this railing are groups of figures in stone—those on the right representing France victorious over Austria, by Marsy, with the statue of Peace; those on the left, France victorious over Spain, by Grardon, with the figure of Plenty. The Court itself slopes from the Palace, and on each side is a plain range of buildings erected by Louis XIV. for the use of his ministers. In front of these stand sixteen marble statues: on the right, Richelieu, Bayard, Colbert, Jandon, Massina, Jounville, Duc Gray, Trounin and Touren; on the left, Suger, Du Greschin, Sully, Lalles, Mortier, Suffren, Duquesne and Condé. In the midst of the upper part of the Court is a colossal equestrian statue of Louis XIV. The lofty building on the right is the chapel, the architecture of which is remarkably florid and elegant. It is ornamented with Corinthian pilasters and a balustrade crowned by twenty-eight statues.

The Grand Trianon is a villa at the extremity of the Park, and was built by Louis XIV. for Madame Maintenon, after the design by Mansard. It is in the Italian style, consisting of one storey and two wings united by a long gallery pierced by seven arcades, fronted with Ionic columns and pilasters of Languedoc marble.

The garden of the Grand Trianon is laid out in a style similar to that of Versailles, and contains seven fine fountains in Carara marble. There are many excellent pieces of sculpture in various parts. The grounds in the rear are laid out in groves cut into labyrinths.

The Grand Trianon was always a favorite residence of Louis XIV., XV. and XVI. Napoleon also frequently resided in it, and made a direct road from there to St. Cloud.

As no opportunity was lost during the week of seeing all the sights, Versailles was the point of attraction on the 25th of August.

The Royal party were in the Park in the rear of the Palace, while immense crowds thronged the square in front. A determined effort had to be made to get through the gateway. A procession of officials appeared from another part of the Palace marching towards the main entrance to the Park. Seizing the opportunity we fell into the procession and soon found ourselves on the Grand Terrace, close to the Royal carriages, with only a select few standing around, while the splendid band of the Cent Gardes performed. Shortly afterwards the party drove towards the Grand Trianon along lines of statuary flanked by evergreen yew trees, forming perpendicular walls pierced with arches. This effect is produced by clipping the trees. As the carriage of the Queen and Prince Albert passed each fountain a salute burst from the water works, producing a most beautiful effect. These water works, commenced by Charles X., are the finest in the world, and have cost fabulous sums in being brought to their present perfection, receiving constant additions and improvements from the various reigning sovereigns.

As a reminiscence connected with Toronto, on entering a restaurant at Versailles, we noticed at a table close by Mr. and Mrs. William Henry Boulton.

After inspecting various grand galleries in the Palace, including the great hall of paintings, which if spread out would cover seven miles, we left this grandly historical building, having a delightful run to Paris by rail, some of the carriages having seats for passengers outside, on the top.

The rush to leave Paris after the departure of the Queen, was far greater than on her arrival. It seemed as if everybody wanted to get away at the same time, and here a hint may be given that might be useful in similar crowds, should they ever be witnessed in Paris again. Even if a knowledge of the language is possessed, it is an advantage sometimes to appear to know nothing about it.

The Paris gens d'armes, with cocked hats and swords, are formidable looking individuals, but if there is a rush for a train, and you are kept back, with the risk of losing your connection with the tidal train at Dieppe (which was to be our point of departure for Newhaven), a volley of English will be found to confound the policemen, and to gain the victory. This plan was never known to the writer to fail, except on one occasion. The rule on all omnibuses and tramways of limiting the number of passengers is strictly enforced, and each passenger, no matter what the rush may be, is only admitted by ticket in the order of consecutive numbers. When the conveyance is full the board with the word "*complet*" is shown.

A story was told of a gentleman waiting at a certain point to get a 'bus for the Grand Exposition, but all appeared with this board at the back. At last he remarked that all the conveyances appeared to be going to "*Complet*," and he wanted to go to the Exposition. On going to the waiting room he got on in his regular order.

The writer undertook to jump on a 'bus having the word referred to, and hoped by the free use of English to confound the conductor, but this attempt proved a failure, and a firm "*Descendez vous, monsieur, si vous plait,*" compelled a descent.

When will the Toronto Street Car Company adopt the French and English system of finding a seat for every passenger?

Departure from Paris.

This occurred on Monday, the 27th August. As the brilliant staff of Generals, headed by a squadron of mounted Chasseurs, turned down the Rue Castiglione, it became evident that a splendid show was behind them. Very imposing the staff looked, backed by the scarlet uniform of the band of the Guides. After the Guides came four Piqueurs preceding four elegant carriages drawn by two horses, and three state carriages drawn by six horses. The splendor of these equipages, literally covered with gold, led the crowds to believe that they must contain the Queen and the Emperor, but glancing along the line they saw that the point of attraction lay still in the distance.

These carriages contained the suites of the two Courts. They were followed by eight splendidly-equipped Piqueurs, who were before a gorgeous state carriage, the body of which was green, richly relieved by gilt ornamentation. In this vehicle sat the Prince of Wales, wearing over a black velvet tunic a tartan scarf. He appeared to take a boyish delight in the affair. In the same carriage with him was Prince Napoleon.

The next carriage, drawn by eight splendid horses, contained the Queen of England, the Emperor, Prince Albert, and the Princess Royal.

As this magnificent carriage, made for the Emperor's wedding, advanced, the most lusty cheers arose to greet the Royal party.

The Imperial carriages were followed by the Generals of division and brigade, the Cent Gardes, and a squadron of Cuirassiers of the Guard, preceded by their band.

From the railway station, where the ceremony of parting took place amid great enthusiasm, the Queen and party left for Boulogne *en route* for England.

Incidents During the Queen's Visit.

The Queen, accompanied by the Emperor, admired at the Exhibition a fine group in bronze, "*Le Lion Amoreux*." Immediately on the departure of their Majesties, it was removed to St. Cloud and placed in the apartments occupied by the Queen.

On the evening of the representation at the Grand Opera, just before starting, the Emperor sent to the Queen a bouquet of splendid exotic flowers, contained in a *porte-bouquet* of gold ornamented with diamonds and pearls, being one of the most exquisite productions of jewellery that could be conceived. The Queen was so enchanted with it that during the evening she was continually admiring it, and remarked, "I cannot describe the amiability with which I am received here; all is so magnificently and at once so delicately done, that it is impossible to find a fitting expression."

Upon her entrance into the gorgeous saloon of fountains at the Hotel de Ville, the Queen remained a moment breathless, speechless with admiration and surprise, and at last uttered these words: "Our English language has no word, no term, to express the feeling excited by such wonders. It is a dream, the realization of one of the Arabian Nights tales!"

The Imperial Cent Gardes,

as their name indicates, were one hundred in number, and nearly all six feet in height. When mounted they wore a light blue tunic, with crimson facings, a cuirass, and bright, silvery looking helmets, profusely decorated with gold, and carrying a double red and white feather. The epaulettes were gold and fringe gold, mixed with crimson silk. The breeches were white leather, the boots similar to the Horse Guards, the saddle-cloths crimson, richly embroidered with gold.

The writer on one occasion seeing them at night, observed that over all this gorgeous uniform they wore long cloaks of pure white cloth. Being attracted by their appearance at the entrance to the Gymnase Theatre, and hearing that the Emperor and Empress had just gone in, the temptation was too great to be resisted, and I soon found myself in a place nearly opposite the Royal box. With the free use of a "binocular" I had a splendid sight of the Royal pair, which was really the object I had in view at the time. The Empress was then in the very prime of her celebrated beauty, and being mourning, without any ornament whatever, showed to thater advantage. This circumstance occurred during a previous visit to Paris.

The cost of lighting the Palace and Gardens at Versailles amounted to $31,250, and the ball at the Hotel de Ville to $60,000.

In a few days after the departure of the Queen from Paris, the second bombardment of Sebastopol—which Prince Gortchakoff profanely designated as "a fire of hell"—commenced, on the 5th of September, and on the 8th the Russians fled.

When day dawned on the 8th, the flames of a great conflagration were seen in the centre of the city, and in a short time it was a mass of ruins. On the same day the assault of the Malakoff was undertaken by Marshal Pelessier, assisted by Generals Bosquet and McMahon, to whom the Marshal gave the credit of the assault. The taking of the Malakoff Tower compelled the Russian evacuation of Sebastopol.

Toronto can boast of two of the trophies which were dis-

tributed through England and her colonies, in the possession of
two guns in the Queen's Park.

Paris Universal Exhibition.

The building erected for the finer productions, remaining
still, is familiar to visitors to Paris, situated on the Champs
Elysees, close to the Place de la Concorde; it is now used as a
fine arts gallery. The annexes, extending for nearly a mile
along the banks of the Seine, and used for machinery and heavy
exhibits, were removed.

The splendor of the Panorama building, with its long line
of jewellery, gold, silk, satins, paintings, sculpture, musical instruments, etc., was in some respects superior to London in
1851, but was surpassed by the Exhibition in 1867

During the week, as far as time permitted, all the grand
sights were witnessed and the various places of interest visited.
The Palace of the Luxembourg, the Hotel des Invalides, and the
Tomb of Napoleon, where streams of visitors passed in and out.
Under the magnificent dome is the open crypt, on the polished
granite walls of which are inscribed the names of the hero's
great victories. In the centre stands the massive sarcophagus
with marble statues around it. "Before you is the superb high
altar, flooded with golden light from the painted windows,
and around are the stately columns which support the lofty
dome. The tomb is gorgeous in marble and gold."

Notre Dame Cathedral, with its jewelled splendors, the solid
gold and silver utensils on the altar, the splendid robes of Popes,
Bishops, and Coronation robes of Kings, including that of the
Emperors Napoleon I. and III. Then the Louvre, with its
frescoed walls and ceilings, marble pillars and long halls of
paintings and statuary by the great masters, marble tables
covered with rich cabinets of the rarest specimens of jewels and
enamels. The Madeleine, the Palace of the Tuilleries, the
Grand Exposition itself, which it would be vain to attempt to
describe, were all done and thoroughly enjoyed before leaving
the beautiful city on this visit.

The return to England was by way of Dieppe to Newhaven,

and in another week we were on board one of the Allan steamers for Quebec, having again as a fellow-passenger, also returning to Toronto, our friend Col. R. L. Denison. After re-

NOTRE DAME CATHEDRAL, PARIS.

maining in Toronto till the close of the fall trade we returned to England, making St. Helens, near Liverpool, our home. This was a convenient point for attending to shipping from Liverpool, and as nearly three hundred trains a day passed the "junction," it afforded constant and easy access to the manufacturing districts of Lancashire and Yorkshire, as also to London, Paris, Ireland and Scotland.

While making my home in England, for the purpose of shipping goods weekly to Toronto, till 1858, two trips were made during that time, and the trade was closely watched. In 1856 the work of railway construction went rapidly on, and trade had never been so good—the importations had increased from $2,286,508 in 1850, to $6,670,500. The duty had increased from 12½ to 15 per cent., and no one foresaw the re-action that was so soon to take place, on the completion of the Grand Trunk and other railways, as well as the close of the Crimean war, when prices of produce returned to their normal condition.

The Queen Opening Parliament, February 1st, 1856,

at the close of the Crimean War, was an event of more than ordinary importance. Crowds of people assembled at all the points of the route from Buckingham Palace to the Palace Yard, and long before the usual time for opening Parliament every available spot in Parliament Street, Whitehall, the Horse Guards and along the Mall was occupied; numbers of ladies crowded the windows, and platforms along the route were filled. On no former occasion was there so monstrous an assemblage or so prevailing a sentiment of loyal curiosity.

At two o'clock Her Majesty left Buckingham Palace amidst the cheers of thousands of spectators who lined the Mall. In the state carriage, which was drawn by eight splendid cream-colored Hanoverian horses, were the Queen and Prince Consort, Her Grace the Duchess of Sutherland, and the Duke of Wellington. The Marquis of Breadalbane, Lord Chamberlain, and Earl Spencer, Master of the Horse, occupied the carriage which preceded that of Her Majesty. The other carriages forming the cortege contained the other high officers of the Queen's Household. Besides the Yeomen of the Guard, the escort consisted of two troops of the 1st Regiment of Life Guards and a troop of the Royal Horse Guards Blue, and the magnificent appearance of this fine body of soldiers evidently sent a thrill of pride through the bosoms of all that beheld them. The procession passed through the dense rows of spectators, who, from time to time, burst forth into cordial cheering, which was graciously acknowledged by Her Majesty and the Prince Consort.

At the Horse Guards and through Whitehall, but more especially in Palace Yard, the crowd was immense. Here, along the front of the Palace, and along Parliament Street, was the line of peeress's carriages, which, in itself, was a dazzling sight. The most beautiful women in the world in full dress, ablaze with coronets of diamonds and jewels, all waiting the arrival of Her Majesty, was indeed a brilliant spectacle. Altogether it was a scene which, in the essential features, it would be impossible to witness outside of England.

Royal and Imperial pageants abroad might outstrip the scene in military pomp and magnificence, but where shall we seek for that warmth of loyalty, that devoted reverence and affection for the monarch, that unaffected interest in the personal welfare of the sovereign, which Queen Victoria's subjects display; and on the other hand, where look for the perfect confidence with which our Queen's womanly virtues and purity of private character, no less than her irreproachable conduct as the occupant of the throne, enable her at all times to meet her admiring people?

Her Majesty's arrival at the Victoria Tower was announced by the discharge of cannon from the Horse Guards' Parade, and a flourish of trumpets by the Royal Trumpeters on splendidly caparisoned steeds, themselves still in scarlet and gold, as also were the Royal coachmen and the grooms who walked at the head of each horse in the Royal carriage.

The Queen was received by the officers of the House of Peers, and entered the House led by Prince Albert and preceded by Lord Viscount Harding bearing the Sword of State, the Marquis of Winchester bearing the Cap of Maintenance, and the Marquis of Lansdowne carrying the Crown. A guard of honor, composed of a body of the Life Guards, dismounted, lined the entrance to the House of Lords, and a company of the Scots Fusiliers Guards was drawn up in front of the Tower.

After the delivery of the Speech the Queen descended from the Throne, and left the House in the same order which had been observed on Her Majesty's entry.

The Great Peace Rejoicings in London.

In April, 1856, peace was concluded, and was announced in London by the firing of guns in St. James' Park, and from the Tower, and the Lord Mayor read the despatch announcing the fact at the Royal Exchange.

A day was appointed for great peace rejoicings, and a general illumination, with a display of fireworks on a scale of magnificence never before attempted.

Being in London that day I first visited the Crystal Palace, when the great water-works were first opened, and played their grand part in the programme. The crowds were immense, and trains every five minutes for London were not sufficient to accommodate the tens of thousands who were rushing back to be in time for the grand display.

Some desperate efforts were made to secure even standing room on the trains. My brother-in-law, who accompanied me, having got into the same carriage, was suddenly pushed out in the scramble, and nothing more was seen of him till the next morning.

THE FIREWORKS IN GREEN PARK.

As the hour approached for the introductory discharge of fireworks, thousands entered the Park by the six new entrances which had been made to prevent accident. Deepening and thickening with wonderful rapidity, the huge mass extended itself on the soft and verdant carpet, and the large spaces in front of Buckingham Palace, the Mall and Constitution Hill, were crowded with spectators. A few minutes before the commencement of the fireworks, the Queen, Prince Albert, and the members of the Royal Family, Prince William of Prussia, and other persons of rank, took their seats in the pavilion erected at the north end of Buckingham Palace, facing the Park. Her Majesty was received with loud demonstrations of loyalty and enthusiasm. The Royal party had an admirable view of the fireworks, and seemed to participate in the admiration which they excited. To describe the scene would require a large amount of time and space. For upwards of an hour and a half the air was luminous with the blaze of sun-stars and comets, the flight of shells, rockets, and Roman candles, descent of meteors, parachutes, and showers of pearls, silver and golden rain, shining serpents, and fire-flies, chasing each other through a sea of light resting on a bed of upturned human faces. The programme consisted of twenty-four divisions, and was not exhausted till eleven o'clock. It comprised everything new, curious or beautiful in pyrotechny.

Some of the fixed pieces were remarkably elegant. The stars, hoops and crosses elicited bursts of delight; cascades, fountains, and trees were represented with wonderful exactness, and one of the most beautiful devices was the formation in the air of sheaves of golden corn. But the great triumph of art was the concluding exhibition. It consisted of four fixed pieces, all of the most elaborate construction, with the words "God Save the Queen," illuminated in the centre. At the same time there was a grand discharge of Roman candles, batteries of pearls, streamers, and tourbillions, and rockets in red, blue, green and yellow. The effect was magnificent, almost magical, and when in addition to the above no fewer than ten thousand rockets were shot in the air, the scene was one which can only be witnessed once in a lifetime. The display in Hyde Park, Primrose Hill, and Victoria Park were, though all different in design, equally magnificent.

Having seen all four exhibitions, or the larger portion of each, we wended our way through the millions of people who crowded the streets, amid the blaze of illuminations which made it as bright as day, all along Pall Mall, Charing Cross, The Strand, Fleet Street, to Cheapside, arriving at our hotel between two and three o'clock in the morning.

Great Naval Review at Portsmouth.

In 1856 there were ample opportunities for a buyer in Europe to combine business with pleasure in the way of sight-seeing. Having been in London at the opening of Parliament by the Queen, and at the peace rejoicings with fireworks and illuminations, a second journey was made, taking in the great Naval Review at Portsmouth. Leaving Liverpool by the Great Western Railway through Chester, I arrived at Portsmouth the day before the memorable event took place.

Never, at any period of our history, could we boast of a fleet as powerful in numbers and metal as that which floated at Spithead in April 1856. Such a mighty gathering of first-rates and gun-boats may not again be witnessed on these waters.

The people who, in 1854-5, met to cheer our gallant sailors to their duty, again assembled to cheer them from its performance.

In the same proportion as the fleet of 1856 exceeded that of Lord Howe in 1791, so the number of spectators exceeded that of sixty-five years ago. It was then considered a splendid effort to bring together a single line of ships extending for five miles; here we had a double line for a much longer distance, whilst hundreds of gun-boats, floating batteries, and mortar vessels, crowded the outer spaces off Ryde and Portsmouth.

On Saturday the fleet anchored, a stately line, with the *Duke of Wellington* at its head, bearing the Admiral's ensign. The *Rodney* and *London* had already taken up their position near the Nab as pivot ships round which the fleet was to sail. In the open spaces between the two divisions the water was sprinkled with boats carrying spectators, steamers filled with visitors, steering like pigmies through their colossal sisters; gunboats puffing like locomotive engines; while in a mass off Ryde lay a host of craft forming clumps with their masts, relieved in yellow on the houses and trees of the town.

At no great distance off Southsea Castle lay the heavy forms of the floating batteries, rising and falling on the swell like whales, and stretching from their vicinity far away past Monckton towards Browndown, where lay the heavy, round hulls of the mortar vessels in the grim gray rest that seemed to have its attractions.

The sun shone brightly on the white walls of Southsea Castle, with its tower soaring away above the embankments, bristling with guns, and on the varied crowd that covered the Esplanade. The entrance to the harbor was thronged with boats, some of which, filled with merry bearded faces, were carrying liberty men from the ships of war to the shore. Others were crowded to the thwarts with curious spectators, anxious to gain a view from the water.

Passenger steamers, gun-boats, and tenders to the fleet were perpetually passing in and out of harbor, bewildering the eye by their rapidity of motion and quick successions. Streaming down the streets of the town, visitors from London and elsewhere, curiously viewing the great guns in the embrasures, and peering into their muzzles, did not wait long, but rushing to the pier, invaded the steamers, which left the quays swaying to and fro in an alarming manner.

It is almost needless to say that the usual accommodation to travellers at hotels had long been pre-engaged and taken. Those who trusted to chance to find a bed were woefully disappointed in the endeavor to find a resting place.

The streets were filled with people who seemed totally at a loss how to spend the night. Tired groups might be seen wandering from street to street, making fruitless attempts at admittance at various houses, where the price seemed too exorbitant to any but millionaires. While wandering about the streets in this way the writer had offers of beds at a guinea apiece, or to be rowed over to the Isle of Wight for the same price, but the appearance of our soliciting friends not bespeaking extra accommodation, we declined their kind offer, and the night being fine, with the exception of a rest on a chair at an hotel, was spent in promenading the city.

The weather was most suitable, and never did a more delightful day shine upon the millions of spectators congregated at the various points, commanding a view of the fleet and its evolutions. And splendid was the sight it was destined to shine upon, for never was there a more magnificent and gorgeous spectacle in ancient or modern times.

The "Great Cleopatra," could she have risen from her sarcophagus and been witness to it, would have envied our Island Queen her rule of a nation which can boast possession of the greatest and most splendid armament that ever floated, of which it might well be said :

> "Britannia needs no bulwarks,
> No towers along the steep ;
> Her course is o'er the ocean wave,
> Her home is on the deep."

Although for days before the railways had been bringing thousands of visitors from all parts of the kingdom, and steamers from every port on the southern coast, teeming with human freight, had been day by day discharging their living cargoes, yet it was on the morning of the Review that the town presented the most extraordinary appearance.

From an early hour, and up to midday, thousands of excursionists were seen issuing from the various railway depots and wending their way in one continued stream toward the shore to secure a good position to witness the sight. Southsea common was literally teeming with human beings. From the ramparts and along the Esplanade to beyond the Castle, was one dense living mass. An immense grand stand was erected on the Esplanade for the accommodation of those who preferred to witness the Review from the land. The admission to the stand was ten shillings, a moderate demand compared with prices required for accommodation on board the steamers. But it was not only upon the land that the scene was interesting, nor was the interest on the waters confined exclusively to the Royal Fleet. There was another fleet important in itself, which contributed greatly to the splendor of the scene.

Our mercantile steamers are of a class that astonish and command the admiration of all who behold them. Several of these were present, belonging to the Oriental and Peninsular Navigation Company, and the *Atrato*, the largest paddle-wheel steamer in the world, *La Plata*, *Trent* and *Tay*, belonging to the Royal Mail Steam Packet Company, were all thronged with visitors. The Directors of the Royal Mail Steam Packet Company and their friends were on board the *Atrato*. The steamers of the South-Eastern Company, from Folkestone, and those belonging to the South-Western Company were also present, together with many others from various ports, all swaying with passengers.

The French steamer *L'Imperatrice*, from Calais, with a numerous company of ladies and gentlemen on board, was among the list. She had a splendid brass band, which, in passing the Admiral's yacht, struck up "Rule Britannia"—a graceful compliment.

Nearly all the large steamers carried the French flag at the fore, in compliment to our gallant allies. On the arrival of Her Majesty she was at once conveyed by her state barge on board the Royal yacht, accompanied by Prince Albert and the other members of the Royal party and suite. The *Victory* and the other ships in the harbor manned yards and fired a salute as soon as the Royal Standard was seen flying at the masthead. Her Majesty was accompanied on board by the Lords of the Admiralty. The yacht then moved rapidly out of the harbor, when the forts immediately saluted.

The Queen's Arrival.

Never had monarch a greater opportunity of witnessing a people's loyalty and devotion than our august and beloved Queen had on the occasion of her reviewing her mighty and magnificent fleet on that day. The moment of Her Majesty's appearance in the port was a signal for that enthusiasm which is always displayed whenever she is graciously pleased to appear among her subjects. Simultaneous cheers burst from tens of thousands of loyal hearts, showing the hearty welcome of the "Sea Queen" by her delighted people. The review of such a fleet as the world never before beheld, equipped with an efficiency which all the newest appliances of art and science had given to each of these powerful engines of war which composed it, and manned by seamen whose services our vast commercial wealth enabled us to command without limit, was most gratifying to all who witnessed it. This gorgeous and truly national pageant was a fitting spectacle in celebration of peace, and one which illustrated the greatness of our triumph, the immensity of our resources, and the solid basis of our strength.

The fleet as it appeared at anchor on the morning of the review, extending in a line east and west from pivot ship to pivot ship, covered a space of more than twelve miles, and comprised line-of-battle ships, frigates, corvettes, sloops, floating batteries, mortar ships, mortar boats, and gun-boats, and upwards of two hundred and forty sail, of which not more than ten were without steam power.

There never had been a time when the British Navy was more efficient than it was at that time.

The Queen was most enthusiastically cheered by the assembled thousands on the shore as the yacht pursued her way toward the Spit buoy, on rounding which the whole of the fleet manned their yards and commenced a royal salute. The scene was most imposing at this point.

The yacht then proceeded rapidly towards the westward, followed by a large fleet of steamers which were desirous of keeping pace with her, but which her superior speed rendered a matter of impossibility. As she passed along the line each of the men-of-war manned their rigging and cheered Her Majesty.

The French corvette of war *La Chavalor* manned yards and joined in the cheer of welcome. Then followed the sham-fight, and after the signal was made to cease firing the Royal yacht proceeded to the harbor under the salute of the fleet.

Southsea Beach, extending for many miles, afforded a splendid opportunity for the immense multitude, numbering fully half a million, to witness the whole spectacle. As the Royal yacht *Victoria and Albert* steamed close to the shore, the writer had a distinct view of the Queen and Prince Albert sitting on the deck.

The following is the list of the fleet with their order of sailing :—

STARBOARD DIVISION.

VICE-ADMIRAL SIR G. SEYMOUR, COMMANDER-IN-CHIEF.

Name.	Guns.	Crew.	Name.	Guns.	Crew.
Royal George	102	920	Cossack	20	250
Nile	91	850	Esk	21	240
Conqueror	100	930	Falcon	18	160
Cressy	80	750	Conflict	8	165
Cæsar	91	850	Harier	17	160
Algiers	90	850	Eurolas	12	200
Sanspariel	70	626	Seahorse	12	200
Centurion	80	750	Vulture	6	200
Ajax	70	600	Magicienne	16	220
Hawke	60	600	Samson	6	200
Hastings	60	600	Vesuvius	6	160
Imperieuse	51	530	Basclisk	6	160
Amphion	34	342	Gorgon	6	160
Pylades	20	260	Firefly	5	100

PORT DIVISION.

REAR-ADMIRAL SIR R. DUNDAS.

Name	Guns	Crew	Name	Guns	Crew
Duke of Wellington	131	1100	Brunswick	80	750
Orion	91	850	Edinburgh	60	600
James Watt	91	850	Hogue	60	600
Majestic	80	750	Bleinheim	60	600
Exmouth	90	860	Russell	60	600
Colossus	80	750	Euryalus	51	530

REAR-ADMIRAL R. L. BAYNES.

Name	Guns	Crew	Name	Guns	Crew
Arrogant	41	450	Retribution	28	300
Pearl	20	200	Centaur	6	200
Tartar	20	250	Dragon	6	200
Archer	14	175	Bulldog	6	160
Desperate	8	165	Geyser	6	160
Cruiser	17	160	Merlin	6	110
Rattler	11	130	Hecla	6	135
Forth	12	200	Hydra	6	135
Horatio	8	200			

FLOATING BATTERIES.

Name	Guns	Crew	Name	Guns	Crew
Meteor	14	200	Thunder	14	200
Glatton	14	200	Trusty	14	200

SAILING SHIPS.

Name	Guns	Crew	Name	Guns	Crew
London	90	830	Belleisle	6	244
Rodney	90	820			

GUN-BOAT FLOTILLA.

CENTRE, RED—Algiers, 91; Flying Fish, 6; Ringdove, 6; Biter, 4; Starling, 4; Snapper, 4; Bustard, 4; Dove, 4; Loveret, 4; Fervent, 4; Beaver, 4; Opossum, 4; Firm, 4; Blazer, 4; Brazen, 4; Rainbow, 4; Redbreast, 4; Havoc, 4; Pioneer, 6; Lapwing, 6; Swinger, 4; Skylark, 4; Pincher, 4; Charger, 4; Grasshopper, 4; Mackerel, 4; Forester, 4; Whiting, 4.

VAN, WHITE—Colossus, 81; Victor, 6; Peter, 4; Thistle, 4; Sandfly, 4; Plover, 4; Carnation, 4; Insolvent, 4; Mayflower, 4; Spanker, 4; Traveller, 4; Louisa, 4; Erne, 4; Mastiff, 4; Lively, 4; Ruby, 4; Tickler, 4; Seagull, 4; Bulldog, 4; Hasty, 4; Herring, 4; Griper, 4; Thresher, 4; Julia, 4; Sepoy, 4; Manly, 4; Mistletoe, 4; Magnet, 4.

REAR, BLUE—Brunswick, 81; Intrepid, 6; Mohawk, 6; Stork, 4; Dapper, 4; Gleaner, 4; Magpie, 4; Redwing, 4; Badger, 4; Skipjack, 4; Forward, 4; Banterer, 4; Haughty, 4; Assurance, 6; Procris, 4; Goshawk, 4; Grappler, 4; Hyena, 4; Violet, 4; Weasel, 4; Jackdaw, 4; Hind, 4; Lark, 4; Snap, 4; Sheldrake, 4; Cockchafer, 4; Stanch, 4; Charon, 4.

LIGHT, STRIPED—Sanspareil, 71; Surprise, 6; Cheerful, 2; Daisy, 2; Pert, 2; Drake, 2; Angler, 2; Pet, 2; Rambler, 2; Wanderer, 6; Chub, 2; Onyx, 2; Janus, 2; Ant, 2; Nettle, 2; Decoy, 2; Partridge, 4; Coquette, 6; Beacon, 4; Brave, 4; Bullfinch, 4; Raven, 4; Hardy, 4; Tilbury, 4; Sparrowhawk, 4; Goldfinch, 4; Delight, 4; Bouncer, 4; Nightingale, 4.

This list of vessels, taken from the programme of the day, will give a good idea of the strength of the British Navy, especially when it is borne in mind that these ships were ordered only from convenient naval stations, and many more were scattered all over the world on every sea.

Since that time a new fleet, comprising the most magnificent specimens of naval architecture, has been built, and England's claim to the supremacy of the sea cannot be denied, and never since "first, at heaven's command, she rose from out the azure main," did Britain more triumphantly "rule the waves," than at the present time.

The most interesting feature in the day's movement was that reserved for the night, as an Emeralder might say, and was a thorough novelty to all who witnessed it. The illumination was effected by simultaneously lighting up the yards and portholes with blue lights.

At nine o'clock gun-fire, the whole fleet at anchor burst into light as if by magic. The jets one above another, main topmast-high aloft, and the port of each opening at once, showing a vivid glare between decks, caused an unusual roar of cheering from the shore, which was echoed and given back by the boats and the legion afloat. This, in the stillness of the calm night, had an effect as imposing as it was rare. Cheer upon cheer applauded the spectacle. From nine till ten, rockets were sent up thickly from the ships and rained a golden shower upon the "floating capital."

The Close of the First Decade.

After making his purchases for the Fall trade of 1856 the writer came out to Toronto and found everything apparently prosperous. The importations for the year exceeded those of any previous year, reaching a point equal to 1866, ten years later. Sales were large and payments good, and none seemed to anticipate hard times.

The progress of Toronto during the ten years ending in 1856 was accelerated by the opening of railways, east, west and north, and by that time its population was 45,000, showing an increase of 23,000 in ten years; the number of its houses was 7,476; the assessment of property had increased from $69,000 to $515,000, and the imports from $750,000 to $6,670,500.

Toronto had been reaping the first fruits of her connections through the Grand Trunk and Great Western Railways, and the close of this, the first decade, contained in this sketch, found Toronto improved almost beyond recognition to those who had not seen it during that time. The wide streets, containing splendid shops, and the number of handsome churches, all conspired to impress a visitor with the growing character of the place.

Dr. Mackay writes of it at this time as "a thing of yesterday, a mushroom, compared with the antiquity of Montreal and Quebec, though rivalling the one and exceeding the other in trade and population. It is built on the American plan of straight lines, preferring the chess board to the maze, and the regularity of art to the picturesque irregularity of nature. The streets are long and straight. There is a Yankee look about the whole place which it is impossible to mistake, a pushing, thriving, business-like, smart appearance in the people and the streets, in the stores, and in the banks and churches.

From 1847 to 1857. 143

"Looked upon from any part of itself, Toronto does not greatly impress the imagination, but seen from the deck of a steamer, it has all the air of wealth and majesty that belongs to a great city. Its numerous churches, stores, and public buildings, its wharves, factories, and tall chimneys, mark it for what it is, a thriving place."

During this decade the following buildings had been erected: The General Hospital, Normal and Model Schools, St. James' and St. Michael's Cathedrals, Knox Church, St. Lawrence Build-

FORMER POST OFFICE (PRESENT OFFICE OF RECEIVER-GENERAL).

ings, Nordheimer's Buildings on Toronto Street, the Exchange, Free Library Building, Post Office, City Schools, the University, several Banks, and the Rossin House Hotel.

Toronto was now the headquarters of the Royal Canadian Rifles. The science of photography had lately been discovered, and artists styled photographers and ambrotypists began to multiply.

Manufactures had not shown much progress, and consisted chiefly of wood-working and planing mills, boots, shoes, safes, soap, spices, paper, and blank books.

From the time of the introduction of the bonding system through the United States, British goods to Boston generally came to Toronto *via* Ogdensburg, and from New York *via* Lewiston, until the opening of the Suspension Bridge, and passengers sometimes had difficulty in making connections in winter.

In the winter of 1856-7 the writer had secured his passage to Liverpool by Cunard steamer from Boston, and started in good time to Prescott, intending to cross to Ogdensburg to connect with train for Boston. On arriving at Prescott a violent snow storm prevailed, and the captain of the steam ferry refused to cross. On telegraphing across to our agents, Messrs. Stark, Hill & Co., Mr. Stark, who had been a sea captain, immediately came across in a small row boat and offered to row me across. As the storm grew worse, while thanking the captain for his kindness and courage, I declined to risk both our lives when the steamer would not risk the crossing, and telegraphed to Messrs. Hill, Sears & Co., of Boston, to write to my family in England the cause of my detention. Not wishing to return to Toronto, I went on to New York and waited for the next Cunard steamer from that port.

TORONTO FROM 1857 TO 1867.

Financial Crisis in 1857.

Returning to make the spring purchases in Europe, and back to Toronto in February, 1857, there were indications of an impending change.

The stoppage for the time of railway operations and the circulation of money was soon felt all over the country, and the testing time of the 4th of March was the crisis, when payments at the banks were so bad as to cause a number of failures. In a short time the panic ensued with full force, and the whole picture suddenly changed. Railway enterprise suddenly came to an end; some of the largest houses were compelled to suspend payment. Old established houses smashed like glass bottles, and mercantile credit collapsed.

To show, however, that this state of affairs was not confined to Canada, one fact may be stated. During this year the deficiency in remittances from the United States to England amounted to nearly fifty millions sterling, the great bulk of which was never paid.

So depressed was trade in Toronto that hundreds of persons in the city who had heretofore enjoyed all the ordinary comforts of life, for the first time felt the sharp pinch of poverty. There was much suffering and want amongst the laboring classes, with a corresponding amount of drunkenness and crime. There is good reason to believe that several persons died of sheer starvation. For the first time in her history her streets swarmed with mendicants.

The *British Colonist* of August 4th says : " Pass when you will, you are beset with some sturdy applicant for alms. They dodge you round corners, follow you into shops, they are to be found at the church steps, and at the door of the theatre. They infest the entrance to every bank. They crouch in the lobby of the post office, assail you on every street, knock at your private residence, walk into your place of business, and beard you with a pertinacity that takes no denial.

" In this, our good city of Toronto, begging has assumed the dignity of a craft. Whole families sally forth and have their appointed round. Children are taught to dissemble, to tell a lying tale of misery and woe, and beg or steal as occasion offers."

This picture is far from attractive. The advent of brighter days, however, brought in a very perceptible change, and when trade assumed its normal condition, our streets ceased to be suggestive of poverty and mendicancy; but it was not till 1859 that business resumed its healthy appearance. The writer returned to Europe in May 1857.

The Desjardins Canal Accident.

During the writer's stay in Toronto at this time the most terrible accident which had happened since the opening of the railroads, occurred at seven o'clock of the evening of the 12th March, 1857, at the bridge over the Desjardins Canal, a mile east of Hamilton. The train from Toronto, consisting of a locomotive, tender, baggage car, and two passenger coaches, the latter containing about ninety-three persons, left about five p.m. When this train reached the junction just above Hamilton, it was ascertained that the train from Detroit had not gone down to Hamilton, as it was entitled to do before the Toronto train. After waiting twenty minutes the Toronto train came on. Just before reaching the bridge over the Desjardins Canal, the train left the track by the misplacement of a switch or some other cause, and ran upon the bridge. The force of the train knocked the bridge down, and engine, cars and all plunged into the canal thirty or forty feet below.

The catastrophe was sudden and awful, and the work of death was instantaneous and complete. The locomotive and tender were entirely submerged, and the baggage car partially so. The forward passenger coach turned bottom upwards, and sank so deep that the floor was but a few inches above the water. The rear passenger coach rested upon one end and was about half submerged. Most of the passengers in the rear of this coach escaped; the remainder were drowned.

The writer had a description of the scene inside this car, from one who escaped, by the wood-work being cut through with axes within a few inches of his head, and the scene described was terrible in the extreme.

Every person in the first car perished except four—two men and two children. One of the children was thrown out of the window on to the ice; the other was dragged out of a window, having been up to its neck in water for fifteen minutes. They were brother and sister; their father, mother and uncle perished,

Among those who were killed were Samuel Zimmerman, the great Railway King of Canada, and Captain Sutherland, owner of the well-known iron steamer *Magnet*, with other prominent men, both American and Canadian.

Mr. Hugh McSloy, of St. Catharines, having come over in response to a circular to see the spring opening of new goods, had made some purchases, and bid the writer good-bye, stating he would soon be back to complete them. At about 7.30 a telegram came from his brother to know whether he had left by that train, when a reply was sent accordingly. He was amongst the victims of the terrible tragedy.

British capital to the amount of $450,000,000 was invested in the United States at this time.

The whole gold coinage of the United States from 1793 to t January, 1856, was only $396,895,574; the silver coinage t. same period was $100,729,602, and copper $1,572,206; the th e together amounting to $498,197,383.

All the gold would not suffice to pay back the capitalists and more than half of the silver would be required for the purpose.

Art Treasures Exhibition in Manchester.

"A thing of beauty is a joy forever."

The history of painting and its close identity, from the earliest periods, with the interests of religion and morality, and the rapidity with which the art is increasing its influence upon current opinion and thought, would render it nothing less than a scandal if nineteenth century religionists and moralists were indifferent to its tendencies and claims.

That will indeed be an evil day in which the range of moral sympathy is not wide enough to comprehend a love of all the pure and noble forms of art.

It is the duty of religion to cherish every delicate art which tends to embellish and reform human life and character. Piety is never more unwise than when she expels beauty from her tents, and by that act of excommunication drives her fairest sister into alienation and profanity.

Only a shallow observer of human society will lightly estimate the painter's power on the domains of human morals. Under what an obligation are we placed by some of the giant names of historic art—Fra Angelico, Botticelli, Guido, Bassano, Raphael, in his cartoons and pictures of the Divine Incarnation; Rembrandt, in his setting forth of Christ as the poor man's Saviour and friend, habited in coarse garments, concerting alternately with angels and men of low estate; and an amiable Caracci, in his overwhelming picture of "The Three Maries."

It is not possible to conceive a scoffing Michael Angelo, or a flippant Raphael. What masculine blows at drunkenness, debauchery, coxcombery and cruelty were dealt out upon canvas by Wm. Hogarth, long before philanthropy and temperance reform had become the rage.

English art has touched with subtle skill a wide range of religious emotions,—the form of a pure and beautiful woman transferred to canvas, the picture of a good man's face, the vision of a godly mother, busy in the hallowed sphere of home, are surely powerful side-lights upon the question of religion in daily life.

Never was a blow more fearlessly and directly dealt at the ruinous vice of gambling than was given by Mr. W. P. Frith R.A., when he portrayed on canvas in five divisions, the "Road to Ruin."

Every picture that denounces evil, that attracts to good, that kindles sympathy with pure and innocent pleasure, that awakens in us higher and holier affections, and makes us more kind to the brotherhood of men is, in a broad and healthy sense, moral and religious art.

In the entire history of the fine arts, there never occurred such a wonderful display as that which took place in Manchester in the year 1857. Amidst the throes of a commercial panic, which shook the world to its centre, when banks, public companies and mercantile establishments were tumbling down, bringing ruin and destruction in their fall, the merchant princes of Manchester undertook to collect from the private galleries of Great Britain, for the purpose of exhibition, the priceless gems of art, hitherto only seen by a select few, and to accomplish this a palace was erected and all expenses guaranteed by these gentlemen.

On the 5th of May, "I declare this Exhibition opened," were the words which, uttered by Prince Albert, gave to Manchester, the first city in the Empire in regard to its manufactures and the second in respect to its population, an Exhibition of its own, and differing in some respects from those held in London, Cork, Dublin, New York, and Paris, where industrial and art gatherings had been held. The treasures of art alone constituted this wonderful exhibition, such as the world had never beheld.

The birth of Princess Beatrice, on the 14th of April, caused the postponement of Her Majesty's visit till the beginning of July. Her Majesty was entertained during her visit at the mansion of the Earl of Ellesmere, Worsley Hall.

It so happened, the day of the Queen's visit to the Exhibition, the writer was removing from among the smoky chimneys of the celebrated glass and chemical works, and the furnaces of the copper and silver smelting works, of St. Helens, to the heart of the cotton manufacturing district of Manchester, and, anxious to see the pageant, arranged by a study of "Bradshaw" to strike the spot where the procession would pass at a certain time; and with the Queen's well-known punctuality, not a minute was lost. The sight was very fine.

For seven miles, with crowds ten deep on the pavements, through which she had to pass before she reached the Art Treasures Exhibition, which the taste and wealth of Manchester had been the means of bringing together, every window was filled with human beings anxious to see Her Majesty. The whole city seemed to have ceased from the untiring, energetic labors of its manufactures, and appeared with one consent engaged in the more pleasing occupation of welcoming the Queen. Gigantic mills, with their enormous extent of bare walls, assumed a gay and festive appearance. Forests of flagstaffs grew as if by magic out of the factory roofs, while strings of banners between opposite windows bore devices of welcome.

Her Majesty, accompanied by the Prince Consort, the Prince of Wales, the Princess Royal, Prince Alfred, the Princess Alice and Prince Frederick William of Prussia, left Worsley Hall in the following order: First carriage, containing Mr. Gibbs, tutor to the Prince of Wales and Lieut. Cowell, tutor to Prince Alfred; second carriage, the Hon. C. B. Phipps, C.B., and the two equerries-in-waiting; third carriage, the Lord Chamberlain (the Marquis of Breadalbane), Sir George Grey, Bart., Baron Moltke, in attendance on Prince Frederick William of Prussia; fourth carriage, the Marchioness of Ely, lady-in-waiting to Her Majesty the Queen.

Reception in the Building.

As the audience rose and Halle, supported by Miss Novello and Sims Reeves, looking and feeling musical, began to attune their ears and voices for the Coronation Anthem—in glancing round we observed the following noteworthy people at the foot of the dais erected for the Queen: The Prince Consort, Lord and Lady Palmerston, Lord and Lady Stanhope, Lord Burlington, Lord Wilton, Lord Ward, Mr. Granville Harcourt, M.P., and Frances, Countess of Waldegrave, Mr. Ex-Chancellor Gladstone and Mrs. Gladstone, Lord Talbot De Malahide, Messrs. Peto and Paxton, Sir Roderick Murchison, Williams of Kars, etc., etc.

The Queen was accompanied by the Prince Consort, the Prince of Wales, the Princess Royal and her intended, Prince Frederick William of Prussia; Princess Alice and Prince Alfred, Sir George Grey, Secretary of State; the Lord Chamberlain, Marquis of Breadalbane; the Mistress of the Robes, Duchess of Sutherland, and the Hon. Eleanor Sutherland, daughter of Lord Stanley of Alderley.

Her Majesty then knighted Mr. James Watts, merchant of Portland Street, and at the time Mayor of Manchester. This ceremony was performed by the Queen with the Peninsular and Aliwal sword of Sir Harry Smith, with two strokes given with wonderful grace—James Watts rising into Sir James, (here Lady Watts blushed, smiled and looked down). Sir Harry, retaking his sword, kissed the hilt recently touched by the fair hand of Her Majesty.

This done, Her Majesty commenced her walk through the Exhibition. The route was, of course, chronological, beginning with Van Eyck, and ending with Leighton and Millais.

It was noticed that she lingered longer over the early German School than any other part of the Exhibition. As for the Royal children, it was easy to see, as the policemen observed, that Mulready's "Boy having his hair cut," and Webster's "Slide" were more after the children's heart than the best Raphael or the finest Mabrise.

Amongst modern paintings, the greatest crowd seemed to collect around the "Death of Chatterton," where several policemen were stationed to keep back the crowd. The Royal party then, retracing their steps, studied the series of British portraits, also chronologically arranged, forming a perfect English history; afterwards the Enamels, Venetian Glass, Metal Work and Ivories.

Her Majesty before leaving the building partook of a handsome luncheon served by Mr. Donald, and is said to have praised most highly a particular mixture, which, on Her Majesty enquiring what it was, Mr. Donald immediately called "Donald's Royal Art Treasures Nectar, patronized by Royalty." Her Majesty smiled at the "patronized" and left the building amid enthusiastic cheers, and blushes from Mr. Donald such as Scotchmen alone can blush.

"To wake the soul by tender strokes of art."

The works of art contained in the Exhibition were divided into the following sections: 1. Paintings by Ancient Masters; 2. Paintings by Modern Masters; 3. British Portrait Gallery; 4. Collection of Historical Miniatures; 5. Museum of Ornamental Art; 6. Sculpture; 7. Water Color Drawings; 8. Original Drawings and Sketches by the Old Masters; 9. Engravings; 10. Photographs.

The number of paintings by ancient masters, commencing with Cimabue in 1240, and ending with Jean Baptiste Greuze in 1805, including the Marquis of Hertford's contribution of forty-four, was 1,123. The number of what were classed as modern masters, commencing with Hogarth in 1740, up to 1857, was 689. The number of portraits, 386; of water colors, 969; works of sculpture, including a few bronze, 160. The collection comprised works by every great artist, ancient and modern, and of every school of art. The whole of these works of art were insured for five millions sterling, much below their real value. The number of visitors was 2,500,000.

Royal Mail Cunard Steamer "Persia."

The voyage to New York by the Cunard steamer *Persia* in the winter of 1857-8 was unusually stormy, as may be judged from the report of the ship's "log" published in New York papers on our arrival. The statement of having encountered "tremendous hurricanes," although rarely reported, was no exaggeration. For several days we "lay to," making about two knots an hour—just enough to keep the engines in motion. One of the immense paddle-boxes, forty feet in diameter, was carried away with one sea, and other damage done. The voyage lasted over sixteen days, nearly double her usual time. Lord and Lady Napier and suite were passengers, and his lordship suffered greatly from sea-sickness, while her ladyship, whose cabin was nearly opposite that of the writer, scarcely ever missed her morning salt water bath, and was present at almost every meal at the table in the saloon.

As this magnificent ship was then the finest afloat, and was the last of the paddle steamers, except the *Scotia*, a notice of her may not be out of place.

This leviathan vessel, then the largest steamship in the world, left Liverpool on the 26th June, 1856, commanded by Captain Judkins, the Commodore of the Cunard Mail Packets, on her first voyage across the Atlantic. This Company having the exclusive contract for carrying the mails, the position of Commander of one of these steamers was at that time one of great importance, and the rank equal to a commander in the Royal Navy.

As the whole Continent was on the *qui vive* for the arrival of these steamers at Boston or New York, when the signals went up by firing guns by day or rockets at night, a whole fleet of steamers and boats of every size were seen racing for the great object. Then the scramble up the ladders, the rush for the latest papers and despatches, and the rush back to the city of news reporters for the daily papers, and the competition to publish the latest news, was a lively scene.

The Captain, in full naval uniform, giving orders through his silver trumpet, before the days of electric bells, as he stood on the bridge was the observed of all observers. If we are about to start, I see him on his elevated position, and it is interesting to notice how quickly and completely the inward thought and purpose alters the outward man. He gives a quick glance to every part of the ship. He casts his eye over the multitude coming on board, among whom is the English Ambassador and suite. He sees the husbands and wives, mothers and children, entrusted to his care, the valuable cargo, the carefully counted mail bags, all pouring in, and his form as he gives orders for our departure seems to grow more erect and firm. The muscles of his face swell, his eyes glow with a new fire, and his whole person expands with the proud consciousness of his importance and responsibility.

In these days of cablegrams, the importance of a Commander is chiefly dependent on the shortness of the passage made by his ship, as is described on the arrival of the *Etruria* at New York, on having made the fastest passage on record. "The steam was puffing out of her sides in short, painful gasps, like the quickened breath of a grand race-horse, tired, and resting after a great burst of speed. Commodore Theodore Cook was proud as the proudest man in America, as he walked down the noble ship's gang-planks, and then stood up so straight that he nearly fell backwards. No one seems to have been prepared for the phenomenal time she had made."

In November, 1858, "Westward!" was the cry. The more that was learned of the great countries to the North-West, the stronger w the desire to establish uninterrupted communication therewith. The means of access to the Eastern seaboard were already numerous and easy. An open route to the banks of the Saskatchewan and to the shores of the Pacific was wanted. The feeling was that more would be gained in a single year by trading with the North-West than by ten years of the closest communication with the lower Provinces. The Mediterranean would not bear upon its bosom so great a burden of wealth as would our lakes and rivers, should the country become the highway between the two great oceans—the connecting link between China and Europe. In this year the Buffalo and Lake Huron Railway was opened.

The first Toronto City Directory was published by William Brown, the writer having lent him a copy of the London (England) Directory as a model. It was only copied in the classification of the names, the addition of the street directory, as at present, not being adopted for several years afterwards.

In July of this year the writer went to Quebec to meet his

family coming out from England by the *North American*, Captain Grange, and had the pleasure of meeting Rev. John Maclean, now Bishop of Saskatchewan, Rev. Dr. Hellmuth, late Bishop of Huron, and Rev. Mr. Fleury, Chaplain of the Molyneux Blind Asylum in Dublin, to whom I frequently had the pleasure of listening in the chapel attached to the institution, as also the delightful music of the choir, the members of which, including the organist, were all inmates. These gentlemen had been exceedingly kind and attentive to my family during a long and stormy voyage, and on their arrival in Toronto all paid us a visit, expressing, at the same time, their surprise and delight at the fine appearance of the city.

In this year the 100th Regiment, to which Toronto contributed a large quota, was enrolled in the Regular Army as the Prince of Wales' Royal Canadian Regiment of the line; Major-General Viscount Melville was appointed Colonel-in-Chief. The Regiment sailed in three detachments, the first from Quebec, by the Allan steamer *Indian*, nearly 500 strong; the second per *Nova Scotian*, 435 strong, and the third per *Anglo-Saxon* with remainder.

In July, 1859, the *Agamemnon*, in laying the Atlantic cable between Valentia Bay, in Ireland, and Trinity Bay, Newfoundland, a distance of 1,650 nautical miles, was in great danger; the coils broke adrift and the cable was displaced, as she was nearly thrown on her beam ends; the electric instruments were all injured and the deck boats got adrift.

On the successful accomplishment of the undertaking, on the 17th of August, messages were exchanged from the Queen to the President of the United States. Lord Napier was then British Minister at Washington.

Fetes were given at New York, and a reception to the officers of the *Agamemnon* by the City Council; on that occasion, amongst the toasts proposed was the following:

"The people of Great Britain and Ireland, joined to us in the Court of Neptune. May that nuptial tie never be put asunder."

Visit of the Prince of Wales to Canada, 1860.

On the 9th of July, the Prince, accompanied by the Queen and Prince Consort to Plymouth, embarked on board the line-of-battle ship *Hero*, ninety-one guns, Captain Seymour, having as an escort the ship *Ariadne*.

The suite of His Royal Highness consisted of the Duke of Newcastle, Secretary of State for the Colonies; the Lord-Steward of Her Majesty's Household, Earl of St. Germains; His Royal Highness' Governor, Major-General Hon. R. Bruce; equerries-in-Waiting, Major Teesdale, R.A., and Capt. Gray, Grenadier Guards; Dr. Acland, His Royal Highness' physician.

The Prince was commissioned to represent Her Majesty in the opening of the Victoria Bridge, and on all public occasions; to hold levees and receive addresses while in Canada; and in travelling through the United States he was to assume the title of Baron Renfrew.

The squadron arrived at Halifax on the 29th of July, and after visiting Prince Edward Island and New Brunswick proceeded to Quebec, where, leaving the men-of-war, they proceeded to Montreal, arriving on the 25th of August. The Royal party remained there for several days, during which the Prince opened the Industrial Exhibition in the Crystal Palace, attended a magnificent ball given in his honor, laid the corner stone, being also the last stone, of the Victoria Bridge, and clinched the last bolt of the Bridge (a silver rivet) with stout and sturdy blows.

After stopping at Ottawa, Brockville and Kingston on the way up, the Prince arrived at Toronto on the 7th of September, and met with a magnificent reception, the preparations being on a scale far surpassing those of the other cities he had visited. The Prince disembarked at the western extremity of the Esplanade. Here a splendid pavilion was erected facing the city; the hangings were of crimson, blue and white, and the building was adorned with green leaves and festoons of flowers. The whole was surmounted by a Royal crown, on all sides protected by flags.

The greatest charm was the entrance arch, which spanned the

street and was really magnificent. It was of the Grecian order, but exceedingly rich in ornament, and stood sixty feet high. The pillars were massive, palmated at the top. The interior of the arch was adorned with beautiful fresco paintings, and the whole surmounted with a shield bearing the Royal Arms and a Royal crown supported on each side by a fine display of flags. A semicircular platform was erected, with tier upon tier of seats, and was ornamented with shields and banners, and more than 10,000 people were in position it.

In the open space was a troop of cavalry, and in the centre was a great level platform, with the dais and throne under a gorgeous canopy.

Here the Prince was received by the Mayor, Corporation, Judges, Members of Parliament, Officers of the Army and Volunteers, etc.

After the reading of the address the National Anthem was sung by 5,000 children, under the leadership of Mr. John Carter, the Cathedral organist.

It is impossible to do justice to the imposing spectacle presented when the vast assembly stood up and united in one tremendous burst of cheering, which lasted several minutes, the ladies waving their handkerchiefs and men nearly killing themselves with shouting the loyal hurrahs, while several bands played the National Anthem.

The Prince was intensely affected at this glorious welcome, which was so hearty and magnificent.

A procession of militia, firemen and national societies filed past, drooping banners and cheering vociferously. The Prince's carriage followed the procession through the principal streets, cheered by the people, while flowers were strewed before him. Night having come on by this time the city was most brilliantly illuminated, and the whole formed a spectacle which, for magnificence, was never surpassed in Canada. The Prince and suite were entertained during their stay at Government House.

On Sunday the party attended divine service in St. James' Cathedral, and were met at the door by Bishop Strachan, Rector

Grasset, and other clergymen. The sermon was preached by the Bishop, from the text, "Give the King Thy judgments, O God, and Thy righteousness unto the King's son." The demeanor of the Prince during the service was what might have been expected. He joined heartily in the responses, and his entire manner might be copied by some church-going young men with decided advantage.

The Orangemen had erected a splendid arch at the intersection of Church and King Streets, with a large painting of King

GOVERNMENT HOUSE AND ST. ANDREW'S CHURCH.

William III. in a conspicuous position. Instead, however, of the party driving under the arch along King Street, the carriage went down Church to Wellington, and so to the Government House. It transpired that this was done by the positive order of the Duke of Newcastle.

During the week the Prince visited all the principal objects of interest, and planted a tree in the Horticultural Gardens, at the same time opening the rustic arbor then recently erected He also planted an English silver oak in the Queen's Park.

which stands to the east of the guns, and laid the foundation stone of the statue to the Queen, surrounded by civic, provincial and other dignitaries; and in addition to all he turned the first sod of the Toronto Grey and Bruce Railway.

He attended a public ball, given in his honor, in the Crystal Palace, wearing the uniform of a colonel of the British Army, unattached, and led off the dance by taking the hand of the accomplished wife of Mayor Wilson, one of the present Chief Justices of Ontario. The ball was a brilliant scene, and wound up the entertainments given in honor of the Prince in Toronto.

He next visited Hamilton, and then proceeded to New York, where the demonstrations were almost extravagant, and did the people of that city much credit.

The squadron sailed from Portland in November, arriving in England in a short time.

1860 to 1865.

Outside of general events, the local history of Toronto from 1860 to 1865 was that of the proverbially happy country that has no history. The close of the decade of the fifties had witnessed commercial depression, stagnation in trade and manufactures, starvation and misery. The first half of the decade of the sixties brought commercial vigor, activity in trade and manufactures, abundance and prosperity.

It was the story of Pharaoh's kine reversed. The American war caused the country to be overrun with commissariat agents purchasing stores for the army. American gold poured in in steady streams, and produce of all kinds could not be supplied to meet the demand.

Farmers and merchants reaped a golden harvest, and many a fortune was accumulated by trader and speculator. Toronto had its share in the general prosperity, and the condition of the city was one hitherto unexampled.

During this period the speculation in gold reached its climax. Fortunes were made and lost in exchanges between New York and Toronto. Goods bought in American currency and paid for in gold at a high premium, corresponding with the depreciation in American currency, gave the importers of American goods room to realize immense profits.

As an illustration of the difference in the values of the currency at one time, the writer and the late Mr. A. W. Lauder, M.PP., when starting to New York to meet our families, who had been visiting in England, took $40 each to a broker on King Street, for which we received $100 in American currency, and as the price of everything on the American side had remained unchanged—their argument being that a dollar was still a dollar, which they soon found to be rather a delusion—the fare to New York, which fro   the Suspension Bridge was $10, was to us only $4, while a charge of $4 a day at the St. Nicholas' Hotel, New York, was to us just $1.60. Travellers to Canada soon found out the real value of their currency, compared with ours, when coming off the boats to make their purchases.

One gentleman, on purchasing an article on King Street, the price of which was 25 cents, and getting 15 cents change out of his dollar bill, was so chagrined that he vowed he never again would put his foot on Canadian soil.

The return to specie payments was much more rapid than any one had anticipated.

Mr. J. G. Bowes, who had filled the civic chair in 1848-49-50, and had been described as the ablest man who ever filled the office of Chief Magistrate up to that time, was again honored with the confidence of his fellow-citizens by being elected in the years 1861-62-63.

Mr. Bowes spared neither time nor expense in keeping up the dignity of his office and attending to his duties; his hospitality and benevolence extending far beyond the emoluments attached to the office. The respect in which he was held was most marked whenever he made his appearance, and the almost universal recognition accorded him was proof of his great popularity.

On public occasions Mr. Bowes always appeared in official costume, which, although not ornamented with the gold chain, as the Lord Mayors in England, was most appropriate and becoming.

Dr. Russell, of the London *Times*, writes: "The city is so very surprising in the extent of its public edifices that I was fain to write to an American friend in New York to come up and admire what had been done in architecture under a monarchy, if he wished to appreciate the horrible state of that branch of the fine arts under his democracy. Churches, cathedrals, markets, post office, colleges, schools, mechanics' institute rise in imperial dignity in the city. The shops are large and well furnished with goods.

"In the winter time the streets are filled with sleighs, and the air is gay with the carolling of their bells. Some of the sleighs are exceedingly elegant in form and finish, and are provided with very expensive furs, not only for the use of the occupants, but for display. The horses are small, spirited animals, of no great pretension to beauty.

"The people in the street are well dressed, comfortable looking, well-to-do; not so tall as the people in New York, but stouter and more sturdy looking. Their winter brings no discomfort, as fuel is abundant, and when the wind is not blowing high the weather is very agreeable."

Anthony Trollope says: "Toronto, as a city, is not generally attractive to a traveller. The country around it is flat; although it stands on a lake, that lake has no attributes of beauty. The streets of Toronto are paved with wood, or rather planked, as are those of Montreal or Quebec, but they are kept in better order. I should say that the planks are first used in Toronto, and then sent down by the lake to Montreal, and when all but rotted out, they are again floated off by the St. Lawrence, to be used in the thoroughfares of the old capital."

This is somewhat hard upon Quebec, but is highly flattering to Toronto. But there is no rose without its accompanying thorn; at this time another writer informs us that if the streets of Toronto are better than those of other towns, the roads around it are worse.

"I had the honor," he writes, "of meeting two distinguished

members of Parliament at dinner some few miles out of town, and returning back a short time after they had left the host's house, was glad to be of use in picking them up from a ditch into which their carriage had been upset."

The Death of Prince Albert.

On the 14th of December, 1861, occurred the most mournful event in the reign of Queen Victoria, the death of the good and universally beloved Prince Consort, Prince Albert, a double calamity to the kingdom, since it also removed for a long period from public life and public usefulness the affectionate and inconsolable Queen.

Not Britain alone, but all Europe, and distant India and America, felt this blow as the shock of an earthquake. In every place of worship throughout the land, on that fatal Sunday morning, the congregations met in deep sorrow, and the tears of multitudes were shed in regret for the bitter loss, and compassion for the heart-broken widow.

For even the distant homage due Her Majesty's high estate was swallowed up in the sympathy of woman for woman. Nor was she less revered as the mighty sovereign when recognized by all as the weeping widow, and true and earnest were the prayers raised for Her Majesty and her fatherless children.

England never saw King or Consort who so greatly won the respect, the confidence and love of his people. Under his quiet, unassuming and profoundly judicious influence the kingdom was blessed with prosperity and domestic tranquility, his children were trained in the paths of virtue, honor and religion, and the Royal Consort became not only an example to the country, but to all Europe. The blessings conferred on society by the good Prince Albert can never be forgotten, and posterity will regard with reverence the name of a Prince who, though early removed from earth, left behind him the glory of a holy and useful life.

> "Only the actions of the just
> Smell sweet and blossom in the dust."

Buying in Europe.

ITS PLEASURES AND RESPONSIBILITIES.

It has been said of a celebrated New York millionaire and merchant prince, that during his visits to Europe he would never turn aside to witness any exhibition or display that had not immediate connection with his own business; and yet it is a question whether, in the case of his own buyers who regularly visited the markets, such a course would not have deprived them of using one of the very best means of educating their taste and informing their judgment as to the results of the skill and the beauty of the productions of those who contribute to these exhibitions. Besides, all work and no play, in this as in every other department of labor, is not good policy.

There may be a few to whom a sea voyage is a pleasure, but to most persons crossing the Atlantic becomes a weary and monotonous duty, altogether apart from the dangers incurred. Not a few of the buyers with whom the writer was acquainted met with a watery grave. Wilson, of Toronto, Silver, of Halifax, and Cameron, of Montreal, are amongst the number.

The rule is, that the pleasure of the trip is confined to *terra firma*, and to combine business with a reasonable amount of pleasure is both desirable and profitable.

As one of the magnificent ocean steamers floats at anchor in the Mersey, or the St. Lawrence, or her dock in New York, she appears to the beholder a "thing of beauty," and on going on board, how often the exclamation is heard from untried passengers and their friends when they enter the main saloon, and gaze on the elegant carpets, luxurious sofas and arm chairs, mirrors, panels and gilding, the racks of shining glasses, satin damask curtains, handsome piano, etc., " How beautiful everything is, and how nice it must be to cross the ocean in such a vessel!"

Their admiration increases as they view the steward's pantry adjoining, with its glittering electro-plate and piles of earthenware, all fitted in so as to weather every storm, with a place for everything and everything in its place. Then the houses on deck for butcher, baker, pastry cook, ice, vegetables and meat, and the perfection of ranges in the cook's gallery, are all inspected with pleasure. The bedrooms are next visited, with the purest of bed linen, toilet utensils, marble basins, damask curtains, electric bells, and so on to the engine room, and from stem to stern, the size of a pin's head of anything cannot be found out of place; all that art and skill, combined with wealth, can do to make a voyage pleasant and comfortable has been done.

And now the hour of sailing has arrived, and under a full head of steam the noble vessel moves out seaward, a thing of life as well as a thing of beauty. If sailing from New York, the decks are crowded with passengers as they pass Staten Island and view the charming villas and merchants' mansions so thickly studded all over that beautiful suburb. Soon outside of Sandy Hook, now for the first time the heavy swell and roll of the Atlantic is felt, and presently the scene changes. The indefatigable stewards are already at work. The elegant crimson silk-embroidered table-covers give place to the plain "Turkey red," and the satin damask to worsted. The linen covers are soon doing duty on sofas, where wet boots would prove fatal to rich plush covering, and the ominous guards are attached to the dining-tables, something which all sea-goers understand.

A certain lady writer has said that in naming the Cunard steamers in some of which she crossed, while there was a *Persia, Gallia, Etruria*, etc., it was a wonder that none had been named the *Nausea*; and Dickens said that on his first trip to America he counted twenty distinct smells; but that was long before the late improvements in ventilation and other matters, and must have included the smell of beautiful flowers in the saloon, and the fragrant odors of the cuisine; and yet there is something on board every ship to justify the lady's remark as to the feelings that are experienced when once on the "rolling, foaming billows." At the worst, at the present time, the voyage is short, and enjoyed greatly by most after the first *désagréments* are over, and England is soon reached.

The buyers who go to Europe from Toronto are chiefly

confined to the dry goods and millinery trades; while a few visit the markets for fancy goods and toys, a few more for china and earthenware, and one or two for jewelry, watches and watch materials; in these branches of business a visit twice a year, or once at least, is indispensable; and while a good share of pleasure may be enjoyed, in the variety of scene, the attentions of business men, and the delightful scenery through which the journeys lie, yet the responsibility is very great.

In the dry goods and millinery trades especially, the buyer is thrown very much on his resources as to whether he shall risk the novelties which are constantly coming forward, and then as to the quantity that would be safe. This applies, of course, to fancy goods, while as to goods of a staple character he must be wide awake as to *price*, which is the main point.

The responsibility is enhanced where one buyer has to select every class of goods; but even where the ground to be gone over only includes the goods for one large department, a buyer must not only possess judgment and taste, but have a quick perception of the value and suitability of the goods. Promptness of decision is absolutely necessary, as his time is valuable and limited.

Every buyer of dry goods must make Manchester one of his principal points; here, in the very heart of the cotton trade of the world his contracts must be made for printed and plain cotton goods, and many classes of dress goods and small wares. If he has time to go through the various mills and manufactories, he cannot fail to be instructed and interested; and as every experienced buyer has his eyes and ears open, he will gain information of great practical value.

The print trade must be regarded as one of the greatest importance, and the perfection to which these goods have been brought during the present century is one of the greatest triumphs of art and science, whether regarded as to the finish and style, or their marvellous cheapness.

As late as 1860, in the very district where calico printing is now carried on so extensively, Squire Raven owned the parish of Ravensborne, a fine estate in the most rural part of Lancashire.

In this parish he ruled supreme. By his orders, in the Squire's servants' pew on Sundays was ranged a row of serving-maids in the old Lancashire costume—a calico jacket, a Lancashire bed-gown, and a striped linsey-woolsey petticoat—a very pretty costume, no doubt, and formerly a costly one, for the old-fashioned chintz, in the good old days of Queen Charlotte, would have cost five shillings instead of five pence a yard. If the Squire's ukase had been as powerful in Parliament as in his own parish, the long line of manufacturing towns and villages which, beginning at the green oasis of said Squiredom, stretches into Yorkshire, and gives employment to millions of operatives, might be still in the future.

The cheapness of machinery has swept away a crowd of prejudices and flooded us with comforts and luxuries unknown to past generations. The reference to Lancashire takes the writer back to his former residence at Bran lesholme Hall, near Bury, just nine miles from Manchester.

From my hall door one could look out on a forest of factory chimneys, extending for miles in every direction. Yonder is the old seat of the Peel family, in which the late Sir Robert Peel was born, and here the calico printing, from the hand block work to the copper cylinder productions, has been carried on from its commencement. Just behind is the Peel monument on Holcomb Hill; on the other side is the Grant monument, erected in honor of the family of that name who, coming here from Scotland, by wonderful skill and industry in this trade, accumulated an immense fortune.

Away in the distance is Bolton, where, amongst a wilderness of factories, only one can be named—the firm of Barlow & Jones, who have supplied the world with quilts and counterpanes, all made and bleached in their own works. A little nearer is Ratcliffe, where the firm of R. Bealey & Co. divide some of the business with Barlow & Jones; and a buyer from Canada, and especially from Toronto, will be sure of a cordial welcome to the beautiful mansion, and grounds and conservatories of Mr. Bealey, as the writer can abundantly testify from happy hours spent in that delightful home.

The same may be said of the cotton spinning works of Mrs. I Robinson Kay, at Summerseat, the town being entirely occupied by the employees of the firm, some 5,000 finding employment and the kindest treatment.

In the Wesleyan Church a tablet to the memory of the late Rev. J. P. Hetherington, a most intimate friend of the family, is placed in the chancel, and in the adjoining yard is seen the tomb beneath which he is buried. This church is the free gift of the firm for the use of the work people, who with the family are the sole worshippers.

Walmersly House, the family residence, is a fine specimen of the princely mansions of these manufacturers; the furniture and decorations inside corresponding with the beauty and magnificence of the surroundings. Here has ever been found the most unbounded hospitality without ostentation, and finest style without a particle of affectation and here delightful evenings were spent, which are pleasant to the memory of the writer.

Five miles on the other side is Rochdale, where the river Roche, after the water has been used in various ways, carries off the off-scourings of hundreds of factories including those of Mr. John Bright and others, in the flannel and drugget trade.

Yonder are the paper works of Messrs. Wrigley & Co., who supply the London *Times*, and pay to the excise about £80,000 sterling a year.

All around are the works of the Rylands, Bannermans, Henrys, Westheads, Phillips's, Barbours, Hoyles, Ashtons Watts', etc. The sight at night, when the factories are lighted up, forms a fairy scene which is quite indescribable. The thousands of windows, as far as the eye can reach, illuminated, which, with the hum of machinery on all hands, show the enterprise of the capitalists (nearly all self-made men) who control this trade and give employment to such vast masses of people.

From Bury to Manchester trains can be had about every ten minutes, by a choice of three lines of railway, besides omnibuses, from the top of which a splendid view may be obtained, and a delightful ride on one of the finest roads in the world.

The nephew of the writer, Mr. J. C. Kay, proprietor of one of the oldest and most extensive foundries and engine works in Lancashire, will introduce any Canadian buyer who may call to any of these large manufactories, which will well repay a visit. His residence is Heaton Grove, and the works are on Bolton Street, Bury.

It will be evident from the advantage of being in the centre of this district, that a house with large capital and being in a position to place orders of from 50,000 to 100,000 pieces of prints, can always get bottom prices, besides being able to avail themselves of opportunities of a depression to get even below the cost of production.

The Tuesday meetings of the Lancashire manufacturers in the Exchange in Manchester is a sight which, once witnessed, is not soon forgotten. The hum of thousands of voices by which, without any visible signs in the way of goods or samples, and in the quietest manner, yarns and goods to the value of millions of pounds sterling change hands, is something marvellous. East Indian, Turkish, Greek, Australian, Canadian, and other resident merchants contract for goods for their different markets, while the spinner contracts with the weaver, and the weaver with the finisher or printer; the cotton is bought on the spot by telegraph to Liverpool for cash. The merchant or manufacturer in this way can calculate to a penny what his profit will be, and sometimes as many as 500,000 or 750,000 pieces of one line of shirtings, for Calcutta, are bought and sold in a few minutes.

A transaction was mentioned to the writer, in Manchester, in which such a lot of goods was sold in Calcutta in the morning and repeated four times in twenty-four hours by telegraph. A large portion of the trade of Canada in this class of goods has been lost to England through the competition with Canadian and American manufacturers, who produce on the whole a purer article.

One of the most interesting branches of manufacture in Manchester is the cotton velvet trade. The perfection to which cotton velvets and velveteens have been brought within the last few years would in itself require a separate paper to explain.

Rivalling in lustre the very finest productions of silk velvets from Crefelt and Lyons, they possess a brilliancy and finish that fit them for the use of royalty itself; and yet, wonderful as it may seem, these goods when taken from the looms in Lancashire are simply fustians, such as are worn by bricklayers and other artizans at their daily work: very few would suppose that the process of turning these fustians into velvets is accomplished by boys and girls, thousands of whom are employed in that trade. The cloth is stretched on frames, and these boys and girls, with sharp-pointed knives, cut every thread so as to form the " pile " on the face, (this being done on the silk velvets by the threads being cut each time the shuttle passes through, but it is hand-work in the cotton trade,) and afterwards comes the singeing, dyeing and finishing, which brings them to a state of perfection that is truly wonderful.

Passing from the cotton to the linen manufactures, we remark that while Russia, Scotland, and England are large producers, we must go to the great centre of the flax-growing districts in the north of Ireland for the chief supplies. Not only Canada and the United States, but almost every country in the world, here find goods of every grade to suit their wants. Wherever you travel, by land or sea, alike in the cottage of the peasant and the palace of royalty, every table is furnished with the productions of the thrifty and enterprising linen bleachers and manufacturers of Ulster.

From the rough brown diaper to the finest bleached satin damask, all can be procured in this market. The navy and mercantile marine, and also railway companies of almost every nation, here place their orders for table linen and towels, and orders are taken for every design, whether Royal Arms, crests, monograms, names of vessels, or anything that may be required. These are woven into the fabric with exquisite skill. Cambric handkerchiefs in millions are here produced at prices low enough for the school-child, and others so fine that a microscope would be necessary to count the threads; and lastly, the

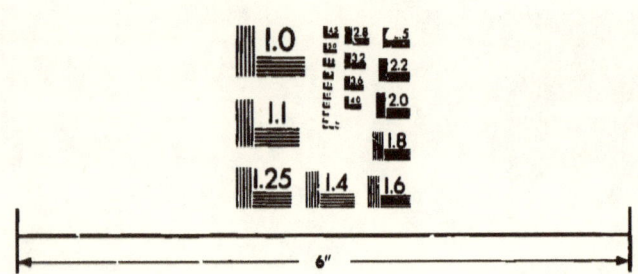

**IMAGE EVALUATION
TEST TARGET (MT-3)**

Photographic
Sciences
Corporation

23 WEST MAIN STREET
WEBSTER, N.Y. 14580
(716) 872-4503

threads (chiefly made in Gilford), as fine as a lady's hair, are produced by the perfection of machinery.

The buyer who visits this district in the season is delighted with the beauty of the plant from which all these fabrics are produced. The delicate blue flowers, as beautiful as the "forget-me-not," waving in millions in the breeze, as far as the eye can reach, is a lovely sight.

The view of immense tracts of country covered with the linen during the bleaching process has been partially changed by the introduction of chemicals.

Leaving the linen district proper, the buyer of shirts and collars, previous to the changes in the tariffs both of Canada and the United States, would visit Londonderry, where thousands of operatives are employed in this trade, although the goods manufactured there are sent to Glasgow to be finished and boxed. The trade in these goods has almost entirely dropped, nearly all the goods of this class being now made in Canada and the United States for home consumption.

To complete purchases in heavy linen goods, a buyer will go on to Glasgow, visiting Dundee, Dunfermline and other places, and will place his orders for white and printed muslins, winceys, handkerchiefs, shawls, and many classes of dress goods.

For Scotch tweeds, the neighborhoods of Hawick and Bannockburn will be visited.

Returning to England, the woollen districts of Yorkshire, including Leeds, Huddersfield, Bradford, Halifax, Heckmondwike, will be ransacked for cloths, blankets, and upholstery goods; and for carpets, Kidderminster and other places.

Nottingham and Leicester will be visited for lace goods and hosiery, and the buyer of millinery will take in Luton and Dunstable for straw goods.

Crossing over to the Continent, he will visit Lyons for velvets and silks, Grenoble for gloves, St. Etienne for ribbons, and in Paris he will select fine dress goods, and a variety of fancy articles of rare beauty and fine workmanship. Here he can select from a stock of fans, from 1 to 3,000 francs each.

The luxury of buying can only be experienced in Paris,

especially if the goods be artificial flowers. In an elegantly furnished room, on a luxurious sofa, the buyer will be waited on by ladies of refinement and taste, who with charming grace submit their samples of flowers for his selection. These are imitations of every natural flower, with many of a purely fancy character, either mounted or unmounted, and of exquisite workmanship. When the order is given and goods made, they are packed in cartoons got up in the well-known style of perfection.

Then visiting Switzerland, he will buy his embroideries in St. Gall, and silks in Zurich.

In Germany there are Chemnitz for fine hosiery, Crefelt for velvets, and Berlin for fancy wool goods.

In London he will complete his purchases, as here, in the great market of the world, he will find every manufacture represented, whether British or foreign.

It will be admitted that the position of a buyer for Toronto is no sinecure, and few require such a combination of qualifications. To be a successful buyer, taste, judgment, tact, promptness of decision, and self-reliance are all necessary; and while there are many pleasures connected with the travels of a regular buyer, there is much responsibility.

In London, buyers are paid from £500 to £5,000 sterling a year, according to their experience, £1,000 being a common salary. Buyers from Toronto for fancy goods, watch materials, electro-plate, toys, and such goods, do not go over as much ground as dry goods and millinery buyers, yet have to visit France, Switzerland and Germany, as well as London, Birmingham, Sheffield, and other places in England.

The grocery and hardware trades do not necessitate a regular system of visiting their sources of supply, the bulk of these trades being done by samples or through agents.

The Fenian Raid.

In March, 1866, the Fenians had formed an elaborate military plan for the capture of Canada, including the seizure of the Grand Trunk Railway by Sweeny, with 30,000 men. A mass-meeting, attended by 100,000 persons, was held at Jones's Wood, New York, and drilling went on openly all over the Northern States.

The most vigorous efforts were made to repel any invasion. Bodies of volunteers were despatched to the principal points along the frontier.

Bishop Lynch issued a circular denouncing Fenianism, and calling upon the people to repel the threatened invasion. A meeting of the St. Patrick's Society was held and Fenianism denounced. A Defence Committee was formed for the protection of the city, and liberal subscriptions were given amid great enthusiasm, the late Mr. William Cawthra heading the list with $1,000.

At this time the Canadian forces consisted of 10,000 regular troops; 11,000 volunteers on frontier service; 15,000 volunteers ready for immediate service, and 80,000 militia balloted for and ready to be called out.

The excitement subsequently subsided for a time, till, on the night of the 29th of May, the demented creatures made a dash across the Niagara River from Buffalo, under Colonel O'Neill, and captured Fort Erie. The number was variously estimated at from 500 to 2000.

When the news reached Toronto the greatest excitement prevailed, as it was supposed by getting a foothold large reinforcements would soon follow, and that they would probably reach Toronto before their progress could be checked. The moment the news was received by the Government, troops, both regular and militia, were despatched as rapidly as possible from Toronto.

Two columns of troops were directed by different routes to Fort Erie; one—consisting principally of regulars, with a battery of field artillery, amounting to about 1,500 men, under the command of Colonel Peacock, 16th Regiment—proceeded by way of Niagara Falls and Chippewa; the other—composed altogether of militia, about 500 in number, under the command of Colonel Dennis—went by the Welland Railway through Port Colborne.

The Fenians remained in possession of Fort Erie till the morning of the 2nd of June, when they advanced towards Port Colborne. Colonel Booker, on whom the command of the militia devolved, found them strongly posted at Ridgeway. He immediately attacked them, at first with success, but finding himself opposed to superior numbers and his ammunition failing, he returned towards Port Colborne with a loss of six killed and forty wounded; the enemy suffering about equally.

Colonel Peacock did not reach Fort Erie till after night, when the Fenians re-embarked, leaving a few of their wounded and a few stragglers, in all about sixty men, in the hands of the Canadians.

The brunt of the battle fell upon the Queen's Own Rifles, five of whom were killed. They were so placed as to be without support, and behaved with the utmost gallantry. The bodies were removed to Toronto, and were displayed in the drill shed for several hours on a platform draped with black. The coffin of Ensign McEachran occupied the middle and front position, covered with the Union Jack; that of Corporal Defries was placed on the right, and that of Private Anderson on the left. The coffins of Privates Alderson and Tempest were placed behind and above, covered with flags. The procession from the drill shed to St. James' Cemetery was led by the band of the 47th Regiment. The Mayor and Corporation, with an immense concourse of citizens, accompanied the funeral. The burial service was read by the Rev. J. H. Grassett. Several other members of the Queen's Own died from the effects of wounds and exposure, amongst whom were Mewburn, Matheson, Leckie and McKenzie.

A handsome monument in the Queen's Park commemorates their bravery.

To prevent further attempts nine steamers on the lakes were temporarily turned into gunboats, and 20,000 troops stationed at different points along the frontier.

Colonel O'Neill, and other ringleaders, including a Protestant and Roman Catholic chaplain, were tried, and the writer was present when the Colonel was sentenced to be hung. The sentence was not carried out, however, having been commuted to imprisonment in the Penitentiary; and so ended the great invasion.

Decimal Currency and American Silver.

During this period the Halifax Currency was abolished and the Decimal System introduced; at the same time all accounts in banks and warehouses were changed from pounds, shillings and pence to dollars and cents, thereby assimilating the whole system to that of the United States, getting rid of the confusion with sterling money and facilitating exchanges generally.

During, and subsequent to the American War, American currency became depreciated, and the premium on gold rose to a corresponding degree, at last reaching to 250 premium. The effect of this fluctuation was to drive the silver and gold in the United States out of circulation, leaving it in the hands of brokers and speculators, and specie became an article only to be bought and sold in the Gold Room in New York, where scenes of intense excitement might be witnessed every day. The effect of this was to send it over to Canada in large quantities, where it passed freely in the purchase of cattle and produce, as well as of every kind of merchandise, at a discount of from four to five per cent. Th "nuisance" commenced when the banks refused to take it, and the greatest inconvenience was experienced by merchants, when making deposits or paying duties at the Custom House, and messengers were running round the city every day to get it changed into bankable funds. At the same time the want of a Canadian silver and copper currency was sorely felt. At this juncture the Hon. Francis Hincks, Minister of Finance, undertook to grapple with the difficulty, his first act being to issue twenty-five-cent paper "shin-plasters," and afterwards to get an Act passed for the issue of a silver and copper coinage, which was shortly afterwards shipped to Canada from the Royal mint. At the same time Mr. Hincks undertook, through the agency of Mr. Weir, of Montreal, to buy up all the American silver in Canada and ship it back to the United States. The value of the same was reduced by the Government, and every precaution taken to prevent its re-importation. This put an end to what was long known as the "silver nuisance."

This decennial period was not marked by any extraordinary progress, being more a time of recuperation of resources than of actual advancement.

The importations at the end of 1866 were a little less than they had been ten years previously, amounting to $6,340,679; the city expenditure was $322,892, compared with $299,848 in 1856; retrenchment and economy had been judiciously exercised and the future made all the brighter in consequence.

The opening of the Street Railway by Mr. Easton in 1861, from Yorkville to the St. Lawrence Market, was hailed with great delight, and a good deal of excitement took place when the first car arrived at the corner of King and Yonge Streets. The undertaking, not proving profitable, was afterwards handed over to Mr. J. G. Bowes, who was the owner up to the time of his death.

One or two locomotive engines had been built by Mr. James Good at his works on Queen Street, from whence they were taken down Yonge Street to the Northern Railway track with quite a display of pride on the part of the citizens generally.

Between 1860 and 1869 Toronto was visited by three Princes besides H. R. H. the Prince of Wales. After him came Prince Alfred, as midshipman in the Royal Navy; leaving his ship at Halifax he paid Toronto an informal visit, and was received with every demonstration suitable to the occasion. As Duke of Edinburgh he has since sailed round the world.

Prince Arthur, Duke of Connaught, arrived in Toronto in 1869, and won all hearts by his princely demeanor. Of more commanding presence than either of his brothers, his appearance created great enthusiasm. He appeared in a public procession and was loudly cheered. The Prince planted a tree in the Horticultural Gardens as a memento of his visit. The Grand Duke Alexis, of Russia, also paid Toronto a visit and was well received.

The increase of manufactures since 1856 was not very remarkable, and consisted of chemicals, brushes, confectionery, engines and boilers, pumps, scales, vinegar, trunks and saddlery, stained glass, carriages, refrigerators, and brass work, all of which gave employment to numbers of operatives, and contributed to the growth and prosperity of the city.

Notwithstanding the financial crisis and consequent depression experienced in Toronto during this period, improvements went on. Churches, banks, several benevolent institutions and private residences sprang into existence. The city continued to extend in every direction, and the population continued to increase. The Esplanade had been built, forming a continuous street, which proved a great convenience in reaching the wharves to which access previously could only be had by coming up from one wharf to Front Street and down to another, and the receiving and shipping of goods were greatly facilitated.

TORONTO FROM 1867 TO 1877.

Confederation.

When the clock struck midnight on the 30th of June, 1867, the joy bells of St. James' Cathedral rang out; it was the 1st of July, the birthday of the new Dominion. Confederation was accomplished and Toronto was once more a capital. The capital only of a Province, it is true, but that Province the wealthiest, the most enterprising, and the most populous in the Union. The day was observed by the greatest rejoicings in the city. What with bonfires, fireworks and illuminations, excursions, military displays and musical and other entertainments, the citizens and the thousands of strangers who crowded the streets did not want for amusement. Since the visit of the Prince of Wales no such day had been witnessed in Toronto.

To celebrate the event a banquet was given in the Music Hall, over the present Public Library room, at which the Hon. John A. Macdonald and Hon. George Brown were the principal guests, as having united for the accomplishment of this grand and crowning work. Their mutual interchange of compliments on the occasion, when each spoke of the other as respectively the greatest statesman and patriot Canada had ever produced, was a striking feature on this memorable and festive occasion.

Paris Universal Exposition, 1867.

From December 1866 to January 1868, the writer crossed the Atlantic six times, keeping up a constant correspondence with Toronto, as far as circumstances would permit, a large portion of the time being spent on the water.

While Toronto was recovering from the reaction caused by the cessation of the American war, with the consequent loss of demand for Canadian products, and the alarm of further Fenian invasions was subsiding, important events were transpiring in Europe, some of which are memorable as matters of history.

The most remarkable trial of modern times, that of the Tichborne claimant, was going on in the Westminster Hall, London. London and Paris were visited by the Sultan of Turkey and the Viceroy of Egypt. The splendid Exhibition in Paris was the great centre of attraction for visitors from all parts of the world, amongst whom were numbers from Canada, and many from Toronto.

The building of the Paris Universal Exposition of 1867 was erected in the Champ de Mars. The palace consisted of eight elliptical galleries, intersected by sixteen transversal avenues, each about five hundred feet long, and all radiating from a central garden. These avenues were described as streets, named after the various countries whose particular section of the palace they abutted on.

There were the Rue d'Alsace, Rue de Normandie, Rue de Flandres, Rue de France, Rue de Lorraine, Rue de Provence, Rue de Belgrave, Rue de Russia, Rue d'Afrique, Rue de Prusse, Rue d'Austriche, Rue de Swisse, Rue des Indes, Rue d'Angleterre, Rue des Etats Unis, Rue de Canada, and the Grand Vestibule.

The palace had sixteen different entrances. The Exhibition Park filled the whole of the Champ de Mars from the Point de Jena to the Ecole Militaire, and was covered with buildings erected by all nations, representing the exact mode of life in each country, both as to the style of the interior and the costumes of the inhabitants.

The Russian stables and post-house were elegant looking buildings. The marble steps that led to the elegant ornamented polished steel doorway, were beautifully engraved and inlaid. The majolica balustrades were remarkably handsome. The stables contained stalls for twenty horses, which were led every day by a Russian groom in the Czar's livery, and put through their paces. The Emperor's Pavilion was furnished and decorated in gorgeous style, and was an object of great attraction.

There was the Palace of the Bey of Tunis, the Prussian Garden and Pavilion, Egyptian Okel, and model of the Catacombs of Rome, model of the house of Gustavus Vasa, in the Swedish quarters, Turkish Mosque and Palace of the Pacha of Egypt, the Egyptian department with costumes and figures, the establishment of the Bey of Tunis, and the English Cottage and Terra Cotta Boiler-house. The outer of the seven concentric ovals, in the vast range of buildings, about one mile in circumference, was entirely taken up with restaurants of every nation in the world, where the attendants, in native costumes, served their own countrymen and others with refreshments to which they had been accustomed in their own country; and in addition, there were the magnificent Spanish, Swedish, Austrian, Turkish, Japanese and Chinese cafes in the Park.

No attempt is made to describe the wonders of the exhibits; one article only can be mentioned from amongst the long line of cases of Lyons silks, which were purchased by Grant & Gask of London—a silk dress, richly embroidered, was sold by that firm at their grand display after the Exhibition was over for £1100 sterling. This particular dress the writer saw, and was credibly informed of the price at which it was sold when in London.

The Sunday before leaving Paris on this trip was spent with several Canadians, amongst whom was Mr. Richard Brown, of Brown Bros., of this city. Having met at the Wesleyan Chapel in the Rue Roquepine, a visit was paid to the celebrated cemetery of Pere La Chaise, where repose the ashes of kings, queens, emperors, statesmen, poets, philosophers, musicians, painters, and all ranks of Parisians, down to the humble workman; and here crowds of people resort on Sundays to decorate the tombs. In the evening the sight of the Champs Elysees, at ten o'clock, being still daylight, was such as even Paris herself has never witnessed before or since. The climax of splendor had been reached. From the Place de la Concorde to the Arch of Triumph was one stream of carriages, while on both sides the various exhibitions were in full blast.

The following Thursday, the 11th of July, may be regarded as the turning point in the history of Napoleon III. He had seen Paris arise under his direction, as with a magician's wand, to a point of unparalleled grandeur. Mile after mile of magnificent new boulevards had sprung into existence. The Exhibition had eclipsed all those which preceded. Paris had been visited by kings and emperors, and on the day named a grand review of the troops took place in the presence of Abdul Aziz, then the Sultan of Turkey; Ismael Pacha, G.C.B., Viceroy of Egypt, being there the same week.

This was the last peaceful military display ever witnessed by the Emperor. Not very long after the Franco-Prussian war broke out, terminating in the surrender at Sedan. "*Sic transit gloria mundi.*"

The same day the writer left Paris for London, accompanied by Mr. Richard Brown and the late J. H. Mead, who, being an excellent French scholar, as well as a gentleman of very general information, made a very agreeable fellow-traveller.

As an incident of the Exhibition, the writer had an opportunity of seeing the Empress Eugenie in one of the picture galleries, where from the peculiar shape of the building allowing no long views, the Royal party had the advantage of a quiet inspection. The Empress had become quite matronly in appearance since 1855, but still retained marks of beauty which were very attractive.

Fenianism in Manchester.

While residing in Manchester, in 1867, the trial and execution of Allen, Larkin and O'Brien, for the murder of Policeman Brett, took place.

Two Fenian head centres, Kelly and Deasy, —who were styled Colonel Kelly and Captain Deasy, officers of the Fenian Army—

having been arrested, we ᷉ put in irons and locked in the police van with a number of other prisoners.

The van proceeded over Ardwick Green, and along Hyde Road, a fine open street nearly a mile in length, toward the prison. It was drawn by two horses and was guarded behind by seven policemen, with Brett inside the door, while each prisoner was locked in a separate compartment.

The van had proceeded about half up the road, when, in passing under the viaduct of the London and North-Western Railway, a volley of shots was fired at both horses and men. The policemen dropped from the van and spread themselves out wide. There was a rush of thirty or forty men (said to be Irish) upon the police and the van. One had a hatchet, another a hammer, and a third a bayonet, with which they set to work to break open the van; one man took a revolver and fired it into the lock. At last several men, with large stones, broke through the top of the van and the panels of the door behind, and set all the prisoners, including the Fenians, at liberty. The policemen collected in a body to prevent the prisoners from being liberated, and Brett refusing to give up the key, several revolvers were discharged. Sergeant Brett was shot over one of his eyes and died shortly afterwards. It was proved that Allen fired the fatal shot.

The trial which followed was one of the most remarkable in history. The Fenians threatened to burn up the city, and the greatest excitement prevailed.

Troops, including dragoons, hussars, and infantry, amongst which were the 42nd Highlanders, with artillery, poured into Manchester, while policemen from the surrounding towns were ordered into service. The splendid new assize courts, where the trial was held, was guarded by immense bodies of police, who were heavily taxed to keep back the crowds.

After every day's trial the police van was escorted to the prison by a strong body of military marching before, behind, and on each side, the whole width of the streets, while policemen stood on the van with loaded revolvers to meet every or any attack that might be attempted.

After the fullest and fairest trial Allen, Larkin, and O'Brien were found guilty and sentenced to be hung.

The writer—using his unfailing talisman to gain admission to every place of interest after working on the feelings of a policeman for nearly two hours, and speaking of Canada and America—succeeded in getting admittance to the Court Room, and was present when the death sentence was passed.

Larkin, amid the shrieks of some of the female relatives of the prisoners, jumped up in the dock and shouted "God save Ireland!"

The morning of the execution of these three men was so foggy that those on the opposite side of the street could not see the terrible spectacle. The streets around the Old Bailey at Salford, where they were hung, were barricaded with immense beams of timber, and all traffic was suspended till all was over.

The judges at the trial were Justices Blackburn and Mellor. For the prosecution, Sir J. B. Karslake, Attorney-General, and Mr. Hinman; for the defence Mr. Digby Seymour, Q.C., Mr. Sergeant O'Brien, Mr. Cottingham and Mr. Ernest Jones.

Assassination of Thomas D'Arcy McGee, M.P.

Having, when a young man of twenty-three, been one of the accomplices of the Smith-O'Brien rebellion in 1848, Mr. McGee escaped in the guise of a priest to America, and when the amnesty was granted became a loyal citizen of Canada; and at the time of his assassination represented Montreal West in the House of Commons. He was a man of high personal character, and of remarkable talents and accomplishments.

Mr. D'Arcy McGee was most earnestly opposed to the Fenian Conspiracy, and by speech and writing warned his countrymen against it.

On the night of April 7th, after an eloquent speech in the House of Commons in favor of loyalty and unity, he was shot dead from behind, at the door of his lodgings. The agent of the bloody deed was James Whelan. The murder was planned by forty Fenians in Montreal, among whom lots were cast as to who should execute the deed, and the lot fell upon Whelan. He was hanged on the 11th of February, 1869.

Sir John Young was sworn in as Governor-General on the 2nd of February.

Tariffs of England, United States and Canada from 1869 to 1876.

Having retired from the direct importing trade in 1869, the writer accepted the agency of the firm of Potters & Martin (Limited), of Manchester, England, for the United States and Canada. This firm had been established nearly a century before, the head at one time being Sir John Potter, under the style of Potters & Norris, and subsequently of Potters & Taylor; the present Mr. Thomas Bailey Potter, M.P., continuing the business till the introduction of Mr. Martin as partner, is well known as the friend of Mr. Cobden and Mr. John Bright, and is still the chairman of the Cobden Club, and a representative free trader.

Having been a buyer of American goods for many years, I had a good knowledge of the leading lines of their domestic manufactures, which up to a comparatively recent period had been limited in both number and extent; and having engaged three travellers to look after the Canadian business, I undertook to do all the American trade myself, and with this view got up an immense line of samples weighing some five hundred pounds, and comprising a full assortment of British dry goods, besides everything in French and German goods for which an order was likely to be obtained. During six years of this business I had the best opportunity of seeing the operation of the tariffs of the three countries. Every invoice passed through my hands, and all the correspondence, extending from Halifax to Winnipeg, and Baltimore to St. Louis, was carried on by myself directly, while the ground gone over twice a year was about 5,000 miles each journey.

The amount of business done in the States may be judged from the sales of the year 1875, representing in American money about $300,000. That amount was done from a very few lines of the samples carried, and if a fair proportion of the goods previously imported from England had been ordered the amount could have reached the millions. But the rapid growth of their manufactures from season to season, under the high tariff, gradually excluded line after line, and instead of having six hundred pounds of samples, one hundred pounds would be amply sufficient to represent all the goods there was any chance of selling, and by the end of 1876 the United States were independent of the world for all necessary goods; those which might be called luxuries only being required for their wants.

The firm which I represented did not seem to appreciate the real position of affairs, and in the face of these facts would supply me with lists of members of the Cobden Free Trade Club, amongst whom were a few American names, including that of Rev. Henry Ward Beecher.

To circulate literature of that kind amongst my clients would have been as ineffectual as the efforts of Free Traders in 1885, described by the Philadelphia *Free Press*, which says:— "The Free Traders are preparing to smash the tariff again. The performance will resemble the efforts of an over-ripe tomato to smash a stone fence."

In taking orders, it was necessary to take the American tariff constantly as a *vade mecum*. This required constant study, with its endless distinctions in specific and *ad valorem* rates, and both combined. It was evident that no branch of industry had been overlooked, and that every manufacturer, small and large, had been at Washington and had a clause inserted for his own benefit, and so the manufactures spread and grew with amazing rapidity. The average rate on our goods was about 60 per cent. *ad valorem*, and this was always payable in gold, the premium on which, during this period, averaged nearly 20 per cent. To illustrate the actual cost of foreign goods to the importer, it may be stated, that at the highest rate of duty paid this year (1886) in Canada, goods can be laid down at about 65 per cent. advance on the sterling cost, or $3\frac{1}{4}$ cents to the penny.

The simplest way the leading importers in the States used to arrive at the probable cost of goods, in giving their orders, was the latter calculation of so many cents to the penny. As nothing in dry goods paid less than 35 per cent. *ad valorem*, no goods could be laid down at less than 4 cents, while most cost 4½ to 5 cents. The effect of this high rate of duty was to bring some British manufacturers to establish their works in the States.

Messrs. Coats and Clark, the great thread manufacturers, finding the difference in duty between thread in hanks and on spools to be so great (on the latter the duty, being specific, reached to an average of 72 per cent. *ad valorem*), opened large establishments in New Jersey, where now their thread is all spooled, giving employment to hundreds of operatives, and by so much depriving Paisley of the payment of these people's wages, and all the corresponding advantages. All this time American goods were being shipped to England free of duty, and the climax was reached when, on my last trip, I was asked to take samples of American cottons, these being largely sold close by the warehouse in Manchester, and offer them for sale in Canada (!) while not a yard of similar goods made in England was sold in the whole of the United States. This proposal I at once begged to decline; it would have been too humiliating. The goods referred to, admitted free into England, were liable at the time in the States to a duty of five cents a square yard, and ten per cent. *ad valorem*. This did not appear to me to be in any sense "fair trade" the opinions of the great Manchester manufacturers to the contrary notwithstanding. About the same time the firm of Randall, Farr & Co., of Hespeler, Ontario, who were extensively engaged in the manufacture of Alpaca cloths, not being able to compete with British goods, removed their whole machinery to Massachusetts, and never returned.

Metropolitan Church.

During the residence of Rev. Dr. Punshon in Toronto, the congregation worshipping in the old Adelaide Street Church, corner of Toronto Street, feeling the necessity of increased accommodation, as well as of having a building of more modern style, in looking round for a site, fixed their attention on McGill Square, then about to be sold. The late Rev. Dr. Taylor and Dr. Punshon, with other members and trustees, soon secured the property, relying to a great extent on the services and influence of Dr. Punshon to raise funds for the erection of a church in the centre of the square.

The corner stone was laid in 1870, and soon the present magnificent structure appeared in its grand and beautiful proportions.

The building has so often been described, and is so familiar to both citizens and visitors, that any present description is quite unnecessary; besides, any attempt to describe the churches of Toronto would involve a larger amount of space, from the vast number that has sprung up of late years, than these pages could afford.

The Metropolitan Church with its beautiful grounds, so splendidly ornamented with trees and flowering shrubs, as well as flower beds, belongs not only to the Methodist body, but to the whole city of Toronto, forming, as it does, an open square, which is at once a boon and ornament to Toronto, and remains a lasting monument to the memory of Dr. Punshon, and also to Drs. Taylor, Ryerson and Green, as well as laymen who contributed liberally towards its erection.

While some churches in Methodism are more elegant and greatly more expensive, there is not one in the world—take it altogether, internally and externally, the grounds included—which, in all its appointments, is so complete as the Metropolitan Church of Toronto. Messrs. Langley & Burke were the architects.

A beautiful stained glass window, in memory of Mrs. Punshon, who died at their residence on Bond Street, was placed by Dr. Punshon in the south-west gallery.

In 1870 and 1871

Toronto had become a very important commercial centre. The principal streets wore an aspect of staid, unpretentious prosperity. They had begun to spread out indefinitely; the area of

METROPOLITAN CHURCH.

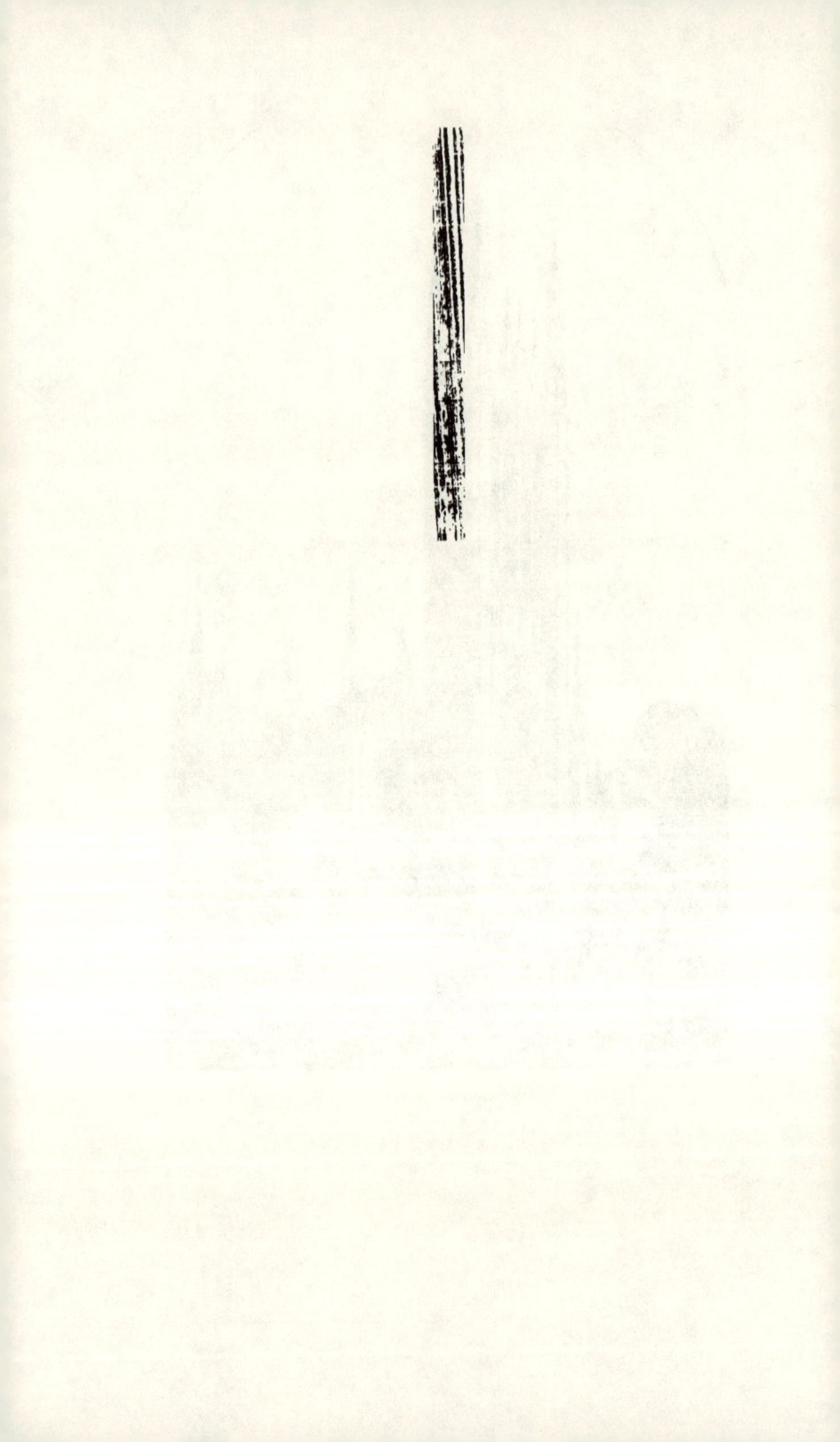

the population had been widely and rapidly extended. From the Provincial Lunatic Asylum on the west, to far eastward beyond the Don, stretched mile upon mile of densely populated thoroughfares. To the northward, Bloor Street had long since ceased to be anything more than a nominal boundary between Toronto and Yorkville. The Esplanade on the City front had become a hive of railway and general industry. Jarvis Street had been beautified with elegant and stately residences. King and Yonge Streets continued to monopolize the lion's share of the retail business; but Front and Wellington had developed into the centre of the wholesale trade, and many large and wealthy establishments had headquarters there.

A writer in the *Canadian Illustrated News* (Montreal), at this time indulges in some rather severe strictures on the aspect of our streets, which he describes to be, generally speaking, either dirty or narrow, with the light of heaven almost shut out; or broad, wretchedly paved, certainly with a number of sufficiently handsome houses, but at the same time with an undue preponderance of common, and generally having the appearance of being laid out on the sand-flat. He admits, however, that Toronto possesses two principal streets, sufficiently broad, well lit, and well paved, and lined with handsome shops. Some of this gentleman's comments on the social aspect of the streets are suggestive and entertaining.

" Between the two principal streets of the Western Capital is a great gulf, made by the inflexible laws of society and fashion—a gulf as great as separates the Bowery from Broadway, the Rue de Rivoli from Rue Mont Parnasse, or Regent Street and Rotten Row from the humble thoroughfares of Pentonville and the City Road.

" The buildings on King Street are greater and grander than their neighbors on Yonge; the shops are larger and dearer; and last, but not least, King Street is honored by the daily presence of the aristocracy, while Yonge is given over to the business of the middle-class and the beggar. Amid the upper classes there is a performance that goes on daily, that is known among *habitues* as ' doing King.' It consists principally of marching up and down a certain part of that street at a certain hour, performing, as it were, 'Kotow' to the goddess of fashion, and sacrificing to her sister divinity of society.

"At three o'clock in the afternoon the first stragglers appear on the scene, which extends perhaps a quarter of a mile. These consist principally of young ladies, whose proper place should be at school, and young men attired in the height of fashion. By the time these ardent devotees have paraded a few times, the regular *habitués* make their appearance, and till six o'clock in the evening one side—for one side only is patronized—is crowded to excess.

"It is rather considered 'the thing' to patrol King Street in this manner; and of a fine evening every one who belongs to the *elite*, as well as many who do not, may be seen perseveringly trudging up and down, no doubt to their great comfort, and to the intense discomfiture and dismay of others less smiled upon by nature or less favored by their tailors or their dressmakers. King Street is in a way a great social 'Change,' where everybody meets everybody and his wife; where the latest fashions are exhibited, and the last quotations of the matrimonial market are exchanged.

"Would you see the newest style in hats or panniers? They are to be seen on King Street. And would you know how many young swells are doing nothing for a living? You are sure to find them on King Street. Would you wish to hear the last imprudence of young Harum Scarum, or the progress of Miss Slowcome's engagement? You may be sure before you take half-a-dozen turns some conversant, intelligent busy-body of your acquaintance will have whispered the facts of the case in your ear, all of which he has 'on the best authority, sir.' It is on King Street that Clelius makes his appointment with Clelia for their afternoon walk; that Thersites, jealousy stricken, scowls at Adonis; and that Pomponia depreciates the value of her dear friend Amaltheus' new silk and trimmings. There Cornelia, the careful mother, brings out her treasures and exhibits to the public gaze those desirable lots of which she is so anxious to dispose on advantageous terms. While far above all, Diogenes, in his garret, little more roomy or commodious than the ancient 'tub,' looks down upon the motley throng, notices their petty follies and foibles, and thanks his lucky stars that he is not as other men."

In 1871 the population was 56,000, an increase in ten years of 11,000. During the next three years Toronto, in common with the Province, enjoyed an unexampled epoch of prosperity. A remarkable impetus was given to all the usual branches of trade; and the commerce, both wholesale and retail, assumed such proportions as not even the most sanguine had hoped for. More than 13,000 were added to the population, and both public and private enterprise kept pace with this rapid increase. The streets were full of bustle and activity.

Mercantile palaces were built by some of the leading houses, and many of the finest mansions and most beautiful churches in the city were erected.

The progress made since Confederation had been amazing. Not only had its area and population largely increased, but it had been greatly beautified by the erection of huge business establishments, and palatial private residences; and it had developed a commercial enterprise and energy which seriously endangered the pretensions of Montreal to the mercantile supremacy of the Dominion.

It was during 1872-74 that Toronto began to make the rapid strides in commercial enterprise that placed her in the proud position she now occupies. They were years of unusual prosperity, and trade of all kinds received a remarkable impetus. Happily the foundations then laid of the city's mercantile greatness were sufficiently solid to resist the shock of the reaction that followed.

In July, 1873, a delightful passage was made to England in the Allan steamer *Polynesian* from Quebec. After passing through the Straits of Belle Isle large icebergs were seen, while the weather was that of summer. Amongst the passengers were Dr. and Mrs. W. T. Aikens, of Toronto, and the family of Mr. and Mrs. Gammon, of Chicago, visiting Europe for the first time. The fine weather gave an opportunity for games of various kinds on deck, those of shuffle-board and quoits being the favorites. A very pleasant time was spent in London in sight-seeing.

Return of Rev. Dr. Punshon to England.

During my stay in Manchester, in 1873, the late Rev. Dr. Punshon—who, had he lived, would have done as much to recommend Canada, and Toronto in particular, to the attention of the English people as any other man, having frequently stated he was bound to the country by the dead and the living—returned to England. In company with Dr. Gervase Smith and other friends, we met him at the railway station on his arrival from Liverpool.

The Wesleyan Conference being then in session in the Free Trade Hall, the Doctor was expected to attend one of the evening meetings. The Conference, numbering about six hundred ministers, occupied the great platform, while the audience was fully six thousand in number.

Dr. James occupied the presidential chair, and all were on the *qui-vive* for the appearance of Dr. Punshon, who was known to have arrived. Soon he entered quietly at the back of the platform and took a seat, but was instantly recognized, when the immense audience stood up, and between clapping of hands and waving of handkerchiefs, round after round, the scene baffles description. For the time all the Doctor could do was to stand with head bent down and eyes streaming with tears, until an opportunity was given afterwards for giving expression to his feelings in words. It was a scene never to be forgotten.

In 1874 a voyage from England was made in company with several Toronto gentlemen, including the late Rev. Dr. Jennings. One of the passengers was the now celebrated Mr. Joseph Arch, M.P., who, it is reported, took the oath in the House of Commons dressed in a suit of corduroy, and appeared at a banquet given in his honor, amongst a number of noblemen and gentlemen, dressed in a tweed suit.

Mr. Arch was accompanied by a secretary, and represented

the Laborers' Trade Union of England; himself a working-man. Their object was to get information as to the desirability of emigration on a large scale. After travelling extensively through Canada and the United States they returned to England, but no practical results followed.

On the passage many lively discussions on politics took place, in which Mr. Arch showed himself to be a man of good common sense and of moderate views, with a decided tendency to the democratic side. He is a Methodist local preacher.

St. James' Cathedral Clock.

About ten years ago the citizens of every denomination united to purchase the world's prize timekeeper from Benson & Sons, of London, and succeeded in placing it in the tower on Christmas Eve, 1875.

This clock possesses a threefold movement, viz., keeping time, chiming, and striking the hours and quarter-hours. The combined weights to keep it going are over three thousand pounds; the pendulum is over sixteen feet in length, the end weight being two hundred and fifty pounds. The quarter-hour chimes are a copy of the famous Cambridge chimes in England, composed by Handel one hundred years ago, and may become in time, to citizens of Toronto, what Bow Bells are to inhabitants of London.

The year 1875 had been marked by a very perceptible reaction in the commercial world of Toronto.

The year 1876 came in gloomily, and with murmurs against the trade policy, and yet improvements went steadily on. New streets were being opened up in all directions, and the population went on increasing.

At the close of 1876 the imports to Toronto had reached $11,231,543; the value of taxable property was $47,150,302, and the population had grown to 71,693. It will be seen from the above that the value of the imports had nearly doubled in ten years; the greatest increase having taken place between 1871-72. After a period of prosperity a time of depression set in that continued till 1878, when the city began slowly to recover from the effects of evil times.

Several new and additional manufactures had been introduced, amongst which were fine jewellery, steam gauges, engines and general machinery, watch cases, elevators, rubber stamps, cork cutting and varnishes.

The highest point the duty had reached up to this time was twenty per cent. *ad valorem*, except on one or two articles on which, by way of incidental protection, twenty-five per cent. was charged. These goods were principally ready-made clothing.

TORONTO FROM 1877 TO 1886.

Protection versus a Revenue Tariff.

The question of Protection *versus* a Revenue Tariff, inaugurated in 1878, brought in the Tilley Tariff and National Policy.

Previous to 1858 the manufacturing industries of Toronto were few and small. At this time, in the Parliament of United Canada, then sitting in Toronto, a protective tariff was introduced by Inspector-General Cayley, the rate being twenty per cent., and, as previously stated, on some goods twenty-five per cent. The improvement was soon perceptible in the immediate impetus given to manufactures, which continued till 1866, when Inspector-General Galt cut down the tariff to fifteen per cent., producing a disastrous change. Manufacturers who had invested large capital in machinery, at once losing confidence, became discouraged, and commenced to withdraw their capital from what appeared to be a policy of fluctuation and uncertainty,—a state of things which continued till 1878.

It will be seen by comparison with the Tariff of the United States that in general the principles are the same. Although the rates of duty in Canada are much lower there is evidence of a similar arrangement for the protection of home manufacture, especially those in actual operation throughout Canada.

Exhibition Buildings.

These magnificent buildings were opened by His Excellency the Earl of Dufferin, in September, 1878. The palace is built with solid brick foundations, with sides and roof of glass, and affords admirable accommodation for the display of goods. The cost of the buildings was $250,000.

Through the suggestion of Mr. J. J. Withrow, the indefatigable President of the Industrial Exhibition Association, the whole of the material of the original Crystal Palace was utilised in the erection of the present building, thereby effecting a great saving, and accounting for the similarity in appearance of the two buildings. The design was copied by Mr. Sandford Fleming from that of Sir Joseph Paxton for the London Crystal Palace, in 1851.

The grounds, sixty acres in extent, are the finest in the Dominion. They are most beautifully situated on the shore of Lake Ontario, and from there a splendid view of Toronto and the surrounding country and lake can be obtained.

The other buildings comprise horticultural and machinery halls, apiary, dairy, and horse and cattle pens, etc. The buildings and grounds are kept in the most perfect order.

The Marquis of Lorne and H.R.H. the Princess Louise.

The appointment of the Marquis of Lorne to succeed the Earl of Dufferin as Governor-General of Canada gave great satisfaction.

The Vice-regal party sailed from Liverpool on the 14th of November, 1878, in the Allan steamship *Sarmatian*, and arrived in Halifax on the 23rd, having had a very rough passage. They were met by the Duke of Edinburgh, who, with a naval squadron, had come to meet his royal sister. Leaving for Montreal the following Wednesday, and stopping at various places on the way, they arrived in Ottawa in a few days.

The Governor-General held his first New Year's Day reception at Rideau Hall on the 1st of January, 1879.

Their first visit to Toronto was on the 20th of January, on their way to the Falls, and was quite informal; their object being to get a winter view of Niagara.

The lamented death of the beloved Princess Alice had occurred on the 14th of December. Under the circumstances it

EXHIBITION BUILDING.

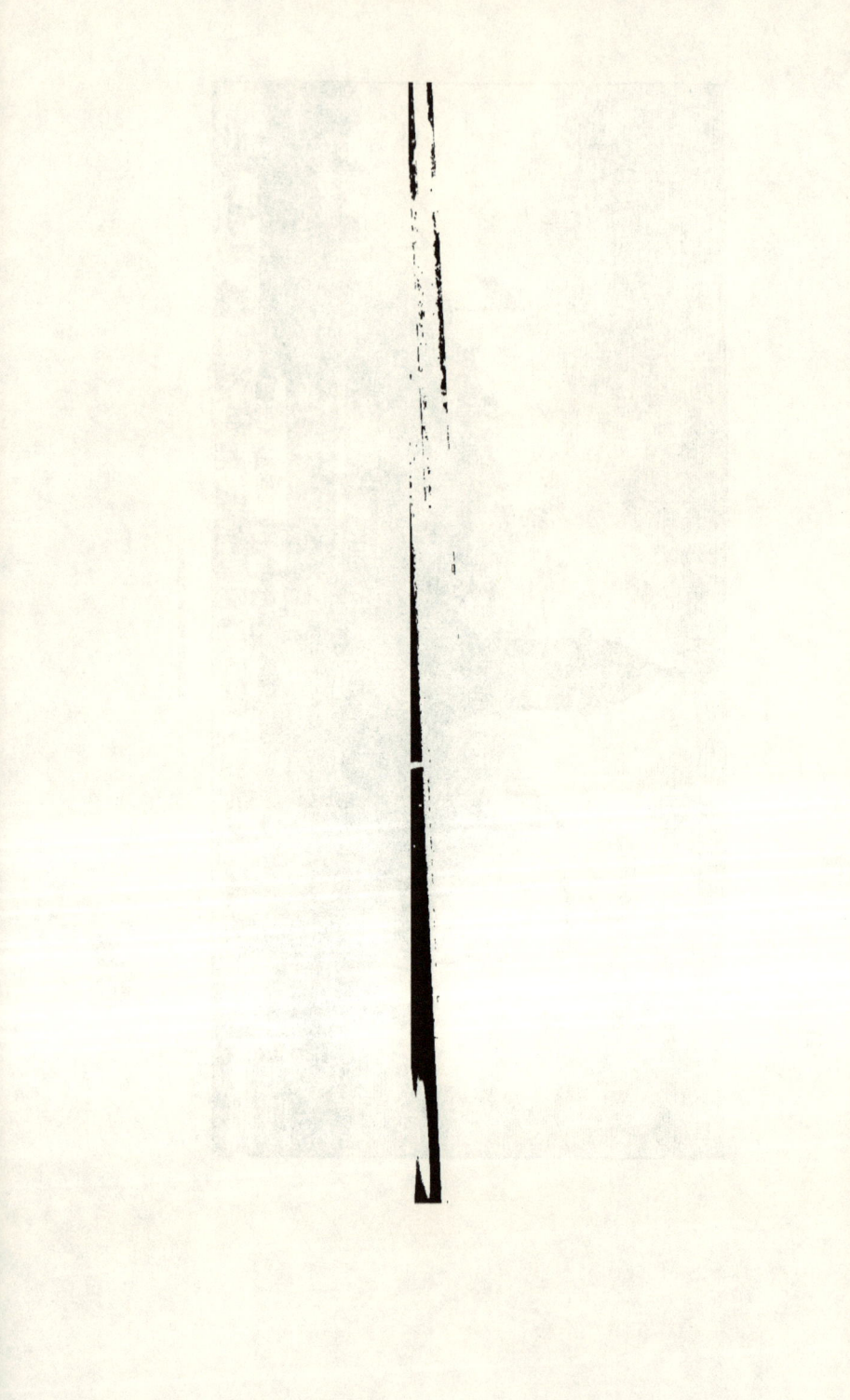

was considered best to defer the Vice-regal visit till after the harvest of 1879, and the Governor-General having consented to open the Exhibition, the date of their visit was fixed for that time.

When Toronto had been visited by three princes it was scarcely expected she would so soon afterwards be honored by a visit from one of Her Majesty's daughters, and when the announcement of the appointment of the Marquis of Lorne as Governor-General was made, it was received with intense pleasure.

The Earl of Dufferin, in his speeches on the occasion, in truly eloquent and beautiful language described the character of the Princess Louise, and congratulated the country on this distinguished mark of the Queen's love and affection for Canada, in consigning her favorite daughter to her care; at the same time portraying the character of Her Royal Highness, from actual knowledge, in colors which he well knew how to use. As an artist, musician, and scholar, she excelled in every accomplishment, and her benevolent and kind disposition was truly and beautifully described.

Her visits to Toronto fully confirmed the description given by His Lordship, and Toronto fully sustained her reputation for loyalty by giving the Vice-regal pair a right hearty reception. The party arrived in Toronto on September the 4th, and were received with a guard of honor, and by all the civic and military dignitaries.

The Exhibition was opened on September the 6th by the Marquis and Princess Louise, amidst great enthusiasm. There was a general illumination at night. They left for London on the following morning. Returning on the 18th, Her Royal Highness laid the foundation stone of the Home for Incurables, and the Governor-General presided at the opening ceremony of the Credit Valley Railway.

During this and subsequent visits all the public institutions were inspected, especial attention being given by Her Royal Highness to those of a charitable and benevolent character, including the General Hospital.

The Grand Opera House was destroyed by fire in November, 1879.

On the 25th of March, 1880, the Hon. George Brown was shot in the thigh and succumbed to the effects the following May. The funeral was attended by an immense concourse of people, and business was almost entirely suspended while the procession was passing. Bennett, the murderer, was tried and executed for the crime.

In June, the Hon. John Beverley Robinson was appointed Lieutenant-Governor of Ontario.

During this year Prince Leopold visited Toronto, accompanied by the Marquis of Lorne and the Princess Louise on their third visit. The Princess and Prince Leopold left for England by the steamer *Polynesian*, on the 31st of July.

On the 6th of August a fight occurred between Roman Catholics and Orangemen, and one policeman was fatally wounded.

Dr. W. H. Russell writes: "Toronto, seen under the most disadvantageous circumstances" (it was pouring rain when his party arrived), "was voted to be very surprising, and my friends were not prepared for such fine buildings and such a great array of wharves and quays on the bay, and the great fleet of craft alongside them. Toronto has increased in all the elements of wealth and consequence by bounds, and since 1861, when I was there, the population has doubled and is still increasing very rapidly."

The Doctor pronounces the University to be worthy of a great nation, a noble Norman pile, beautifully situated.

Farewell Visit of the Vice-regal Party.

Having on several occasions expressed the pleasure with which they visited Toronto, the Marquis of Lorne and Her Royal Highness the Princess Louise, before leaving Canada, paid a farewell visit to the city.

On the 12th September the Vice-regal party arrived at the Union Station, and were received with a guard of honor of one hundred men of the Royal Grenadiers, accompanied by their band. A large number of civic and military dignitaries were present to welcome the distinguished party.

Additional interest was manifested from the fact that another member of the Royal family, Prince George of Wales, second son of His Royal Highness the Prince of Wales, was with the Vice-regal party, and for the first time in Toronto. The first day was spent in visiting the public institutions, including the Home for Incurables, General Hospital, Infants Home and House of Providence

In the evening they attended a concert in the Horticultural Pavilion, given by J. T. Thomson. The artists were Signori Brignoli, Poggi, Adamouski, Madame Teresa Carreno, and Miss Carrie Mason.

The next day the Exhibition was visited, and preparations were made to present the Marquis and Princess Louise with a farewell address. By one o'clock the Queen Street Avenue was lined with immense crowds of people, while detachments from the Queen's Own Rifles and Royal Grenadiers took up their positions around the gates of the enclosure. An archway was erected on the mound which rises in the centre of the flower plot, surmounted with the Royal Arms, hedged in on either side with flags, and decorated with flowers, and having the words "Welcome to Toronto," "Lorne and Louise," artistically displayed.

The steel helmets of the Body Guards were the signal of the approach of the Vice-regal party, and amid a down-pour of rain they entered the enclosure and stood on the dais, in front of which about 3,000 people presented an unbroken covering of umbrellas. As they made their appearance, cheer after cheer arose from the assembled multitude, the pouring rain being ineffectual to dampen their enthusiasm. When the cheering for the Marquis and Princess had subsided, some one called out for three cheers for Prince George. Not catching the words at first, as referring to himself, the Princess turned towards him and pleasantly said, "That's you." The cheers were given heartily, and Prince George bowed his acknowledgment.

When the ceremonies were ended the Princess drove to the

Hospital for Sick Children, and the Marquis to the Exhibition. They left Government House on the 14th ; Toronto, as usual, having done herself honor in this display of genuine loyalty.

Arrival of the Marquis of Lansdowne.

The new Governor-General, Lady Lansdowne and suite arrived by the Alian steamer *Circassian*, at Quebec, on the 23rd of October, and were met by Lord Lorne and the Cabinet. The Marquis of Lansdowne took the oath of office the same day, after which they proceeded to Ottawa.

FIRST VISIT TO TORONTO.

On the 9th of January, 1884, His Excellency the Governor-General, Lady Lansdowne, Lord and Lady Melgund and suite arrived at the Union Station, where they were met by His Honor the Lieutenant-Governor and Captain Geddes, A.D.C.

A guard of honor from the Queen's Own Rifles, composed of one hundred men and the Band, assembled to meet the distinguished party, who were immediately driven to Government House.

The first day was spent in sight-seeing. The route taken was through the principal streets to the University. In the evening a large number of the leading citizens were invited to meet the party at Government House.

The next day they went to the Falls, and crossing the new Suspension Bridge, were landed on American soil for the first time in their lives. On their return to Toronto on the 12th, His Excellency proceeded to the City Hall to receive the Address of the Corporation, to which he replied in the most felicitous terms. The Vice-regal party visited the Hospital and other institutions. The Marquis and Lord Melgund visited the Granite Rink and attended the ball of the Royal Canadian Yacht Club.

In letters to the London *World* addressed to eminent persons, an independent critic said, at the time of his appointment as Governor-General of Canada, to the Marquis of Lansdowne :—

" There is no Englishman of your age whom I could congra-

HIS EXCELLENCY THE MOST HONORABLE THE MARQUIS OF LANSDOWNE,
G.C.M.G., ETC., ETC., GOVERNOR-GENERAL OF CANADA.

t
b
an
pr
18
til

bu
an
sir
to

tulate with equal warmth and sincerity upon the assumption of an arduous and anxious post. Everything is in your favor. You carry with you more than promise, more even than the first fruits of performance.

"A singularly blameless youth was crowned with the highest honors at the first University of the world. The advantages to which you were born, and which are not possessed to the same extent or in the same degree by any but the peers of historic English titles, have been turned by you to admirable account. You have acquired a valuable insight into the routine of office, and you have shown, both in the House of Lords and elsewhere, that you possess that power of speaking which is indispensable to public men of your race.

"The Canadians will recognize in Lady Lansdowne a guarantee that they are about to welcome a Vice-Queen after their own heart."

The Semi-Centennial Celebration

took place in Dominion week. The 6th March was celebrated by the opening of the Free Library by the Lieutenant-Governor, and a reception by the Mayor in the City Hall, this being the proper day for the commemoration of the birth of the city in 1834; but it was deemed advisable to postpone the celebration till Dominion week.

The celebration commenced on Monday, 30th June. Flags, bunting, mottoes, and evergreens were used in the decorations, and the scene, looking down one of the principal streets, was simply a vista of fluttering colors. The whole week was given to pleasure, and thousands of sight-seers, from all parts of the Province and the United States, crowded the city.

Monday, June 30th, was the municipal and historical day, specially commemorative of the city's municipal organization and progress. The procession comprised municipal bodies, police, fire brigade, etc.

Tuesday, July 1st, military day; grand street parade and review, comprising visiting and city corps to the extent of over four thousand men.

Wednesday, July 2nd, trades and industrial day, specially commemorative of the progress and standing of the commercial interests of the city. The parade comprised members of the different labor organizations of the city, each with a tableau, illustrative of the trade followed; also representatives with illustrative tableaux from all the mercantile and manufacturing establishments of the city. It consisted, in part, of waggons, on which various mechanics were plying their daily vocations.

Thursday, July 3rd, "U. E. Loyalists" day, commemorative of the settlement of the U. E. Loyalists in Canada, one hundred years ago. In the afternoon there was a reception at the Government House, and in the evening the Oratorio of Redemption was given at the Horticultural Gardens, also a grand display of fireworks in the harbor, and imitation naval combat.

Friday, July 4th, benevolent societies day; parade comprising uniformed and un-uniformed lodges of Masons, societies of all kinds, etc.

Saturday, July 5th, commemorative of our educational institutions. The parade comprised over 8,000 children from the public and separate schools of the city.

Captain Joseph Dutton, R.N.

This popular and favorite Commander, as Commodore of the Allan Line, always took charge of the newest ship; and having had the pleasure of his personal acquaintance, I desire to pay some small tribute to his memory.

On land an accredited local preacher of the Wesleyan Church, he never failed to fulfil the duty on board his ship, except by consent to give place to regularly ordained clergymen. Those who have crossed with him will remember his appropriate sermons and his leading of the singing, while he accompanied himself on his melodeon, which he always had in addition to the piano belonging to the ship. Not alone in the saloon did he study to please and profit the passengers by getting up concerts, but on certain nights in the week, and also on Sunday afternoons, he got the sailors to carry his melodeon into the steerage, much to the delight of the passengers. Here, accompanied by a number of the saloon passengers, he would sing and play and then call on those around for a song or recitation, the response to which often showed a wonderful amount of talent, scarcely to be expected from such a motley crowd, many of whom, who, from necessity or economy, were travelling in this way, would put to the blush those who would not deign to associate with them on the saloon deck.

As a total abstainer Capt. Dutton was a pattern of firmness and consistency. On his ships no sailors were allowed any intoxicating liquors, and in his place at the head of the table, while surrounded constantly by the most distinguished passengers who had the place of honor, neither wine nor other liquors ever passed his lips. At the same time he never interfered with the chief steward, who attended to the wine list—and every passenger ordered what he wanted *ad libitum*—but kept on the even tenor of his way, always ready to "crack a joke" when chaffed on his temperance principles, giving offence to none and setting a good example to all. Once a week he delivered a temperance address in the steerage. His genial manners, united with the fearlessness and bravery of the true seaman, inspired every passenger with the most perfect confidence in times of danger. When relieved from the severe duties incident to stormy weather, all his efforts were directed to make the time pass pleasantly for the passengers, a contrast in this respect to many who were almost unapproachable beneath the weight of their responsibility. His pleasant humor turned at one time on composing what himself and his intimate friend, Dr. Punshon, called "logograms," which consisted in making the name of a town or city out of a sentence given impromptu.

The writer, having on one passage lost his perpendicular by a sudden lurch of the ship, saved himself from an actual fall by grasping a rope attached to one of the life-boats, but in doing so was caught by another rope, taking the skin off his legs, and causing him to lie on a sofa in the saloon for several days. Capt. Dutton soon propounded as one of his logograms, "Mr. T. has a sore leg." The answer was shortly given in the name of the town "Sorel." Many a dull hour was relieved and enlivened by such innocent amusement.

In these days of fast sailing a passage made in the *Polynesian*, under command of Capt. Dutton, in five and a-half days from sight of land to land, is worthy of mention. Although faster sailing has been made from Sandy Hook to Queenstown, this was the shortest sea passage of which there is any record.

Those who have seen the Captain's family come out from New Brighton on the Company's tender to meet him, and have seen the joy of all, will sympathise with them in their loss, which will also be felt by those who waited for his ship to have the pleasure of crossing with him.

Population of British Cities.

Professor Seeley, speaking of the expansion of England, says: "As an instance of a lack of a due conception of the spread of the British race, how many people, on being asked to enumerate the twenty most populous British cities, would think of including Melbourne, Sydney and Montreal. And yet, leaving London with its five millions out of the list, the following are the fourteen chief cities and towns in the order of population:

City.	Population.	City.	Population.
Glasgow	671,595	Sydney	250,000
Liverpool	573,202	Dublin	249,602
Birmingham	421,258	Edinburgh	236,002
Manchester	338,296	Bristol	215,457
Leeds	327,324	Bradford	209,504
Melbourne	305,000	Nottingham	205,298
Sheffield	300,563	Montreal	200,000

And in the next fifteen would be found Adelaide and Toronto, each with over 100,000 inhabitants."

He proceeds to remark of Toronto, that it is "a political centre of great activity, where originate plans and projects that largely influence Dominion politics; the tone of its intellectual life is higher, and it is generally admitted that there is a more assured type of culture and urban refinement by the shores of Lake Ontario than even in the Island of Montreal."

Comparative Population of Seven Canadian Cities.

	1871.	INCREASE IN TEN YEARS.	1881.	PER CENT. OF INCREASE	1884.
Toronto	56,092	30,323	86,415	54.05	102,000
Montreal *	107,225	33,522	140,747	31.21	200,000
Quebec	59,699	2,741	60,440	4.60	65,000
Hamilton	26,716	9,245	35,961	35.06	42,000
Halifax	29,582	6,518	36,100	22.03	40,000
Winnipeg	241	7,744	7,985	3213.21	30,000
Ottawa	21,545	5,867	27,412	27.23	29,700

* Since 1881 Montreal added Hochelaga with 40,000.

In reference to Toronto, the Fredericton (N.B.) *Reporter* says, "The growth of Toronto is something astonishing. The census of 1881 gave that city a population of 86,415. In 1885 the assessors' returns place it at 111,800, and this may be regarded as under the mark, as the census would be taken in a more liberal manner. That city is now fast approaching Montreal in the number of its inhabitants, and when the next census is taken, if it continues to make the same rapid progress it has in the past five years, it may be the first city in the Dominion in numbers. Its growth in wealth and its substantial improvement are very remarkable."

Climate of Toronto, 1885.

FROM THE METEOROLOGICAL RECORDS.

		Av. 45 yrs.
Average temperature for year	41.57	44.17
Warmest month, July.		
Average of warmest month	68.30	67.58
Coldest month, February.		
Average of coldest month	11 08	22.60
Difference between the warmest and coldest	57.22	44.91
Warmest day, July 25th.		
Average of warmest day	75.45	77.41
Coldest day, February 11th.		
Average of coldest day	5.90	2.00
Date of highest temperature, July 17th.		
Highest temperature	88.6	90.73
Date of lowest temperature, January 22nd.		
Lowest temperature	16.1	12.00
Mean temperature, winter, 26 4 ; summer, 63.6.		

N.B.—The year 1885 was the coldest on the records except 1875.

Number of hours of possible sunshine	4,463
Number of hours of actual sunshine	1,931 *
Number of fair days	184

* Over 43 per cent.

Toronto is situated in North Latitude 43.49, and West Longitude 79.71; 5 hours, 17 minutes and 26 seconds later than Greenwich time.

While writing the above, on the 19th of January, 1886, at one o'clock in the afternoon, the thermometer stood at thirty degrees, just sufficiently below freezing-point to prevent a thaw. The universal desire was expressed that we would not lose our snow, the sleighing being good and everybody wishing it to continue. The disappointment felt by the absence of snow at New Year's would seem strange to people in Britain, but is well known to those who have resided in Canada any length of time. The thermometer is in this respect a sure indicator of the state of trade, which rises or falls according to whether we are favored with a good fall of snow or otherwise, its absence being regarded as a calamity by all business men; so any feeling of compassion towards us by those at a distance on the ground of climate would be entirely thrown away.

As to the fall of rain, it will be sufficient to mention that nature is very propitious; there always appears to be a supply of the right degree and at the right seasons for all agricultural purposes.

In 1885 the number of days on which rain fell was 103; the average in forty-five years, 112 days.

As to whether more rain is desirable or beneficial there will be a difference of opinion. The writer never left his home in Lancashire, summer or winter, without an umbrella, and it was said that rain fell in the neighborhood of Manchester about 250 days in the year. The effect of this was to keep every bit of grass in a state of constant verdure unknown in America, but it may have disadvantages as great as the absence of such a quantity has in Canada.

The quantity of fruit shipped to England will show that the climate is well adapted to the ripening of all vegetable productions, which abound in perfection in the neighborhood of Toronto.

The pictures representing Canadian winter costumes are very misleading, and a plain statement of facts from actual experience will form a more correct standard than that of any thermometrical character.

If I were asked in England why the ladies in Canada wear furs, I should reply that they also wear them there, and very nearly to as great an extent, and partly because it is the fashion as well as for comfort. If asked why men wear heavy fur caps and coats, I should say it was the fashion also, and not so much a necessity. In no city in the United States, where the cold is quite as great as in Toronto, can you find men wearing the headgear referred to, and a Canadian is instantly recognized when appearing in this costume; so that it is evidently not because of the rigor of the climate, and yet it is one of those things that tend to fasten this idea on the minds of people abroad.

The first winter the writer spent in Toronto he was much struck with this fact, and not to possess a "set" of furs—consisting of a great cap, a pair of gauntlets up to the elbows, and a fur muffler, made out of a whole mink or fox skin with the head carefully preserved and worn as an ornament in front—was to make yourself a marked man and altogether unfashionable. Nevertheless, the writer, who soon commenced going back and forward to England and France, persisted in wearing his usual clothing, and from that time to the present has never worn one single article different from what he wore on the other side of the Atlantic, and on the ocean in winter.

The heaviest outer garment was a heavy beaver coat with a fur collar, and this did service on land and sea in the most severe weather, and was found just as necessary on a night journey from Manchester to Glasgow as in an open sleigh in Canada. An ordinary felt hat was the warmest head covering, and no inconvenience was felt from want of fur.

I will state one fact for the information of those who pity Canadians who have to travel in winter. I have driven from Toronto to Kingston, in what I will call a one-horse sleigh (known here as a cutter), 180 miles in three days, and returned in the same time; with snow so deep that I was in danger of overturning in the drifts, and with no warmer clothing than I have described, except to have a buffalo skin for knee covering; and felt no more discomfort than I have experienced in one of the journeys from London to Liverpool. I have told this many times in England, but friends who were in the habit of "baiting" their horses every ten miles on their beautiful roads were so incredulous that they would not be convinced the thing was possible, and yet it was a simple fact.

Mr. Burdette, under cover of what is intended as a humorous strain, unwittingly represents every soul in Toronto as swathed in furs. The London *Times* could have done no more and no worse.

A walk along our principal streets any day, the coldest that comes, will demonstrate the fact that the great majority of the people do not find it necessary to wear furs. There are comparatively few days during the winter when a man who knows how headaches and baldness are superinduced finds it prudent to wear so much as a fur cap. The people of Ontario generally have less need of furs than their friends of many of the States of the Union where the plug hat prevails all the year round.

The custom of wearing furs by gentlemen must have originated at the time when the beaver, mink, otter, fox, wolf, raccoon, and the bear were trapped by the Indians in the neighborhood of our present cities, and being found useful for articles of clothing, have continued in use and will do so till these animals are gradually exterminated from the country.

Not many years ago the same ideas were entertained in Toronto of the climate of Manitoba and the North-West as are now held by many in Great Britain with regard to Ontario, and yet the Canadian Pacific Railway Co. assert of the climate of Manitoba, that "it is healthy: there are no epidemic diseases, no malaria; spring, clear and bright; summer, warm with cool nights; autumn, balmy and pleasant; winter, uniform, dry and bracing."

It would be just as incorrect to put down the whole of Canada as having the same climate, as to compare the State of Florida, where flowers bloom all the year round, with northern

Minnesota. It must be remembered that the whole of England is farther north than Toronto, and that Aberdeen is seven degrees still farther.

That fur coats are not confined to Canada, it may be stated that a Boston gentleman, last winter, purchased an overcoat costing $4,000, and it is declared that it could not be duplicated for a much larger sum. It contains sixty-nine Russian sable skins of the finest quality. The overcoat, which is quite large, is of the finest German castor; the body and sleeves being lined with sable, while a broad collar and deep cuffs of this costly material give a rich finish to the garment. Although so warm that the wearer would not feel the most intense cold, the overcoat is much lighter than our ordinary ulster.

Much misapprehension certainly exists in England with respect to the climate of Canada, including Toronto. The imperfect knowledge possessed by the great mass of the British people as to the immense extent of this Dominion has led to the error of giving to each portion the character of the whole; and when travellers who happen to be in Montreal during the "ice carnival" describe ice palaces, toboggan slides, and skating rinks, and when snow-shoes, blankets coats, and tuques are represented in pictures and photographs, the general idea conveyed to persons at a distance is one of discomfort, whereas the very contrary is the fact.

At what season is there so thorough enjoyment as when all this goes on? Young and old alike enter into the spirit of the season; and the very horses in the sleighs seem to keep time in their prancing with the musical tinkle of the sleigh bells.

Every resident in Toronto knows that the absence of snow and frost in the winter is regarded, instead of a boon, as little short of a calamity. The bracing air, with the thermometer verging towards zero, instead of having a depressing effect, is quite exhilarating, and everybody is more healthy and hearty.

The writer, after a residence in Toronto of over thirty years, can positively assert, that he has suffered more discomfort from the climate of England and France in one winter than all he has spent in Toronto, and this is true, whether applied to travelling or staying at home.

In the former the want of heat in the railway carriages, (except the hot water tins for the feet, which soon cool, and are altogether inadequate to impart comfortable warmth on a night journey,) affords a striking contrast to the comfort in our Canadian cars, where, if there be any discomfort, it is from excess of heat; and leaving out the higher class of hotels and private residences of Europe, which are heated by all modern systems of steam and water, the great bulk of houses are entirely unprovided with proper heating arrangements, such as are common all over America. The writer knows well from experience the feeling in England, in cold, raw weather, of crouching over a fire in a grate, when the face is burning while the back is almost freezing; and to go to bed was something to be dreaded, unless, indeed, a fire was ordered specially in the grate, and the warming pan applied to the bed linen before you ventured in.

The most intense cold experienced by the writer in his life was during a night spent at a manufacturer's house in Staffordshire. An extra supply of bed-clothing seemed ineffectual to keep up the desired warmth during sleep, and in the morning, on lifting the water jug, instead of water, a solid lump of ice, having burst the jug, rolled on the floor. The second jug was tried, with the same result, but the gentleman being a manufacturer of these articles, did not suffer as much as his guest. Such a thing has never happened in all my travels in Canada, the arrangements for heating bed-rooms being so much more complete and convenient. Such a thing could scarcely ever happen in Toronto, and it is of Toronto I am writing, and not of some of the Hudson Bay stations.

In churches and public halls the same difference is perceptible. The custom of wearing overcoats in these places, so prevalent in Great Britain, not being necessary in Canada, they are all so comfortably heated.

Snow.

Snow ! snow ! beautiful snow !
It falls upon king and pauper alike,
Regardless of station, of wealth, or of might.
The white cloaks of courtiers it contrasts to shame ;
To the blush of the cheek it adds freshness and flame.
To the festive in age, or the sportive in youth,
Earth's winter garlands are atoms of mirth.
Then welcome the snow, though heavy the fall,
God's emblem of purity, power over all.
—*Shearl.*

In England it is a common expression that it is cold enough for snow. We say in Toronto that it is too cold for snow, by which is meant that snow is never accompanied by intense cold ; and what in London is little short of a calamity, by the obstruction of traffic, when a heavy fall of snow takes place, in Toronto the event is hailed with joy ; no one is inconvenienced, but, on the contrary, traffic is more easy and travelling more pleasant. The sleigh-runners immediately take the place of wheels, and heavier loads can be drawn with less fatigue to the horses, which the animals seem to understand quite as well as to feel, and everything is delightful and exhilarating.

So carefully is the snow guarded that in Montreal there is a law to impose a fine for using wheels when runners can be used ; and in Toronto the Street Railway Co. is prohibited from removing the snow off their tracks, and compelled to put on sleighs.

The winter enjoyments consist of skating, curling, tobogganing, and ice-boating, and for all of these the facilities are unlimited. The bay in front of the city, with its thousands of skaters, with numerous rinks in all parts of the city, which, under cover of splendid glass roofs, with comfortably heated dressing rooms, and every convenience, might well excite the envy of skaters who, for want of better, hasten to the "Serpentine" in London when ice has formed, and continue to use it long after it has lost its native purity, and when it would not tempt any small boy in Toronto to skim on its dark surface. Canada is indeed beautiful in her winter aspect.

One cannot imagine how animated and brilliant is Toronto when she puts on her snow-shoes, and gets herself up on runners, and fills all the air with the chimes of the sleigh-bells. There is an endless variety in design, and pattern, and color of sleigh, and robe, and bell, and plume, and the streets look like Christmas as long as the snow lasts. Even the street cars feel the infection, and mount themselves on bobs (short runners), and jingle the loudest bells, and take the best half of the street.

Robt. J. Burdette, after a visit, asks: "Who are these in blanket suits? It is pleasant to tarry among people whose girls wear satin slippers when they dance, and 'arctics,' when they wade through the snow. Our fair Canadian cousins have no dread of comfort. The snow has no terrors for them. They dress for the storm as sensibly as for the reception. They dress prettily; and if there is a prettier figure on the North American Continent than a daughter of Canada, apparelled for the ice or the toboggan-slide, herself a part of the snow-drifted landscape, a picture of health and comfort that fairly softens the piercing wind into a sense of warmth, I have not seen it.

"She dresses in perfect harmony with the winter and landscape. She has a complexion clear as the ice of Ontario, and her warm blood shines through it rich as the flashes of the Aurora, graceful and free in every movement. Everybody dresses for the winter when it comes, and yet it is a climate no more severe than that of York state.

"I was the only man in Ontario," says Mr. Burdette, "with a stiff felt hat and a cloth overcoat" (this is hyperbolical, as stiff felt hats and cloth overcoats are in the majority), "and felt all the time I was in the Province as though I was a lost Arctic explorer and had eaten my fur overcoat, cap, mittens, and boots, and was waiting for a rescuing party to find me."

It will be evident that the following description is also written by this most celebrated of American humorists:—

The Toboggan

is a sled with a single runner which spreads clear across the bottom. The top of the toboggan is just like the bottom. It is somewhat thicker than a sheet of writing paper, and about as long as an after-dinner speech. Its seating capacity is only limited by the number of people who can get on it.

The urbane and gentlemanly conductor sits aft and uses one of his lithe and willowy legs for a steering apparatus, by which he guides the toboggan some way or "rudder." It is easy to slide down hill on a toboggan; in fact, after you start down you can't do anything else. True, you could fall off: that is easily done. The flying-machine is not high, so that you have not far to fall; still, if you have to fall from a toboggan half way down the slide, or else fall down stairs with a kitchen stove, you take the stove and the stairs every time; it isn't so exciting, and it isn't so soon.

The prince and I walked up the stairway for the purpose of sliding down the bannister on a toboggan. The president of the Club took his place aft; somebody said "Let her go." Then we stopped and the president said, "How did we like it?" I left my breath at the top of the slide and we had to go up and get it. There it was, a great gasp, three and a half inches long, sticking in the air like an icicle just where I had gasped it when I started. I took it down, stuck it in my left lung and began to breathe again with great freedom. The toboggan is to any other way of getting down hill what flying is to going to sleep. If I was in a hurry and it was down hill all the way, I would rather have a toboggan than a pair of wings any day.

Departure of Toronto Troops for the Northwest.

When the rebellion, led by Louis Riel, had assumed such proportions as to demand a call to arms, the Government order to prepare for immediate departure reached the commanding officers in Toronto on the 27th of March. During Friday night and the early hours of Saturday, the 28th, orderly sergeants were busily engaged in scouring the city informing the men of the startling news. At an early hour the drill shed presented an animated appearance, the men having flocked to their answer to the roll call. Such was the enthusiasm manifested that great disappointment was felt that only two hundred and fifty men of each regiment could be sent to the front. As the sentiment displayed was one of cheerful alacrity in responding to the call to arms in the country's defence, there was no holding back or hesitation, and the number required was soon made up.

On the 30th March tens of thousands gathered at the Union Station to see the gallant volunteers depart for the scene of action, and all through their dreary route their progress was looked for with the deepest anxiety and most heart-felt sympathy. The march over the ice, and the heroic fortitude displayed through intense cold and fatigue throughout the entire journey, as well as the bravery displayed in the different engagements with the enemy, have all become a matter of history. Thousands of hearts in Toronto throbbed in sympathy with her citizen soldiers during those memorable months, and prayers were constantly offered in all the churches for the success of our arms and the safe return of our sons, when victory had crowned their efforts.

Return of the Toronto Contingent.
WELCOME HOME—JULY, 1885.

War-worn, sun-scorched, stained with the dust of toil,
And battle-scarred, they come victorious.
Exultantly we greet them, cleave the sky
With cheers, and fling our banners to the wind;
We raise triumphant songs and strew their path
To do them homage. Welcome home!
We laid our country's honor in their hands
And sent them forth: undoubting, said farewell,
With hearts too proud, too jealous of their fame,
To own our pain. To-day glad tears may flow;
To-day they come again and bring the gifts,
Of all earth's gifts most precious—trust redeemed.
We stretch our hands, we lift a joyful cry,
Words of all words the sweetest, "Welcome home!"
Oh brave, true hearts! oh steadfast, loyal hearts!

> They come, and lay their trophies at our feet ;
> They show us work accomplished, hardships borne,
> Courageous deeds, and patience under pain,
> The country's name upheld and glorified,
> And peace, dear purchased by their blood and to l.
> What guerdon have we for such service done?
> Our thanks, our pride, our praises and our prayers,
> Our country's smile, and her most just rewards ;
> The victor's laurel laid upon the brows,
> And all the love that speaks in "Welcome home ; "
> Bays for the heroes, for the martyrs palms ;
> To those who come not, and though dead yet speak,
> A lesson to be guarded in our souls
> While the land lives for whose dear sake they died
> Whose lives, thrice sacred, are the price of peace ;
> Whose memory, thrice beloved, thrice revered,
> Shall be their country's heritage,
> To hold eternal pattern to her living sons.
> What dare we bring? They, dying, have won all ;
> A drooping flag, the flowers upon their graves,
> Are all the tribute left ; already theirs
> A nation's safety, gratitude and tears,
> Imperishable honor, endless rest.
> —*Annie Rothwell.*

Should some Rip Van Winkle have fallen asleep in 1850, waiting for the hourly omnibus for Yorkville, at the corner of King and Yonge Streets, and awaked on the 23rd July, 1885, he would not have been surprised at the sight of a "Union Hotel, by Jonathan Doolittle;" nor would he have mistaken any other face on a signboard in place of Her Majesty, Queen Victoria, as did that mystic individual mistake the sign of George Washington for the ruddy face of good King George. The evidences all around would soon undeceive him, and he would quickly discover that Queen Victoria still reigned over a happy and contented people.

The return of the Queen's Own, Royal Grenadiers, and Governor-General's Body Guard, amidst the spontaneous display of welcome by the tens of thousands of Toronto's citizens, was a sight seldom equalled, and one to be remembered by the present generation, and to be recorded in Canadian history and perpetuated by the well-earned tokens of the appreciation of Her Majesty and the English people, by the medals worn on the breasts of the heroes, these having been struck in the Royal mint and with the immediate sanction of Royalty.

On this day, amid a blaze of bunting, under triumphal arches from north to south and east to west, the return of the citizen soldiers was greeted with an ovation only equalled by that given to the Guards in London on their return from the Crimean War covered with blood stains and martial glory.

ARRIVAL AT NORTH TORONTO.

The movement of the Governor-General's Body Guards towards the ground indicated the arrival of the train and the commencement of the cheering.

The troops disembarked amid the strains of "Johnny comes Marching Home," and "Home, Sweet Home," by the bands of the regiments. The cheers were taken up by the spectators along the streets as the column came into view.

On Yonge Street the sight which met the eye was one which had never before been presented. Looking southward the view was beautiful. Arches, flags, banners, festoons of flowers and evergreens, with multitudes of spectators in windows and on housetops, as well as on the crowded thoroughfares, as street after street was passed, under arch after arch, formed a scene which could only again be repeated under like circumstances, and which will in all probability never occur. It was joyful, enthusiastic and loyal, and will live in the memory of all who witnessed it while life shall last.

Under any circumstances the return of volunteers to their homes and friends would be a cause of rejoicing; but when they come having bravery, victory and peace inscribed on their banners, their march is a triumphal procession.

Our gallant defenders, under the command of Colonels Miller, Grassett, Otter and Denison, with General Middleton as Commander-in-chief, will have their names and deeds recorded on the page of history as examples of heroic endurance and bravery. The distance travelled, hardships endured, battles fought and won, thorough discipline without a single act of insubordination, cool courage, steadiness under fire, and the crowning result in the capture of the leaders and the entire suppression of the rebellion—all distinguished this short campaign of less than four months as one of the most remarkable of ancient or modern times.

How to see Toronto in 1886.

In order to get a correct idea of the city, let a visitor enter an open carriage at the Queen's Hotel, and proceed eastward. He first sees the Union Station, a fine modern building, and the Walker House, a large hotel at the corner of York Street. In front is the extensive factory of Ewing & Co.; in the rear of which are the large new stables of the Dominion Transport Co., and on the opposite side of Lorne Street, those of Shedden & Co., carriers to the Grand Trunk Railway.

Proceeding to Bay Street, passing a splendid block of warehouses, and looking north to Queen, the site of the new Court House, and perhaps City Hall, comes into view. This, when completed, will form a new square, and be an ornament to the city. From Bay to Yonge, passing spacious and elegant warehouses, the Custom House and new Bank of Montreal are reached.

At this point, on looking up Yonge Street, the traveller will be reminded of the view up Broadway, New York, the appearance of the street here being very fine and imposing. Splendid wholesale warehouses, banks and public offices, with stores of every description, stretch away far beyond the reach of vision, giving the impression of a thorough business city, the traffic at this point being very great.

From Yonge to Church he will find continuous lines of handsome warehouses, occupied by the large wholesale grocery merchants and boot and shoe manufacturers. On passing Scott Street a view of the Great North-Western Telegraph Co.'s building, the Ontario Bank, and several large Insurance and wholesale dry goods warehouses, is obtained; and, in passing on to Church, the Front Street entrance of Messrs. John Macdonald & Co.'s wholesale dry goods warehouse.

From Church Street to the Market are more wholesale grocery and provision houses.

Passing the St. Lawrence Market, the City Hall, and Drill Shed, the largest building is the immense premises of the Street Railway Co., with a variety of manufacturing establishments, including a spice factory, canned fruit and pickle warehouse refrigerators, oil and boiler works, soap and candle factory, and Taylor's safe works; also the extensive distillery and other premises of Messrs. Gooderham & Worts.

The large building used as a glucose factory, recently burned down, has been re-erected, and is now in operation as a syrup factory.

Turning north to King Street, and going east to the Don, the large brewery of the Thos. Davies Co., with fine private residence and grounds, are to be seen. Then westward, passing the St. Lawrence Market and buildings, he will see the St. James Cathedral, with its celebrated clock, and the highest spire in America, the height being 316 feet; thence along ranges of the finest retail stores, with their plate glass fronts, will be seen the favorite promenade.

On passing Church Street a view will be had of the Public Library, and in the distance the grounds of the Mpolitan Church.

At Toronto Street the view as far as Adelaide Street is very fine: in front is the Post Office, and on either side are handsome and lofty buildings occupied by Building Societies, Land Companies, Insurance Companies, and the former Post Office which is used as the offices of the Deputy Receiver-General, the Inland Revenue Department, and the Inspector of Weights and Measures.

Proceeding to Yonge Street, on the north the *Globe* office as also that of the *World* are passed, and on the south the palatial stores of Walker & Sons and W. A. Murray & Co., when the fine view north and south is again obtained, the Dominion Bank being especially noticeable; at this junction the traffic of the Street Railway Company and of general business can be best appreciated.

Still westward, the splendid buildings of the *Evening Telegram* and the *Mail* strike the eye; and at the corner of York, the Rossin House occupies a most commanding position, having two frontages, affording separate entrances, which are most convenient.

Next come in view the Government House and grounds, St. Andrews Church and Upper Canada College.

By extending the drive in this direction, the immense works of the E. & C. Gurney Co., the Silver Plate Co., Mason & Risch's piano factory, H. E. Clarke & Co.'s trunk factory, are all seen; and still farther are the engine works of Inglis & Hunter, the agricultural implement works of the Massey Manufacturing Co., the Abell Engine and Machine Works, and

ROSSIN HOUSE.

the Gutta Percha and Indian Rubber factory. The drive here would end at the Exhibition grounds, including the Zoological Gardens, which should certainly be visited.

Leaving Parkdale and Brockton, and turning north from Queen Street at Spadina Avenue, after passing the Asylum and Trinity College, at the head of this splendid avenue—the future "Champs Elysees" of Toronto—Knox College appears, and from this point it is difficult to select the best route in which take in all the splendid private streets which would well repay an inspection.

Taking College Street, and passing Beverley, St. George, and other handsome streets, to reach the University, a visitor can not fail being impressed with the beauty and magnificence of

KNOX COLLEGE.

the surroundings. The University buildings, Meteorolcgical Observatory, Divinity School, and splendid mansions, follow in rapid succession. The Queen Street Avenue, rivalling in beauty the finest in Europe, and the Queen's Park, are such as Toronto citizens may feel proud to show to visi'ors to the city.

Driving north are seen the monument to the Queen's Own and the fine statue of the Hon. George Brown, and a little to the westward of the Park gate the beautiful building of the Baptist College and McMaster Hall stands.

Thence eastward to Sherbourne Street a view may be had of the romantic ravine separating the city from Rosedale. If the latter suburb is visited, the ravine may be crossed by either of three handsome bridges, and the scenery here cannot fail to delight the eye in summer.

In Rosedale are some elegant mansions, and here are the new and spacious grounds of the Athletic Association, with a grand stand and all suitable appointments.

Sherbourne Street itself has become the residence of many leading merchants and manufacturers, and will impress a stranger most favorably.

The streets intervening between Sherbourne and Yonge are Jarvis and Church, the former still retaining its character for beauty and style, and the latter steadily rising in importance, which will be enhanced by the new block paving. Both of these latter streets ought to be traversed, especially as sight-seers invariably visit the Horticultural Gardens, and the Normal and Model Schools.

On Bond Street, bounded on the south by Queen, and on the north by Gould, a view of the finest churches in the city may be had. The splendid proportions of the Metropolitan, with its fine tower and beautiful grounds; the magnificent Roman Catholic Cathedral of St. Michael, with its lofty and graceful spire; the elegant and substantial Congregational Church of Bond Street, with its tower and dome, are all in full view on this street. While in the distance may be seen the spire of St. James' Cathedral, and the tower of St. James' Square Presbyterian Church on Gerrard Street; also the new Orange Hall on Queen Street, and the Normal School grounds, having the principal entrance on Gould Street, and forming the square surrounded by Gould, Gerrard, Church and Victoria Streets.

A traveller from England taking this route in summer cannot fail to be struck with the beauty of the shade trees on all the principal private streets, and the profusion of flowers displayed on every hand, which have become a source of rivalry, and the cultivation of which is now studied as a science.

Toronto the Centre of the Dominion.

A few years ago a book was written to prove that St. Louis was geographically the central city of the world, and that eventually it must become the commercial centre, and very plausible reasons were given to prove the statement.

The immense resources of the country of which it was the centre, in iron, coal, gold, silver and cotton, and its growing manufactures, were used to show its probable destiny.

Toronto puts forward no such claim, and yet, while Winnipeg may more properly be considered the geographical centre of the Dominion, a glance at the map will show the splendid position of Toronto as a commercial centre, and as a resort for tourists; and it is safe to say that, in the near future, no city on the continent will be more celebrated for general attractiveness, and that the present hotel accommodation will soon be altogether inadequate for the crowds who will flock here in the summer. The contiguity to the Falls, with the prospect of a Free Park on the Canada side, will attract travellers from Hudson Bay to the Gulf of Mexico, and from Halifax to Vancouver.

As a central point of arrival and departure, either east, west, north or south, her advantageous position cannot be exaggerated.

The chain of lakes north and west, the Canadian Pacific and Grand Trunk Railways, and the navigation through to the Atlantic Ocean, via the St. Lawrence, all promise a future for Toronto such as has never been dreamed of before.

Who would have predicted ten years ago that a traveller could take a car at the Union Station, or at the foot of Yonge

NORMAL SCHOOL.

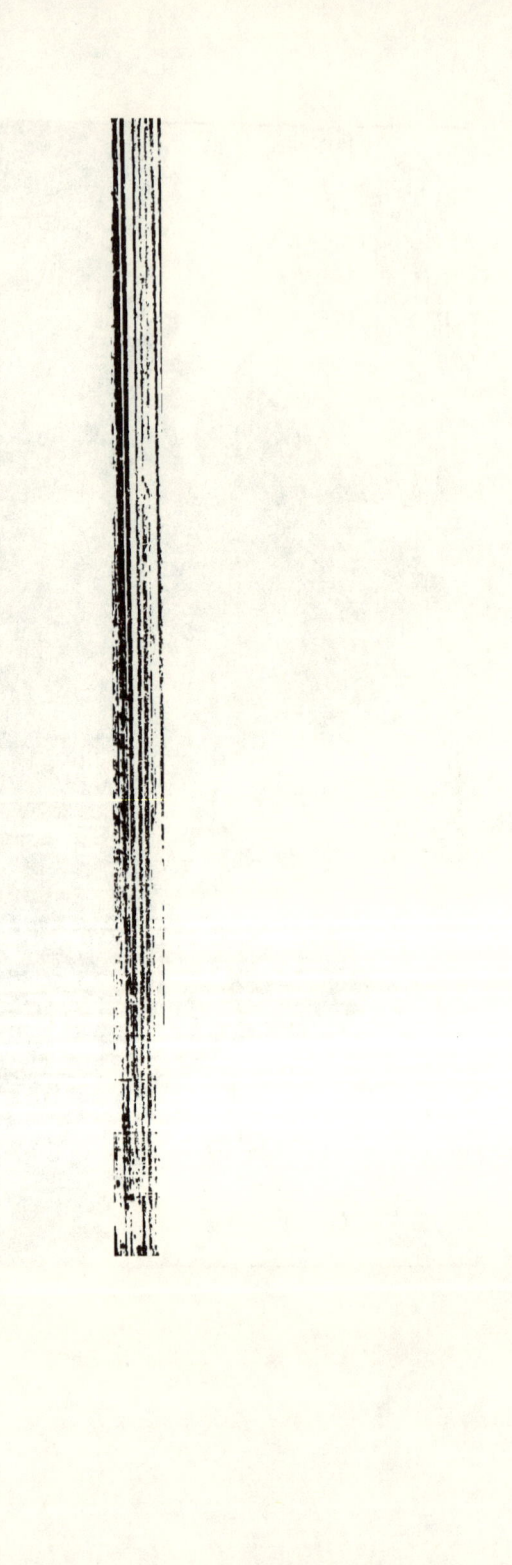

Street, and by going to North Toronto Station purchase a ticket, and perhaps even check his baggage, for China or Japan? And yet all this will be an every day occurrence within a short time.

The completion of the connection at Callander, making the route from New York to Winnipeg *via* Toronto the most direct, will at once give her all-rail communication with the great North-West and the Pacific, equally good in winter as in summer.

Toronto is fast becoming the wholesale centre of the Dominion. Once Quebec enjoyed the good luck, but for some reason or other a blight fell upon the ancient capital, and the business houses that flourished on St. Peter Street forty years ago are there no longer. Montreal for years back did the bulk of the business, but for the last fifteen years Toronto has been gradually taking it away from her. At the present rate of progress Toronto will lead Montreal in ten years, perhaps in five.

Toronto possesses one advantage which alone is sufficient to account for her success. We have a choice of seaports, and the competition in freight and charges which such an advantage confers. We can receive our importations either by the St. Lawrence or by New York, and have the same advantage with regard to our exports. If Toronto becomes the wholesale centre many other things must follow. The headquarters of the Grand Trunk Railway must come here before long.

Many Montreal houses are now opening branches, or removing their whole business to Toronto, and there are certain indications besides that Toronto is now the wholesale centre of the Dominion, and is going to march at the head of the procession.

Population and Assessment Returns.

Toronto commenced business as a city fifty-one years ago, with a population of 9,254. To-day, according to the just completed assessment rolls, the population is 111,800. An increase of 102,000, or the multiplication of the population by twelve in half a century, is a pretty good record, and Toronto people may well be proud of it.

Should the rate of increase not diminish, another half-century will see in the site of the present Toronto a city of almost half a million. As it is, Toronto takes a place with the cities of the second class as to population in the empire.

There are only forty-seven larger cities in the British Dominions, and England herself can boast of only eighteen which have a greater population. We are larger than Aberdeen, Cork, Derby, Greenock, Halifax, Huddersfield, Northampton, Norwich, Plymouth, Preston, Southampton, or Stockport.

There are only seven larger cities in Germany, nineteen in the United States, seven in France, and seven in Russia. We rank with Detroit, Milwaukee, Bremen, Stuttgart, Blackburn, Oldham and Sunderland, all of which stand in the neighborhood of 111,000.

The following grand annual total assessments will show the gradual increase which has been made in the value of taxable property in the city for the years indicated:

ASSESSMENTS.		ASSESSMENTS.	
1871	$29,277,235	1879	$49,753,402
1872	32,487,772	1880	50,165,539
1873	41,775,844	1881	53,559,910
1874	43,472,512	1882	55,064,899
1875	46,506,280	1883	59,561,143
1876	47,150,302	1884	65,083,877
1877	47,614,393	1885	69,225,114
1878	49,053,765	1886	72,721,559

TORONTO STREET.

The realty and personalty on this street is assessed in round numbers at one million dollars, one-seventieth of the total assessment of the city, and is only a block in length.

POPULATION OF TORONTO AT DIFFERENT PERIODS.

1817	1,200	1850	25,000
1826	1,677	1854	40,000
1832	4,000	1857	45,000
1834	9,000	1871	56,000
1842	15,000	1881	86,000
1845	19,000	1884	100,000
1847	22,500	1886	110,000

VALUE OF BUILDINGS ERECTED DURING THE YEARS

1882	$1,757,630	1884	$2,033,235
1883	1,506,740	1885	3,449,375

Of the buildings erected in 1885 the proportion was:

	NO.	VALUE.
For miscellaneous manufacturing and others	33	$168,000
Social and charitable institutions	22	230,000
Schools and churches	9	61,000
Hotels	5	17,000
Business buildings	181	488,000
Residences	900	2,028,375
Various improvements		465,000
		$3,449,375

Commercial Travellers' Association.

There are five Commercial Travellers' Associations in Canada: Toronto, with a membership of 2,300; Montreal, 1,500; London, 500; Winnipeg, 150; Halifax, N.S., 150.

We give the following statistics of the Toronto C. T. A.:

Reserve Funds	$100,000
Gain for last year	13,930
Membership	2,300
Increase last year	77

As an interesting item, showing the growth of commercial travelling in the United States, the history of which nearly corresponds with its date in Canada, one of the leading men says, "There are now about 80,000 travelling salesmen in the United States; their expenses are $1,500 each, which means an outlay of $120,000,000 a year, and if you count on an average salary of $1,000 a year each, it will swell the total to $200,000,-000 a year. This immense sum is scattered all over the country. It keeps up the hotels and is one of the most important items of railroad passenger receipts. The character of the travelling salesman has changed in these ten years; you will find very few boys and fewer drunkards on the road. The competition is so great and expenses so heavy that firms have to send out their best men, and salaries of from $3,000 to $5,000 a year are by no means uncommon."

With some modifications the above figures will apply to Canada according to its numerical proportions.

Toronto Custom House.

In any country or city where the revenue is raised by indirect taxation, the history of the Custom House is, to a great extent, the history of its growth in trade and manufactures.

There was a time in the history of the importing trade of Toronto when the duty was five per cent. *ad valorem*, and the Government of the day, with great liberality, took the importers' note at six months in payment.

No doubt this gave a stimulus to the trade, which has resulted in placing Toronto at the head of all American and Canadian cities of its population in the extent of its imports.

About the same time that the importations commenced in this way to Toronto, the non-importing merchants got their supplies in what is now called "Niagara by the Lake," where merchants went regularly to make their purchases up to the time when the seat of government was changed to Toronto, in 1821.

Others got their goods in Montreal, and these were brought up the St. Lawrence and along the shore of Lake Ontario in batteaux; while over the portages they did the best they could in the way of transport.

The intelligence of some of these gentlemen may be judged from the following incident, which is given on the best authority, the writer giving nothing from personal knowledge previous to 1847.

One of the firm of McDougal Bros. having made his purchases in Montreal, returned home in advance of the goods, having his invoices with him; the brother, who remained in Toronto, on looking over one invoice discovered a line of cloth, with number of yards and prices stated, and immediately underneath was the word "ditto" also having the length and price. On enquiring from the buyer what "ditto" meant, he replied he could not tell, as he was quite sure he had not bought any such goods as "ditto." Steps were immediately taken to have the article returned on its arrival, as the goods appeared to come to a good deal of money.

TORONTO CUSTOM HOUSE.

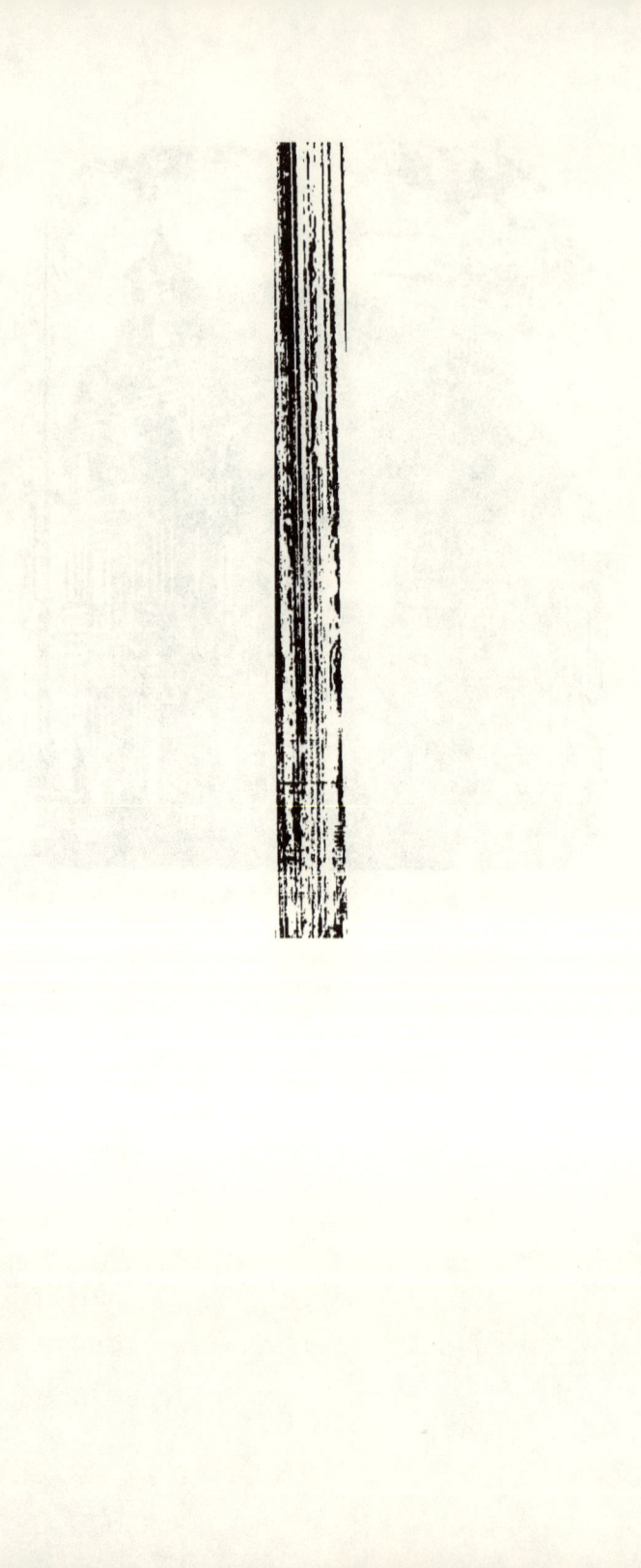

My first entry at the Custom House was made in the fall of 1848, being a little over twelve months from the time of arriving in the country, and being the youngest man who had made direct importations to the city. My faith in the future of Toronto was based on two facts: first, the water communication in front, with a beautiful harbor, and second, the fine agricultural country stretching away in the back; and in addition to this there was confidence in the taste and wealth of the people sufficient to warrant the importation of a fine class of goods, as shown by the fact that one case alone was valued at £800 sterling, the contents of which, with all other goods, were speedily disposed of.

Mr. Stanton was the collector at this time, and the duty was 12½ per cent. *ad valorem*.

As the whole importations that year were under a million dollars in value, the Custom House staff, inside and outside, did not exceed four or five, not one of whom remains in the service.

Mr. Stanton was succeeded by Mr. Mendell, and in 1851 the staff had slightly increased; Mr. T. McCarthy, still in the service, being the only one remaining of the number in the service at that time; Mr. Thomas Scott was surveyor, Mr. John Cameron, chief clerk, and Mr. Robert Emery, landing waiter.

Shortly after the introduction of the "bonding system" through the United States, the private bonded warehouses were authorized as a convenience to importers, who, commencing to receive goods at all seasons of the year, discontinued the custom of opening their whole importations at one time: country merchants visiting the market more frequently, and importers taking their goods out of bond as orders were given from samples, or, in the case of dry goods, by opening only a portion of any class of goods at one time.

The appointment of "lockers" followed this arrangement, and the first who acted in that capacity were Mr. James Stitt, some time superannuated, Mr. R. G. A. Paton, the present polite and courteous cashier, and Mr. Alex. Duff, now gauger; all of whom were justly popular for their obliging and attentive manners, as well as the faithful discharge of their duties. Of the former and the latter the writer can speak from experience (Mr. Paton having to do with the grocery trade). On the arrival of goods, these gentlemen were always ready to lend a hand and use a truck to get a lot of goods off the street sometimes after ten o'clock at night, when by getting the goods in they would be covered by insurance.

The conscientious discharge of duty, the unvarying readiness to oblige and willingness to impart information, on the part of Mr. Scott, are all well known to present as well as past importers. When it was necessary to see Mr. Meudell he was to be found at his post, and if a question arose on any point in which he differed with an importer, if he showed any disposition to act in an arbitrary manner, a gentle reminder that as the servant of the public he must be accommodating invariably resulted in the offer of a friendly pinch of snuff, a box of which he always kept on his desk, and the matter came to an amicable conclusion.

The gradual increase in the importations, with the rate of duty at various periods up to the present time, when they have reached such a large figure, will be found in another place.

The Custom House staff in 1854 consisted, in addition to the gentlemen already named, of Hon. Captain Curzon and George Henderson, clerks; J. P. Dunn, landing waiter, and A. Macpherson, who succeeded Mr. John Boyd, father of the present Chancellor, who was the first appraiser.

The present surveyor, Mr. John Douglas, entered the service in 1855, having occupied the position of chief clerk before his present position, which he assumed on the death of Mr. Scott. The long and valuable services of Mr. Douglas are, and will be, associated with the history of the importing trade of Toronto, long after the present time. His uniform courtesy and gentlemanly deportment are too well known to the merchants of Toronto to give the statement even the shadow of flattery. Having known Mr. Douglas during the whole of his connection with the service, the writer can say he never heard a breath of complaint, but, on the contrary, universal respect always expressed towards him.

Mr. Meudell was succeeded by the Hon. Robert Spence, and after his death Mr. T. C. Scott acted as collector. An effort was made to have him appointed to the collectorship, but the petition for the object was never presented, a number of merchants and others, including the Hon. George Brown, refusing to sign, on the ground that the appointment of collector should continue to be a political one. Mr. J. E. Smith was appointed to the office, and on his retirement Mr. John Douglass acted as collector till the appointment of the Hon. Jas. Patton, Q.C., LL.D., who now occupies the responsible position.

In 1886 the Custom House staff consists of collector, surveyor, chief clerk, cashier, assistant cashier, seventeen clerks, three acting clerks, three appraisers and two assistant appraisers, two gaugers and lockers, three lockers, one engineer and two assistants, eighteen landing waiters, nine packers and porters, one housekeeper and messenger, and four messengers.

CIVIL SERVICE EXAMINATIONS.

The time has now happily gone by when, by an act of political legerdemain, persons from mechanical, agricultural or other pursuits, without any training or qualification, might have been metamorphosed into civil service officers, and placed in positions for which they were entirely unfitted, contrary to every recognized principle of trade or commerce.

Should a contractor for any large undertaking require skilled workmen, as carpenters, plumbers or bricklayers, and the best accountant in the Dominion apply for an engagement, it is easy to know what his answer would be. Why the rule should be reversed in the case of public departments is peculiar, and could only be applied on the ground of their having the power to conduct the business on a principle that would inevitably lead to the ruin of ordinary commercial undertakings; experience and competency being indispensable in every business where private capital is invested.

The Civil Service examinations must ultimately result in

greater efficiency and economy when the infusion of the new element shall have had time to develop. It is said that already the effect is apparent in the introduction of a more advanced system, in accordance with modern ideas of mercantile life, and resulting in quicker and more correct returns being made to the Government. Should the reform result in a system of remuneration corresponding with services actually rendered, as is the rule in every well-ordered mercantile establishment, and promotion given only on the ground of merit, it will prove alike advantageous to the service and beneficial to the officers, and in a few years the whole service will be purified and improved so that Canada may claim to have established a system of Civil Service equal to that which is styled "the pride and glory of Britain."

Total Imports to Toronto Since 1849.

The fiscal year ending 31st December, 1863, and ending 30th June, 1885. The year 1864 showing six months to 30th June.

Year	Amount	Year	Amount
1849	$1,280,549	1868	$6,833,132
1850	2,286,508	1869	6,658,867
1851	2,778,389	1870	6,833,991
1852	2,020,080	1871	9,968,546
1853	4,723,972	1872	13,097,863
1854	5,830,480	1873	14,590,125
1855	5,495,613	1874	14,717,898
1856	6,670,500	1875	14,807,948
1857	5,303,523	1876	11,231,343
1858	3,530,198	1877	13,376,257
1859	3,976,888	1878	12,611,334
1860	4,138,518	1879	12,141,812
1861	4,763,970	1880	12,192,942
1862	4,253,286	1881	15,090,629
1863	4,436,291	1882	19,110,222
1864	2,387,761	1883	18,634,451
1865	4,342,737	1884	17,000,369
1866	6,340,679	1885	18,032,110
1867	7,031,541	Six months ending Dec. 31	9,418,022

COAL IMPORTED TO TORONTO IN 1885.

	TONS.
Anthracite	238,320
Bituminous	116,178
Total	354,498

INTO THE DOMINION.

Anthracite	909,121
Bituminous	1,080,536
Total	1,989,657
Value	$3,888,548

Coal produced at Nanaimo, B.C.

	TONS.		TONS.
1874	81,000	1880	268,000
1875	110,000	1881	228,000
1876	159,000	1882	182,000
1877	154,000	1883	213,000
1878	171,000	1884	394,000
1879	241,000		

Shipped chiefly to San Francisco, Portland, Oregon, Washington Territory, Alaska, Hawaiian Islands and China.

The Imports of Toronto Compared With Cities in the United States.

FOR FISCAL YEAR ENDING 30TH JUNE, 1885.

	VALUE.	DUTY.	AVG. PER CT.
Milwaukee	$407,452	$160,979.00	39.50
Detroit	2,062,598	284,198.00	13.30
St. Louis	2,601,001	1,036.77	39.88
Buffalo	4,744,610	873,323.00	18.20
Cincinnatti	1,930,000	762,917.00	39.50
Chicago	10,585,347	4,133,675.00	39.05
Toronto	**18,032,110**	**3,274,950.00**	**18.17**

It will be noticed that the average of duty at Detroit and Buffalo is much below the other ports, which can accounted for because of the large bulk being of the produce of Canada, and less from foreign countries.

The above figures were received through the kindness of the Collectors at these ports. It will be noticed that the Toronto imports are nearly equal to all the others put together.

Exports from Toronto in 1885

include the following goods manufactured in the city:

BOOKS.	VALUE.	CARRIAGES.	VALUE
Australia	$7,065	British West Indies	$727
New Zealand	2,044	MACHINERY.	
Bermuda and West Indies	118	Australia	3,829
Spanish West Indies	46	Argentine Republic	450
Newfoundland	88	New Zealand	203
South Africa	1,168	Chili	200

This trade will receive an impetus through the Indian and Colonial Exhibition that may develop into large proportions, especially with the facilities for shipment *via* the Canadian Pacific Railway and its ocean connections.

FOR YEAR ENDING 30TH SEPTEMBER, 1885.

Produce of the Fisheries	$914
Produce of the Forest	308,463
Animals and their Produce	991,874
Agricultural Products	1,284,657
Manufactures	280,276
Miscellaneous	16,573
Total Exports	$2,891,757
Quarter Ending 31st December	$1,411,514

9030

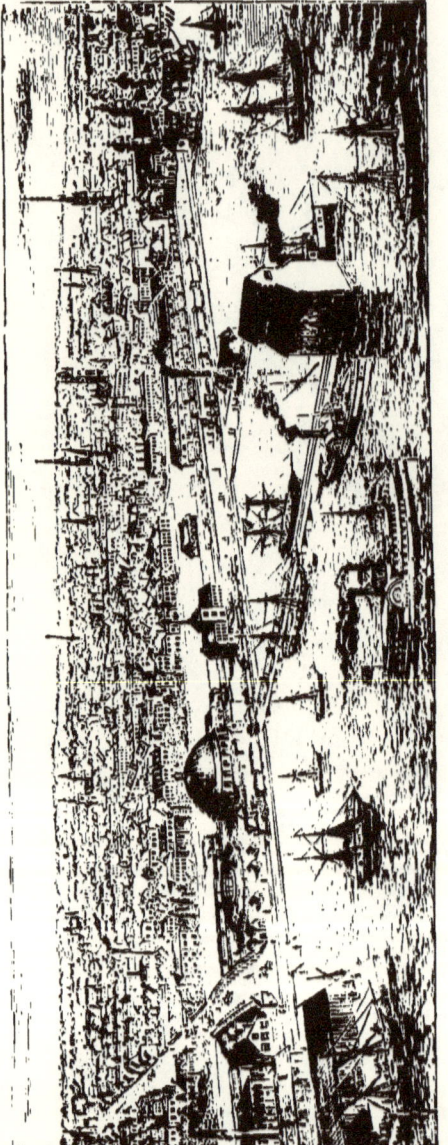

VIEW OF TORONTO, 1856.

TORONTO IN 1886.

> FAIR TORONTO! Queen City of the West,
> Of all thy sister-cities thou art best;
> As far as eye can reach, from Don to Humber,
> Rise towering spires in goodly number;
> Cathedrals, churches, schools, and mansions rise
> In stately grandeur towering to the skies.
> A noble harbor fronts thy southern bound,
> And gentle hills encircle thee around;
> From north to south, and east to west expand
> Streets, avenues and roads, so wisely plann'd,
> That strangers visit thee with ease, and find
> In thee a home at once just to their mind;
> Long live Toronto! loud her praises swell,
> Here Commerce, Art, and Nature love to dwell.
>
> —*Imrie*.

It will be no exaggeration to say that no city on the continent is making greater progress than the City of Toronto. Within ten years the population has doubled. Not only has this increase occurred within the limits, but the city has thrown off shoots east, west and north, which are now rapidly assuming the proportions of towns.

Indeed, one suburb, which a decade ago was a series of farms, with cottages scattered here and there, has been recently incorporated, and its large population, its populous streets, its handsome stores and private residences well entitle it to the dignity of a town,—and this is Parkdale.

The population within the limits now reaches 111,000. That without will no doubt very shortly bring it up to 140,000. Ten years ago Toronto extended from the Don to Bathurst Street, and from the Bay to College Avenue. Spadina Avenue north of St. Patrick Street was a field, where the troops were reviewed, and Sherbourne Street above Carlton resembled the "forest primeval."

It is possible now to walk from half a mile east of the Grand

Trunk crossing on the Kingston Road to within half a mile of
the lake shore, on Queen Street (a distance of about four miles),
through an avenue of shops, and to inspect store windows on
Yonge Street from the Bay to the hill north of the city, which
was formerly regarded as the country.

Nothing illustrates the growing opulence of the city more
than the character of the places of business and the architectural
improvements on the private residences. A shop is not a shop
now unless provided with the metropolitan plate glass front,

OSGOODE HALL.

and the tendency in every business is in the shape of extension,
—in short, to occupy two or three buildings where formerly
one was sufficient.

Where many cities have one fine street of which they are
justly proud, as Euclid Avenue in Cleveland, and Wabash
Avenue in Chicago, none can boast of so many fine streets or
private residences of finer build or more elegant design.

The old square house which was the palace of a merchant
years ago, has given place to a building of Elizabethan or other

fashionable style, in which the taste for ornamentation is fully gratified.

Formerly Jarvis Street was the home of the wealthy, and then Sherbourne laid claims to rivalry ; and while these go on improving constantly, new competitions for style and elegance are springing up both on the north and west.

To the person whose business confines him to the centre of the city, a visit to what recently were fields is at once a revelation and surprise. New streets have been opened out, new and magnificent mansions have been erected, comfortable houses for the middle classes have been built, and places of business to meet all local wants have been provided. In addition to this, there are very few points which are not within five minutes' walk of the street cars.

The enormous development of Toronto of late years is largely the result of a liberal policy which has brought the railroads of the Province, and with them a large portion of the northern and western sections, to our doors. There are to be added to this, the public spirit of the people, the business enterprise of the merchants, the good sanitary condition of the city, and the presence of all those religious and other metropolitan advantages which persons retiring from active business life elsewhere naturally seek. Toronto is making great strides toward being the Chicago of Canada.

The Ontario Assembly in 1886.

Ontario's Legislature was convened with the old time civil and military display. The cannon of the Toronto Field Battery, stationed on Wellington Street, thundered a salute as Lieut.-Governor Robinson, attended by Capt. Geddes, A.D.C., drove from Government House, under escort of Denison's troopers, to the legislative headquarters of the Province, there, for the sixth time in his gubernatorial capacity, to present the Government bill of fare to the people's representatives for digestion during the session.

As His Honor's sleigh made its way through the throng of

spectators in front of the building, the guard of honor from C Company, Infantry School, presented arms to the strains of the National Anthem, while the cannon kept on booming. The Legislative Chamber overflowed with civil and military magnates, legislators, politicians, and the beauty and fashion of the Provincial Capital as represented by upwards of two hundred of the fairer sex. All the galleries were jammed. It was generally remarked that the ceremony was unusually large and brilliant.

STATE DINNER AT GOVERNMENT HOUSE.

The festivities that followed the opening were on a larger and more brilliant scale than usual. Government House was the scene of a magnificent state dinner, which eclipsed anything hitherto attempted in that line at Government House. The table was a perfect gem in the way of decoration and arrangement. It was laid in the ball room with covers for fifty-six. Mrs. Robinson herself designed and superintended the work. The centre piece was a miniature lake, in which fragrant flowers of rare delicacy and hue floated amidst tender green vines and lovely leaves, being refreshed by a gentle spray from a rockery, surmounted by a device in which the word "Ontario" glittered in gas. The lake was flanked by a profusion of flowers, and numerous little ornaments and devices added to the beauty and effect of the display, the *tout ensemble*, under a brilliant flood of light, being really magnificent.

Toronto Board of Trade

was incorporated in February, 1845, the council being composed of the following gentlemen:—Thomas Clarkson, President; E. F. Whittemore, Vice-President; John Harrington, Treasurer; Charles Robertson, Secretary; Messrs. W. P. Howland, James Brown, jun., William McMaster, William Henderson, John Shaw, Charles Robertson, J. G. Worts, T. D. Harris Rice Lewis, George A. Piper, Henry Fowler, John Henderson. Members in 1886, 822; total income last year, $5,553.35.

Banks in Toronto.

	CAPITAL.		CAPITAL.
Bank of Toronto	$2,000,000	Quebec	$2,500,000
Central	1,000,000	Federal	1,250,000
Canadian B'k of Commerce	6,000,000	Standard	2,000,000
Ontario	1,500,000	Dominion	1,500,000
Bank of Montreal	12,000,000	Traders	1,000,000
Merchants'	5,725,000	British North America	5,000,000
Imperial	1,500,000		

SAVINGS BANKS.

Assistant Receiver-General's Office.
Canada Permanent Loan and Savings Company.
Dominion Savings Bank.
Farmers Loan and Savings Company.
Freehold Loan and Savings Company.
Home Savings and Loan Company.
People's Loan and Deposit Company.
Post Office Savings Bank.
Toronto Savings Bank.
Union Loan and Savings Bank.
Western Canada Loan and Savings Company.

PUBLIC COMPANIES.

Toronto General Trust Company	$500,000
Toronto Land and Loan Company	1,000,000
Union Loan and Savings Company	1,000,000
York Farmers' Colonization Company	300,000
British Canadian Loan and Investment Company (Limited)	5,000,000
Building and Loan Association	750,000
Canada Permanent Loan and Savings Company	2,200,000
Reserve fund $1,100,000; assets	8,539,476
Credit Foncier (Franco-Canadian)	5,000,000
Freehold Loan and Savings Company	2,000,000
Home Savings and Loan Company	2,000,000
Imperial Loan and Investment Company	1,000,000
London and Canadian Loan and Agency Company	5,000,000
London and Ontario Investment Company	2,250,000
Ontario and Industrial Loan and Investment Company	500,000
Ontario and Qu'Appelle Company	1,000,000
People's Loan and Deposit Company	500,000
Commercial Building and Investment Society	
Loan and Investment Company	
Canada Company	
Canada Landed Credit Company	
Farmers Loan and Savings Company	
Land Security Company	
Trust and Loan Company	
Western Canada Loan and Savings Company	
National Investment Company	

ASSETS OF BANKS IN CANADA.

In January 1886	$222,905,522

Toronto Gas Works.

The Gas Works of Toronto were originated and built by the late Albert Furniss, in 1842, who was also the builder of the Water Works. The present Consumers' Gas Company originated in 1847, and the first meeting of the subscribers for stock was held on the 29th October, 1847, when Directors were appointed for the management of the Company. The Act of Incorporation was passed in 1848. The Directors had not proceeded far with their arrangements for the construction of the Works before they ascertained that the Gas Works then in use could be purchased, and they unanimously decided on concluding the bargain for their purchase. The late Charles Berczy, Postmaster, was the first President of the Company. The Directors in 1852 were Charles Berczy, Hugh Miller, John T. Smith, David Patterson, J. Arnold, M. Betley, I. C. Gilmor, W. Mathers, S. Alcorn, E. C. Hancock, S. Platt, and James Strange. When the Company took over the Gas Works the price of gas was $5 per thousand, net, besides a large meter rent, and the quality from ten to twelve candles.

On September 30th, 18 there were one hundred and sixty-four street lamps and three hundred and seventeen gas consumers, and the total amount of rental for gas for fifteen months—two quarters at 25s. and three quarters at 20s.—amounted to only £4,619 7s. 10d. The first manager was Mr. John Watson, who only occupied the position for a short time, when he was succeeded by the late Henry Thompson, who occupied the position until 1874, when he was succeeded by W. H. Pearson. The gas manufactured up to September 30th, 1854, was 14,000,000 cubic feet.

The quality of gas now supplied is from seventeen to eighteen candles, and the price charged to small consumers $1.25 per M., medium size consumers, $1.15, and very large consumers, $1.10. Gas stoves and engines, $1 per M. No charge now is made for meters. Over one hundred and twenty-six miles of pipe were laid up to September 30th, 1885. There are two thousand five hundred and fifty-seven street lamps, and six thousand seven hundred and seventy eight consumers. Gas rentals amounted to $353,498.26 for the year ending September 30th, 1885, and the gas made was 273,483,000 cubic feet.

The present officers of the Company are: James Austin, President; Larratt W. Smith, Vice-President, and W. H. Pearson, Secretary. There are one hundred and fifty-four hands now employed by the Company, and its business is rapidly increasing.

Toronto Water Works.

Toronto is supplied with water from Lake Ontario by means of pumping engines, manufactured by Messrs. Inglis & Hunter, of this city, having a capacity of 12,000,000 gallons per twenty-four hours; also two Worthington Duplex Engines of a capacity of 12,000,000, making a total of 24,000,000 gallons. The building of the Water Works in which they are placed is a handsome structure at the edge of the bay.

The reservoir at Rose Hill, from which the water is distributed, is beautifully situated to the north of the city. The wonderful growth of the city will be seen by a comparison of the following statistics with the system in 1847:

Total mileage of water pipes	144
Number of hydrants	1,414
Number of services	22,000
Number of hydraulic hoists	140
Gallons of water pumped in 1885	3,543,735,410

It is interesting to notice that in 1847 there was no hoist of any kind in any building in Toronto. All goods and furniture were carried to the different floors, while passengers had to walk up stairs. The first two hoists were of the old wheel and rope pattern, and one was placed in the present Bank of Commerce building by Messrs. Ross, Mitchell & Co., and the other in the warehouse at present occupied by Mr. P. Jacobi by Taylor & Stevenson in 1853.

Meat Markets and Horses of Toronto.

Contrasting with the inferior meat of former times, the markets of Toronto, for splendid supplies of first-class meats, cannot be surpassed anywhere. The display at Christmas time is another evidence of Toronto's great progress, and would do credit to any city in the world.

In connection with this, reference may be made to the wonderful improvement that has taken place in all classes of horses, which are to be seen in such numbers on our streets. Whether for saddle, carriage, or heavy draught, no city in America can show finer specimens of horse-flesh, and it is only in point of size that they are excelled in Britain. The finest display of heavy draught horses in the world is to be seen on the first of May in Manchester, when, in splendid new brass-mounted, shining harness, and gaily decorated with ribbons and flowers, the proud teamsters display their leviathian animals, sleek and fat, in a procession extending for miles in length. Toronto horses belonging to the railway companies are quite equal in symmetry and condition.

Toronto a Manufacturing City.

A Sheffield teacher gave a school girl, for a home lesson, a composition on the question of trade. Next morning she brought an excuse for not having done her task, and also handed to the teacher a note which her brother had sent, and which contained the following:—"'Trade is the substance of things hoped for, and the evidence of things not seen.' It will come 'in the sweet by-and-bye.' Trade! trade! where art thou? Come forth and show thyself."

This is the problem which the greatest political economists in the world are trying to solve to-day. An Imperial Commission has been appointed in England to find out where her trade has disappeared to, and the cause of its decline; with this only result so far, that new markets must be found to supply the place of those that have been lost.

It is probable the youth knew nothing of the theories of Free Trade and Protection, and did not know that Sheffield goods were excluded by a hostile tariff from what had formerly been the largest market for these goods; nor that the manufacturers of Connecticut and Rhode Island were sending in similar goods to England entirely free; he only knew the sad fact of poverty and all its attending evils.

When—either by defective legislation or some unfortunate circumstance, as the Cotton Famine during the American War—tens of thousands of industrious operatives are reduced to the verge of starvation, it is a dreadful state of things, and it must be gratifying to the citizens of Toronto, that happily no such state of things exists here; trade is a visible and tangible reality, and there appears every prospect of steady progress in the future as there has been in the past. While no class is oppressed all are benefitted.

List of articles manufactured in Toronto, the importation of which has fallen off in a ratio corresponding with the home production:

Agricultural Implements	Electro-plated Ware.	Ornamental Iron Work.
Bagatelle Tables.	Envelopes.	Paper Manufactures.
Baking Powders.	Fire Works.	Paper Bags and Boxes.
Bed Comforters.	Furniture, all kinds.	Paper Hangings.
Bedsteads.	Fur Caps, Hats, Muffs, &c	Pianos.
Billiard Tables.	Gas Fixtures.	Pickles and Sauces.
Bird Cages.	Gloves, leather.	Rasps and Files.
Biscuits.	Gutta Percha Goods.	Saddlery.
Blacking.	Hats and Caps.	Satchels.
Blankets.	Hollow Ware.	Scales and Balances.
Blank Books.	Horse Shoes.	Shirts.
Boots and Shoes.	Horse Shoe Nails.	Show Cases.
Boot Laces.	India Rubber Manuf'res.	Skates.
Building Brick.	Ink, writing & printing.	Soaps.
Bridges, iron.	Iron Bolts and Nuts.	Spices.
Candles, tallow.	Jellies and Jams.	Stoves and Furnaces.
Carpet Bags.	Jewellery, manuf'res of gold and silver.	Suspenders and Corsets.
Carriages and Sleighs.		Telegraph Supplies.
Cloaks, fur.	Linen Clothing.	Tin Manufactures.
Cloaks, cloth.	Meats, smoked and dried.	Trunks and Valises.
Clothing, Cotton.	Mill (& other) Machinery.	Whips.
Collars and Cuffs.	Mouldings, gilded.	Wire Work.
Colors and Paints.	Mouldings, wood.	Wooden Ware.
Copper Manufactures.	Musical Instruments.	Woollen Clothing.
Corks.	Oil, lubricating.	Woollen Hosiery.
Cottons, grey and white.	Oil, illuminating.	Woollen Underclothing.
Earth Closets.	Organs, parts of, & reeds.	Woollen Yarns.

The cottons mentioned, although not manufactured in the city, are largely sold here by manufacturers and their agents, and are controlled by Toronto merchants; this also applies to denims, drillings, and other lines of goods. The list could be greatly extended if goods manufactured in the Dominion were enumerated.

When it is remembered that at the commencement of our sketch there was just one stove foundry, one soap and candle factory, and one or two other unimportant kinds of goods manufactured in Toronto, the list speaks for itself. It must be borne in mind, however, that this does not by any means include all the branches of manufactures, as new industries are starting up constantly, for which we have no comparison to make in imported goods.

It would be impossible to over-estimate the importance of these manufactures to the city, not only giving employment to thousands of the population, but forming a large market for the agricultural productions in the surrounding country, and also attracting buyers of every class of goods; all tending to the circulation of money, and contributing to the general prosperity.

No thoughtful person can walk down any of the leading thoroughfares in the morning, or at six o'clock in the evening, without being struck with the crowds of well-dressed men and women, all tending toward or returning from the centre of these industries; and he must, indeed, be void of patriotism, whose feelings are not thrilled by the sight of so much enterprise and industry, making our streets vie with those of Manchester or Nottingham. Nor is there any reason to doubt that, before long, we may see the numbers greatly increased. While the extension of manufactures may embrace those not so cleanly, no one would object to see even the linen overalls and the wooden clogs which, in other cities, although corresponding with the work of the operatives during the week, are often replaced by silk and patent leather on Sundays and holidays.

A spool of cotton may appear trifling, but few people, except the initiated, are aware of the gigantic business done in this article. In Paisley, Scotland, there are employed in the trade thousands of operatives,—one mill alone employing over 3,000 hands, earning good wages, and employed all the year round. When factories in other trades are shut down for lack of orders, the spool cotton mills do not suffer much, if any, from depression. Torontonians will be pleased to hear that this important branch of manufacture is to be established in Toronto by Kerr and Co., the well-known Paisley manufacturers. Machinery of the newest and best description will be imported from home, and workers brought out from Paisley to teach others here.

TORONTO MANUFACTURES.

Account Books	5	Flour Mills	3
Agricultural Implements	2	Furnaces and Ranges	2
Artificial Limbs	3	Furniture	10
Awnings, Tents, etc.	3	Glue	1
Baking Powder	4	Hardware	1
Barb Wire Fencing	1	Harness	28
Baskets	5	Hats	9
Belting	6	Heating Apparatus	2
Billiard Tables	1	Hosiery	2
Blacklead	1	Hoop Skirts	2
Blacking	2	Hydrants and Valves	1
Boats	12	Iron Bedsteads	1
Boilers	7	Iron Fencing	2
Boots and Shoes	8	Iron Gates and Guards	2
Boot and Shoe Uppers	3	Iron Working Machinery	1
Boxes, cigar	3	Japan Ware	2
Boxes, fancy	2	Jewellery	24
Boxes, packing	3	Jewel Cases	2
Braces and Belts	1	Lamp Fixtures	2
Breweries	10	Lasts	2
Brick	24	Leather Belting	2
Bridges	1	Letter Files	1
Brushes and Brooms	10	Lithographs	11
Carpets	1	Mantles and Grates	1
Carriages	13	Marking Ink	1
Chemicals	6	Matches	1
Cigars	11	Metallic Roofing	1
Coffee and Spice Mills	9	Matrasses	11
Coffins	2	Mill Machinery	2
Collars	1	Mouldings	6
Confectionery	7	Mustard	1
Coppersmiths	3	Office Furniture	1
Cordage	1	Oils	3
Corks	1	Organs	6
Corsets	4	Organ Reeds	1
Drugs	2	Ornamental Iron Work	2
Electrotypes	5	Overalls	6
Elevators	1	Paints	2
Engines	7	Paper	2
Files and Rasps	3	Paper Bags	2

Pattern Making	3	Spring Beds	8
Pianos	5	Stained Glass	2
Pickles and Sauces	4	Stamps	4
Picture Frames	8	Stencils	5
Planing Mills	23	Stereotypes	3
Printing Ink	1	Stoves	3
Printing Presses	2	Straw Goods	3
Publishers	45	Tanners Supplies	1
Pumps	3	Tassels	1
Rattan Goods	1	Telegraph Supplies	2
Refrigerators	2	Trunks	1
Roller Skates	2	Trusses	2
Ropes	2	Varnish	3
Rubber Goods	2	Vine	3
Saddlery Hardware	1	Wa...	20
Sa..s	1	Wall Papers	1
Sanitary Appliances	1	Washing Machines	1
Sash, Doors and Blinds	12	Watch Cases	1
Saws	1	White Lead	3
Saw and Shingle Mill Machinery	1	Wire Matts	1
Scales	1	Wire Works	2
Sculptors	3	Window Shades	5
Shirts	6	Wood Turning	7
Show Cases	2	Wooden Ware	4
Silversmiths	1	Wood Working Machinery	1
Silverware	4	Wool Knit Goods	1
Soap	4	Yeast	1

Great Britain having, through hostile tariffs, lost access to the markets of many countries which were formerly the best outlets for her trade, is now turning her attention to new fields for her enterprise, and in the future will look to India, China, Japan, Burmah and Siam to take her surplus productions. As these countries comprise about one-third of the population of the earth, there is abundant scope, and it will indeed be a novel sight to find the young Dominion competing with the mother country for this very trade, with all the advantages on the side of Canada, in being so much nearer the field of operations.

PER CENTAGE OF GROWTH OF MANUFACTURES IN 50 YEARS.

1836 to 1846	5	1866 to 1876	25
1846 to 1856	10	1876 to 1886	45
1856 to 1866	15		
Total			100

From the long list of Toronto manufacturers a few old-established firms are selected as representing the "wonderful growth and progress" of the city in its manufactures:—

J. & J. TAYLOR, TORONTO SAFE WORKS.

This is one of Toronto's representative institutions, whether as it regards the enterprise of the firm or the growth and progress of the city in substantial wealth.

The demand for safes as security against fire or burglary has kept pace with the accumulation of gold, silver, bank notes, bonds, mortgages, and jewellery and watches, all of which are now protected from all harm and danger.

It was indeed a sight worth seeing, to be permitted to inspect the nineteen safes at present being exhibited at the Indian and Colonial Exhibition in London. For beauty of finish, both internally and externally, these specimens of Toronto workmanship need fear no competition at such an exhibition; and even if England were admitted to the friendly rivalry, it is a question whether anything finer could be produced.

It is now over thirty years since the firm of J. & J. Taylor commenced the manufacture of safes in Toronto. During that period over forty thousand have been distributed throughout the Dominion, from British Columbia, Manitoba, and the North-West Territories, to Newfoundland and the Maritime Provinces.

It has been their constant aim from the first to keep pace with the times by adopting every improvement that would make security, if possible, doubly secure in all the work that might pass through their hands. That they have succeeded beyond their most sanguine expectations is evidenced by the fact that for many years they have done by far the largest portion of the bank safe work and the Government work of the Dominion; and in offering their safes to the general public, this is, perhaps, the best guarantee that their safes stand unrivalled in the Canadian market.

The burglar-proof bank safes shown by J. & J. Taylor in

London are of the quality used by all the best monetary institutions of Canada, and embody all the best-known materials and points of construction in general use, as well as several additional improvements that are peculiar to themselves, and patented by them. In brief, these safes are made without seam or joint of any kind on the outside corners, the frames and body being welded continuously around the entire safe. They are also fitted in all corners with J. & J. Taylor's improved solid triple corners of five-ply welded steel and iron. The safes are locked with revolving bolts on all sides of door, secured with back shaft combination locks capable of some forty-one million (41,000,000) changes. The spindles and arbors are of J. & J. Taylor's patent enlarged centres. Door jambs are stepped and rabbetted, also tongued and grooved, and fitted with improved rubber tube packing. Doors operate on J. & J. Taylor's improved Crane hinges and Cam lever bars. Also, after careful and expensive actual tests with dynamite, this firm have adopted the new Holmes' electric time lock with Newbury's dynamite safety devices.

The fire-proof safes also present special features. They are all made with J. & J. Taylor's patent non-conducting steel flange doors and fronts, solid round corners, and continuous angle iron frames. They are fitted with combination locks, and hardened steel plates for protecting the locks. The filling is of the best fire-proof resisting qualities.

The firm devote their attention exclusively to the making of burglar-proof and fire-proof securities, combination locks and bank locks. They employ about two hundred hands, and have capacity for making about fifty safes per week. The factory has a working floor of about 68,000 square feet, and faces on Front and Frederick Streets.

The locks on the vaults of Dominion Finance Department, Ottawa, St. John, Winnipeg, P. E. I., and Toronto, are all made by them, also the vault doors, etc. The safes of the firm are a credit to themselves, to the city of Toronto, and to the Dominion.

TAYLOR BROTHERS.

The Don Paper Mills may be considered the oldest established manufactory of importance in Toronto, dating back to 1845. The manufacturing plant is situated on the River Don, three miles from the city, and comprises three mills, the united production of which is about four tons of paper every twelve hours. The lower mill is devoted to the manufacture of roofing and carpet felt, grocers', dry goods, and express wrapping paper; the middle makes all kinds of printing, colored, and book paper, and at the upper mill is manufactured manilla and hanging papers. There is also a paper bag factory in connection with the works.

The location of the mills was selected on account of the running water which is essential to the manufacture of paper, and the entire establishment is replete with the most improved machinery and appliances, amongst which is a Harper Improved Fourdrinier Paper Machine. The trade of the firm is co-extensive with the Dominion, and Toronto may justly pride herself in this representative establishment, as supplying every want connected with the trade.

In connection with the paper trade, the firm operates an extensive steam saw-mill, and altogether gives employment to a large number of operatives, all contributing to the growth and prosperity of the city.

BROWN BROTHERS & CO.

In the manufacture of book and the publication of every form of diaries, this firm is the longest established in the city, and in the latter trade stands unrivalled in the Dominion. The house was founded in 1846 by the father of the present firm, which was formed ten years later. The business includes every branch of book-binding, from the plainest to the most ornamental and highly finished work. The most improved and labor-saving machinery is employed, and the general facilities for production are unsurpassed.

The business is thoroughly systematized in departments, and the stock comprises every description of paper, stationery, and a full and complete stock of book-binders' and printers' materials. The trade extends all over the Dominion, and has latterly been pushed to the far east,—the greater portion of the books shipped to Australia and New Zealand, as well as to foreign countries, are the productions of this establishment, which holds a front rank amongst the numerous manufacturing establishments of Toronto.

The exhibits at the London and Colonial Exhibition are attracting much attention, and reflect much credit on the firm and on Toronto.

ROLPH SMITH & CO.

While the principle laid down in "Toronto Called Back," of giving the history of the importing trade and manufactures, is strictly carried out, this firm is selected as being exceptional.

The history of lithography and engraving is so inseparable from both of the above-named interests as almost to be included in them. The work executed for all other branches of trade, and for banks and public institutions, stamps it with great importance, and exhibits in a remarkable manner the progress of trade and its constantly increasing requirements, and this applies in a very special manner to Toronto.

For many years the writer or his partner, on their half-yearly trips to Europe, made a rule of placing their orders for stationery and all printed, lithographed, or engraved matter in the hands of some large house in London or Manchester, immediately on their arrival, so as to have it ready for shipment with goods. This necessity no longer exists, as everything in the way of account-books, invoices, cards, cheque-books, promissory note forms, and circulars, which were then ordered in England, are now done quite as well in Toronto, and the duty and freight saved besides.

The business of this firm was originally founded by Mr. John Ellis, in 1840, in a small engraving shop on King Street, and from him it passed into the hands of Mr. J. T. Rolph, the senior member of the present firm. In 1873 Mr. Rolph admitted his brother, Mr. Frank Rolph, and Mr. David Smith, as partners, under the present style of Rolph, Smith & Co.

The exhibits of the firm forwarded to London for the Indian and Colonial Exhibition are a fair representation of the regular work executed in the business. They consist of twenty-one large walnut frames, containing specimens of their work, comprising colored show cards, labels, lithographed portraits, and all kinds of commercial work, such as cheques, notes, drafts, letter, note and invoice headings, lithographed menu cards, copy book head-lines, embossing, etc. These specimens are alike creditable to the skill and enterprise of the firm and to the business men of Toronto, and will undoubtedly attract much of the attention of the colonies, as well as of this Dominion. The extensive new premises in course of erection on Wellington Street West will afford increased facilities for carrying on the business.

HEATING OF BUILDINGS IN TORONTO.

This is of so much importance, combining health and comfort with the beauty and adaptation of house furnishing, as to have become a matter of scientific skill, as well as one of the ornamental arts.

In 1847 the only stove in use was the square, unsightly, box-shaped article, and these were of all sizes, from the smallest up to those large enough to admit a whole stick of wood without being sawn or split. The gradual introduction of coal, which at this time was only used by blacksmiths, led to great improvements in the shape and designs of stoves. Some were made as open grates, which added much to the cheerfulness of sitting rooms.

To witness the display at one of the annual exhibitions, or in one of the large manufacturing establishments, is to see in a most remarkable manner, as much as in any other branch of manufacture, the progress of taste and refinement, as well as in arrangements for comfort. The rarity and beauty of the designs, as well as the arrangements for promoting health, and the convenience of "self-feeders," in which the fire need never go out the whole winter, are truly marvellous.

The stoves of the present day are not only useful but highly ornamental, and other heating arrangements, whether from furnaces supplying hot air, or by steam, or hot water, all are made to appear as part of the furnishing of hall or drawing room.

THE E. & C. GURNEY CO. (LIMITED),

was founded originally in Hamilton, in 1843, for the manufacture of stoves and other castings suited to the requirements of that time.

Since then the firm has taken the lead in introducing every improvement and new design, till at the present time the business has extended to Toronto, Winnipeg, Montreal, and has also extensive scale works at Hamilton, and also carries on the manufacture of agricultural implements at Dundas.

The Toronto branch was established about sixteen years ago, by Mr. Edward Gurney, junior, under whose management it has grown to its present gigantic proportions.

The buildings on King street, erected by the firm, four stories high and 400 x 60 feet, are occupied as store-rooms and mounting shop, and another of the same dimensions utilized as a foundry. These have been supplemented by a large addition the present year, making the whole arrangements complete in every department.

The very best talent and unlimited capital are employed in producing every article of the most approved and artistic construction for the heating of buildings, from the cottage to the palace. Stoves and ranges of every description, combining beauty with utility, are manufactured, and shipped all over the Dominion; and as a result of their exhibits in London, no doubt a large trade may be anticipated with Australia, and possibly with Great Britain, the stoves now in use in Canada being equally suitable for all these countries.

The specialties of the firm are steam and hot water boilers, with the Bundy radiators, adapted to every building and to every part of any building, and these, when ornamented with the new coil screens, whether in hall or drawing-room, may be made to correspond with the most luxurious furniture, and become an attractive feature in the general effect.

The firm in Toronto employs from 175 to 200 hands.

THE GRAND "TRUNK" HOUSE OF THE DOMINION.

If any person would like to have proof of the wonderful development of commercial travelling within the period of the present reminiscences, let him read of its first commencement, and then take a walk through the baggage-rooms of the Union Station and inspect the vast piles of iron-bound, grimly-defiant, smasher-proof contrivances which contain the samples of home and foreign manufactures, used by the army of 2,300 commercial travellers of the Toronto branch alone, by which the large manufacturing and wholesale establishments are represented from the Atlantic to the Pacific, and the comparison will be found to be rather surprising. The history of the firm of

H. E. CLARKE & CO.

is intimately connected with this branch of trade.

Mr. Clarke commenced business about thirty years ago, in a small store on Yonge Street, his staff consisting of one boy. The writer recollects distinctly of his purchase from Mr. Clarke of the first commercial trunks for the firm, on the opening of the Northern and Grand Trunk Railways, and since that time the demand has steadily and rapidly increased, with a corresponding improvement in the manufacture and convenience of these articles. No less remarkable has been the progress of the trade in trunks, satchels and valises for the tourist, and especially in everything to suit the convenience of ladies.

The old flat-bottomed scow has given place to the noble three-decked "Saratoga," where everything appertaining to ladies' dress, from tip to toe, parasol and fan included, may be arranged in compartments from which they will emerge without crease or wrinkle.

Messrs. H. E. Clarke & Co. occupy large premises as a factory, employing a large staff of workmen, and have recently enlarged and beautified their retail store on King Street, making it the leading establishment of the kind on the continent.

The Queen's Hotel,

founded by Captain Thomas Dick in 1862, received its name, no doubt, from the well-known loyalty of its founder, and while a "rose by any other name would smell as sweet," there is an appropriateness in this being applied to the leading hotel in the Queen City of the West that will always strike a traveller, especially from Britain. This attachment to everything appertaining to royalty was further evidenced by Capt. Dick in the name given to the steamer built for him on the Clyde, which he called *Her Majesty*.

The writer crossed to England with him when going over to place the contract, and when all had been completed, and the steamer was on her way out, she was unfortunately lost. This was regarded as matter of great regret, not only by the Captain, but by all Toronto citizens.

From the commencement the aim of Captain Dick was to provide a comfortable home for his guests, as distinguished from the "caravansary" style of most hotels in America, and in this he was most successful, even to the minutest detail. The present proprietors, Messrs. McGaw & Winnett, have followed up the original design, making constant improvements in every department. This popular hotel has recently been renovated and changed in many respects from the first to the third story. A year ago its elegant and commodious dining-room was very handsomely frescoed. During the last three months many of the parlors, corridors and halls have been tastefully decorated and painted. New private staircases have been fitted up in the Queen Anne style. Each landing has a magnificent stained glass window, and as one ascends these unique windings the idea must flash upon him that he has mistaken the Queen's Hotel, and is ensconced in some baronial hall. The halls and corridors have all been relaid with costly and luxurious carpets.

From 1877 to 1886.

When all these changes are added to the previous commodious and handsomely furnished drawing-rooms and bedrooms, with bathrooms, to say nothing of the fine suites of rooms which were fitted up for the Princess Louise and the Marquis of Lorne on the occasion of their first visit to Toronto, as well as other suites that were prepared several years ago, in a magnificent style, for the reception of the Grand Duke Alexis, then heir apparent to the crown of Russia—the Queen's stands unrivalled in this respect by any hotel in the Dominion, and as

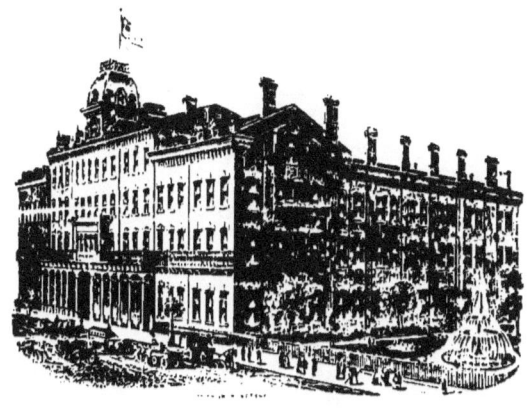

THE QUEEN'S HOTEL.

regards the *cuisinerie* and the daily *menu*, nothing is left to be desired.

Need we wonder, then, that the Queen's is largely patronized, not only by guests of the first standing from all parts of the Dominion, but also from the United States, England and the Continent. In May, 1880, their Royal Highnesses Prince Leopold and Princess Louise occupied a suite of apartments at the Queen's. His Excellency the Earl of Dufferin, Governor-

**IMAGE EVALUATION
TEST TARGET (MT-3)**

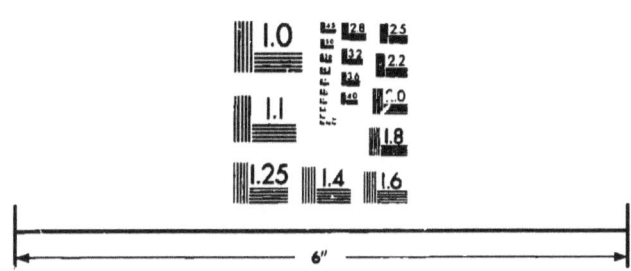

Photographic
Sciences
Corporation

22 WEST MAIN STREET
WEBSTER, N.Y. 14580
(716) 872-4503

General, and the Countess of Dufferin, also occupied apartments at this hotel.

The situation is delightful, commanding a splendid view of Toronto Bay and Lake Ontario, and from its proximity to that splendid sheet of water, the cool breezes can be enjoyed all through the summer, making it a most desirable resort for visitors from the south.

The beautiful grounds around are both spacious and airy, and with croquet and chevalier lawns, nothing more pleasant could be desired by business men, pleasure seekers or tourists. The Queen's is furnished with all the latest modern improvements, having a handsome passenger elevator and electric bells, and in addition will be found the most polite attention to every wish of its guests.

The building being only three stories high, covering a large area of ground, and used exclusively as a hotel, having lawns on either side, with means of exit from the house, in addition to those in front and rear, renders it almost impossible for an accident to take place from fire, and consequently the Queen's is looked upon as the safest hotel in the Dominion of Canada, and is regarded with pride by the citizens of Toronto as an establishment worthy of a great city.

Toronto's Natural Advantages.

We get here no earthquakes such as those of which the San Franciscan sleeps in nightly dread. We get no fervid heat, such as in New York often slays its scores in a day by sunstroke. We get no excessive degree of cold, such as all places to the east, west and north, and some to the south, including Chicago and St. Louis, suffer from. We get no cyclone or windstorm, such as all the cities west of us, even as near as Detroit, are subject to. No western cyclone ever yet reached this district. We get no floods, such as periodically inflict loss and suffering beyond calculation upon many of our sister cities. Nature has done everything for our comfort, providing even for the absence of the mosquito, which is just beginning to ply its proboscis elsewhere.

Toronto a City of Churches.

<blockquote>
Wherever God erects a house of prayer,
The devil always builds a chapel there ;
And 'twill be found upon examination
The latter has the larger congregation.
—*Daniel Defoe.*
</blockquote>

If this celebrated man, the father or founder of the English novel, was living in Toronto to-day he would scarcely venture to introduce the above lines into a satire on churches and church-goers. The congregations worshipping in Toronto churches would show a very different result from what is implied in the above verse. In no city in the world are churches more numerous, or the congregations larger, in proportion to the population, and it is safe to say that in this respect the church accommodation is larger than in any other city. Taking the average capacity to be one thousand, and the number of churches in Toronto and suburbs at one hundred and twenty, the entire population, if present at one time, could nearly be accommodated; and this cannot be said of any other city. Although this can never happen, it is evident the average attendance must be very large and the accommodation abundant.

It is safe to say, that nowhere else can such a sight be witnessed on a fine Sunday evening, within the same limits, as in Toronto, when the churches are emptied of the crowds of worshippers and the sidewalks are blocked with the throngs returning to their homes.

The writer having spent Sundays in every large church-going city on both sides of the Atlantic, can make this statement without fear of successful contradiction; nor is there anywhere to be seen better dressed or more respectable looking congregations than worship in Toronto churches.

What the feelings must be of those who absent themselves from Toronto churches on Sunday I cannot imagine, never having such an experience, but it seems as if that very absence would preach a sermon which, to every freethinker or agnostic, would be as powerful in favor of Christianity as if a sermon were listened to inside the walls of a church.

The ringing of the bells is at an end, the rumbling of the carriage has ceased, the pattering of the feet is heard no more, the flocks are folded in the numerous churches. For a time

ST. ANDREW'S CHURCH, KING STREET WEST.

everything is hushed, but soon is heard the deep pervading sound of the organ, rolling and vibrating through the buildings and out into the streets, and the sweet chanting of the choirs makes them resound with melody and praise, while it is poured forth like a river of joy through the recesses of the city, elevating and bearing the soul on a ti... of triumphant harmony to heaven. The wanderer about the streets at such a time is not a proper subject for envy.

In writing of Toronto as a city of churches, the men who, by their faithful discharge of duty and their advocacy and influence, have been to a great extent instrumental in educating the religious element up to the present high standard of church-going in Toronto, ought not to be forgotten. The following are amongst those to whom much of the credit is due, and as the names are given entirely from memory, and none given whom the writer has not heard preach since 1847, any omission will be overlooked:—

BAPTIST.

Rev. Messrs. Piper, Fyfe, Caldecott, Castle, and Thomas.

CONGREGATIONAL.

Rev. Messrs. Roaf, Ellerby, Marling, Lillie, Burton, Powis and Wild.

PRESBYTERIAN.

Rev. Messrs. Burns, Topp, Barclay, Gregg, Taylor, Parsons, King, McLeod, MacDonnell, Kirkpatrick, Milligan, Robb and Kellogg.

EPISCOPAL CHURCH.

Bishops Strachan, Bethune, McLean and Sweatman; Rev. Messrs. Grasett, Baldwin, Lett, Givens, Sanson, Williams, Darling, Pearson, Scadding, Lewis, Jones, Rainsford, Dumoulin, Langtry, McCollum, McCarrol, Bilkey, Boddy, A. H. Baldwin and Morgan Baldwin.

METHODIST.

On account of the itinerant system of the Methodist Church, the array of names will necessarily be much greater than of the others.

Rev. Messrs. Hetherington, Cooney, Harvard, Richey, Evans, Wood, Rice, Stinson, Wilkinson, Squire, Bishop, Douse, Douglas, Elliott, Ryerson, Rose, Taylor, Green, Spencer, Sanderson,

Borland, Howard, Williams, Hall, Lavell, Stevenson, Punshon, Cochrane, McClure, Savage, Potts, Briggs, Dewart, Dorey, Johnston, Antliff, S. J. Hunter, W. J. Hunter, Clarkson, W. W. Ross, Jeffrey, Jeffers, Hannan, Learoyd, McRitchie, Stafford, Poole, Bridgeman, Harper, Laird, Starr, Blackstock, S. P. Rose, and Shorey.

ROMAN CATHOLIC.

Not having heard any preachers of this Church except Archbishop Lynch and Rev. Mr. Teefy, I can only say that both of these gentlemen are distinguished for literary ability and devotion to the interests of their Church.

The improvement in the numbers and respectability of the worshippers since they were confined to the comparatively insignificant church on Power Street is something marvellous, and no one visiting any of the handsome Roman Catholic churches in Toronto can help being struck with the decorum and reverence observed during the service.

CHURCHES.

The total number of churches at present in Toronto is one hundred and ten, divided as follow:—Episcopal, 26; Presbyterian, 18; Baptist, 11; Methodist, 25; Roman Catholic, 9; Hebrew, 1; Congregational, 7; Reformed Episcopal, 2; Unitarian, 1; Lutheran, 1; Catholic Apostolic, 1; Plymouth Brethren, 2; Miscellaneous, 5.

THE SALVATION TEMPLE.

The Salvation Temple just completed is quite an imposing structure with its castellated bastions, combining in appearance the castle, the barracks and the temple. The frontage is 106 feet, with a depth of 100. It is built of red brick with stone facings. A space of 22 feet has been divided off in front to be used as offices. Through this portion three entrances reach the Temple; the central one being broad and lofty. The height of the ceiling inside is 32 feet, and the width 96, with no roof columns. This is the widest span without support of any public building in Canada. The walls are four feet thick, and are capable of standing an enormous strain.

The auditorium will hold about 2,500 people, and there is not a bad seat in the house; the ventilation is perfect, as are also the acoustic properties.

The Temple is constructed in amphitheatrical form and has one gallery at the back. The ground floor rises from the centre, and a passage runs entirely round next the wall.

The officers conducting the services sit on the north side, with the soldiers and audience all about them. The soldiers for the most part occupy the pit, or dress circle. This latter

THE SALVATION ARMY TEMPLE.

arrangement is in accordance with the system followed by General Booth in England. The ceiling of the Temple is of varnished wood, while the walls are finished stucco work in plaster. Texts and mottoes will be used as additional ornaments. The entire height of the building, which comprises four stories, is 80 feet to the top of the tower, and 50 feet to the centre and slates. The windows are all stained glass with Scripture mottoes. A pair of iron gates close in the front entrance, over which appears in stone letters the single word "Hallelujah." The entire cost will be about $40,000.

THE SALVATION ARMY

reports that the organization is at work in one hundred and fifty-one cities, towns and villages throughout the country. It has outposts in fifty-three places. In five places land has been secured for building purposes, while there are barracks in forty places. The number of officers in 1885 was 418, number of corps 148, and outposts 47. The attendance numbered 269,000, being an increase over the previous year of 76,612. The amount of money received and expended weekly on the local corps was $2,905.

The Temple was formally opened on the arrival of Marshall Ballington Booth, who came this way from Australia (on his return to England) to dedicate the building. The "Council of War" continued from the 1st to the 8th of May, and was the occasion of enthusiastic demonstrations. The daily processions accompanied by bands of music, were witnessed by immense crowds of people, and at night the vast auditorium of the Temple was crowded to excess. On Sunday, the 2nd, the formal dedication took place, and each succeeding day and evening through the week there was a change of programme, including a Hallelujah Wedding and Infant Dedication.

On the night of the latter ceremony a number of officers and soldiers who had been imprisoned for noisy demonstrations appeared in prison costume and related their experience. In connection with the presentation of the infant the Marshall stated that twenty-eight years ago he was taken by his parents sixty miles in England to be baptized by the Rev. Jas. Caughey, so well known in Toronto, who is still living, and commencing again to preach as an evangelist.

The Marshall gave a striking account of his opening campaign in Manchester,—the extraordinary language used in the posters having brought immense masses of the people to see and hear,—and then of his arrest and imprisonment; all of which had a thrilling effect on the vast audience. He left for England the following week, accompanied by Commissioner Coombs and William Gooderham, Esq., of this city.

Toronto an Educational Centre.

This position claimed for Toronto will be admitted by all. From the lowest step in the ladder to the highest, no city can boast of equal advantages in the shape of education. The Common School system, a lasting monument to the ability, wisdom, and indefatigable exertions of the late Dr. Ryerson, has been brought to a state of perfection perhaps unequalled in the world. Framed on the models of all the best systems in every

UNIVERSITY OF TORONTO.

other country, it combines the best feature of all, and improvements on most.

Rising in the scale, it will be found that no educational want has been left unsupplied; whatever the pursuit or profession the student may intend to follow through life, he will find a school, academy, college or university in which he will have full scope for his ambition. From the Public Schools, there is a step upwards to the Model Schools, then to the Collegiate Institute, Upper Canada College, and to the University of Toronto. Then there are technical schools, including the School of Practical Science and the Ontario School of Art.

A city possessing so many advantages for students must afford increasing attractions from year to year, the high standing of its professors, and the honors to be obtained, whether as medals, scholarships, fellowships, or other degrees, offer inducements superior to those of any other city in the Dominion, and must lead ultimately to the federation of other colleges with the University of Toronto.

In addition to the colleges named are Knox College, Trinity College, the Baptist College, and St. Michael's. There are also the College of Pharmacy, Toronto School of Medicine, Trinity Medical College, Veterinary College, Canadian Institute, and School of Divinity, or Wycliffe College.

The Normal School, for the training of teachers, was established in 1847. The present buildings were erected in 1851, the corner stone being laid by the Earl of Elgin, and in the month of November, 1852, the buildings were opened. They were then described as being elegant in architectural appearance, commodious in their accommodations, and healthy in their situation. They are at present an ornament to St. James' Square, the grounds surrounding the building being beautifully laid out with trees and flower beds, and in addition there is a handsome conservatory.

The Educational Museum is a source of attraction to visitors, as well as valuable to the students, and contains paintings, statuary, and curiosities of various kinds, plaster casts of Egyptian, Assyrian, Babylonian, Persian, Grecian and Roman antiquities. It also contains philosophical apparatus, being representative, on a small scale, of the South Kensington Museum.

Great North-Western Telegraph Co.

Miles of lines	34,000
Number of offices	2,000
Number of messages in 1885	2,446,000
Number of words in press reports	63,500,000
Number of miles for messages at twenty-five cents	1,275
Number of miles controlled by connection with Western Union Co.	450,000
Employees of the Company	2,500
Toronto staff	174

CANADIAN INSTITUTE, RICHMOND STREET WEST.

Toronto a Musical City.

High on the shore sate the great god Pan,
  While turbidly flowed the river,
And hacked and hewed as a great god can,
With his hard bleak steel, at the patient reed,
Till there was not a sign of a leaf, indeed,
  To prove it fresh from the river.

He cut it short, did the great god Pan,—
  How tall it stood in the river !
Then drew the pith, like the heart of a man,
Steadily from the outside ring,
  Then notched the poor dry, empty thing,
In holes, as he sate by the river.

"This is the way," laughed the great god Pan,—
  Laughed while he sate by the river,—
" The only way, since gods began
To make sweet music, they could succeed."
Then dropping his mouth to a hole in the reed,
  He blew, in power, by the river.

Sweet, sweet, sweet, O Pan,
  Piercing sweet by the river,
Blinding sweet, O great god Pan !
The sun on the hill forgot to die,
And the lilies revived, and the dragon-fly
  Came back to dream on the river.

Elizabeth Barrett Browning.

Prior to the period when the present reminiscences commence there was little to note of the musical history of Toronto. The writer is indebted to the Toronto *Mail* for some account previous to 1847.

It appears by the earliest records, that as far back as 1818 the sole instrumental artist of Toronto was a Mr. Maxwell, distinguished "for his quiet manner, for the shade over one eye, and for his homely skill on the violin."

With military music the townspeople were familiarized by the occasional performances of the regimental bands which were stationed here from time to time. The ecclesiastical music was entirely destitute of organs or melodeons.

At the Church of St. James' a Mr. Hetherington officiated as clerk, and his mode of procedure was to announce the psalm or hymn, give out the tune on the bassoon, and then accompany the vocalists present with original and often grotesque improvisations on that instrument. At one time a choir was formed at this church with a bass viol, clarionet and bassoon as the accompanying instruments. The music was almost entirely confined to the churches that then existed; the choirs being accompanied by flutes, violins, violoncellos, and occasionally a trombone. It is said that Mr. James Baxter organized and led a choir at the old Methodist church on King Street, near the present site of R. Hay & Co.'s establishment, in 1831.

The first impetus of a permanent character given to music was through the services of the late Mr. John Ellis and Dr. McCaul; the former distinguished by his performance on the violoncello, with which Toronto audiences were favored gratuitously for many years, and the latter on the piano, showing himself to be an accomplished musician as well as composer.

For many years Dr. McCaul was the patron of every enterprise which contributed to the pleasure and advantage of the citizens. No meeting for any object of a literary, benevolent, or pleasurable character was considered complete without the presidency of Dr. McCaul, and whenever he took the lead his felicitous remarks, always mingled with real Irish humor, invariably resulted in success.

Through the influence and efforts of Dr. McCaul, selections from the oratorios were first given in 1845, in the Parliament Buildings. Monsieur Bley, a talented violinist, was brought over from New York to conduct, and with him were engaged Miss Andrews, Miss Northrall, and Mr. Miller, as principal vocalists. Two concerts were given, which were very successful and excited great enthusiasm. Dr. McCaul presided at the piano, and the Toronto *Mail* says, "was received with a burst of applause on making his appearance on the platform." The result of this new venture led to the inception of the idea of establishing a Philharmonic Society. Monsieur Bley, having been induced to remain in Toronto, was appointed conductor of the new organization, which started in 1846. Dr. McCaul was the President and Mr. Ellis the instrumental manager.

This Society gave a concert in the University Hall, Parliament Buildings, on St. George's Day, April 23rd, 1847, a few days after the writer's arrival in the city, for the benefit of the Irish and Scotch relief funds. Among the vocalists were Mr. J. D. Humphreys, who became Toronto's favorite tenor, Mrs. Searle, and Messrs. Ambrose and Barron.

After a short stay in Toronto, Monsieur Bley returned to France, and the Society was started afresh in 1848, with Dr. Strathy as vocal conductor and pianist, and Mr. Schallehn as "*chef d'attaque*" of the orchestra.

The first concert was given in the City Hall on the 28th of December, 1849, which created quite an excitement; some of the most difficult morceaux of the great masters were given with fair success. The second of these concerts was given in the Temperance Hall, on the 31st of January, 1850, under the patronage of the Earl and Countess of Elgin. Mr. Schallehn was a clever clarionet player, and was bandmaster of the 71st Regiment.

In 1851 the Toronto Vocal Music Society was formed in the room of the old Philharmonic. Dr. McCaul was the President, the late Chief-Justice Draper, Vice-President, and Dr. Clarke, Conductor. At the first of the reunions of this Society, in May of that year, the solo vocalists were Miss Davis (afterwards Mrs. F. Thomas) and Miss Harris; among the choral numbers given was Handel's "Hailstone Chorus," from "Israel in Egypt." These meetings culminated in a public concert in the following December. The programme embraced selections from the works of Handel, Weber, Rossini, and Mendelssohn. The soloists were Miss Davis, Mr. Hecht, baritone, and Mr. T. Cooper, tenor.

The second concert was given in June, 1852, in the St. Lawrence Hall, which had just been opened. This concert was given in commemoration of Moore, the poet. Mr. Paige, tenor, and Miss Paige, soprano, made their appearance and became great favorites with the public.

After this a new organization was formed under the old title of the Philharmonic Society. Dr. McCaul was elected President, Mr. Fred. Widder, vocal manager, Prof. Croft, instrumental manager, Dr. Clarke, conductor, and Mr. F. Griebel, leader of the orchestra.

Mr. Griebel, who came to Toronto with the Jenny Lind concert troupe, was one of the greatest violinists ever resident in the city.

The first open meeting of this Philharmonic Society was held on the 25th of April, 1854, in the University Hall, Parliament Buildings. On the programme was a symphony of Beethoven's, the "Hallelujah Chorus" from the "Mount of Olives," a cornet solo from Mr. Harkness (bandmaster),the overture to" L'Italiana', and a violin solo, "The dying scene," from "Lucia," by Herr Griebel.

At the third meeting, Herr Griebel played De Beriot's first concerto for violin, and one of Paganini's concert solos. The Chorus sang Handel's "Fixed in his everlasting seat."

This society next figured at a concert in aid of the patriotic fund for the Crimean War sufferers, in the St. Lawrence Hall, February, 1885. The programme included the "Funeral March," by Beethoven, piano solo, Mr. Haycraft; song, "Oh, God, preserve the mourners," Miss Davis; solo and chorus, "Qui tollis,' Mr. Hecht; fantasia, on the "Cujus animam," Mr. Hayter; song " Ruth," Mrs. Beverley Robinson; song, "I would be a soldier," Mr. L. W. Smith; piano and violin *duo* on "William Tell," Messrs. Griebel and Haycraft; "Heroes of the Crimea," Mr, Humphreys; piano solo, "La Violette," Mr. Klophel; song "The sea is Merry England's," Mr. Barron, (then late Principal of the U. C. College). This concert excited unbounded enthusiasm, and was very successful.

The patronage of music lovers was at this time diverted from the society by the introduction of subscription concerts given by Mr. and Miss Paige. This resulted in the fall of the Philharmonic Society, and musical matters were comparatively neglected till the arrival of Mr. John Carter, who accepted the post of organist at the Cathedral Church of St. James, then newly built. Mr. Carter arrived in Toronto in October, 1856, and the aspect of the musical world of Toronto was soon completely changed.

Mr. Carter was not long in developing the resident talent, for in the following year he gave the first oratorio performance ever given in Upper Canada. The oratorio selected was the "Messiah," and was given on the 17th December, 1857.

The work was accomplished in twelve weeks, and such was the enthusiasm created, that the concert room was filled to the doors.

Mr. Carter was assisted by Herr Griebel, and Messrs. Noverre, Maul, Schmidt, and Martin Lazare, amongst the instrumentalists, and by Miss Davis, Miss Kemp (afterwards Mrs. Cobban), Miss Robinson, Mrs. Poetter and Mrs. Scott. Among the vocalists were Messrs. Jacob Wright, Sugden, Barron, C. Grasett, Briscoe, Lang, Jas. Baxter and F. Roche.

"Judas Maccabeus" was performed in 1858, under the direction of Rev. Mr. Onions, who started an opposition scheme which divided musical society into two parties, known as the Onionites and the Carterites. The feud, however, was of rather an amicable nature.

The Rev. Mr. Onions had Mr. Noverre as leader of the band, and Mr. G. F. Graham as organist. His vocalists were Mr. and Mrs. Hickok, Mr. Lindsay, Mrs. Dunlevi, C. J. Martin, Mr. Humphreys, Mr. John Baxter, the Misses Robinson, Madame Wookey, Mrs. Hastings, Miss Scarle, Mrs. Emerson, and Messrs. Briscoe, Sugden and Vial. The band and chorus were advertised as numbering two hundred.

At one of these oratorios, the writer and his party sat near a, gentleman of the legal profession, recently out from London, who criticised the performance of each vocalist, and during the performance of one tenor singer, not appreciating his efforts, he made himself conspicuous by shrugging his shoulders and screwing up his countenance, at the same time exclaiming loudly enough to be heard, "Oh, Sims Reeves!"

Having lately heard that celebrated tenor, in Exeter Hall, we could partly sympathize with his feelings, but not so far as to lose the enjoyment of the Toronto performance, which was highly creditable to all concerned.

The rivalry resulted in each party giving the "Creation." In 1861 Mr. Carter formed the "Toronto Musical Union," and Mr. Onions the "Metropolitan Choral Society," under the direction of Mr. Martin Lazare, a most able musician. Some of the performances of this gentleman on the piano were truly marvellous, especially "medleys" and "fantasia" with one hand.

In 1863-4 Mr. Carter, as director of the Musical Union in connection with the Mechanics' Institute, in the Music Hall over the present Free Library, gave occasional concerts; and among the works produced were the "Messiah," "Judas Maccabeus," the "Creation," the "Lay of the Bell," the "Stabat Mater," and the operas "Il Trovatore," and "Martha."

In 1872 Mr. Robert Marshall, in connection with Mr. Alex. Mills, undertook to reorganize the Philharmonic Society, and succeeded in inducing a sufficient number of instrumentalists and vocalists to combine for this purpose.

Dr. McCaul was appointed President, the veteran Dr. Clarke, Conductor, Mr. Robt. Marshall, Vice-President, and Mr. John Hague, Secretary.

The first concert of this new society was given in October, 1872, when the "Messiah" was given in Shaftesbury Hall. The chorus consisted of twenty-eight sopranos, twenty-six altos, forty-eight tenors, fifty basses, and eight principals—in all one hundred and fifty.

The orchestra, under the direction of Mr. Marshall, consisted of twelve violins, three violas, three basses, two double basses, two flutes, two clarionets, one bassoon, one horn, two trumpets, and two drums—total thirty.

The solo vocalists were Messrs. J. G. Sheriff, Marriott, Martin and Pearson, and Mrs. Grassick, Mrs. Cuthbert, Miss Hillary, Miss Clarke and Miss Thomas.

The pianist was Mr. H. G. Collins. This was the last occasion on which Dr. Clarke conducted at an oratorio.

Mr. Marshall wielded the baton, until the arrival of Mr. Torrington in 1873. This event marked a new epoch in the musical history of Toronto.

F. H. TORRINGTON.

This gentleman received his musical training as Cathedral organist, choirmaster, pianist, etc., under James Fitzgerald, of Kidderminster (pupil of Dr. Corge, Bristol), under whom he was articled for four years. As violinist he was a pupil of Geo. Hayward, Birmingham. In 1854, Mr. Torrington was elected a member of the London Society of Sciences, Literature

F. H. TORRINGTON.

and Arts, for which he has a diploma. After a successful career in England he came to Canada, and was engaged in Montreal as organist of Great St. James' Street Methodist Church, a post he held for twelve years. During this period he developed his musical talent, and worked hard to cultivate public taste for the best class of music. For a considerable portion of this time Mr. Torrington was bandmaster of the 25th Regiment, and as founder and director of various vocal and instrumental societies, his services as solo organist and violinist were in constant demand. His reputation brought him to the notice of Mr. Gilmore, and he was engaged by that gentleman to form a representative Canadian Orchestra to take part in the first great Peace Jubilee at Boston. During this visit Mr. Torrington was asked by Mr. Gilmore to take up his residence in Boston, and a short time afterwards was offered and accepted the position of organist and musical director at King's Chapel, which position he left for the one he now holds at the Metropolitan Church, Toronto. During Mr. Torrington's residence in Boston he was engaged as teacher of the piano and organ at the New England Conservatory of Music, solo organist at the Music Hall Concerts, one of the first violins in the Harvard Symphony Orchestra, solo organist at the Saturday afternoon organ concerts in Henry Ward Beecher's Church, Brooklyn, N.Y., concurrently with Messrs. S. P. Warren, Geo. W. Morgan and other eminent organists. His services as conductor of musical societies were in much demand in and around Boston, and in the last Great Jubilee, six societies which Mr. Torrington was conducting took part. In connection with this event he was extensively engaged as conductor of the Mass-rehearsals preparatory to the great gathering of the *twenty thousand* voices which met together on that occasion. During the period of his residence in Toronto his work speaks for itself, as, in addition to the palpable improvement in church and choir music which he has effected, and the training of pianists, vocalists, organists and choirmasters now to be found occupying positions in Toronto and other Canadian cities, he has produced with large chorus and orchestra, through the medium of the Toronto Philharmonic Society, the following works of the Great Masters, many of them heard for the first time in Canada, and some for the first time on this side of the Atlantic :

Messiah, Elijah, Creation, Lay of the Bell, Fridolin, St. Paul, Stabat Mater, May Queen, Hymn of Praise, Walpurgis Night, Naaman, Fair Ellen March and Chorus (Tannhauser), March Cortege (Reine de Saba), March and Chorus (Life of the Czar),

Miserere Scene (Trovatore), Mors et Vita, Israel in Egypt, Spring's Message, Bride of Dunkerron, Rose of Sharon, Judas Maccabeus, Gypsy Life, The Last Judgment, Acis and Galatea, Preciosa, Redemption, Rose Maiden, Crusaders.

Mr. Torrington is also Conductor of the Hamilton Philharmonic Society, and in that capacity has produced in Hamilton, Romberg's "Lay of the Bell," "The Messiah," "Elijah," "Hymn of Praise," "Naaman," "Rose of Sharon" and "Samson." And with the Toronto University Glee Club Mendelssohn's music of "Antigone," in the original Greek, and Max Bruch's "Frithjof."

CHAMBER MUSIC.

The extent to which classical music is cultivated in private in the shape of trios, quartettes, and quintettes for stringed and other instruments, is generally considered a fair indication of the degree of musical taste that has been developed in a community.

The earliest quartette party in Toronto consisted of Herr Griebel, first violin; Mr. Noverre, second violin; Mr. Childs, tenor, and Mr. Ellis, bass.

After the death of Mr. Griebel, a piano quartette party was formed as follows: Mr. Carl Pieler, piano; Mr. Ernest Pieler, violoncello; Mr. Thomas, tenor, and Mr. Noverre, violin.

Although the amateur players on stringed instruments were few, there were in proportion to their number many fine and valuable instruments among them. Mr. Thomas had the Walmsly bass that belonged to Mr. Ellis (who died in 1877, at the age of 83,) and an Amati tenor; Mr. Marshall had a beautiful Testore; Mr. E. R. Parkhurst had a Johaine Baptiste Guadagnini, date 1751; Mr. H. Parkhurst, a Jacob Stainer, and Mr. Torrington is the owner of an Amati.

From a host of star artists who have appeared in Toronto since Jenny Lind's arrival, we name the following:

Piccolomini, Mario, Santley, Carlotta Patti, Rudersdorff, Parepa Rosa, Catharine Hayes, Cary, Lucca, Canissa, Madame Anna Bishop, Di Murska, Kellogg, Thalberg, Rubinstein, Vieuxtemps (the king of violinists), Arabella Goddard, Wieniowski, Sauret, H. C. Cooper, Lichtenberg, Theresa Liebe, Alfred Jaell, Camilla Urso, Prinne, Listerman, Remenyi, Joseffi, Teresa Carreno, Brignoli, Nillson, Lehmann, Musin, Rummell, Wilhelmj, Fabre, Leopold D'Meyer, Paul Julien, Brega.

Among the clubs, the Mendelssohn and Beethoven Quintette, the Damrosch and Thomas Orchestras, and Gilmore's Band have appeared from time to time in Toronto.

The Toronto Quartette Club is composed of Mr. J. Bayley and Herr Jacobsen, violins; Mr. Fisher, viola; and Mr. Correll, cello.

JENNY LIND.

The arrival of Jenny Lind, the "Swedish Nightingale," in America, in 1853, created such a sensation as was never known in the musical world. The sale of tickets for her first concert in New York was a great event. The first choice of a seat being set up for competition, was purchased by Genin, the Broadway hatter, for five hundred dollars.

On her first appearance she carried all hearts by storm, not for her great beauty, either of face or figure, but the irresistible charm of her simple and natural manner. Once heard, Jenny Lind could never be forgotten. Nor was her wonderful gift as a songstress the only cause of the royal ovations she received wherever she made her appearance. Everywhere she was fairly worshipped for her goodness and benevolence.

Although she had hundreds of letters every day asking her for help from all sorts of applicants, no worthy cause was overlooked. Her purse was always open to afford relief, and no request to give her services towards any charitable object was denied.

The foundation of the Protestant Orphans' Home in this city is due to her kind-hearted benevolence. In New York especially, the Jenny Lind mania became so strong that fabulous prices were paid for anything that might be preserved as a memento of her visit.

It was said that chambermaids at the hotel sold the combings, and even stray hairs from her hair-brushes, at large prices, and so of every article of which she had made use at the table.

Jenny Lind was the first and greatest star artiste Toronto has ever seen. Her one concert was given in the St. Lawrence Hall, in the fall of 1853.

Before the time announced, on the sale of tickets at Nordheimer's, the window shutters were put up, and the door strongly barricaded to keep back the crowd and allow applicants to enter in batches. So great was the scramble that coats were literally torn on men's backs; and to the great amusement of the crowd, one gentleman, determined to secure his prize, hoisted a small boy over the heads of the people, and in this way the boy procured a ticket. The price of admission was ten shillings, or two dollars.

Those who were present at the concert will remember her rendering of the simplest and most familiar songs. "Comin' through the rye," and "John Anderson, my Jo," were given, although with a slightly foreign accent, with great beauty and simplicity of expression; but while the air was so familiar, the variations, from the lowest to the highest range of the voice, were such as were never heard in Toronto, and were perfectly indescribable; and so of all the other numbers on the programme.

THE "SWEDISH NIGHTINGALE" AT WASHINGTON IN 1853.

The immense National Hall was crowded to its utmost capacity, notwithstanding big prices and inclement weather. Among the notabilities in the front seats, were President Fillmore, Daniel Webster, Henry Clay and John Howard Payne.

Jenny opened with the "Flute song," her voice contesting rivalry for purity and sweetness with a flute in a duett; then the once famous 'Bird song," and next the "Greeting to America." The volume of plaudits which followed each piece was emphasized by Mr. Webster, who rose and made the singer a profound bow, as if responding for the country to her greeting.

In response to a rapturous encore, Jenny Lind turned in the direction of John Howard Payne, the author of the song, and gave "Home, Sweet Home," with all the wonderful tenderness, purity and simplicity fitting both the air and the words of the familiar song. Before the first verse of the song was completed, the audience was fairly off its feet. People ordinarily demonstrative clapped, stamped and shouted as if they were mad, and it really seemed as if the uproar would never end.

Meantime, all eyes were turned upon Payne, a small-sized, gray-haired man, who blushed violently at finding himself the cynosure of so many glances. It was the most thrilling episode in his life.

Jenny Lind (Mdme. Goldschmidt) has been importuned by her friends and admirers to appear once more in public. Her voice is said to have lost none of its sweetness, and to retain much of its power.

She sings a good deal in private, so that she has preserved the flexibility of her voice, and the command of it which made her famous in her younger days. She has finally yielded to the solicitations which have been forced upon her, and has consented to re-appear in a concert in London.

This event will take place during the summer season, and is looked forward to with very great pleasure by all musical people in the metropolis.

MRS. JOHN BEVERLEY ROBINSON AND MRS. J. G. BEARD.

Any account of the progress of vocal music in Toronto would be incomplete without the name of Mrs. John Beverley Robinson, wife of the present Lieutenant-Governor of Ontario.

This gifted and accomplished lady, possessing a fine appearance and exquisite voice, was ever ready to respond to the call of the citizens on every occasion, on behalf of any charitable or benevolent enterprise, and her singing always elicited the most hearty applause. The amounts raised by Mrs. Robinson's services for these noble objects were very large, amounting to many thousands of dollars; one excellent institution here, "The Home for Incurables," having, in 1874, received the sum of $2,000, the result of one of her charitable concerts. Only a comparatively small number of citizens know how much they are indebted to this lady for the existence of some of the institutions of our city.

Mrs. J. G. Beard also contributed largely to the same objects, especially the Girls' Home. Her services as leading soprano in the choir of St. James' Cathedral, as well as at all such concerts as have been alluded to, are well known to many in Toronto.

As amateurs these ladies have never been surpassed, and even by the great artistes who have visited the city, seldom excelled.

THE MUSICAL FESTIVAL.

To Mr. Torrington is due the conception of establishing a series of musical festivals in Toronto, after the model of those given in England and the United States, and the first of these, which took place on the 15th, 16th and 17th of June, will be memorable in the musical history of Toronto. The first concert consisted of the opening chorus of God Save the Queen, followed by Gounod's sacred trilogy, "Mors et Vita;" the second was a miscellaneous concert; the third was Handel's sublime oratorio of "Israel in Egypt," and the fourth the Children's Jubilee and miscellaneous concert, in which 1,200 children took part.

The solo performers were as follows: Soprano, Fraulein Lilli Lehmann, Mrs. E. Aline Osgood, Mrs. Gertrude Luther; contralto, Miss Agnes Huntington; tenor, Mr. Albert L. King; baritone, Mr. Max Heinrich; bass, Mr. D. M. Babcock; organ, Mr. Frederic Archer; piano, Mr. Otto Bendix; harp, Mme. Josephine Chatterton; violin, Herr Henri Jacobsen.

The festival chorus comprised 1,000 voices, and the orchestra 100 performers. Mr. F. H. Torrington was the musical director.

Whatever Mr. Torrington's ambition may be in the future, unless some grander compositions appear than Gounod's "Mors et Vita," and Handel's "Israel in Egypt," he can expect no greater success than he has already achieved in the performance of these great works.

The interpretation of the conception of these great composers, and the thorough execution of their great works, is only second to the compositions themselves, and in the Toronto festival, the masterly manner in which, in every part of light and shade, whether of vocalization or instrumentation, Mr. Torrington rendered every word and note in the programme, has placed him in the front rank of musicians.

To sum up in one word, the whole festival was perfect in all its parts, and the delighted audiences who had the opportunity of listening will look forward to a repetition of the musical feast with confident anticipation.

The best building the city afforded, having been utilized, proved to be most adequate to the occasion. While it would be most desirable that a music hall could be built to accommodate double the number which attended the festival concerts, yet as there is a limit to the powers of the human voice and ear, the whole advantage was on the side of the building used for these concerts, and of both performers and listeners who were present. It is well known that at the Crystal Palace and other large places, no matter what the number of the performers may be, the outside rim of the 20,000 people who attend do not enjoy the music, from the fact that it is impossible to hear at such a distance.

Toronto could afford to have a hall sufficient to accommodate six thousand people, and at prices within the reach of all; and chorus and orchestra might then be increased in a corresponding degree, without loss of the general effect so delightful on the late occasion.

The officers of the Musical Festival Association, who so ably carried out the arrangements, were as follows: Geo. Gooderham, Honorary President; S. Nordheimer, President; J. B. Boustead, J. Herbert Mason, P. Jacobi, Vice-Presidents; James McGee, Treasurer; Jas. C. McGee, Assistant Treasurer; John Earls, Honorary Secretary; Edmond L. Roberts, Secretary; A. L. Ebbels, Recording Secretary.

The festival was successful financially as well as artistically, and reflects the highest credit on all concerned.

The musical festival orchestra comprised twenty first violins, fourteen second violins, ten violas, ten cellos, ten double basses, two flutes, one piccolo, two clarionets, two oboes, two bassoons, four horns, six cornets, three trombones, two tubas, kettle drums, big drums, side-drums, cymbals, triangle and gong.

At the Children's Jubilee a most interesting programme was successfully carried out, several of the celebrated soloists taking part. The children, however, were the chief attraction. When their youthful voices, with pleasing freshness and simplicity, struck the chorus "Hark to the Rolling Drum," the vast assemblage listened with marked attention, and many a father and mother looked with pride upon their children, whose appearance and behavior reflected much credit on the city.

Mr. Torrington, taking the place of Mr. Schuch, next conducted them in singing the national song of his own composition, entitled "Canada," the first verse of which runs :—

> O Canada, fair Canada!
> Name ever dear to me;
> A home for all who leave the shores
> Beyond the bright, blue sea.
> We love our land, though young it be,
> Its sunshine and its storms,
> Its faces fair, and hearts sincere,
> Affections strong and warm.
> We love our land,
> We love our flag,
> Beyond all others seen;
> God prosper our Dominion fair,
> Our country and our Queen.

At a particular part in the closing verse each child suddenly produced a small Union Jack and waved it in the air. The beautiful sight of 1,200 flags, together with the patriotic sentiment and excellent singing of the song, created the greatest enthusiasm, and the last verse had to be repeated.

It was a pretty sight to see 2,400 little hands waving in the air in the action songs, led by Mrs. J. L. Hughes, in illustration of the words being sung at the same time. At the close of the concert the entire chorus joined in God Save the Queen.

THE TORONTO VOCAL SOCIETY,

Founded last season by Mr. W. E. Haslam, for the practice of glees and unaccompanied part songs, is the latest enterprise.

TORONTO CHORAL SOCIETY.

This society was organized in 1879 by Mr. Edward Fisher, and has during its existence performed many of the greatest works of the great composers, including the principal oratorios, compositions for chorus and orchestra, and solos with orchestral accompaniment.

THE TORONTO PHILHARMONIC SOCIETY.

The principal soloists are Mrs. Bradley, Mrs. (Corlett) Thompson, Mrs. Jenkins, Mrs. (Torrington) Parker, Miss Hillary, Miss Corlett, Mrs. Caldwell, Mrs. J. B. Baxter, and Messrs. Warrington, Blight, Taylor, Curran, Schuch, and Sims Richards.

The principal instrumentalists of the Philharmonic Society are: Messrs. Bayley, Jacobsen, R. Cowan, T. Aikenhead, and Mr. Campbell, violins; Mr. Obemer, viola; Messrs. Correll and Daniels, cellos; Mr. Claxton, bass; Mr. Young, trombone; Mr. Williams, tuba, and Mr. C. Reiddy, tympani.

ST. MICHAEL'S AND ST. BASIL'S.

In these churches the very highest class of sacred music is performed, under the direction of Vicar-General Laurent. The grand masses of Mozart and Haydn, the Gregorian Chant, and other works of the great masters are given with splendid effect. Mr. Lemaitre is organist of St. Michael's, and amongst the soloists in these churches are Mrs. Petley, Miss Bolster, Mrs. O'Hara, Miss Meyers, Miss Murphy, and Messrs. Ward, McNamara, and McCloskey, with forty chorus singers.

In church music the two organs of 1847 have increased to fully one hundred; and the choirs are now composed of trained voices from the various musical societies.

The removal of the regular troops from Toronto by the English Government caused the want of a military band for several years, the last being that of the 13th Hussars, under command of Colonel Jennings. That want has been well supplied of late years by the splendid bands of the volunteers: the Queen's Own, Mr. Bayley bandmaster, and Royal Grenadiers, with Mr. Toulmin, also the Governor-General's Body Guards, and the Garrison Battery of Artillery. Besides the fine band of "C" Company, Infantry School, which completes the list of military bands, there are the bands of Heintzman & Co., the Massey Manufacturing Co., and Christian Brothers, all of which contribute to the pleasure of the citizens, and show a wonderful development of musical talent in our midst.

The Manufacture of Pianos in Toronto.

In a work professing to give a sketch of the wonderful growth and progress of Toronto, and the development of its manufacturing industries, and also of its present character as a "musical city," nothing can be more appropriate than to refer to the manufacture of musical instruments, and especially of pianos. No better evidence of the advancement of Toronto in wealth, culture, and refinement could be found than in the existence in her midst of extensive establishments for this branch of manufacture, and in the prospect of constantly increasing demand. The specimens forwarded to the Indian and Colonial Exhibition in London must remove every trace of misconception as to the state of society in the Queen City of the West, and of Canada in general, and show a state of educational refinement that no other class of exhibits could possibly do.

HEINTZMAN & CO.

The first piano made in Toronto was manufactured by Mr. John Thomas, about 1847. In 1860 Mr. T. A. Heintzman, the founder of this firm, removed to Toronto from Buffalo, where he had been engaged in the manufacture of pianos for the previous ten years. First in connection with Mr. Thomas, and then on his own account, he entered energetically into the business, having no competition in the manufacture of pianos for several years. From that time to the present the growth of the business has been marked by steady progress, and during the past few years has shown an increase of fifty per cent. every year, and especially in the last ten years, has shown a total increase of 800 per cent.

The present staff numbers one hundred and forty men, who turn out an average of from twelve to fifteen pianos a week. The perfection to which this firm has brought their instruments is shown in the magnificent specimens now being exhibited at the Indian and Colonial Exhibition. These consist of one "concert grand" piano, and one "semi-grand," and five different styles of upright pianos. On the grand pianos there are two very important patents. First, the patent bridge, which gives a very brilliant, distinct and beautiful singing quality to the treble notes. Second, the improved action, which makes it less complicated, and less liable to get out of order. The upright pianos are all constructed in different styles, and the workmanship and designs of the cases are excellent. One is in American blistered walnut, which looks very neat, and another upright is finished in mahogany and satin wood, with carved fretwork. Another smaller upright piano is got up in a very pretty figured French burl walnut, with beautifully carved trusses. Two more of the ordinary stock pianos are finished in rosewood.

All the upright pianos have Mr. Heintzman's patent desk, a very complete arrangement for supporting music. Many professors of music, both in London and elsewhere, have examined these instruments, and pronounce them first-class in every respect. No doubt many of them will find their way into the English and colonial markets.

J. E. Adkins, Royal College of Music, London, says: "I can bear testimony to the excellence of Messrs. Heintzman & Co.'s piano, both as regards workmanship and tone."

Herr Max Blume, F.S.S., London, from the Conservatory of Music, Leipsic, writes: "Having tried the pianos made by Messrs. Heintzman & Co., at the London and Colonial Exhibition, I must say, without hesitation, that they are, without doubt, to my liking, the finest pianos I have ever tested; their tone, touch, and mechanicism are perfection, whilst the solidity of their construction and workmanship is the finest I have ever seen in the pianoforte making."

Henry Wienkowski, from the Vienna Conservatory, says: "I

have the most sincere pleasure in saying that I have never met with a piano I can so confidently recommend for quality of tone and delightful touch, and can really say that it more than surprises me to see that so perfect an instrument is made in Canada. Having travelled through the United States for three years, I had the opportunity of trying the very best American pianos, and gave recitals at Chickering Hall, playing on Steinway and Weber pianos, and consider the Heintzman piano equal to the very best in the world."

The exhibit of pianos has been visited by several members of the Royal family, including the Crown Princess of Germany, and the Princess Louise, also the ex-Empress Eugenie, all of whom, having tested them personally, have given them unqualified praise. Before the Toronto Industrial Exhibition opened, these pianos always took first prize at Provincial Exhibitions, and at the Industrial have carried off first honors, also medals at Centennial in Philadelphia, and Sydney, N. S. W.

MASON & RISCH.

"Triumphant success! Our pianos are greatly admired for their true tone quality and beauty of design. The Queen, Princess Louise, and other members of the Royal party delighted with them," were the contents of a cable despatch from London to the above firm, on the opening of the Indian and Colonial Exhibition.

This exhibit is displayed within a handsome canopy, occupying six hundred square feet of space, and consists of eight pianos. Four are out of the ordinary stock, two being uprights, one a concert upright, and one a grand. Of the other four it may be said, they are magnificent and beautiful specimens of workmanship: one is a finely polished mahogany grand, supported on elegantly carved legs. Around the sides run eleven carved panels, each of a different design. Two other pianos are uprights, one finished in silver and green, the other in gold and olive, both elaborately and delicately carved and fretted in metal and wood carving. The last is a polished walnut upright of fine finish and tone.

The pianos of Mason & Risch are noted for their rich, sympathetic, and flute-like tone quality and durability. The business was established in 1871, and assumed the present style in 1878, during which time it has steadily increased, till at present one hundred hands are employed in all the branches.

From the commencement of the business, the aim of Mason & Risch has been to secure a substantial and enduring success by deserving it. The Mason & Risch "Parlor Grand Pianos," are instruments of the highest artistic excellence. In their development the best scientific skill of the firm has been employed, and in the results attained, it is safe to say that new problems in tone science have been successfully solved.

Musicians who have examined these instruments are unanimous in their expressions of praise; the great master, Dr. Franz Liszt, pronouncing them "excellent, magnificent, unequalled." As a token of his high appreciation, he had his portrait painted by Baron Joukovsky, son of the renowned Russian author, and personal instructor of the Emperor Alexander II., and presented to the firm. This portrait is now in London in connection with the Piano Exhibit. At the Toronto Exhibition in 1879 the Mason & Risch pianos obtained two special diplomas and the gold medal.

From their manifold excellence of tone, touch and workmanship, the Mason & Risch pianos have received from the highest musical authorities in Europe, United States and Canada, the most unqualified recognition.

The Mason & Risch factory is one of the most extensive in the country, and is complete in every department. It is supplied with the best labor-saving machinery, and with every facility for superior production. The lumber yard is stocked with the best material, which is seasoned for three or four years before being used, and in addition has been subjected to a patent drying process, for the use of which the firm has had a large royalty.

OCTAVIUS NEWCOMBE & CO.

This firm does not claim to be one of the pioneers of piano manufacturing in Toronto, but to have commenced operations with all the benefit of the experience gained by experiments made previously in piano building. In 1871 Mr. Newcombe, with two others, established a first-class pianoforte business in Toronto. It was continued with success during a partnership of seven years, after which the firm assumed its present style.

Beginning in a careful way, with a staff of skilful and experienced artisans, their aim was to manufacture a superior class of pianofortes, strong, durable, and of true musical quality, that would in time take the place of the costly American instruments, and supersede the inferior ones, whether of Canadian or foreign make. By adopting the latest and most approved system of construction, endeavoring to produce only the very best grade, and sparing no expense in making any possible improvement, their pianos have gained a position and reputation that has secured for them an increasing demand.

Their factory is conducted on the principle of a division of labor, the work passing through many hands before it is completed, each man being required to make his part perfect before it is received by the next, and each department being in charge of an experienced foreman, and all under the supervision of the firm. As their pianos have become known, their merits have been recognized and acknowledged by the musical public.

They have been selected by teachers for their own use, and for the severe work of schools, convents and colleges, which is the best evidence of their substantial character, thoroughness and durability, as well as their superiority in touch and tone. A tone clear and liquid in the treble, mellow and well sustained in the centre, and resonant in the bass, and affording in all the registers a harmony clear and equal, and of that sympathetic nature which, under the hands of an artist, arouses the enthusiasm of the listener, and demonstrates that the Newcombe pinafortes are unsurpassed in these qualities.

At the World's Exhibition in New Orleans, in 1885, a striking illustration of this effect occurred in a piano recital by Mrs. Marguerite Samuel, whose great talent as a pianist was recognized by all musicians in that city. The programme selected was strictly musical. The vast space of the building did not prevent her *finesse* of execution and delicacy of tenor being immediately apparent to her critical audience. All the numbers were choice and conscientiously rendered. There was the prayer of Lohengrin, arranged by Liszt, with its orchestral tones and immense difficulties; Weber's Barcarole of Oberon, full of poesy; the Polonaise of Chopin, brilliant and at the same time thoughtful; Les deux Alouettes of Lecktizki, a warble of birds in springtime, with fresh perfumes in it of vernal breezes; the Rondo Capricioso of Mendelssohn, ideally representative of that composer's dreamy and finished style; and the "Suis moi" of Gottschalk, so passionately nimble.

Here was enough to try not only the best piano, but even the distinguished pianist. Both stood the test victoriously. The "Newcombe" piano expressed all that was asked: the vigorous sonorities of Wagner, the agility and brilliancy of Liszt, the thoughtfulness of Chopin, the grace of Weber, the sparkling melody of Lecktizki, the sweetness and polish of Mendelssohn, and the passionate lightness of Gottschalk.

The *Musical Courier*, of New York, says of the Newcombe pianos exhibited at New Orleans: "Toronto is noted for its advancement in education and musical taste, and has, within the last decade, made remarkable progress in manufactures, and is now the centre of pianoforte industry of Canada. There are a number of piano factories in Toronto making the various styles of these instruments, and doing such a successful business that the importation of instruments from Europe has almost ceased.

The enterprise of Messrs. Newcombe & Co., and their confidence in the substantial character of their work, is shown by the fact of their placing their pianos where they can be compared with the best instruments of United States makers.

The style of these pianos indicates a Northern degree of solidity and strength that ensures durability, and they possess a pleasing symmetry of design at once graceful and appropriate. The woods used in the cases are American wave walnut, and French burl, an agreeable change from rosewood. The actions of these pianos are creditable specimens of material and workmanship, and give a full round satisfying tone which is much admired."

The Newcombe pianofortes sent to the Exhibition in London comprise some half-dozen instruments selected from their regular styles. From a musical point of view these pianos are magnificent specimens of skill and industry, and will, no doubt, create as favorable an impression in London as they did at the World's Exposition, New Orleans, 1884-5. In external appearance they are everything that could be desired, evidencing the practical good taste for which the firm has already earned a good reputation. The large grand and small parlor grand are both in rosewood, the latter being an exceedingly pretty model. One upright is chiefly of French burl walnut, relieved with plain walnut, so as to set off the rich coloring and figuring of the natural burl in fine relief. Another upright is in mahogany —a richly-panelled design, some fine emblematical carving in the centre panel, but with a fret running straight across the front of the upper frame; brass continuous hinges and candelabra are attached at each side to a fret work of crystals. The design is both unique and elegant to a degree. The other styles are in rosewood and American wave walnut, and are chaste and beautiful in appearance, and perfect in tone and finish.

On "awards on musical instruments" at New Orleans, the *Times-Democrat* says: "The Newcombe Pianoforte heads the list with the first silver medal, and jurors' report of commendation for construction, quality of material, workmanship, even tone throughout the instrument, and general excellence from a musical as well as a mechanical point of view. This is a genuine triumph for the manufacturers, who have not only had to compete with other foreign makers, but with the wealthy and enterprising exhibitors from the great centres of pianoforte manufacture in the United States, New York, Boston and Baltimore."

LANSDOWNE PIANO CO.

Messrs. A. & S. Nordheimer having acquired such high reputation for American pianos of the most celebrated makers, for whom they have been the exclusive agents, amongst which are the Chickering, Stodart & Dunham, the Steinway, Haines & Gabler, that, notwithstanding the high rate of duty on these instruments, their customers being willing to pay the higher prices so as to secure an instrument of first-class quality and excellence (some of these pianos having been in use for forty years), still continue to supply these instruments.

Nevertheless, to meet the demand for instruments less expensive, and yet such as they could recommend, they established the present firm for the purpose, appointing Mr. Gerald Heintzman as managing partner, who, from his well-known practical experience as a manufacturer, will co-operate with Messrs. Nordheimer in placing the enterprise in the front rank of the manufacturing industries of Toronto.

Their capital being practically unlimited, and their facilities unsurpassed, a bright future is in prospect for the company, and another star in the galaxy of Toronto's manufacturing establishments now shines at the grand display of Indian and Colonial exhibits at Kensington, London.

The Lansdowne Piano Co. have sent to the Indian and Colonial Exhibition six instruments. They are all "cabinet grands," and form a magnificent collection, both as regards beauty of finish, and perfection of tune. One of these possesses a handsome case, consisting of inlaid work, carving, and other ornamentation in lavish profusion, yet with such exquisite taste and skill that it stands as a perfect gem of workmanship.

The others are from the Company's stock of inlaid and polished walnut, and are a credit to the manufacturers and to Toronto. Many musical critics have pronounced these pianos to be without equal in the country, and their superior excellence is attested by all competent judges who have tried them.

In addition to other advantages possessed by this firm, with its great manufacturing facilities, they have secured several important additions to their staff, including one of New York's best tune and action regulators.

Hitherto the success of the Lansdowne Piano Co. has far exceeded their expectations, and, according to the judgment of competent connoisseurs, they seem destined to play a prominent role in the manufacture of pianos in Toronto.

In connection with the manufactures and exhibits of the Lansdowne Piano Co. is a novelty in the shape of an "upright grand," patented by Mr. A. Gunther, of this city, and manufactured by this Company. The patent consists in producing an instrument having all the internal construction of a grand, with the convenience in shape of an upright. This object is gained by the sounding board being cut obliquely from left to right under the keyboard, and having a peculiar scale of strings in connection, the strings and bass being very long.

It was in compliance with Mr. Gunther's solicitation that the Lansdowne Co. undertook the manufacture of these instruments which has been accomplished with such unqualified success in the completion of several of these "upright grands."

The style of the "Lansdowne Piano Co." was adopted with the approval of His Excellency the Governor-General.

Benevolent Institutions.

General Hospital, Home for Incurables, House of Industry, House of Providence, Girls' Home, Boys' Home, Protestant Orphans' Home, Infants' Home and Infirmary, Andrew Mercer Eye and Ear Infirmary, Industrial Refuge, News Boys' Lodging and Industrial Home, Dental College and Infirmary, Haven and Prison Gate Mission Home for Aged and Infirm, Burnside Lying-in Hospital, Magdalen Asylum, Hospital for Sick Children.

THE LAKESIDE HOME.

The Lakeside Home for Little Children, the convalescent Home in connection with the Hospital for Sick Children, occupies a site on the West Point of Toronto Island, nearly one

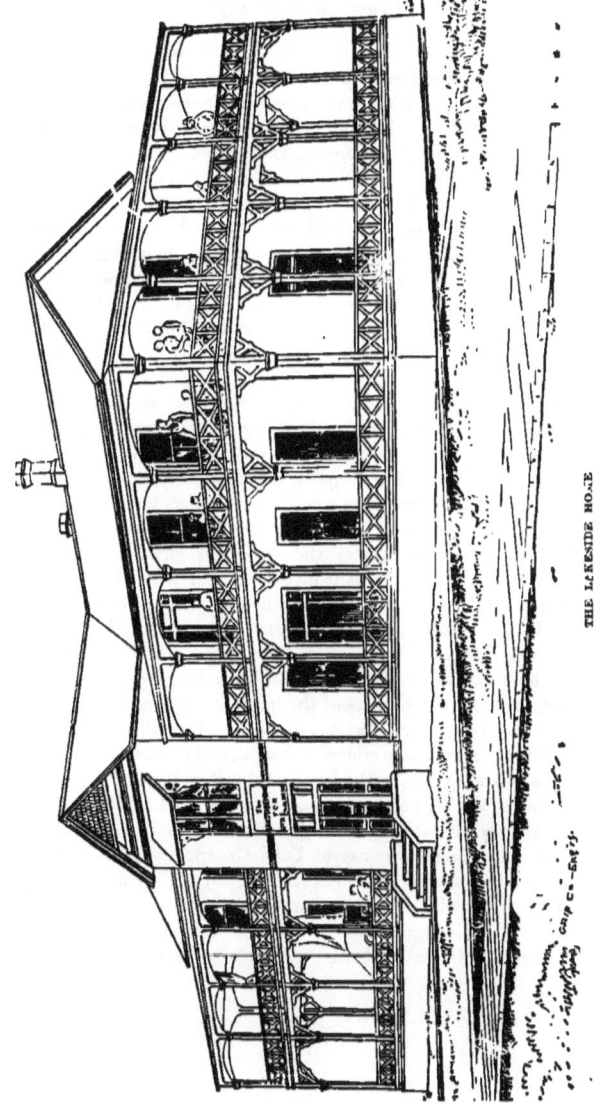

THE LAKESIDE HOUSE

hundred yards north-west of the light-house and the same distance from the south shore of the island. The building is twenty minutes' walk from the dock at Hanlan's Point, and the plot of ground on which it was built was leased by the Corporation of the City of Toronto, as the deed states, so that "a convalescent Home for Sick Children" should be "erected thereon, in connection with the Hospital for Sick Children." The Lakeside Home is very prettily situated, just on the spot where the little sick ones can have all the advantage of the invigorating and health-giving breezes of Lake Ontario. The building, as will be seen by the engraving, is of very attractive appearance. It is constructed of wood, and built in that light and airy style which architects consider best suited to places designed for summer residences. It has two stories, and each floor has a space of twenty-eight hundred square feet. It is lighted throughout with large windows, and a broad stairway leads from the entrance hall to the second story. On the ground floor there is a large dining room, a pantry, kitchen, board room and two large wards for forty children. On the second floor there is a large hall, on either side of which is a large ward for the use of the boys and girls respectively. Opening from these wards is a smaller room, which is occupied by children in advanced stages of disease. At the east end of the hall is a commodious bath-room, which is fitted up with the most improved appliances. The interior of the building has been finished in Canadian pine, and every provision has been made for the comfort of the inmates. A broad and shady verandah runs round the north-west and south sides of the building. This is two stories in height, and is reached by wide doors which open from the boys' ward. Here the little invalids are placed during portions of each fine day, and on the hottest day they receive the full benefit of the cool breezes which blow in from the broad expanse of Lake Ontario. A laundry and washhouse has been erected at the east end of the building, and an ample supply of pure water is brought from the lake by means of a windmill on the lake shore. The entire expense of building the Home and bringing it to its present state of completion has been borne by Mr. J. Ross Robertson, of the Toronto *Evening Telegram*, who attaches to his gift the condition, "The Lakeside Home as well as the Hospital for Sick Children, Toronto, shall be open without any charge to the children of Freemasons. Seven brethren, members of the Grand Lodge of Canada of Ancient, Free and Accepted Masons, have been named as those who have the privilege of presentation. Each applicant must have the endorsement of any one of the following :—Messrs. Daniel Spry, Barrie ; Dr. J. A. Henderson, Kingston ; George Birrell, London ; J. J. Mason, Hamilton ; David McLellan, Hamilton ; J. G. Burns, Toronto, and Wm. J. Hambly, Toronto." Mrs. S. F. McMaster is the President of the Hospital for Sick Children, and to her is due a great deal of the success that has attended that institution.

Toronto a Literary City.

Were Toronto to be judged by the number of people who read the party political articles in the daily papers, it would rank high in the scale of literature, and if the demand for works of fiction were a proof of literary taste, then our Public Library and its branches would bear testimony that the citizens of Toronto were a truly intellectual people ; but while these tests may be applied to indicate the taste of the majority, and would certainly show the tendency to be in the line of both of these habits, it is a pleasing fact that a large number cultivate a taste for literature for its own sake, and for the improvement of their minds.

The number of non-political newspapers, and of those representing the various religious denominations, is as great as in any other city of its population. The number of book stores and publishing houses, together with the large amount of books imported throughout the year, is a good indication of the extent of the private libraries which exist in the city and of the number of their readers.

It cannot be said that, in proportion to the population, there is a greater taste for literature than in previous years. Although there was no literary institution of a popular character, except the Mechanics' Institute, that was always well patronized, and the average intelligence of the people of Toronto was quite equal to what it is at the present time, at least in book literature. While efforts were made to encourage a taste for reading generally, especial attention was given by the managers of the Mechanics' Institute to impart technical knowledge. Nor was the cultivation of the faculties for appreciating the beautiful in art, thought and feeling, as well as for enjoying the truths of physical science, neglected.

That elegant and reflective literature which tends to moralize, to soften and adorn the life and soul of man, and the *belles lettres*, which operate for the advancement of the mental condition of the middle and humbler classes of society, might now as well as then hold a higher place in public estimation, and with advantage be more generally called into practical requisition. The Canadian Institute, which now ranks so high as a literary and scientific institution, did not come into existence till 1849, since which time it has done much in the higher sphere of literature, and takes the highest rank amongst Canadian literary societies.

Amongst the literati of Toronto may be named Drs. Wilson, Scadding, Loudon, Hodgins, and Withrow, and Prof. Goldwin Smith, who is contributing largely to the literature of the city. The *Week* newspaper, of which he is editor-in-chief, holds a place between the ordinary newspaper and the magazine; the latter being represented by only one, The *Canadian Methodist Magazine*, which is alike creditable to the publishers, the contributors, to Toronto and the Dominion.

It is an interesting question, whether the taste for solid reading is more cultivated amongst the young men of 1886 than those of 1847 and whether their general intelligence is greater. The number of amusements and attractions of various kinds which Toronto now affords may have a tendency to reduce the hours spent in study, and thereby prevent the acquisition of knowledge which, in the absence of these surroundings, made the old Mechanics' Institute itself the leading attraction for young men.

It cannot be denied that the newspaper is the great educator of the nineteenth century, and that no literary power can compare with it.

Rev. Dr. Talmage says: "The newspaper is the 'flying roll' of the Apocalypse. It is book, pulpit, and platform, all in one. And there is not an interest, religious, literary, commercial, scientifical, agricultural or mechanical, that is not within its grasp. All our churches, schools, colleges, asylums, and art galleries feel the quaking of the printing press. The vast majority of citizens do not read books.

"How many treatises on constitutional law, or political economy, or works of science are read? How many elaborate poems or books of travels? How much of Boyle, or De Tocqueville, Xenophon, Herodotus, or Percevil? Whence, then, this intelligence and the capacity to talk about themes secular and religious—the acquaintance with science and art—the power to appreciate the beautiful and the grand?

"Next to the Bible, the newspaper,—swift-winged, and everywhere present, flying over fences, shoved under the door, tossed into counting-houses, laid on the work bench, read by all—white and black, German, Irishman, Spaniard, American, old and young, good and bad, sick and well, before breakfast and after tea, Monday morning, Saturday night, Sunday and weekday. The man who neither reads nor takes a newspaper is a curiosity."

The literary taste of the people of Toronto may be judged by the value of the importation of books for the year ending 31st December, 1885. The value for the first quarter was $47,761; the second, $50,076; third, $57,234, and fourth, $63,299, making a total of $218,370, or an average of two dollars a head of the population. The addition of the value of books published in Canada would show a considerable increase in the amount.

The Globe and Mail.

These two great leading political papers—the former representing the Liberal Reform, and the latter the Liberal Conservative party—are published daily, morning and evening, and also weekly. Both wield an immense influence, and have extensive circulation throughout the Dominion, and also in

Great Britain. For literary talent and enterprise, these papers compare with the first-class leading press of New York and London, nothing being wanting to furnish the latest news through the associated press despatches, and through special correspondents, several times a day.

The *Globe* newspaper contains its own history.

THE GLOBE BUILDING.

From 1847 to the time of his death, the writer had a good opportunity of observing the career of the late Hon. George Brown. While the principle of *de mortuis, nil nisi bonum* was not adhered to in his paper, it is only just to say of himself, when he is gone, that, apart from politics, he was a man highly respected for every generous and noble quality. He was genial and pleasant in manner, honorable in his dealings, kind and benevolent in disposition.

In the days when business men were thrown together in the Montreal steamers for a couple of days at a time, the writer has spent pleasant hours in his company, in conversation and chess playing, a game in which he excelled.

THE MAIL BUILDING.

The glory of his career culminated in his coalescence with Hon. John A. Macdonald and the other gentlemen who founded the Confederacy, and the painting now opposite the main entrance to the Parliament Buildings, in commemoration of the great event, and in which the Hon. George Brown is one of the most prominent figures, will perpetuate his name even more than the monument to his memory in the Queen's Park in Toronto.

The World and News.

The *World* has well supplied a want previously felt, in the shape of a one-cent morning paper, and is remarkable for the full reports of all leading topics, as well as ably written editorials, which display a large amount of literary ability and sound common sense, on all questions of the day.

The *News* is the only one-cent paper published both morning and evening, and is fast rising in i... ence, and shows a rapidly increasing circulation both in ... and the city.

The Evening Telegram.

The *Evening Telegram* has for some years past been commonly recognized by the public as the principal paper in Toronto. It is now in the ninth year of its existence. The first number was issued on the 17th April, 1876, and from that time down to the present six editions of it have appeared every afternoon, except on Sundays and holidays. It was founded by its present proprietor, Mr. John Ross Robertson, who had previously been connected with several newspaper enterprises in Toronto, and had acquired a reputation as an energetic and capable man of business. During the first year of its existence it was issued at two cents. It filled an acknowledged want in local journalism, and met with considerable success from the first. In 1877 the price was reduced to one cent, and the effect was at once apparent in a largely extended circulation, which, from that time forward, grew with rapid strides. Advertising patronage was a necessary accompaniment of increased circulation, and by the time the paper had been established three years it had begun to yield a large and lucrative revenue from this source. Of late years it has been subjected to very keen rivalry, but as a local advertising medium it has fully held its own, and is to-day one of the most profitable newspaper enterprises in Canada. It is read by people of all classes, and is more extensively sold on the streets and in the news stores than any other paper in the city. Its present circulation ranges from 17,000 to 19,000; on Saturdays it runs up to 21,000 and 22,000. The *Telegram* was the first daily paper started in this Province on independent or non-partisan political principles. From the date of its first issue until now it has kept itself entirely untrammelled by party ties, and has always been ready to award its approval or its censure upon considerations of merit alone. Speaking in general terms, its pervading tone is decidedly liberal, but it is in no sense the organ of any hard-and-fast school of politicians, and it criticises both sides with the utmost freedom. It has from the first devoted special attention to municipal matters, a feature which has had no slight share in contributing to its very remarkable pecuniary success. It has also been noteworthy for the freshness and comprehensiveness of its local news, in which respect it has generally distanced its larger and older contemporaries. Its editorial notes and articles are light and readable, the writers carefully avoiding the ponderous, unwieldy

THE TELEGRAM BUILDING.

style which mars the effect of so many of the articles in the morning dailies.

The fine building in which the *Telegram* has its headquarters, at the south-west corner of King and Bay Streets, was erected expressly for its accommodation. The structure was completed in 1881, and was fitted up with all the latest improvements, and with little regard to the mere question of expense. The counting-room and the private offices are the handsomest for their size of any in Canada, and the private office of Mr. Robertson is considered by connoisseurs the most artistically furnished office in the Dominion. Indeed, outside of one or two offices in New York and Philadelphia, there is no office in America that will compare with the private office of the *Telegram*. Within its walls there are thousands of dollars' worth of statuary, oil paintings, etchings and bric-a-brac. The etchings of the "Breaking up of the Agamemnon," and "A Lancashire River," by the celebrated etcher, Seymour Haden, are gems; and an oil painting entitled "The old Politician," by Guzzardi, is regarded as one of the finest specimens of that kind of work in the Dominion. This office also contains a marble bust entitled "The Coquette," a veiled figure, by Bazzanti, of Florence, which is so perfect that the lines of the face may be seen distinctly through the marble veil. The velvet decorations, and the leaded glass screen which separates the private office from the main office, are highly commendable pieces of work. The furniture is in keeping. The front office is finished in cherry, mahogany, and Hungarian ash, and the ceiling and cornices, in plaster, are so finished in detail and design, that they attract the attention of not only those who are interested in that kind of work, but the thousands of visitors who yearly visit the office to inspect its contents. The *Telegram* is printed on a Scott Webb Perfecting Press, which has capacity for printing from 25,000 to 30,000 impressions per hour. The appointments of the establishment are fully commensurate with the spirit of enterprise which characterizes the general management. The editorial department is, beyond comparison, the most comfortable to be found in the city. The library and chief editor's room are artistically furnished, and no expense has been spared to render them pleasant for the gentlemen who occupy them. Of the business of the *Telegram* it is almost unnecessary to write. It is not an unusual thing of a Saturday to see sixteen to eighteen columns of the paper occupied by small type advertisements, varying from one to three lines each. The returns from this source are considerable, and it has been stated that they average over one hundred dollars a day which is certainly a large amount for a paper published in Toronto. Take it all for all, the *Evening Telegram* is an honorable monument to the energy and enterprise of its proprietor.

The "Christian Guardian" and Methodist Book and Publishing House.

The *Christian Guardian*, the chief paper of the Methodist Church in Canada for many years, and now the sole organ of United Methodism in Ontario, Quebec, the Northwest, and British Columbia, was started in the fall of 1829. Its first editor was the late Dr. Egerton Ryerson. In 1879 the present editor, Dr. Dewart, issued a jubilee number, for which Dr. Ryerson wrote an article, giving an account of the origin of the paper. He took the long and toilful journey to New York to obtain printing material, spending six days and nights between Lewiston and New York. The first number of the paper was issued on November 22, 1829.

During these early years the *Guardian* did valiant battle for equal religious rights and privileges. Dr. Ryerson was editor for nearly nine years with some breaks, which were filled by Revs. James Richardson, Franklin Metcalf, and Ephraim Evans. In the earlier years of the *Guardian*, before the establishment of the political papers that have since become famous, it was a leading organ of public opinion in a greater degree than since it has become more strictly a religious paper. During its whole course it has vigorously contended for all moral and social reforms, as well as defended the doctrines and usages of

Methodism. Of the editors which succeeded those already named the Rev. Jonathan Scott was in office four years ; the Rev. Geo. F. Playter two years ; the Rev. G. R. Sanderson five years : the Rev. James Spencer nine years ; the Rev. Dr. Jeffers nine years ; the Rev. Dr. Dewart, at the present date (1886), has been in office seventeen years.

REV. EGERTON RYERSON, D.D.

The Wesleyan Book Room was begun at the same time as the publication of the *Guardian*. The publication office was on " March Street, north of the new court-house." It was afterward removed to the present stand on King Street East. At first it was a small bookstore doing a very limited business. But it has steadily grown, till it has become an extensive publishing house. It probably publishes a larger number of books and other publications than any other house in Canada. It gives employment to over one hundred fifty hands; and does a great deal to supply both Methodists and others with wholesome religious literature. The present Book Steward, Rev. William Briggs, D.D., has done much to extend the business.

Free Library.

The good the Free Library is accomplishing in informing and brightening the life of large masses of people should make its operations welcome. The growth of the Toronto Library, owing to its efficient management, has been steady and onward, and its future seems bright and assured. The increasing rate of its book circulation is very marked, and the interest taken by its promoters, is manifested in a practical way by a handsome addition to the reference department in the shape of a donation of some 2,000 volumes, the valuable private collection of Mr. John Hallam, of this city. It may be hoped that others will follow his example, and multiply the resources and attractions of the Public Library until it becomes the pride of Toronto.

The largest private library in the city is that of Professor Goldwin Smith. The Ontario Parliament Library ranks first in importance amongst those of a public character, and contains 25,000 volumes. Next comes Osgoode Hall with 20,000 volumes, chiefly on legal subjects. The University Library is in every way worthy of that splendid institution, and occupies one of its handsomest rooms.

The Canadian Institute has 4,000 volumes; Normal School, 5,000; Free Library, 38,000; Trinity College also possesses a large library which is steadily increasing. There are seventy-two newspapers and periodicals published in Toronto. The five daily papers are the *Globe, Mail, Telegram, World* and *News*. These are all published every morning, except the *Telegram*, which continues as it commenced, as an evening paper. As such it is, perhaps, both as to its popularity and circulation, without an equal in any city of the size of Toronto in the world.

King Street in 1886.

In every city there is some street which is the special resort of ladies for promenading and shopping. Here strangers and visitors first receive their impressions of the wealth and taste of the citizens, and in reporting their opinions to their friends, the effect will be favorable or otherwise just as they are struck with the elegance of the shops and the richness of the goods displayed.

King Street, Toronto, has long been known to travellers as the centre of attraction, but the tourist of 1886, in describing the splendid plate glass fronts of immense establishments especially in the dry goods trade, would completely cast in the shade all previous descriptions.

To illustrate the subject of Toronto's growth and progress, two of the King Street stores are selected, and the first is that of

MESSRS. ROBERT WALKER & SONS.

as being the oldest established house in the trade. While scores, if not hundreds, of dry goods stores on King Street have either changed their entire form, or failed, as the writer knows by experience and losses, there is only one which can date its existence back to 1847, when this sketch commences. The firm of Walker & Sons was originally established in 1836 by the late Mr. Robert Walker, and in 1847 the firm was Walker & Hutchinson. In that year two stone-fronted buildings, the first in the city, were erected by Mr. Peter Paterson and Mr. Walker, at a cost of $30,000. In 1867 Mr. Walker acquired the whole site, pulled the two buildings down and erected the present magnificent building, at a cost of $50,000, and since that time it has been enlarged and increased to its present immense proportions. Every visitor to the city is at once struck with the imposing appearance of this establishment, which is, indeed, an ornament to the city, and a self-evident proof of its wonderful progress and advancement. The front of the building is of ornamented cut stone, surmounted by a large figure of a lion, the trade mark of the firm. For the first thirty feet the front of the structure is entirely composed of plate glass, running from the sidewalk up to a massive ornamental iron girder, extending the entire width of the building. The windows and doorway contain over 1,500 square feet of glass. The interior is beautifully finished, and in addition to the front, light is supplied still further from an ornamental dome, which adds greatly to the general effect.

The premises extend to Colborne Street, where there is another entrance, and altogether it may be said to be the finest retail dry goods and clothing house in the Dominion. The staff consists of nearly one hundred salesmen, cashiers and bookkeepers, and the average stock amounts to about a quarter of a million dollars.

In 1847 this firm and Mr. Peter Paterson were the only retail importers in Toronto. The business is conducted on the departmental system, and the European markets are visited semi-annually by one of the firm, their immense capital giving unsurpassed advantages in purchasing direct from the manufacturers.

While King Street has always had the reputation of possessing the finest shops, as London has Regent Street, New York its Broadway, Boston its Washington Street, and Chicago its State Street, there are in each of these certain houses distinguished as the leaders of fashion and as caterers to the highest taste. The house of

W. A. MURRAY & CO.

may, in this respect, be considered as the "Swan & Edgars," or " Marshall & Snelgroves," of Toronto, as in this splendid establishment may be found the richest classes of goods, to meet the requirements of the most refined and wealthy or the most fashionable. From the "layettes," to the "trousseaux," for wedding or christening, ball or opera, every want can be supplied by "modistes," "costumieres," and "coiffeures," not excelled by Mr. Worth himself. So perfect are the arrangements in every department, that a special room is provided, where may be seen, by artificial light, the effect of shades for evening dresses, at any hour of the day.

The senior partner, Mr. W. A. Murray, having graduated in some of the large houses in Britain, two of which are already described, and having been a buyer in 1854, when the present business was established, brought to Canada all the experience and judgment already acquired; and, devoting all his attention to the buying department since that time, by continuous visits to the British and foreign markets has not only kept abreast of the fashions, but has had the advantage of leading them in Toronto by anticipating the styles and designs in course of preparation for the coming season.

The fact of Mr. Murray having crossed the Atlantic this season for the one hundred and twenty-fifth time, is a sure guarantee of the experience he brings to bear on this department of the business.

The splendid plate glass front of this establishment extends from 17 to 27 King Street East, and here are displayed the finest productions of British and continental manufactures. The interior arrangements are simply perfect in every detail, the departments being so connected that each harmonizes with the other, and the light has been studied with such artistic skill as to be adapted to each class of goods, advantageous alike to the buyer and seller.

Every article in woollen and linen drapery, silks, hosiery, lace goods, haberdashery, house furnishings, including the finest curtain materials, millinery and mantles, is to be found in this well-regulated establishment.

The staff consists of about one hundred salesmen, besides cashiers and bookkeepers, and from one hundred to two hundred workwomen are employed, according to the season, in the dressmaking and millinery departments. Mr. John Drynan, a member of the firm, has the general management, and Toronto may well take a pride in this, as a representative house in its line, of the wonderful growth and progress that are still going on.

The Art of Pottery.

While other arts, as painting and sculpture, have been cultivated to please the taste and delight the eye, the art of making vessels of earthenware for domestic use, and in particular of turning them into shape on a wheel, is of very remote antiquity, and was undoubtedly suggested by the instinct of necessity.

In Egypt, all the processes of mixing the clay, of turning, baking, and polishing vessels and vases, are represented in the tombs of Thebes and Beni Hassan, and to-day may be seen in the potteries of Staffordshire—as witnessed by the writer in his frequent visits to the pottery district—the same kind of wheel, and the potter moulding the clay into beautiful shapes of great variety by his manipulation while the wheel revolves. No art has a more wonderful record of self-sacrificing and heroic perseverance and endurance in experiment, nor more wonderful success in discovery in bringing it to its present perfection, than the art of pottery.

The Palissy's, Wedgewoods and others, by their chemical research have produ*** the variety of enamelled and variegated ware which rival *** eauty the finest china, which, according to Chinese chronology, has been made in that country for thousands of years.

In Chelsea, porcelain was made so beautiful that George II. bestowed the light of his countenance upon it, and it became all the rage; one service was purchased by the King for £1,200.

Then comes the Wedgewood ware, manufactured by the Wedgewood's, of Burslem (a place well remembered by the writer as having spent the coldest night of his life there),—at first, tableware, dense, durable, well glazed and cheap; then the Queen's ware; then terra cotta, a kind of pottery in which Wedgewood was enabled to imitate porphyry, granite, Egyptian pebble, and other beautiful stones; then basalt, or black ware; then white porcelain biscuit, having a smooth wax-like appearance; then jasper, or white porcelainic biscuit, of exquisite delicacy and beauty.

But although the Chelsea and Wedgewood ware were both

beautiful, and are now sought out by connoisseurs,—as much as five guineas a piece for dessert plates, and twenty-five guineas for a couple of tea cups having been paid,—it was a West-of-England man who discovered the clay in Cornwall from which the pure porcelain is made, and the clay is largely shipped to Staffordshire to be manufactured.

The discovery of felspar, at Belleek, County Donegal, Ireland (only celebrated before for the catch of eels), led to the establishment of the pottery there, and the most beautiful ware is produced. Hand-painted dishes were shown to the writer when visiting this establishment (just six miles from the Atlantic coast), the prices of which were from twenty to fifty guineas each; the painting being done by first-class artists.

The terra cotta ware at Torquay, in Devon, is very beautiful and fashionable, as are also the Royal Worcester and Royal Derby ware, placing the English manufactures high up in the scale of pottery, as seen at Kensington and other places, where the largest collection of the productions of all countries are on permanent exhibition. To add one more to the list of enterprises in Ireland, the Vodrian ware, manufactured in Dublin, deserves special notice, being awarded the first prize medal at Cork Exhibition, in 1883.

MR. GLOVER HARRISON,

of the China Hall, King Street, has for the past twenty-five years made this art his study, and in catering for the citizens of Toronto has done much to educate the taste of the people in this branch of trade, combining the useful with the ornamental more than in any other department; while on the other hand his efforts have been appreciated by all classes, from the highest, who have expended their wealth in furnishing and decorating their houses (showing as much as in anything else the wonderful progress of Toronto), down to the humblest, who have suited themselves in every article necessary for comfort and convenience. Mr. Harrison visits all these sources of production periodically, including Limoges and Sevres in France, and Dresden, in Germany. A visit to his galleries of art treasures will be found exceedingly interesting and instructive and everything in glass, as well as earthenware, to furnish the mansion, hotel, or cottage, will be found in endless variety and beauty.

New Buildings Approaching Completion.

Bank of Montreal, College of Pharmacy, Manning's Arcade, Orange Hall.

Buildings Proposed to be Erected this Year.

Young Men's Christian Association Building, St. Alban's Cathedral, St. Mary's Roman Catholic Church, Sherbourne Street Methodist Church, Parliament Buildings, Court House, Quebec Bank.

The Manning Arcade

is of the Italian Renaissance style, ornamented with polished granite pillars, and sculptured emblematic figures, two being caryatides supporting entablatures on each side, and one male figure in the centre representing Labor, which add much to the beauty of the design.

To form a perfect arcade, it will be extended to the north, and is an ornament to King street.

New Bank of Montreal.

This beautiful building illustrates in a remarkable manner the progress of architecture in the city.

The material is Ohio stone, and the style of the composite order of architecture, in which the Corinthian largely predominates, and is the most ornate of all classical styles. The Corinthian is the most elaborate of all Grecian orders. The merit of its invention is ascribed to Callimachus, a celebrated sculptor of Athens, about 540 B.C. He is said to have taken the idea from observing the leaves of the acanthus, growing round a basket which had been placed with some favorite trinkets upon the grave of a young Corinthian lady—the stalks which rose among the leaves having been formed into slender volutes by a square tile which covered the basket.

The capital is larger and more ornamental than in the other orders, spreading in the form of a basket, and commingling the richest and lightest vegetation with the decorations of previous orders.

The pilasters of the Bank of Montreal are richly sculptured, the designs, surmounted by mask heads, emblematic of various subjects. On the south are: (1) Commerce, (2) Music, (3) Architecture, (4) Agriculture. On the east front are: (1) Industry, (2) Science, (3) Literature, (4) Arts; and over the main entrance are the arms of the Bank of Montreal.

This splendid work has been executed by Messrs. Holbrook & Mollington, architectural sculptors, who also performed the fine work on the Custom House. Messrs. Darling & Currie are the architects.

The interior will be superbly finished in stucco, and being one complete room, with dome light, will present a magnificent appearance.

Toronto Post Office in 1886.

No greater evidence of the growth and the expansion of the commerce of Toronto can be given than by a comparison of the business of the Post Office Department during the period covered by the present sketch.

When the present office of the Receiver-General, on Toronto Street was built for a new post office, none but the most sanguine doubted its capacity for all its requirements for many years to come, but while it was still a comparatively new building it was soon found to be quite inadequate to the rapidly-growing business of the city, and in 1873 the present beautiful structure was erected.

A more suitable situation could not have been chosen than that on which it stands, surrounded, as it is, by buildings in every way worthy of the neighbourhood, and in close proximity to the business portion of the city.

The building is of three stories, faced with cut stone, elaborately ornamented, and the internal arrangements are admirably adapted to the never-ceasing business transacted.

A side door at the western end of the building leads, by a handsome staircase, to the offices of Mr. M. Sweetnam, the Post Office Inspector, and his assistant and other officials.

The present staff consists of Mr. Thos. C. Patteson, postmaster; Mr. John Carruthers, assistant-postmaster; 5 first-class 12 second-class, and 49 third-class clerks.

There are 74 letter carriers, 3 caretakers, and 7 porters; 95 street letter boxes, and 3 branch post offices.

Through the politeness of the postmaster the following statistics are given for the year ended 31st December, 1885:

Amount of money orders issued	$309,203
Amount of money orders paid	1,356,163
Number of orders paid	80,086
Amount of deposits in Post Office Savings Bank	$495,364
Amount of postage stamps sold	228,751
Number of letters delivered by letter carriers, exclusive of box holders and general delivery	7,937,461
Number of letters posted	11,288,680
Number of post cards posted	3,328,260

In the month of February no less than nineteen English mails were despatched from Toronto—fifteen *via* New York and four *via* Halifax—and this in twenty-four working days, and in March, April, and May about twenty each month; so that a daily mail to England from Toronto may be looked for in the near future.

Toronto as a Place of Residence.

If the city possesses all the advantages to which reference has been made, it will be admitted that no element in the constitution of a great city is wanting. The capitalist who would invest money to advantage can here find a promising field for enterprise. There is also plenty of room for more manufacturing industries.

The man of leisure, with fixed income, may find in Toronto a

TORONTO POST OFFICE.

delightful home, and live just as his means may allow, even to the enjoyment of luxury. The mechanic and tradesman can, by industry and economy, secure a comfortable home on easy terms, and in Toronto every reasonable wish may be gratified, and the new settler find a welcome to any class of society which may be congenial to his taste.

Governors-General of Canada since 1847.

Earl of Elgin, Sir Edmund Head, Lord Monck, Sir John Young (Lord Lisgar), Earl of Dufferin, Marquis of Lorne, and Marquis of Lansdowne.

Lieutenant-Governors of Ontario.

Major-General Stisted, Sir W. P. Howland, Hon. John Crawford, Hon. D. A. Macdonald, and Hon. John Beverley Robinson.

Mayors of Toronto.

William Lyon Mackenzie, R. B. Sullivan, George Gurnett, John Powell, George Munro, Henry Sherwood, William Henry Boulton, John G. Bowes, Joshua G. Beard, John Beverley Robinson, G. W. Allan, John Hutchinson, David B. Reid, Adam Wilson, Francis H. Medcalf, James E. Smith, S. B. Harman, George D'Arcy Boulton, Joseph Sheard, Alexander Manning Angus Morrison, James Beaty, jun., W. B. McMurrich, Arthur R. Boswell, Alexander Manning, W. H. Howland.

Extent of City.

Total number of miles of streets, one hundred and sixty-six; of which forty miles are cedar blocked, ten miles are cedar and gravel, fifty-four miles are macadamized, and the remainder graded or unimproved. Miles of sidewalks, two hundred and fifty. The work of substituting stone and other material in place of wood has commenced, and the experiment of granolithic *versus* stone will soon be tested on King Street. The stone now used is quarried in Pelee Island, and is consequently cheaper than imported stone. If blocks sufficient to extend the whole width of the sidewalk could be procured in Canada it would be found the most durable.

Toronto Street Railway Company.

Those who are acquainted with Philadelphia know that with its population of nearly three-quarters of a million, there are no tenement houses of four to eight stories, in which a number of families are crowded together, with the terrible risk from fire. Covering more ground than New York, it affords space on which every family can have a home, and this is almost entirely due to the street car service affording easy access to the farthest limits of the city, and around Fairmount Park, with its 3,000 acres, and to the manufacturing suburbs of Germantown.

Applying this to Toronto, it must be admitted that the spread and expansion of the city has been in proportion to the extension of the street car service, and the increase in the value of property in the suburbs is due to the same cause. No city in America can boast of a more efficient street car service than that furnished by the Toronto Street Railway Company, and nothing but very large capital and enterprise could have brought it to its present state of efficiency.

To interrupt this traffic would be to throw Toronto back to the "jolting" times of a quarter of a century ago, and reduce the value of property in all the distant portions of the city. A company which has contributed so much to the health, comfort and convenience of the citizens, and to the enhancement of the value of property in and around the city, as well as giving employment to such a large number of men, must be regarded as public benefactors, and are fully entitled to every financial benefit that may accrue from their enterprise while lawfully and justly carried on.

The Company owns sixty miles of track, and employs three hundred and seventy-five men. The number of horses in the service is seven hundred and fifty, number of cars one hundred and sixty-five sleighs and omnibuses one hundred and sixty. The value of the buildings erected by the Company is about $250,000, with others in course of erection. The entire stock of the Company is owned by Hon. Frank Smith and Mr. R. M. Keiley.

Street Traffic.

There is no city of the size of Toronto, in Great Britain or America, which shows so extensive street traffic, as the writer knows from personal observation. Having said this, the rest of the world might be included. This arises chiefly from the position Toronto occupies as the great distributing centre of the Dominion. The receiving and shipping of imported and manufactured goods, which are sent to every point from Halifax to Vancouver—the representatives of Toronto houses now regularly visiting the whole of this immense field—have created this wonderful amount of business traffic on our streets, evidencing the solid and substantial progress the city has made in a comparatively short time.

Had our Rip Van Winkle, instead of coming from Holland, been acquainted with the topography of London, and in some day during the week of the Industrial Exhibition "waked up" from his long sleep, at the Dominion Bank (leaving out the powdered wigs, plush breeches, silk stockings, and gold-headed sticks of the footmen, and throwing in continuous lines of street cars), he might naturally fancy himself at Oxford Circus, with Oxford Street stretching away at one side, and the Regent Street Quadrant at the other; or should a "block" occur, as in the case of some procession, might imagine he was standing somewhere between the Bank of England, the Royal Exchange and the Mansion House; and as to the wholesale trade, if at the corner of Scott and Front Streets, might imagine himself in St. Paul's Churchyard, with a view from Ludgate Hill on the west, to New Cannon Street on the east, where are to be seen the finest specimens of warehouse architecture in London.

Returning to Yonge and King Streets, he would find carriages of every style, private and public, including phætons, broughams, waggons, coupes, market carts, dog carts, rockaways, pony carriages and hansoms in endless variety, also drays, lorries, merchants', manufacturers', express, and tradesmen's delivery wagons,—all producing a scene of bustle and activity only to be witnessed in a great and prosperous city, and showing a marvellous contrast with the appearance of the streets in 1847.

The Model Wholesale Dry Goods Warehouse of the Dominion.

It is no disparagement of other large wholesale importing dry goods houses, of which Toronto is so justly proud, and to which much of the description that may be given will apply, to select one as *par excellence* the model house of the Dominion; and if a knowledge of its history from the commencement furnishes a qualification for the work, the writer can safely undertake it.

Having had the pleasure of knowing Mr. John Macdonald before he commenced business, and having been our best customer for the two years he remained in the retail trade, I had an opportunity of witnessing the success of his first venture. His rare judgment as a buyer, and carefulness as a financier, gave him, from the very first, a sound position, resulting in a decision to seek a wider field for his enterprise. The "pent up" confines of a retail store did not afford scope for his ambition, and while becoming parties to the transfer of his business, it was with regret we lost a customer who had, in addition to meeting every engagement, promptly and honorably acquired sufficient capital to embark in the wholesale importing trade.

On his first visit to Britain his arrangements were made on such a solid basis as to be a guarantee of the success which followed. The system of buying from large general houses had prevailed almost entirely in Canada and the Maritime Provinces, and this Mr. Macdonald, at the very outset, avoided. He saw no reason why he should not go to the fountain-head of supply, and give his customers the benefit of the intermediate profits previously enjoyed by these large houses in London, Glasgow and Manchester, and whatever commission he paid for his introduction to manufacturers was more than made up by cash discounts.

The saying that "goods well bought are half sold" was in this instance soon verified. Taking Mr. Lyle as a junior partner and buyer, with goods purchased on such advantageous terms,

JOHN MACDONALD & CO.'S WAREHOUSE.

the firm had no occasion to "push trade," but, as Mr. Macdonald at the time remarked to the writer, he "would wait for customers to come, and then dictate his own terms," or in other words, "the goods would sell themselves."

On the retirement of Mr. Lyle from the firm, and his departure for Africa, where he is now doing a lucrative trade in ostriches and coffee, the facilities afforded by the bonding system through the United States led Messrs. Macdonald & Co. to introduce the system of having a resident buyer in Europe and by weekly shipments afford merchants an opportunity of assorting their stocks from time to time, thereby precluding the necessity of laying in a stock for the whole season, as had hitherto been the rule, and also saving a large amount of interest and the accumulation of bad stock.

This formed another element in the rapid growth and extension of the business, as buyers were attracted from all parts to select from the weekly arrivals. From that time to the present, the business has been marked with uninterrupted prosperity, and has attained to a magnitude unequalled in the Dominion, and a fame co-extensive with the great inter-oceanic highway, now successfully completed from the Atlantic to the Pacific.

If a visitor to New York wants to see a grand business and splendid system, he finds his way to A. T. Stewart & Co., or H. B. Chaffin & Co.; if in London, he will go to Cook, Sons & Co., St. Paul's Churchyard, the Fore St. Warehouse Co., or J. & R. Morley's; if in Manchester, he will visit Rylands & Sons, Bannerman's, or Philips's; and so in Toronto he will be directed to the house of John Macdonald & Co. The situation of the warehouse is quite unique, having equally fine frontages on Wellington Street, Nos. 21-27, and on Front Street, Nos. 28-34.

The building, which is six stories in height, is massive and plainly elegant, and in every respect adapted for the business. The light is perfect, both from the north and south, with additional advantages in this respect from the west side, thus affording buyers the greatest facility for inspecting the stock, while the arrangements for the display of goods, affording perfect access to each section, make it easy and pleasant.

To most people visiting an establishment of this kind, their ideas are influenced either as consumers, who look upon these goods as supplying one of the great wants of mankind, or as producers, who are interested in the sale of the goods, and wish for more orders, while to the buyer the chief consideration is as to how much profit he could make out of such or such a lot of goods.

To anyone who has had connection with the home markets and manufacturing districts, his associations immediately connect him with the sources of supply, and as every article, from a pin or needle to the finest productions of the looms of Lyons or Nottingham, has a history which would in itself form an interesting paper, he cannot resist the impression made on his mind of the immense influence which a great distributing centre such as this, between the producers and the consumers, must necessarily have on the thousands who are dependent not only for the comforts but the necessaries of life on the success of such a business. All through the process of manufacture, from the inventor to the designer, and then through the manufacturer and shipper, till the retail merchant and consumer are reached, what vast interests are concerned in the management of such an enterprise on both sides of the Atlantic!

What buyer, who has taken a run through some of the large manufactories of Lancashire or Yorkshire, and conversed with some of the humble yet intelligent operatives, has not been asked whether he had brought good orders from Canada, and has not seen their faces brighten up if he could give an encouraging answer? While they have the world for a market, they know more of Canada and Australia than of any other country.

The aim of the firm throughout has been to systematize the business after the model of first-class British houses, and to accomplish this successfully the departmental system has been most efficiently adopted and carried out.

To give to each buyer the entire management of his own department, and throw on him the responsibility, is the principle which has been found to work so successfully in all the British warehouses, and Messrs. Macdonald & Co.'s business has been no exception to the rule. The business is divided into departments, from the entering room to the warehouse and counting-house, each having a recognized head, and the discretionary power afforded furnishes a motive to excel which no other principle could effect.

To attempt a detailed account of the working of the business would far exceed the limits of these pages, and nothing beyond a cursory glance can be given. There are six principal departments, which, with their subdivisions, are as follows :—

STAPLES.—Prints and general Manchester goods, flannels and blankets, linens and jute goods.

DRESS GOODS.—Hosiery and gloves, ribbons and corsets, gents' furnishings.

MANTLES AND SHAWLS.—Silks, satins, crapes, laces, muslins, and embroideries, british and German knitted goods.

WOOLLENS.—Canadian tweeds, imported woollens, rubber goods.

HABERDASHERY.—Wools and wool work, British and foreign fancy goods, Japanese and papier mache goods.

CARPETS AND OIL CLOTHS.—Brussels and tapestries, supers and three-ply carpets, Dutch and hemp carpets, upholsterers' goods, raw silk and jute coverings, damasks, reps, ferries, plushes, piano and furniture felts, etc.

These six departments are managed by experienced buyers, who visit the markets periodically, making the home office in Manchester their rendezvous, and where orders are sent between seasons to the resident buyers.

A reference to the chapter on "buying in Europe" will show the ground to be gone over by these gentlemen in making their purchases, and, in addition to this, large orders are placed for goods manufactured in other countries, as China and Japan, which are not visited.

The firm employs thirteen travellers, extending their operations from the Atlantic to the Pacific, and altogether the staff comprises about 100 in all departments.

Mr. Paul Campbell has the entire management of the financial and general conduct of the business.

Corsets.

Whatever may be the opinion as to the use of corsets, from a hygienic point of view, whether as improvers or supporters of "the female form divine," it is certain that the trade is one of vast proportions, and perhaps with the exception of Japan and some barbarous or semi-civilized nations, the corset is considered as an indispensable part of female attire in every country. Germany, France, Great Britain, the United States, and Canada give employment to thousands of girls in this suitable and appropriate branch of industry.

THE TELFER AND HAROLD MANUFACTURING CO.

of this city is selected for special notice as an evidence of the progress of the city in this branch of manufactures, in giving employment to a large number of operatives, and as being devoted exclusively to the manufacturing for the wholesale trade of the Dominion, no goods being sold to the retail trade.

The premises occupied by this firm were built especially for them, having every appointment and arrangement for the carrying on of the business in the most convenient manner, and for the comfort of the employees.

The writer, who for several years represented in America the leading corset manufacturers of England, had much pleasure in inspecting the various processes through which these goods pass, in the establishment of Messrs. Telfer & Harold, and found the division of labor so perfectly carried out, and the machinery so complete, as to reduce the cost of production to a minimum. The insertion of eyelets by a machine is done so rapidly as to be well worth a visit, and all through the various stages to the fine embroidery work, which is a marvel of skill and taste, every arrangement is perfect and the best talent employed.

The firm has agents in Victoria, B.C., Winnipeg, Man., Montreal, and Halifax.

The Lace and Embroidery Trade.

Having been the first exclusive importer of these goods in Toronto, and having had an intimate acquaintance with the trade for twenty-five years, the writer has pleasure in noticing the establishment of the firm of

WHITE, JOSELIN & CO.

who are at present, and have for many years been the only exclusive importers of these goods in the wholesale trade in the Dominion.

The enormous capital required to pay designers who are constantly employed to produce novelties to meet the insatiable demands of fashion and trade, and the necessity of a large export trade such as England has to all the markets of the world, renders it probable that in this branch of trade Canada must continue to import for many years to come. Even the United States, with its immense population, cannot in this particular manufacture compete with Nottingham, only one factory of lace curtains having so far attempted the production of lace goods.

Lace is not a describable article. Malines has long been famous for a lace coarser and stronger than that of Brussels. Mechlin lace, properly so called, has been surpassed by that of Nottingham.

Malines lace is made on a cushion with a battalion of pins stuck into it. Each young worker has two small knobby sticks in her hand, to which are attached shining white threads, and with these she manoeuvres among the pins with a rapidity that is surprising. Thread by thread the delicate fabric progresses to its completion. All this work is done by the girls in their own homes, there being no manufactory. In contrast with this is the Jacquard loom, which is a most wonderful piece of mechanism. The patterns of Nottingham lace being registered, each manufacturer jealously guards against any infringement of his designs; and yet a single thread of difference may be sufficient to evade the penalty of infringement. A case occurred some years ago where a suit was entered for infringement, and before a decision could be given, a lawyer was commissioned to go from London to Nottingham to see the pattern actually produced on the loom.

The extent of the trade may be measured in millions of yards. France and Belgium supply hand-made pillow lace, as do the English counties of Buckingham, Hertford, Nottingham, and Devon. Limerick, in Ireland, was long celebrated for her lace, which was brought to such perfection that a pair of gloves, enclosed in a silver-mounted and clasped walnut shell, was a usual and very acceptable present, but the great trade at this time is in machine lace from Nottingham, Honiton and Tiverton.

The embroidery trade has also changed its seat. Formerly thousands of females in Ireland and Scotland found employment in what was called "sprigging" muslin, but at present the trade is almost exclusively carried on by machinery in Switzerland, and from these sources of supply Messrs. White, Joselin & Co., who visit the markets regularly, import their goods, which are distributed from Toronto all over the Dominion.

The spacious warehouse occupied by the firm contains four extensive floors, to which access is had by an elevator, and all are fully stocked with complete lines of the various manufactures of Great Britain, France, Belgium and Switzerland, comprising the greatest novelties in the trade.

The senior partner, Mr. White, has brought an experience of 25 years to the successful carrying on of the business, and is ably supported by the Messrs. Joselin Brothers.

In addition to the lace and embroidery trade, the handkerchief department is made very attractive in every class adapted to the ladies' trade.

Yonge Street in 1886.

If the writer on the Montreal *Canadian Illustrated News* in 1871, who spoke of the "great gulf" between the frequenters of King and Yonge Streets, the latter, according to his statement, being the resort of the "middle class and the beggar,' were to make such a statement in 1886, he would deserve to be tarred and feathered. The rapid progress made on Yonge Street as a business thoroughfare has already placed it on an equal footing with the aristocratic King, and the carriages to be seen any day lining this street, testify to the high class of trade it has secured.

By way of contrast with the time of the first dry goods store in 1849, amongst a number of splendid shops which now attract crowds of customers, one is selected as illustrative of our subject, and in accordance with the principle laid down in reference especially to Toronto as an importing centre.

The building known as Page's Block, erected by the late John Hillyard Cameron, was considered the finest block of retail stores in the city.

MESSRS. T. EATON & CO.

having built up a large business at the corner of Queen Street, sought to extend it, and for this object secured the stores where their present building now stands.

When Mr. Eaton commenced pulling down the fine front of the building, people were amazed at what appeared to be folly and destruction, but when the present front, with its splendid plate glass windows and lofty floors, made its appearance, their wonder was turned to admiration, and a splendid addition had been made to the palatial stores of Toronto.

The internal arrangements are complete in every respect. Thirty-five departments, embracing not only everything belonging to the dry goods trade, including carpets, millinery, and house furnishing goods, but also various classes goods a little distinct from the regular branches (as is the custom of the mammoth establishments in Britain to add boots and shoes, perfumery, toilet and fancy articles to the stock of drapery goods), are all managed with perfect system and discipline.

Whoever would have predicted in 1847, when there was not a single dry goods house on Yonge Street, that such an establishment would be found in 1886, would certainly be the subject of ridicule, and especially should he have ventured to say that the sales of one hundred and fifty salesmen and ladies would be all for cash, he would be put down as a dreamer. It is no exaggeration to say that the cash sales of this house exceed those of all the stores in Toronto in 1847. This will be admitted as a proof of the "wonderful growth and progress" of the city during that period.

The facilities for purchasing are on a scale corresponding with the arrangement of the departments. Passenger elevators constantly in operation afford pleasant access to each floor, and the one-price system, now thoroughly established by all first-class houses in Toronto, is at once satisfactory and honorable to buyer and seller.

The system of checking sales and giving change is quite up to the best either in Britain or the United States, and the establishment reflects the highest credit on the enterprise of the firm and on the city of Toronto.

Mr. Eaton is still further extending by connecting with a new wing which will have a front on Queen Street, and, when completed, will compare with the finest stores in Great Britain or America, forming at once a promenade, arcade, and grand bazaar.

Great Increase in Imports.

Comparative imports at Montreal and Toronto for year ending 30th June, 1882:—Toronto, $19,311,210; Montreal, $45,611,927.

Duty on importations for month of January:—

	1885.	1886.
Montreal	$552,804	$497,735
Toronto	281,583	296,350

Total imports for fiscal year ending 30th June, 1886, $18,310,145; duty, $3,419,265; average, 18.67 per cent.

In 1847 Toronto imported one-eighth as much as Montreal; in 1849 Toronto increased to over one-fourth, and as above, in 1886, to over one-half.

The amount of importations at Toronto for the first ten days of February, 1886, was equal to the amount entered during the whole year of 1848, and the duty collected for one week of 1886, equal to the whole of the same year.

The Arcade.

The front entrance is on Yonge street, to the beauty of which its imposing cut stone facade, with its wide archway and Egyptian pillars in bas-relief, are a valuable addition.

The spacious passage-way is furnished with shops, resembling

YONGE STREET ARCADE.

the Burlington Arcade in London, glittering with much that is attractive, and a stairway leads to gallery, offices, and studios.

Let us hope that in the future it will increase in attractiveness, when every spot will be fully occupied, making it a place of resort not unlike the Palais Royal in Paris.

Summer Resorts.

QUEEN'S PARK.

Just west of the Osgoode Hall on Queen Street West will be found a beautiful avenue of nearly a mile in length. Chestnut and maple trees flank the carriage drive and pathway, which in the vista open out upon the Queen's Park. Going north the intersection of the Yonge Street Avenue is reached, and we pass from the grateful shade of the long line of chestnuts into the verduous sunlight of the open Park, one hundred acres in all, including the University grounds, which have been fenced off from the city property. The Park is a favorite resort during the hot weather, and contains the University Buildings, Observatory (Meteorological Office), Wycliffe College, Volunteers' and Hon. George Brown's monuments, and a score of beautiful villas; it is also the site selected for the erection of the new Provincial Parliament Buildings.

EXHIBITION PARK.

These grounds, originally used exclusively by the Industrial Exhibition Association, have for some time been thrown open to the public all the year round, except for two weeks in September, during the Exhibition.

Under the superintendence of Mr. Chambers, the Commissioner of Parks, these grounds have assumed a most beautiful appearance, being laid out in the most artistic manner as landscape gardens, and having a profusion of shrubs and flowerbeds, which increase in beauty from season to season.

Further improvements are in progress this season—new roads are being made, new sidewalks laid down, a number of new flower-beds have been formed, and the whole of the grounds will this year present a more beautiful and attractive appearance than they have at any previous Exhibition.

LORNE PARK.

This favorite resort is beautifully situated on the north shore of Lake Ontario, fourteen miles from Toronto, and can be reached in twenty-five minutes by rail, or forty-five minutes by water. It commands a splendid view of the lake. It has recently been laid out in cottage and camp lots, of which there are two hundred, with main avenue of one hundred feet, and streets of sixty-six feet, leaving fifty acres for recreation grounds.

The grounds will be lighted by electricity, a proper water supply and system of drainage arranged for, and everything has been done to make this the most pleasant summer resort in Ontario.

No intoxicating liquor will be allowed to be sold on the grounds, or on the steamer plying to the park.

Canadian Pacific Railway.

On the first of November a message was received by the Governor-General at Ottawa from Her Majesty, congratulating the Dominion Government on the accomplishment of the great work; and on the ninth of the same month, Sir John A. Macdonald received a telegram from Mr. Van Horne, and the Premier of British Columbia, congratulating him on the completion of the C.P.R. Mr. Sandford Fleming also telegraphed, stating that the first through train had accomplished the journey from Montreal to Vancouver in five days, and that the trip would shortly be accomplished in four days.

At a banquet given in Montreal to Sir George Stephens and Hon. D. A. Smith, the former said in his speech: "When Sir John A. Macdonald stated in London that the termini of the Canadian Pacific Railway were Liverpool and Hong Kong, he was not indulging in a flight of eloquence. He was stating in simple language a sober fact.

By the proposed line of steamers from Vancouver to the far East, the crossing point of the Canadian Pacific Railway will be reached. In 1861 it took from ten to twelve days for troops to be conveyed from Halifax to Quebec. In 1870, during the Red River rebellion, it took eleven weeks from Quebec to Red River, and ninety-five days from Toronto to Winnipeg. Now the whole distance can be traversed in six days. Troops and stores can reach the Pacific coast from Liverpool in thirteen or fourteen days.

In summer, from Montreal to Vancouver can be done in four and a half days; in winter, Halifax to Vancouver in six days. With steamers making fourteen to fifteen knots, the passage from Vancouver to Yokohama can be made in twelve days, from England to Japan in twenty-six days, from England to Hong Kong and Shanghai in thirty-four days. From England to Hong Kong, *via* Brindisi, takes forty to forty-four days, and *via* Gibralter, forty-nine to fifty-three days; from England to Calcutta, thirty-eight days; and *via* Halifax, adding seven days for Atlantic passage, the distance can be done in twenty-eight days.

Lord Lorne, in his article on the Canadian Pacific Railway, says: " Had not the Americans derived new life and hope from the time that civilization was carried inward from the coast, and the mere fringe of the New England colonies and the Carolinas and New York had blossomed into a nation controlling the Mississippi, and master of all the regions which pour their wealth through the great market place on the shore of Michigan—the city of Chicago." And his lordship asks, " Why should not Canada have its Chicago ?"

Either his lordship had forgotten to mention Toronto, or he did not wish to show any partiality, as he must know that Canada has her Chicago, and that can be no other than Toronto, situated on Lake Ontario, in a position corresponding almost exactly with Chicago on Lake Michigan. Toronto is quite as favorably situated as regards her water communication, and much nearer the seaboard; and as a centre of railways equally well situated, and commanding a larger extent of country for trade, which will be secured to Toronto as quickly as the great Northwest is settled. Even now her trade extends from ocean to ocean, whereas Chicago has no trade whatever to the eastward, and is chiefly confined to the States of Illinois, Indiana, Iowa, Wisconsin and Minnesota, and has to compete with St. Louis, Milwaukee and St. Paul; and if her trade has developed to such large proportions in half a century, what may Toronto not expect, with her immense field for enterprise, during the same period? Surely it must become even greater than the trade of Chicago.

From 1877 to 1886. 335

Dominion Day, 1886.

The nineteenth birthday of Confederation, amidst the usual celebrations that took place, was especially remarkable at Winnipeg by the arrival there of the first through passenger train for Vancouver, which left Montreal on June 28th. Its arrival was greeted with a grand military display, the firing of a *feu de joie*, thunder of artillery, and the cheers of the assembled multitude.

The civic address to the President and Directors of the Canadian Pacific Railway contained the following: "We have no doubt as to the influence this stupendous work will have upon the commercial progress of the grand old Empire of which we are proud to form a part.

"We know that the consummation of this work will unite and consolidate an extensive British Colonial Empire in America, and that by placing our own girdle around the Continent territories now lying waste and desolate will be brought under the beneficent influence of civilization and commerce, maintaining in British hands that supremacy that would appear to be the heritage of the Anglo-Saxon and Celtic races."

This was the first train run on the twenty-four hour time system introduced by the C.P.R. Co. The train to connect left Toronto on the 28th at seventeen (five p.m.) o'clock.

This train arrived at Port Moody on the 5th July, and was received with great enthusiasm. The Victoria band playing "See the Conquering Hero Comes."

Toronto Zoological Gardens.

Toronto is the first city of its size to have established zoological gardens. To Alderman Harry Piper belongs the credit of having established gardens in this city.

The nucleus, at first consisting of two white mice, soon became the centre of a collection of a sufficient size to warrant their exhibition, for which a small fee was charged. This collection soon increased to such an extent as to necessitate the use of a large space of ground on Front Street, where it still grew and proved a grand success both financially and as a source of amusement and recreation to citizens and visitors.

In 1884 the Zoological and Acclimatization Society was chartered by letters patent, Mr. Harry Piper being appointed managing director. The removal of the animals to the new buildings in Exhibition Park entitles the institution to the name of Zoological Gardens, and the arrangements for future exhibitions are complete in every respect. Visitors can have access to the gardens by a choice of conveyance both by land and water, and during the time of the Industrial Exhibition the electric railway will land passengers on the spot. The Society has built a station on the Great Western Division of the Grand Trunk Railway, also landing passengers at the gardens.

The buildings are arranged for the classification of animals, carnivorous, herbivorous and omnivorous, with provision for aquatic and amphibious animals also, and will be largely increased to provide for further accessions to the collection.

Queen Victoria's Jubilee.

The year 1886 being the fiftieth year since Her Majesty's accession to the throne in 1837, it was intended to celebrate this year as the jubilee, but in consequence of the Indian and Colonial Exhibition, and to allow more time for the preparations, which will be on a scale of unparalleled grandeur and magnificence, the event has been postponed till 1887, when the full fifty years shall have elapsed. The following lines in honor of the occasion, from a poem composed by Mr. John Imrie, of Toronto, are worthy of a place in this connection :—

> 1. Our noble Queen, all hail !
> On this thy Jubilee;
> True hearts shall never fail
> To love and honor thee.
>
> CHORUS.—Victoria, to thee,
> From loyal hearts and free,
> At this glad time,
> From every clime,
> Come shouts of Jubilee !

The Indian and Colonial Exhibition held in London, England, 1886.

When Albert "the Good," Prince Consort, first conceived the idea of inviting all nations to exhibit the productions of their skill and industry in London, the project was entertained with some doubt, but when the crystal structure was reared in Hyde Park, and all countries poured in their treasures, and after the invocation of a blessing by the Archbishop of Canterbury, the youthful Queen, surrounded by her great ministers of state, and ambassadors from all foreign nations, amid the strains of music and the boom of artillery, proclaimed the Exhibition open, and when for six months the millions of visitors had gazed with wonder and awe at the vastness of the building, so high as to enclose large elm trees, and then had feasted their eyes on all that was rare and beautiful, the grand result showed the wisdom of the undertaking.

This was followed by another in New York in 1853, then came Paris in 1855, London again in 1862, then Paris in 1867, after that Vienna, and the Centennial in Philadelphia, next Paris in 1878, then came Antwerp, and the "Fisheries" and "Inventories" in London.

In all of these Great Britain and her colonies were largely represented, but it remained for the year 1886 to see the British Empire alone in her dignity and grandeur, represented by her Indian and Colonial subjects, and the productions, varied and exhaustless, of their mines, fisheries, forests, agriculture, animals and manufactures, at the great centre of the Empire over which Her Majesty reigns in the happy and appropriate character of Empress of India and Queen of Great Britain and Ireland and all her Colonies.

This Empire, on which the sun never sets, and the roll of whose drum beat never ceases round the habitable globe as it is taken up every hour while the earth revolves on her axis, with a population numbering one-fifth of that of the whole world, will undoubtedly make such a display as will astonish all mankind.

From the continent of India, including the newly annexed Kingdom of Burmah, have poured in countless treasures of gold, silver, jewels, diamonds, ivory, silk and gold embroideries, shawls, tapestries, and other fine manufactures of fabulous value.

From "Ceylon's Isle," where the spicy breezes blow so softly, have come coffee and spices, and from the land

> "Where the feathery palm trees rise,
> And the date grows ripe under sunny skies ;
> And midst the green islands of glittering seas,
> Where fragrant forests perfume the breeze ;
> And strange, bright birds, on their starry wings,
> Bear the rich hues of all glorious things ;
> And from far away, in this region old,
> Where rivers wander o'er seas of gold,
> Where the burning rays of the ruby shine,
> And the diamond lights up the golden mine,
> And the pearl gleams forth from the coral strand."

Will come all that the imagination can conceive of, or the Arabian Nights have pictured of richness, grandeur, magnificence and luxury.

From Australia, embracing New South Wales, Van Dieman's Land and New Zealand, have been sent the great natural productions of these vast countries,—animals and their produce, in the shape of wool, meats and cheese, and the celebrated woollen manufactures of Nelson, with a variety of other specimens worthy of a great nation.

The gold fields of Australia, already represented in the Crystal Palace at Sydenham by a pyramid showing the bulk of gold shipped to England, from its first discovery up to a comparatively recent period, exhibit much that is still more magnificent.

From Africa have been sent ostrich feathers, coffee and ivory, and men of every shade, from the dark Hottentot to the European colonist, unite to make their very best display.

And so, from the isles of the sea, Newfoundland, Bermuda and the West Indian Islands, and some in the Pacific Ocean, have vied with the other in this great peaceful and brotherly rivalry.

The representation of the great Dominion of Canada, the brightest jewel in the Imperial Crown, is already assured in a manner worthy of her greatness, and from the Atlantic to the Pacific the varied productions of her mines, fisheries, forests, agriculture, animals and manufactures is already displayed, to show to the world the vast strides made by this young giant in the march of civilization, arts, sciences, trade, commerce and manufactures; and Canada will undoubtedly be able to give a good account of herself, even when side by side with the rich productions of her sister colonies, and the great continent of India itself.

No one city will excel Toronto in the exhibition of what is both useful and beautiful.

Who can predict the result of this union of the great British family, brought together in this way for the first time ? The Hindoo of India will shake hands with his brother, the red man of the Canadian forest; and the New Zealander, described by Macaulay as one day sitting on London Bridge sketching the ruins of St. Paul's, will be there to falsify the prediction on behalf of his future countrymen, and will see in the wonders exhibited but the beginning of the extension of the brotherly inter-communication of trade and commerce, when Canada, with Toronto as its commercial centre, will be the great highway between India, Australia and the central heart of the Empire, and as Sir George Stephen, quoting the words of Sir John A. Macdonald, has just expressed it the termini of this great highway will be Hong Kong and Liverpool. Then will soon arrive the time when those vast regions, traversed by the iron road, will be peopled by untold millions of happy and contented settlers, all true in their allegiance to the great Empire of which Canadians are now amongst the most loyal subjects.

The Council of the City of Toronto, with his Worship the Mayor, as Chief Magistrate, may well be congratulated on assuming their responsible duties at such an auspicious epoch. So many circumstances happily conspiring and harmoniously uniting to launch our fair city on a career of prosperity and progress hitherto unequalled, and, as the next ten years will undoubtedly show, compared with which the advancement of the past will dwindle into insignificance.

The writer who, in 1896, describes Toronto with a population of 250,000, will assuredly refer to the present year as the most remarkable period in her history.

The completion of the Canadian Pacific Railway, the last rail on Callender Junction spiked down on the 18th of January, making the distance from Toronto to Winnipeg shorter by two hundred and thirteen miles; the commencement of shipments to Australia, New Zealand, China and Japan; the coincidence of the Indian and Colonial Exhibition and the jubilee of Her Majesty's coronation, all combining as happy omens of the great future, augur well for the men who have undertaken to grapple manfully with Toronto's greatest needs, and when the history of the next decade is written, it will contain a description of the great works accomplished by the grand scheme of combining the health of the inhabitants with the encouragement and development of new manufacturing industries, and last, but not least, the enjoyment of the people.

With a grand promenade in front of the city, beautified with shade trees and approached in safety by handsome bridges thrown over the railway tracks, without danger to the thousands of men, women and children who will crowd down towards the steamboat wharves, and affording a prospect finer than that from the Thames embankment in London.

With a fleet of vessels along the wharves of the Don, and trains of cars in the railway yards adjoining, unloading coal from the Saskatchewan, and ores of iron, copper and silver, to be smelted in the furnaces whose chimneys will rise all around, and the same cars and vessels taking in return cargoes of Toronto manufactures to be distributed from Halifax to Vancouver, and to China, Japan, Australia and India; with our streets crowded with travellers from all countries, students from Japan and China at our University, mingling with British soldiers of horse, foot, and artillery regiments, having Toronto as headquarters, and not a few merchants from the far east, as wise men making their purchases, will far exceed what may now be regarded as a fancy picture.

To realize all this as accomplished in the history of Toronto only requires the carrying out of the plan so happily outlined on the occasion of the recent inauguration of the Chief Magistrate, and the support promised by the chosen representatives of the people, who will certainly approve of what is so plainly the interest of the present and future generations, and by judicious management of the finances and credit of the city will impose no heavy burden, while it secures inestimable benefits for the city for all time to come.

The completion of the Canadian Pacific Railway, and, what is sure to follow, a line of ocean steamers from Vancouver to Hong Kong, and thence through British territory to Calcutta, together with the formation of the Dominion of Australia, point to the near approach of what must happen in the closer union of all British countries.

Every thinking mind must look back with wonder and admiration on the past years of the now waning century. These have been years of miraculous progress, of vast revolutions in surrounding empires, of startling discoveries in science, of beneficial changes in social life.

Time and space have become the servants of science. The telegraph enables us to converse with absent friends instantaneously, or by the railway we fly to see them on the wings of swiftness; and England, in the midst of the changes of other nations, rears her proud head, great and glorious, powerful and peaceful, rejoicing in that precious liberty of mind and body which constitutes her the Queen of Nations.

As children separated from the parental home anticipate with joy a reunion, so are England's sons, the world over, looking forward to the grand family gathering of 1886.

HIS ROYAL HIGHNESS THE PRINCE OF WALES.

THE QUEEN'S JUBILEE

AND

TORONTO "CALLED BACK."

Indian and Colonial Exhibition, South Kensington, London, 1886.

"That they all may be one!" That mother and daughters,
   Tenderly linked like the Graces in love,
Girdling the globe, over lands, over waters,
   May be united beneath and above.
Here on this orb's upper hemisphere olden,
   There on that younger half-circle beneath,
Everywhere shall one sweet union enfolden
   England's fair scions in olive-twined wreath.
All to be one! What a blest federation!
   Britain, Imperial Queen of the World,
Sealed as one heart, one life, and one nation,
   Under one cross, one standard unfurled:
Owning one law of religion and reason,
   Speaking one language, and rich in its wealth,
Proud of the past, and the bright present season,
   And the grand future of hope and of health.
So may the whole world's glorious communion,
   Nature, and Science, and Commerce, rejoice;
Growing together in one happy union,
   Filling the welkin with gratitude's voice.
Canada, Africa, Zealand, Australia,
   India, continents, isles of the sea,
Adding your jewels to Britain's regalia,
   One with Old England the home of the free!

            —*Martin Farquhar Tupper.*

Opening Ceremonies.

The Exhibition was formally opened by Her Majesty on the 4th of May, and was characterized by the impressive, peaceful pomp and pageantry of a Royal progress, and was one of the most remarkable the world has ever seen.

The weather was beautiful. Crowds gathered along the route taken by Her Majesty from Buckingham Palace, and greeted her with enthusiastic cheers.

The main hall in which the opening ceremonies were conducted was crowded with the *élite* of London. The large number of foreign princes and diplomats who attended in court dress, combined with scores of British officers present, in full glittering uniforms, made a magnificent spectacle.

The Prince of Wales, Duke of Edinburgh, Prince Henry of Battenburg and his wife (Princess Beatrice), and the Crown Princess Victoria of Germany, led the Royal procession through the building, and were followed by Lord Hartington, the Marquis of Salisbury, Earl Derby, and scores of other distinguished persons. So great was the rush to witness the Royal procession to the Exhibition building that it required, besides a strong force of cavalry, upwards of 1,000 policemen to keep a passage-way for the Royal carriages through the streets. When the Queen's carriage arrived the entrance was surrounded by throngs of distinguished persons. The Royal guard of honor lined the corridors when Her Majesty alighted and passed into the building. When the Queen appeared in the hall she was greeted with enthusiastic cheers.

The opening ceremonies were simple, and consisted of a carefully prepared programme of music, the presentation of addresses to the Queen by the Colonies participating in the Exhibition, and a formal declaration by Her Majesty that the show was open.

The music was grand. Among the numbers was "Home, Sweet Home," sung by Albani. The immense choir, accompanied by the great organ and orchestra, rendered the Hallelujah Chorus with powerful effect.

The chief feature of the opening ceremonies was the singing of the new British Ode composed by Tennyson for the occasion. The poem is in four parts—one of welcome to the exhibitors; one of prayer for the inheritance by the Colonies of England's attributes; the third describing the loss of the United States, and the lesson of it; and the fourth an appeal for the unity of the Empire.

Her Majesty was immensely pleased and much affected by the singing of the ode. She smiled and nodded approval over each patriotic sentiment rendered, and was fairly radiant with pleasure when the vast audience caught up the poet's spirit and vented their joy in deafening thunders of applause. The text of the ode is as follows:

> Welcome, welcome! with one voice
> In your welfare we rejoice,
> Sons and brothers, that have sent
> From Isle, and Cape, and Continent,
> Produce of your field and flood,
> Mount and line and primal wood.
> Works of subtle brain and hand,
> And splendors of the morning land;
> Gifts from every British zone.
> Britons, hold your own!
>
> May we find, as ages run,
> The mother featured in the son;
> And may yours forever be
> That old strength and constancy,
> Which has made your fathers great
> In our ancient Island State;
> And where'er her flag may fly,
> Glorying between sea and sky,
> Make the might of Britain known.
> Britons, hold your own!
>
> Britain fought her sons of yore;
> Britain failed, and never more,
> Careless of our growing kin,
> Shall we sin our fathers' sin.
> Men that in a narrower day—
> Unprophetic rulers they—

> Drove from out the mother's nest
> That young eagle of the west,
> To forage for herself alone.
> Britons, hold your own!
>
> Sharers of our glorious past,
> Brothers, must we part at last?
> Shall not we, through good and ill,
> Cleave to one another still?
> Britain's myriad voices call:
> Sons, be welded, each and all,
> Into one Imperial whole—
> One with Britain, heart and soul.
> One life, one flag, one fleet, one throne.
> Britons, hold your own!
> And God guard all.

All the parts were sung in English but the second. This had been translated into Sanscrit, by Professor Max Müller, as a mark of courtesy to the large number of Orientals attending the Exhibition.

A noteworthy incident in the ceremony was the presentation to Her Majesty, by Sir George H. Chubb, of a master key of the most elaborate workmanship, which could open any of the 500 Chubb locks in the Exhibition. This choice and costly specimen of the locksmith's art is adorned with jewels of all kinds, and decked with many a dainty and symbolic device. It is well worth a minute description. Imagine it, half a foot long, made of burnished gold, set off with enamel and a variety of jewels, the bow being hexagonal in shape. In the centre of the hexagon, as seen from one side, is a golden representation of the head of a lion in high relief, langued with ruby, crowned and set in red enamel surrounded with a band of white enamel, with the inscription, "The Colonial and Indian Exhibition." From this central circle radiate to the angles of the hexagon six shields in raised blue enamel, each bearing a symbol in gold of the colony or dependency—the animals chosen being the sheep, elephant, tiger, opossum, beaver and buffalo. At the bow end of the key, and surmounting the bow, is the Imperial crown, the band of which is jewelled with rubies and emeralds. The pin

of the key as it leaves the hexagon starts from a centre of four
elephants' heads, whose trunks form a socket on either side of
the bow. The radiating shields are of yellow gold and bear the
names of several of the Colonies, whose symbols are of the
obverse, and in the centre of a small nugget of gold. This key
represented symbolically the opening of the Exhibition by Her
Majesty, after which she handed it to the Prince of Wales.

In addition to the distinguished personages named above
Her Majesty was accompanied by several young Princes and
Princesses, including in all thirteen of her children and grand-
children; all the former being present except the Duke of
Edinburgh, who commanded the fleet in Greek waters.

When the Prince of Wales had read the address on behalf of
the Commissioners of the Exhibition, and the Queen had read
her reply, he kissed the hand of Her Majesty, but she drew him
towards her and kissed him on the cheek.

Thus ended a most significant and appropriate celebration,
which, as the first strictly Imperial pageant, attests the strength
and unity of the British Empire, and emphasizes that desire
for still closer union which has become almost a passion of
patriotic hearts, whether they beat in the younger Britain
beyond the seas or in the old Island Home.

International Exhibitions.

Among the institutions which have developed in the long
reign of Queen Victoria, none are, perhaps, more remarkable
than the series of great exhibitions inaugurated by that of 1851,
when all nations were invited to London.

The Exhibition of 1851 was open from May day until the
15th of October, during which time it was visited by 6,170,000
persons, while the receipts were over half a million pounds
sterling, and the surplus profits amounted to £150,000, which
sum was devoted to the promotion of science and art.

The following were the three Exhibitions of 1886, with the
respective attendance up to the end of October, when the
Edinburgh finally closed with a surplus of £17,000:—Indian
and Colonial, London, 5,378,120; International, Edinburgh,
2,740,000; International (Shipperies), Liverpool, 3,132,516.

THE INDIAN EMPIRE.

While the Empire of India held the leading place, from the point of view of antiquity and a past civilization, her romantic history, and the gorgeous coloring which characterized her productions; her gold and silver works that were rich and rare; carpets of exquisite workmanship; cloths interwoven with precious metals; carvings in wood and ivory; models of ox-drawn palanquins and mystical carriages, decorated with gold and silver and rare woods; fans made from the feathers of the Indian ibis,—nevertheless, even India must suffer by comparison when in juxtaposition with the young and vigorous colonies of the Empire.

THE CANADIAN EXHIBITS

Created a profound impression on the British mind. The people of England had never before been able to realize the extent and variety of Canadian resources, and it may be said with confidence, that this country never stood in anything like as high estimation amongst the British people as she does to-day. The magnitude of her public works, the healthfulness of her climate, and the immensity of her territorial extent, were made apparent through the Exhibition as no other means could have accomplished.

Commemorative diplomas and medals have been awarded to every exhibitor at the Indian and Colonial Exhibition, numbering about three thousand of each.

The medals are of bronze, and are very handsome in design and finish. They are about double the size of an ordinary penny. On the obverse side is a profile portrait of the Prince of Wales, while on the reverse are the words, "Colonial and Indian Exhibition, 1886," surrounded by a cluster of oak leaves.

The diplomas are large-sized and of exquisite design and finish, being artistically colored. Britannia is represented, trident in hand, seated on a throne guarded by the British lion. Behind her stand two figures, one with torch in hand, the other spinning cotton, both representing, according to the interpretation, the march of progress and the speed of enlightenment in the British Empire. Directly in front of Britannia, who extends her right hand in friendly welcome, are groups of individuals attired in characteristic costumes of the various Colonies. Here the noble red man, with uplifted head, presents his contribution to the wealth of the Empire; while there his more thinly-clad fellow-subject from the burning plains of India, the lordly Zulu, or under-sized negro, laden with the product of his clime, seemingly vie with one another in their amiable glances in the direction of welcoming Britannia. Without an open window is seen a purple sea, on which is calmly floating a British man-of-war, reminding the Colonists of their security at all times.

TORONTO EXHIBITS.

No city could compare with Toronto in the number and variety of her exhibits, as shown by the large number of medals and diplomas distributed. The number presented through the Education Department alone was 137, and advantage was taken of the presence in Toronto of the Governor-General and Lady Lansdowne to make the presentation. This interesting event took place on the 4th of May, at a conversazione given in the Normal School buildings; the proceedings being interspersed with vocal and instrumental selections. The recipients of medals were connected with the Normal and Model Schools, the Art School, Public and Separate Schools, Collegiate Institute and various Colleges, School of Practical Science and Toronto University, and exhibitors of school supplies, books and musical instruments, and proved a most interesting occasion; the principal feature being the address of His Excellency on fine arts, which was replete with information and both complimentary and encouraging to the students.

An interesting description of the arrangement of the educational exhibits and the general effect was given by Dr. S. Passmore May, who was the Commissioner in charge, under the direction of Hon. G. W. Ross, Minister of Education. Dr. May has published a complete report, and also a catalogue of the whole educational exhibits, which are very valuable and interesting.

The number and variety of Toronto exhibits reflect great credit on our manufacturers and artists, whose names are worthy of being placed on record, and are hereby given, all of whom have also received medals and diplomas.

Abell, John	Machinery and Implements.
Acme Silver Co.	Silver-plated Ware.
Allcock, Laight & Westwood	Fishing Tackle.
Allen & Co., W. H.	Flavoring Extracts.
Anglo-American Art Co.	Colors for Artists.
Boeckh & Sons, Charles	Brushes, Brooms, Woodware.
Booth & Son	Copper and Brass Goods.
Brown Brothers	Account Books, Diaries, Leather Goods.
Brown, James	Stands and Elevators for Maps.
Bruenech, G. R.	Paintings.
Campbell & Son	Photographs.
Canada Printing Ink Co.	Printing Inks.
Canada School Publishing Co.	School Books.
Canadian Manufacturer Publishing Co.	Specimen Sheets of Canadian Manufacturer.
Cheeseworth, J. W.	Clothing of Canadian Cloth.
Cheeseworth, W. L.	Tailors' Compendium.
Christie, Brown & Co.	Biscuits.
Clarke & Co, A. R.	Morocco, Goat and Calf Leathers.
Cluthe, Charles	Ventilator, Chandelier, and Trusses.
Cobban Manufacturing Co.	Picture Frame Mouldings.
Cooper & Smith	Boots and Shoes.
Copp, Clark & Co.	School Books.
Crompton Corset Co.	Corsets in Satin and Jean.
Cross, William	Canadian Birds and Mammals.
Dack & Son, E.	Boots and Shoes.
De la Salle Institute	Photograph.
Department of Education	Organization, Methods and Appliances, Apparatus and Models, Drawings, School Material and Pupils' Work.
Dodge Wood Split Pulley Co.	Patent Wooden Belt Pulley.
Dubois, Louis E.	Model of Plough for Ditching.
Dubois & Son, Mrs.	Ostrich Feathers Dyed, Feather Trimmings.
Edwards, W.	Books of Mechanics' Institutes.
Elliott & Co.	Linseed and its products.
Fletcher, John	Refrigerators.
Forbes, J. C., R.C.A.	Paintings.
Gage & Co., W. J.	School and College Books.
Garrod & Co.	Sauces and Pickles.
Gibson, J.	Brick.

Gooderham & Worts, (Limited)...... Canadian Malt and Rye Whiskey.
Grip Printing and Publishing Co.... Books, Framed Pictures.
Heap's Dry Earth Closet Co .... Dry Earth Closets.
Heintzman & Co................... Pianos.
Industrial Art School .... Fancy Needle Work.
Inglis & Hunter .... Steam Engines.
Jones, J. L .... Wood-engraved Blocks.
Jones, John........................ Red Brick.
Kindergarten Schools .... Children's Work.
Lamb & Co., Peter R .... Glue, Blacking, Fertilizers.
Lansdowne Piano Co.............. Pianos.
Leon & Co., L. K................. Patent Adjustment in Eye Glasses.
Lindsay, J. A..................... Magnetite.
Loretto Abbey .... Oil Paintings, Water Colors, Crayon
                                                Drawings, Embroidery, Wax Work.
McCausland & Son, Joseph........ .. Stained Glass.
McFarlane, McKinlay & Co........ Window Shades.
Map & School Supply Co .... School Maps and Apparatus.
Marshall, George C .... Hat and Coat Rack.
Martin, T. M., R C.A .... Paintings.
Mason & Risch .... Pianos.
Massey Manufacturing Co.......... Agricultural Implements.
May, S. Passmore, M.D........ .. A Red Deer.
May & Co., Samuel... .. .. Billiard Tables.
Methodist Book & Publishing House. Printing, Binding, Electrotyping and
                                                Stereotyping.
Morrison, James............. ..... Gauges, Counters, etc.
More Soap Co .... Soaps.
Newcombe & Co., Octavius........ Pianos.
O'Brien, L. R., P.R.C.A .... Paintings.
Ontario Lead and Barb Wire Co.... Barb Wire Fencing.
Ontario Pump Co.................. Standard Pumping Windmill.
Ontario School of Art.............. Drawings, Modelling, Carving, etc.
Ontario Veterinary College .... Photographs.
Peard, Jessie M.................... Panel Screen, painted in oils.
Perre, H., R.C.A .... Paintings.
Piper & Son, Noah L............. Street Lamps, Lawn Seats.
Pawbone Keyless Stretcher Co...... Patent Keyless Artists' Stretchers.
Rawlinson, P...................... Mantelpiece.
Reid, G. A., A.R C.A .... Painting.
Robertson Brothers .... Confectionery.
Rodwell, George T. B............. Hand Stamp for Etching.
Rolph, Smith & Co............... Lithographing, Wood and Copperplate
                                                Engraving.
Rosebrugh, Dr. A. M........ .... Mechanical Telephone, exchange system.
Schlicht & Field Co. (Limited)...... Office and Labor Saving Furniture.

School of Practical Science	Photograph of Building, Specimens of Drawing.
Sears & Co	White Enamelled Letters for Signs.
Selby & Co	Kindergarten Material.
Sheppard, J	White Brick.
Sloan, James F	Mattresses.
Staunton & Co., M	Wall Papers, Borders, etc.
Steele Bros. & Co	Seeds.
Steiner, N. L	Head of Moose.
Stewart, F. J	Petrified Wood.
Strange & Co.	Sheet Music and Music Books.
Taylor, J. & J	Fire and Burglar Proof Safes.
Toronto Globe	Files of Toronto Globe.
Toronto Knitting Machine Co	Family Knitting Machines.
Toronto Lithographing Co	Lithographing and Engraving.
Toronto Paper Manufacturing Co	Paper.
Toronto Public Schools	Specimens of Pupils' Work.
Toronto School of Medicine	Photograph.
Toronto Silver Plate Co.	Silver-plated Ware.
Toronto University	Photograph of Buildings.
Toronto Wire Door Mat Co	Patent Steel Wire Door Mats.
University Trinity College	Photograph of Buildings.
Upper Canada College	Photograph of Buildings.
Wearne, C. H. A	Galena.
Wellington, W. E	Fruit.
Williams, H	Indian Curiosities.
Williams & Son, R. S	Pianos.
Wishrow & Hillock	Refrigerators.
Wright, J. D	Flavoring Extracts.

MUSICAL INSTRUMENTS.

As might have been expected, the pianos attracted an unusual amount of attention and patronage, several of the instruments having been purchased by the Queen and by wealthy and distinguished persons, for use in palaces and mansions. Dr. John Stainer, in his report on the Toronto musical instruments, says he "was struck by the high standard of excellence, alike in tone and mechanism." A large number of pianos and organs were sold during the Exhibition. Although the cost of making the pianos is greater in Canada than in England, he doubts not but that from their excellence the Canadian instruments will hold their own anywhere.

MESSRS. MASON & RISCH.

His Royal Highness the Prince of Wales complimented Mr. Mason personally on the excellency of their exhibit, and in company with the Crown Princess of Germany (the Princess Royal), his eldest son (Prince Albert Victor), and the Duke of Cambridge, paid a second visit and expressed their approval. The Princess Louise and Madame Albani also inspected the instruments, and Her Majesty the Queen ordered one of their upright pianos to be sent to Windsor Castle.

MESSRS. OCTAVIUS NEWCOMBE & CO.

This firm also had the honor of Her Majesty's command that one of their grand pianos be sent to Windsor Castle to be placed in the Queen's Audience Chamber. The instrument was selected by Sir Arthur Sullivan, and his judgment was confirmed by Dr. Stainer, organist of St. Paul's Cathedral.

R. S. WILLIAMS & SON.

Her Majesty chose one of the pianos of this firm for Windsor Castle. The selection was made by Mr. Dyson, of Windsor, specially appointed tuner to the Queen, their Royal Highnesses the Duke and Duchess of Connaught, and the Duchess of Albany.

Orders for various classes of manufactured goods were received by Toronto firms, amongst which were the Massey Manufacturing Co., for agricultural implements; McFarlane, McKinlay & Co., for window shades; Joseph McCausland and Son, for stained glass; Messrs. J. & J. Taylor, for safes, which have been shipped to Australia, Great Britain and Ireland; and a profitable trade may be looked for in our various branches of manufactures as the result of the display made at the Exhibition.

The financial results of the Exhibition have been extremely satisfactory. The report of the Finance Committee shows a clear surplus of £32,235. This result is largely due to the unceasing pains taken by the Prince of Wales to forward the

**IMAGE EVALUATION
TEST TARGET (MT-3)**

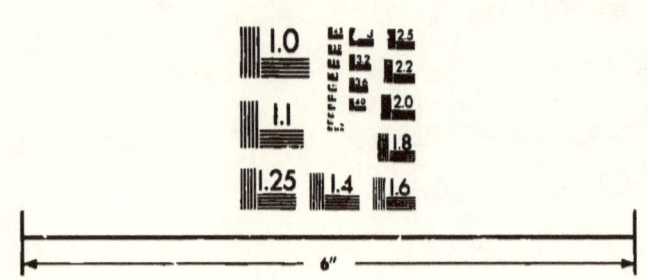

Photographic
Sciences
Corporation

23 WEST MAIN STREET
WEBSTER, N.Y. 14580
(716) 872-4503

HON. SIR CHARLES TUPPER, G.C.M.G., C.B.
(High Commissioner for Canada in London); Executive Commissioner.

interests of the Exhibition. Of this sum £25,000 is assigned to the Imperial Institute, which is the successor and natural heir of the Indian and Colonial Exhibition.

HON. SIR CHARLES TUPPER, G.C.M.G., C.B.

All the exhibitors from Toronto speak in the highest terms of the indefatigable exertions, inexhaustible patience, and uniform courtesy displayed by Sir Charles Tupper during the exhibition.

Rebellion of 1837.

In the session of Parliament at Toronto, in 1836-37, Dr. Rolph used the following language: "Our geographical situation is singular. To the south we are barred from the Atlantic coast by the American Republic; to the north and north-west you pass through barren lands to mountains covered with everlasting snows, and among Indian tribes unknown; and to the east we are intercepted by the sister Province, the very Province with which it is proposed to unite us."

The state of political affairs may be judged from the language used at this time by an English organ of the Opposition: "Henceforth there must be no peace to the Province; no quarter for the plunderers; agitate! agitate!! agitate!!! Destroy the revenue; denounce the oppressors. Everything is lawful when the fundamental liberties are in danger. The Guards die; they never surrender."

At public meetings the Imperial resolutions were denounced as a breach of faith and a violation of right. Resolutions were adopted to use as little as possible of imported articles paying duty, and to raise a Papineau tribute in imitation of O'Connell's Repeal Rent. Such was the state of affairs in Canada while yet His Majesty William IV. sat on the throne of Great Britain.

On the 15th of June, 1837, five days before the accession of Her Majesty Queen Victoria, Lord Gosford tried the effect of a proclamation on the agitation which was convulsing society. He assured the people that the Imperial Parliament had neither violated nor was about to violate the just rights and privileges of His Majesty's Canadian subjects. This proclamation was torn in pieces by the *habitans* in Lower Canada, amid cries of "A bas la proclamation!" The French-Canadians rallied to the popular cries "Vive Papineau! Vive la liberté! Point du despotisme!"

In Upper Canada, William Lyon Mackenzie in his journal declaimed on the condition of public affairs with scathing bitterness. He thus wrote:

"Canadians! Brother Colonists! Your mock Parliament has done its duty; bills and badgerings have followed each other in quick succession.

"Ye false Canadians! Tories! Pensioners! Placemen! Profligates! Orangemen! Churchmen! Spies! Informers! Brokers! Gamblers! Parasites and knaves of every caste and description, allow me to congratulate you! Never was a vagabond race more prosperous! Never did successful villainy rejoice in brighter visions of the future than ye may indulge. Ye may plunder and rob with impunity; your feet are on the people's necks; they are transformed into tame crouching slaves ready to be trampled on. Erect your Juggernaut; the people are ready to be sacrificed under the wheels of the idol.

"The four-pound loaf is at a Halifax shilling (20 cents); the barrel of flour brings twelve dollars. Woe and wailing and pauperism and crime meet us at every corner of the streets. The settlers and their families on the Ottawa, in Simcoe, in the rear of the London district, and many new settlements, seldom taste a morsel of bread and are glad to gnaw the bark off the trees, or sell their improvements for a morsel to keep away starvation.

"The settlers are leaving the country in thousands for lands less favored by nature, but blessed with free institutions and just government. The merchants are going to ruin one after another; even sycophancy and degrading scurrility have failed to save them this time. They cry out, Why is it so? I pity them not. Money, wealth, power, was their god, the Dagon of their idolatry. Let them cry aloud and spare not, perhaps even now he will help them.

"But why are want and misery come among us? Ah! ye rebels to Christianity, ye detest the truth, ye shut your ears against that which is right. Your country is taxed, priest-ridden, sold to strangers and ruined. What then? Ye share the plunders! Like the Lazarroni of Italy, ye delight in cruelty and distress, and lamentation and woe."

Mr. Mackenzie died in 1861, and even at that time he must have been himself astonished at the wonderful changes which had taken place in the condition of the country during the previous twenty-four years of the reign of Queen Victoria; and had he lived during the following twenty-six years and witnessed the Jubilee—with its glorious associations and unparalleled record of progress and prosperity, and nowhere greater than in the Dominion of Canada, and the City of Toronto—no doubt he would rejoice with every other loyal subject—as he afterwards proved to be—at the results of the benign and benignant sway of her who sits upon England's throne and lives in the hearts of her Canadian subjects.

It must not be inferred from the preceding historical extracts that the Canadian people had become disloyal: although a large number joined in the abortive rebellion, they were only a small minority of malcontents, while the great body remained true to the Government, their loyalty being intensified by the insurrection which had taken place.

Toronto's Loyalty.

Toronto, always foremost in her allegiance to Great Britain, manifested her loyalty to the young Queen on the occasion of her Coronation, on the 28th of June, 1838.

The citizens of Toronto, in their expression of joy, joined heartily in the celebration. Public rejoicings, dinners, speeches, and fireworks were the order of the day and evening.

A grand procession of firemen was the principal public feature and formed a fine display, being headed by the bands of the Queen's Rangers and of the Royal Foresters. The fire engines, drawn by two or four horses, were magnificently decorated, and mottoes of loyalty were prominently displayed on flags and banners, amidst which were the names "Victoria," in a wreath of Rose, Thistle, and Shamrock, and "British Supremacy," City of Toronto arms in gold, three gilt lions, gilt Irish harp, and the motto of the City of Toronto in gold— "Industry, Intelligence, Integrity."

The Princess Victoria,

Born May 24th, 1819; baptized same day; vaccinated early in August same year; presented at court, February 24th, 1831; visited Powis Castle, Wynstry, Beaumaris, and other parts of North Wales, and attended the Eisteddfod, 1832; presented Colors to 80th Foot (first public act), August 3rd, 1833; confirmed by Primate, August 30th, 1835; attained legal majority, May 24th, 1837; accession to throne, June 20th, 1837.

The Princess Victoria at the Bazaar.

Miss Martineau relates an anecdote of the Queen when she was a nine-year-old Princess, with no knowledge of the great future before her, and the story shows that she "was reared in as much honesty and care about money matters as any citizen's child," being rigidly guarded against any extra expenditure. At a Tunbridge Wells bazaar, the Princess had bought presents for nearly all her relatives, and spent her last shilling when she recollected one cousin more, and saw a box that she thought would just suit him. The price of the box was half a crown, and the shopkeeper placed it with the other purchases, when the governess admonished him with the remark, "No; you see the Princess has not got the money: therefore, of course, she cannot buy the box." The shopkeeper offered to keep the box for her, and the Princess exclaimed, "Oh, well, if you will be so good as to do that." Next quarter day, before seven o'clock in the morning, the Princess appeared on her donkey to claim her purchase, and this time, having the requisite money, she was enabled to carry off in triumph the box intended for her cousin.

Queen Victoria's Accession.

"The King is dead! God save the Queen."

At five o'clock on the morning of Tuesday, the 20th of June, 1837, the Primate of all England and the Lord Chamberlain reached Kensington Palace, where the Princess Victoria then resided, to inform her that her uncle, William IV., had died at Windsor Castle at 2.12 that morning, and to hail her as Queen.

The messengers had to knock long at the Palace door before the porter could be roused, and when at length admitted they were turned into a lower room and apparently forgotten. They had to ring several times, and an attendant declared that "the Princess was in such a sweet sleep that she could not venture to disturb her." "But," said they, "we come on business of state to the Queen, and even her sleep must give way to that." The young Queen shortly entered the room in a loose white night-gown and shawl; her night-cap thrown off and her hair falling upon her shoulders; her feet in slippers; tears in her eyes, but perfectly collected. The first words of the Queen were a request that the Archbishop would pray for her. They knelt together, and as Miss Wynn states: "Victoria inaugurated her reign like the young king of Israel in the olden time, by asking from the Most High, who ruleth in the kingdom of men, an understanding heart to judge so great a people."

Her Majesty's first act was to write a tender letter of condolence to Queen Adelaide, widow of the late King, and she addressed it to "Her Majesty, the Queen," remarking, when told that this was inaccurate, that she was "quite aware of Her Majesty's altered character, but I will not be the first person to remind her of it."

A Privy Council was held at 11 o'clock, and consequent upon the short notice some of the members had not time to wait for the robes of state; the Duke of Cumberland, Lord Glenelg and others appearing in undress. The Cabinet Ministers and other Privy Councillors then knelt before the throne and took the oath of allegiance. At 10 o'clock next forenoon Her Majesty was formally proclaimed Queen of Great Britain and Ireland, and when she presented herself at one of the windows of St. James's Palace, she was greeted with deafening cheers by the multitude assembled outside. The Queen wore a black silk dress, with a crape scarf over her white tippet, and a little black chip bonnet. Deeply moved by the enthusiastic manifestations of popular loyalty, she repeatedly bowed to the people, who, even while the proclamation was being read, cried out, "God save the Queen."

The Coronation.

The Queen's Coronation took place in Westminster Abbey on Thursday, the 28th June, 1838, with great pomp and ceremony, even the dawn of the day being announced by the guns of the Tower and those of a temporary battery in St. James's Park. All London turned out, and the line of route from St. James's Palace to the Abbey was crowded from pavement to housetop. The procession was long and imposing, and its several branches were separated by mounted bands and detachments of Life Guards. There were numerous grand new carriages of foreign representatives and different branches of the British Royal family. There were twelve of Her Majesty's carriages, each drawn by six horses, attended by four grooms walking, while the state equipage of the Queen was drawn by eight cream-colored Hanoverian horses with a yeoman of the guard at each wheel and two footmen at each door and one at the head of each horse.

The royal progress was marked with continuous enthusiasm, and the young Queen was much affected.

Meanwhile the Abbey's space was utilized to the utmost. The grand procession entered the choir shortly after noon, the Queen wearing a royal robe of crimson velvet furred with ermine and bordered with gold lace, while round her shoulders were the collars of her orders, and on her head was a circlet of gold. She was preceded by the Bishop of Winchester bearing the Bible. Some of the foreign ambassadors were magnificently dressed, especially Prince Esterhazy, whose dress down to his boot heels sparkled with diamonds. The only ambassador who received special attention from the crowd was Marshal Soult, who represented the King of France.

Immediately on the Queen's entrance the National Anthem was performed by orchestra and choir, while the vaulted roofs of the Abbey resounded with the acclamation of the spectators. At the conclusion of the Anthem the Primate announced to the east, south, west, and north, "I here present unto you Queen Victoria, the undoubted Queen of the realm; wherefore, all you who are come this day to render your homage, are you willing to do the same?" Each time the Archbishop made this demand the people loudly acclaimed, "God save Queen Victoria," trumpets sounded and drums were beaten; the Queen meantime remaining standing.

After Her Majesty had made her first offering of an altar cloth of gold, she handed over an ingot of gold, a pound in weight, to the Archbishop, who put it into the oblation basin. The religious service then proceeded. In taking the oath, with her right hand upon the gospel and herself kneeling, the Queen said, "The things which I have herebefore promised I will perform and keep, so help me God." Her Majesty kissed the book and signed a transcript of the oath. While anointing the Queen on head and hands, in the form of a cross, the Archbishop pronounced these words:

"Be thou anointed with holy oil as kings, priests and prophets were anointed; and as Solomon was anointed king by Zadok the priest and Nathan the prophet, so be you anointed, blessed, and consecrated Queen over this people, whom the Lord your God hath given you to rule and govern in the name of the Father, and of the Son, and of the Holy Ghost. Amen."

After other prayers the Bishop placed the crown reverently on the head of the young Queen. Then arose a great shout, "God save the Queen," with cheers and waving of hats and handkerchiefs, while the grandeur of the spectacle was heightened by the peers and peeresses putting on their coronets, and the bishops their caps, and the kings-at-arms their crowns, trumpets meanwhile sounding and drums beating. After

this came the enthronement and the homage, with kissing of
the Queen's hands.

Her Majesty received the two sceptres from the Dukes of
Norfolk and Richmond, on which the trumpets and drums once
more sounded, and the assembly cried out, "God save Queen
Victoria!" "Long live Queen Victoria!" "May the Queen live
forever!"

The Archbishop then presented the Bible to Her Majesty and
again led her to the throne, after which he was the first to do
homage, followed by all the lords spiritual and the lords temporal according to their rank. Each removed his coronet,
touched the crown on the Queen's head, and spoke thus: "I
do become your liege man of life and limb and of earthly
worship, and faith and love I will bear unto you, to live and
die against all manner of folks, so help me God." The last
created baron having sworn allegiance, the Queen showed where
her own homage was due by removing her crown while she
received the Holy Communion. Then the last blessing having
been uttered, with the crown on her head, the sceptre in one
hand and the orb in the other, the Crowned Majesty of England
left the Abbey. The whole gorgeous array swept after her.

The Queen's Crown.

The crown in which Her Majesty appeared at the coronation
weighed little more than three pounds, while the crown made
for George IV. weighed over seven pounds, and was much too
large for the Queen.

The new one made for her was composed of hoops of silver
enclosing a cap of deep blue velvet. The hoops, which were
completely covered with precious stones, were surmounted with
a ball covered with small diamonds, and had a Maltese cross of
brilliants on the top. In the centre of the cross was a splendid
sapphire, while the rim of the cross was clustered with brilliants, and ornamented with rich *fleur-de-lis* and Maltese crosses.
In front of the Maltese cross, which was also in front of the
crown, was the enormous heart-shaped ruby, once worn by the

chivalrous Black Prince. The value of the jewels of the crown was estimated at £112,760 ($563,000), comprising—

20 diamonds round the circle	£30,000
2 large centre diamonds	4,000
54 smaller diamonds at angles	100
4 crosses, each with 25 diamonds	12,000
4 large diamonds on top of crosses	40,860
12 diamonds in the *fleur-de-lis*	10,000
18 smaller diamonds in the *fleur-de-lis*	2,000
Pearls, diamonds, etc., in arches and crosses	10,000
141 diamonds on the mound	500
26 diamonds on the upper cross	3,000
2 circles of pearls on rim	300
	£112,760

The Coronation Chair.

King Edward's Chair, as the coronation chair is called, contains the famous stone from the Abbey of Scone, where the Scottish kings were crowned. This stone is commonly called Jacob's Stone, or the Fatal Marble Stone. It is about twenty-two inches long by thirteen broad, and eleven inches deep, of a steel color, with reddish veins. Tradition says it is the stone on which Jacob laid his head when he slept at Bethel. It was brought to Byzantia, in the kingdom of Galicia, in Spain; thence to Ireland by Simon Brach, who was King of Scots about 700 years before Christ; thence to Scotland by King Fergus, about 370 years later; and in the year 850 A.D., it was placed in the Abbey of Scone by King Kenneth, who caused it to be enclosed in a wooden chair, and a verse to be engraved on it, of which this is a translation:

"Should fate not fail, where'er this stone is found,
The Scots shall monarchs of that realm be found."

The Regalia.

From amongst the crowns and other regalia, carefully kept in the Tower of London, the following were used at the coronation ceremony: St. Edward's staff, the spurs, the sceptre with the cross, the pointed sword of temporal justice, the sword of mercy, the sword of state, the sceptre with the dove, the orb, St. Edward's crown, the palma, the chalice, and the Bible.

The Coronation Medal

Represented the crowned head of the youthful Queen. The medallion was surrounded by a wreath; immediately above it was a crown between the two words "God save," and underneath "Victoria R." An ode was written for the occasion, the first verse of which is as follows:—

> "All hail, Queen Victoria, all hail to this day,
> So teeming with promise, we welcome it here,
> As the bright stream of glory pursues its glad way,
> And the blessing of thousands ascends in that cheer."

The Queen and Her Family.

It was on the 24th of May, 1819, that Victoria Alexandrina, Queen of Great Britain and Ireland and Empress of India, was born at Kensington Palace. She was the only child of George III.'s fourth son, the Duke of Kent; and though her father's death, in 1820, left her heiress to the English throne, she was not acquainted with the fact until she was thirteen years of age, and she cried much on hearing it, while presently remarking, "There is much splendor, but there is much responsibility." She was brought up in strict retirement, but carefully prepared for the high duties which devolved upon her on the death of William IV.

The marriage between the young Queen and Prince Albert, projected by King Leopold and Baron Stockmar, was known to Her Majesty two years before the intention became known to the Prince himself. Writing to her uncle at the close of the Prince's first visit to this country, she begged him "to take care of one now so dear to her."

The marriage was celebrated on the 10th of February, 1840, and in the years of married life which intervened before the Prince Consort's death on the 14th December, 1861, five daughters and four sons were born to the happy couple. "They say," wrote the Queen in 1844, "no sovereign was ever more loved than I, and this because of our happy, domestic home, and the good example it presents."

The first ten years of the Queen's widowhood were spent in seclusion, for though grief did not prevent the necessary duties of the sovereign, it caused her to avoid publicity as much as possible. Besides the loss of her husband and daughter, the Princess Alice, the Queen suffered a severe trial in the beginning of 1871, when her eldest son, the Prince of Wales, had an almost fatal attack of typhoid fever. At the thanksgiving service for his recovery, held in St. Paul's Cathedral on 27th February, 1872, 13,000 persons attended. For the husband she loved so well, and has mourned for so long, the Queen raised the stately Frogmore Mausoleum. The Albert Memorial in Hyde Park, on the site of the first Exhibition building, is also an enduring monument of her love and affection, while statues in London, Liverpool, Manchester, and other towns, are popular memorials of the "Good Prince."

The Heir Apparent.

Of the twenty-three kings who have reigned in England since the traditional incident when Edward I. presented to the Welsh chieftains, at Caernarvon, his infant son as a prince "born in their midst, who could not speak a word of English," only twelve previously bore the title "Prince of Wales."

The title is the principal one attached to the eldest son, or in the event of his death, the grandson of the reigning sovereign; so that it does not invariably fall to the heir apparent, who may not be grandson of the sovereign. Neither James I. nor William IV. was Prince of Wales, and George IV. was the last bearer of the title before the birth of its present holder.

To the Princedom of Wales are annexed the Duchy of Cornwall and Earldom of Chester, in England; the Duchy of Rothesay, Earldom of Carrick, Barony of Renfrew, and Lordship of the Isles, in Scotland, besides the titles of Prince and High Steward; and in Ireland, the Earldom of Dublin.

The present Prince of Wales, and Heir Apparent to the

Royal and Imperial throne of Queen Victoria, is Albert Edward, Her Majesty's eldest son, who was born at Buckingham Palace on Lord Mayor's Day, November 9th, 1841, and was baptized on the 15th of January following; the King of Prussia being one of his sponsors. His Royal Highness received his early education under the Rev. Henry Birch, rector of Prestwich; Mr. Gibbs, barrister-at-law; the Rev. C. F. Turner, and Mr. H. W. Fisher. After studying a session at Edinburgh, he entered at Christ Church, Oxford. After attending the lectures at the latter seat of learning for a year, he, in 1860, paid his visit to Canada and the United States, where he was received with much enthusiasm. Next year he was at Cambridge University, and in the following year he travelled extensively in Europe, Syria and Egypt, accompanied by the late Dean Stanley. It was on the 8th of January, 1862, that he was ordered to be prayed for as "Albert Edward." In the following year he was admitted to the House of Peers, and was also made a Privy Councillor, while on the 10th of March he married the Princess Alexandra, of Denmark, who met with an enthusiastic welcome in England.

The Prince was made a Knight of St. Patrick on the occasion of his visit to Ireland in April, 1868. During his extensive travels in the following year he visited Constantinople and Sebastopol, and in the summer of 1870 he inaugurated the Victoria Embankment on the Thames, besides opening the Workmen's International Exhibition at Islington.

On the 12th of November, 1871, His Royal Highness was attacked with typhoid fever, and his recovery was despaired of from the 6th to the 13th of December, but next day his recovery commenced, and on the 27th of February following he was able to attend with his royal mother the thanksgiving service held in St. Paul's Cathedral.

In the beginning of 1874 he attended the marriage of his brother Alfred, Duke of Edinburgh, at St. Petersburg. On the perversion of the Marquis of Ripon, and his resignation of the Masonic Grand Mastership, that dignity was accepted by the Prince of Wales, who was installed with grand ceremonial in the Royal Albert Hall, on the 28th of April, 1875. In the same year occurred one of the great features of his lifetime—his visit to India—for which Parliament voted £112,000, and this sum more than covered the expenses of his triumphal progress through the great Indian Empire. Like his father, the great and good Prince so long mourned, he has taken a deep interest in the great exhibitions in London and elsewhere. To him belongs the honor of having established the Royal College of Music, and of proving by his visit to Ireland in 1885 that the Irish people are not the disloyalists they are pictured; and to him will also belong the honor of establishing the grand institution in London which is to symbolize the unity of the vast Empire of his mother, the jubilee of whose prosperous reign we celebrate.

His Royal Highness is making to himself friends of something nobler far than the mammon of unrighteousness. He is winning the hearts of the people and their children. He has a marvellous aptitude for translating the teachings of his father into very substantial facts. The Colonies are now in high favor with young men, thanks to the Colonial Exhibition. The working-men, and the boys and girls from the public elementary schools, were there by thousands, and when the Imperial Institute is opened they will continue to go and learn much to their advantage. The people of over-crowded British towns and the great Babylon of London have seen with their eyes how wide and wealthy a place God has given to the Anglo-Saxon race, especially in Canada and Australia. On all sides it may be seen that the set of the popular tide is towards those mighty lands whose people and products the Prince has helped to photograph on the imagination of their hearts. Britain may laugh at revolution and socialistic vagaries so long as the Throne busies itself in caring for the health and wealth of the people.

The Royal Household.

The personal household of Queen Victoria is composed of over a thousand persons, costing a yearly sum of $1,925,000. It consists of a Lord Steward, Lord Chamberlain, a Master of the Horse, each with a salary of $10,000; a Keeper of the Privy Purse at $11,000, with three assistants at $3,000 each; a Treasurer, a Controller, a Vice-Chamberlain, a Controller of Accounts, a Master of the Household, a Master of the Ceremonies, a Master of the Buckhounds, each at $6,000 per annum; a Grand Falconer a. $6,000, an Usher of the Black Rod at $10,000, a Mistress of the Robes at $3,000, eight Ladies of the Bedchamber at $2,500, ten bedchamber women at $1,500 each, ten maids of honor at $1,500 each, fourteen equerries at $3,500 each, eight pages of honor at $750, eight lords-in-waiting at $4,000, fourteen grooms-in-waiting at $2,000, ten gentlemen ushers at $400, ten sergeants-at-arms at a similar salary; a Poet Laureate (Lord Tennyson) at $500 per annum; a painter in ordinary, a marine painter, a sculptor in ordinary, a surveyor of pictures, at $1,000; an examiner of plays at $3,000, a principal *chef de cuisine* at $4,000, a principal cellar master at $2,500; 9 housekeepers, 130 housemaids, and lastly, one official ratcatcher at Windsor at a salary of $80, and another at Buckingham Palace at $60.

Her Majesty's Civil List.

This subject was brought under notice of Parliament on the 22nd of November, 1837. The Queen had placed unreservedly before Parliament those hereditary revenues transferred to the public by her immediate predecessor.

The Chancellor of the Exchequer, Mr. T. Spring Rice, pointed out that while previous sovereigns had inherited considerable personal property, Queen Victoria had not done so, and she would further be deprived of the revenue of Hanover, which had become a separate kingdom. The house voted £385,000, though Mr. Hume made a great effort to have the sum reduced by £50,000.

The Civil List Act provided that while the Queen lived all revenues of Crown lands should be part of the Consolidated Fund, and that "for the support of Her Majesty's household, and the honor and dignity of the Crown of the United Kingdom of Great Britain and Ireland, there shall be granted to Her

Majesty during her lifetime a net yearly revenue of £385,000,"
which sum the schedule thus appropriates:—Her Majesty's
privy purse, £60,000 ; salaries of household and retired allow-
ances, £131,260; expenses of household, £172,500 ; royal
bounty, alms, etc., £13,200 ; unappropriated balance, £8,040.

The Queen's Dominions.

The dominions over which the Queen-Empress reigns, as the
sixth Sovereign of the House of Brunswick, have an estimated
area of 8,991,254 square miles, of which Great Britain and
Ireland represent only 121,115 square miles. Her Majesty's
subjects in all parts of the world number about 316,000,000, or
more than eight times the extent of the British and Irish
population, and nearly one-fourth of the population of the
globe. These vast dominions, on which the sun never sets,
have a yearly revenue of more than £210,000,000 sterling,
their aggregate public debt is nearly £1,100,000,000 sterling,
while the yearly value of their imports and exports is about
£1,080,000,000 sterling. In the fifty years of Her Majesty's
reign, the area, population and the wealth of her dominions
have enormously increased, and her Empire is the greatest that
ever existed in the world's history.

The Year 1887

Will be a year of jubilees. Among the things which will see
their fifty years' lifetime between now and Christmas, and
which have proved of immense advantage to the community,
will be the practical application of electricity as a means of
communication; the introduction of phonography by Isaac
Pitman, and the establishing of building societies.

By means of the electric telegraph the antipodes are practically brought within a speaking distance of our shores ;
Pitman's phonography has revolutionized the newspaper press,
and building societies have proved of immense benefit to the
thrifty among the working classes. The jubilee of these will
no doubt be fittingly celebrated.

The Queen's Jubilee.

The Queen attained her 68th birthday on May 24th, and the 20th of June completed the fiftieth year of her glorious reign. There have been but three similar jubilees in our history.

The jubilee of Henry III. was kept on the 19th of October, 1265, and the festival celebration was hardly a joy-inspiring one. The next royal jubilee was that of Edward III., kept on the 25th of January, 1377, in connection with which also there seems to have been little cause for jubilation. On the 25th of October, 1809, the jubilee of George III. was celebrated with more joyous hilarity than characterized that of the two predecessors. The Queen's Jubilee excels them all in the loyalty and affection of her subjects.

"Carmen Sæculare."
LORD TENNYSON'S JUBILEE ODE.

I.

Fifty times the rose has flower'd and faded,
Fifty times the golden harvest fallen,
Since our Queen assumed the globe, the sceptre.

II.

She, beloved for a kindliness
Rare in fable or history,
Queen, and Empress of India,
Crown'd so long with a diadem
Never worn by a worthier,
Now with prosperous auguries
Comes at last to the bounteous
Crowning year of her Jubilee.

III.

Nothing of the lawless, of the Despot,
Nothing of the vulgar, or vainglorious,
All is gracious, gentle, great and Queenly.

IV.

You then loyally, all of you,
Deck your houses, illuminate
All your towns for a festival,
And in each let a multitude

Loyal, each to the heart of it
One full voice of allegiance,
Hail the great Ceremonial
Of this year of her Jubilee.

V.

Queen, as true to womanhood as Queenhood,
Glorying in the glories of her people,
Sorrowing with the sorrows of the lowest!

VI.

You, that wanton in affluence,
Spare not now to be bountiful,
Call you poor to regale with you,
Make their neighborhood healthfuller,
Give you gold to the Hospital,
Let the weary be comforted,
Let the needy be banqueted,
Let the maim'd in his heart rejoice
At this year of her Jubilee.

VII.

Henry's fifty years are all in shadow,
Gray with distance Edward's fifty summers,
Ev'n her Grandsire's fifty half forgotten.

VIII.

You, the Patriot Architect,
Shape a stately memorial,
Make it regally gorgeous,
Some Imperial Institute,
Rich in symbol, in ornament,
Which may speak to the centuries,
All the centuries after us,
Of this year of her Jubilee.

IX.

Fifty years of ever-broadening Commerce!
Fifty years of ever-brightening Science!
Fifty years of ever-widening Empire!

X.

You, the Mighty, the Fortunate,
You, the Lord-territorial,
You, the Lord-manufacturer,
You, the hardy, laborious,

> Patient children of Albion,
> You, Canadian, Indian,
> Australasian, African,
> All your hearts be in harmony,
> All your voices in unison,
> Singing " Hail to the glorious
> Golden year of her Jubilee!"

XI.

> Are there thunders moaning in the distance?
> Are there spectres moving in the darkness?
> Trust the Lord of Light to guide her people,
> Till the thunders pass, the spectres vanish,
> And the Light is Victor, and the darkness
> Dawns 'nto the Jubilee of the Ages.

Only six sovereigns of England since the Norman Conquest attained an age equal to or beyond that which the Queen attained on the 24th of May, 1887. These were: Queen Elizabeth, who reached 69 years; James II., 68 years; George II., 77 years; George III., 82 years; George IV., 68 years, and William IV., 72 years. Her Majesty's reign has only been twice exceeded in length, namely, by Henry III., who reigned for 56 years, and by George III., who reigned for 60 years; but the reign of one other sovereign, Edward III., equalled it by extending to 50 years.

Queen Victoria is only eighth in descent from James I., a long stretch of history being covered by the seven intervening lives. She is fourteenth in descent from Edward VI., twenty-eighth in descent from Henry I., thirty-fifth in descent from Alfred the Great, and thirty-seventh in descent from Egbert, the first sole monarch of England. The ramifications of her pedigree connect her with many other illustrious personages in addition to those already named.

India.

The fiftieth year of Queen Victoria's reign was celebrated in the capital cities of different Provinces of her Indian Empire, in the most festive manner, on the 16th of February.

At Calcutta, Bombay, Delhi, Lahore, and many towns in the north, western, and central Provinces, and in the loyal Native States, also at Mandalay, in the newly annexed Dominion of Burmah, the utmost loyalty was displayed.

At Calcutta, the Viceroy of India, Lord Dufferin, with the Commander-in-Chief, Sir Frederick Roberts, reviewed the troops on the Parade-ground; afterwards attended with Lady Dufferin a thanksgiving service at the Cathedral, where the *Te Deum* was sung; and in the afternoon, at a public assembly, ninety-two deputations from various bodies, municipalities, and local communities, educational institutions, representatives of trade, of the professional classes, and of different races and religions in Bengal, presented their congratulations to His Excellency to be sent to the Queen.

They were introduced by the Lieutenant-Governor of Bengal. Lord Dufferin made an eloquent speech, assuring them that ' Her Majesty the Queen and Empress watches over the interests of the people of India with affectionate solicitude. The military bands played the National Anthem, and there was a grand display of fireworks in the evening. On the same day thanksgiving services were held at the English, Scotch, Roman Catholic and Greek churches, the Jewish synagogue, and the Brahminical temples.

By order of the Viceroy, 23,307 prisoners for minor offences and for debts throughout India were released upon this happy occasion.

At Bombay, the proceedings commenced with a parade of troops. The streets were crowded with natives, who displayed great enthusiasm. In the evening the buildings were brilliantly illuminated with festoons and coloured lamps, and with gas devices with the words "God Save the Queen," "We are Happy," "England and India United." The triumphal arch over the Queen's statue was magnificently illuminated, and the city generally presented a splendid appearance.

. At Poonah, the Duke and Duchess of Connaught gave a State Ball. The Duke held a grand parade of troops. The Duke and Duchess left for Bombay in the afternoon of Wednesday, when three thousand Eurasian and European children were in procession singing the National Anthem; and there was a general illumination and grand display of fireworks in the evening.

The peculiarity of the Indian celebration has been the heartiness with which the natives, despite the stories of their discontent, have taken part in it. So important a personage as the High Priest of Baidaijanath, one of the most sacred shrines of Lower Bengal, has led in the native observance, and has further issued an appeal to the Hindoos, drafted in true Oriental fashion, to do honor to the Empress. He says, "May that great Empress, under whose protection religious ceremonies have been practised without molestation for fifty years—may that august Empress Victoria live long! The lustre of her reign, which illumines the hollow vales of the wilderness, and the concealed places, and which brightens the night itself, has like a second sun made India blossom like the lotus by dispelling the gloom of injustice originating from the severe tyranny of Mohammedanism.

"May the Empress Victoria, under whose kindness all her subjects have grown strong in the strength of religion and happiness—may she live a hundred years with her sons and friends. May the Empress under whose influence uninterrupted peace reigns in India live long! It behooves you Aryans, one and all, to pray for long life for the Empress. May that Empress in whose Empire men of science sing with delight the manifold blessing of telegraphs, railways and other inventions; may the Empress, whose moonlike deeds spread a halo of light far and wide—may the Empress Victoria be victorious. This is my constant prayer to Shiva."

On the 20th of June, at Madras, the Jubilee was celebrated by the Governor unveiling a statue of the Queen, and the illumination of the city in the evening.

On New Year's Day, 1877, Queen Victoria was proclaimed Empress of India with great pomp and ceremony at Delhi and other Indian cities, and the ten years which have elapsed since that time have fully established the title, as the display of loyalty in the great Indian Empire fully testifies.

Fifty Years' Progress.

No equal period in the history of the world has witnessed such advances in science and speed, such rapid development in the useful arts, such an increase of comfort, liberty and enlightenment. Since Queen Victoria ascended the British Throne the population of Great Britain and Ireland has increased from 26,000,000 to 37,000,000. The acquisition of foreign territory by Great Britain is without a parallel in the history of the human family. She bears rule over one-third of the surface of the globe, and over nearly one-fourth of its population. Her possessions abroad are in area sixty times larger than the parent state. She owns three millions and a half of square miles in America, one million each in Africa and Asia, and two and a half millions in Australia. At the Indian and Colonial Exhibition in London, in 1886, sixty-eight colonies and dependencies were represented, varying in extent from Gibraltar, with its two square miles, to Canada with her three millions and a half. In the fifty years her aggregate wealth has more than trebled, her foreign commerce has increased five-fold ; the imports of the United Kingdom have increased from £66,000,000 to £374,000,000. During the same period the imports of the British Possessions have increased from £26,000,000 to £218,000,000. The public revenues of the United Kingdom have grown since the Queen's accession from £55,000,000 to £93,000,000, and of the British Possessions from £23,000,000 to £115,000,000. In 1837, the shipping of the United Kingdom was 9,000,000 tons, this year it will reach 64,000,000 tons. In the fifty years the average entered and cleared at ports in the British Possessions had increased from 7,000,000 to 78,000,000 tons.

The penny postage was introduced soon after the Queen came to the throne, and in 1839 the total number of letters delivered in the United Kingdom was 82,471,000. In 1885 what was their number ? The total was 1,403,000,000 letters, 496,000,000 newspapers and books, and 172,000,000 post-cards, making a total of 2,065,000,000.

The increase of wealth in the United Kingdom in the fifty

years has been enormous, the taxable income having risen in thirty years from £308,000,000 to £631,000,000, or in the proportion of 105 per cent.

When Queen Victoria ascended the throne, Australia was only a convict settlement, British India belonged to a commercial company, the South African Colony was little more than a barren rock, and the Dominion of Canada was shorn of an immense territory by the Hudson's Bay Company. These are marvellous facts and figures of material progress within one reign, but what is quite as important is the fact that the enlightenment, enfranchisement and bettered condition of the masses, the growth of civil liberty, of art and culture, have kept pace with the vast strides in population, trade and wealth. Newspapers, schools, churches and benevolent societies have grown as never before, and accomplished practical results as they grew. Laws have improved, humanity advanced, wages increased, and the prime necessities of life cheapened, till now it is the deliberate judgment of the most cautious statisticians that the British labourer is 30 per cent. better paid, 40 per cent. better housed, 50 per cent. better clothed, and 150 per cent. better educated, than he was in the reign of William IV.

Royal Jubilee Exhibitions.

The celebration of the Queen's Jubilee in England was inaugurated by exhibitions in Manchester, Liverpool, Saltaire and Newcastle. It was fitting that Manchester should be assigned the first place on the list. The great Lancashire town has long been in the van of the great army of progress. In population, in wealth and independence, it has made vast strides in the last fifty years.

THE MANCHESTER JUBILEE EXHIBITION

was opened by their Royal Highnesses the Prince and Princess of Wales, amidst a scene of great magnificence and unbounded enthusiasm, on the 3rd of May. The Royal visit extended over two days, and the decorations and illuminations were of the most elaborate character. Miles of Venetian masts, triumphal arches with flowers, countless flags and gay streamers, with the hundreds of thousands of spectators, formed a brilliant scene. The second day was given to Salford.

LIVERPOOL.

The Royal Jubilee Exhibition was opened on the 16th May by Her Royal Highness the Princess Louise and the Marquis of Lorne, in the name of Her Majesty. The demonstration in Liverpool was essentially a popular one, being both spontaneous and enthusiastic, and the manifestation of love and affection for the Princess Louise was unbounded.

SALTAIRE AND NEWCASTLE-ON-TYNE.

The Exhibitions in these towns were opened in the name of the Queen by their Royal Highnesses the Duke of Cambridge and the Princess Beatrice respectively.

Opening of the People's Palace.

The first public appearance of Her Majesty in the Jubilee year occurred on the 14th of May, when the People's Palace in the East End of London was opened by the Queen with great pomp and pageantry of ceremonial, and with a full and loud chorus of loyalty and enthusiasm which will in future time mark the 14th of May as a red-letter day in the annals of a glorious reign. The spectacle provided for the East-Enders was of the greatest possible interest. Besides the Queen herself, the Prince and Princess of Wales and nearly the whole of the Royal family then in England graced the proceedings with their presence, and nothing was wanting in the shape of pomp and parade that could heighten the attractions of the scene. Her Majesty was in excellent spirits and visibly enjoyed the hearty acclamations of the myriads of working people who lined the route and filled the great hall of the new Palace.

An interesting incident of the day's proceedings was a visit to the Mansion House, being the first time, since 1838, Her Majesty was entertained by the Lord Mayor of London in his civic residence. The Lord Mayor and Lady Mayoress had invited 800 guests to participate in the ceremony of receiving Her Majesty and the other members of the Royal family. The decorations were superb, and the scene of the grandest description. The Lord Mayor's youngest daughter, Miss Violet Hanson, had the honor of presenting Her Majesty with a bouquet of orchids, roses, and geraniums, the latter being arranged to form the City arms. In receiving the bouquet the Queen made a kindly observation to the young lady and kissed her affectionately. This was the first occasion on which Her Majesty had appeared so far east of Temple Bar, and the hundreds of thousands of cheering voices of the "masses" prove that the rule of the Queen to-day is as surely as at any prior date "firm based upon her people's will."

JUBILEE SERVICE IN ST. MARGARET'S CHURCH, WESTMINSTER.

The State Jubilee Service of the House of Commons was celebrated on the 22nd of May, and was a pageant worthy of the occasion. It was the first time in the reign of any English Queen that such a service had been held, and was celebrated with great pomp. Over 400 members met in the Speaker's House, and 40,000 people assembled to witness the ceremony. The Queen's Westminster volunteers formed an escort, and kept the passage clear. The leading clergy of the city churches and Westminster Abbey, and the Bishops, marched in procession from the House of Commons to Westminster, where 600 ladies had already assembled.

The two ex speakers, Lord Eversley and Lord Hampden, were in the church together with the Archbishops of Canterbury and York.

When all were seated the scene was a remarkable one, such as had never before been witnessed. Speaker Peel, like King Saul, head and shoulders above his fellows, walked in a dignified manner, robed in his State attire and with becoming ceremony, to his seat in front of the mace, which betokened the sitting of the House of Commons in church. Messrs. A. H. Smith, Gladstone, Goschen, Edward Stanhope, Lord Churchill, Sir Henry Holland and other leaders and ministers followed.

When all were seated, "God Save the Queen" was sung with great fervor, and the beautiful service of the Church of England was rendered in the most effective manner. Bishop Ripon preached an eloquent sermon. At the conclusion of the service the Speaker and his attendants returned to the House of Commons. The scene was a remarkable one, and will form a chapter in the history of the nation.

The Queen's Jubilee.

To attempt a detailed account of the various forms of the Jubilee Celebration in different parts of the world would be altogether vain, and would itself fill a volume. A brief reference to what took place in the leading cities on both sides of the Atlantic may, however, prove interesting, and this is all our space will permit.

LONDON.

Never in the world's history did so many circumstances combine to produce a grand and glorious spectacle as on the 21st of June, when all that boundless wealth, military pomp and illustrious rank could do to heighten the effect of a State show of loyalty, or demonstrate the affection of a people for their sovereign, was done, and the result exceeded every display of the kind in ancient or modern times.

London had spent her wealth with a lavish hand; everything that skill and money could do to transform the world's metropolis into a dream city of splendor had been accomplished, and the weather was perfect. Thousands of people sat up all night to secure their places. A steady stream of carriages and pedestrians poured constantly all night until dawn, through the city towards the West End. At five o'clock in the morning every point of vantage along the streets composing the royal procession route was secured. At nine o'clock this line was on each side a compact mass of people.

AT WESTMINSTER ABBEY.

The scene at Westminster Abbey was most brilliant. Every seat was filled, and every person present was a person of distinction. It seemed as if every locality in the world had sent one or more of its representatives to do honor to England's Queen on Britain's greatest holiday. There never, probably, in modern times, assembled under one roof an audience so well and so brilliantly arrayed. Every man present, entitled to wear a uniform or decoration, displayed it. The scene presented was indescribable.

The line of the procession from Buckingham Palace to Westminster Abbey was from the Palace portals along Constitution Hill, Piccadilly, Regent Street, Waterloo Place, Pall Mall East, Cockspur Street, Northumberland Avenue, Thames Embankment, and Bridge Street to the Abbey.

The line of route was kept by nearly 20,000 troops, representing all branches of the service, and in addition 600 boys from the naval training ships were drawn up at the base of the Nelson Monument. At Buckingham Palace the two services were equally honored, the Guards lining one side of the roadway at Buckingham Palace gates, and on the other side the blue jackets were posted. The same services were also represented in a like manner at the entrance to Westminster Abbey.

The first of the Royal procession was composed of Indian princes and a few minor German princes. The second part was composed of fifteen carriages, the occupants being the King of Denmark, the King of the Belgians, the King of Saxony, the King of the Hellenes, the Crown Prince of Austria, the Crown Prince of Portugal, the Queen of the Belgians, the Crown Prince of Greece, Prince George of Greece, the Grand Duke of Mecklenburg Strelitz, with their attendants.

HER MAJESTY APPEARS.

As the Queen, in an open carriage, emerged from the Palace gates thousands of voices were lifted up in cheers, the applause being accompanied by the music of many military bands. The carriage was drawn by eight cream colored horses, and was a large one of chocolate color with red wheels, and having the Royal Arms emblazoned on the panels. Red morocco harness with gilt mounting was used for the horses. The servants wore state liveries of scarlet and gold.

A CAVALCADE OF PRINCES.

The Prince of Wales, the Duke of Edinburgh, the Duke of Connaught, her sons; the Crown Prince Imperial of Germany, the Marquis of Lorne, Prince Christian, and Prince Henry of Battenburg, her sons-in-law; and Prince Albert Victor and George of Wales, Prince Alfred of Edinburgh, and Prince William of Prussia, her grandsons,—all rode in full uniforms beside the Queen's coach as a bodyguard. When the people at the Palace had shouted themselves hoarse cheering for the Queen, they continued to cry out long live the Prince and Princess of Wales.

The other carriages containing members of the Royal Family were of a gorgeous character, horsed with four bays each, and all open. On reaching Regent Circus, where six main streets converge, the sight was a memorable one, the streets being all splendidly decorated. The procession, as viewed from the Duke of York's column passing down the Hill from the Circus to Pall Mall East, was a sight to be remembered. The shouts of the multitude were loudly heard as one vast roar. On reaching Trafalgar Square the crowds were tremendous, and completely eclipsed any assemblage that had ever gathered in that great square. On the procession nearing the Abbey by the Thames Embankment, the troops saluted, the guns fired, and the bells of the churches rang out merry peals, and flags were run up; the cheering continuing till the Queen had reached the Abbey.

A SCENE OF SURPASSING SPLENDOR.

Inside the Abbey the picture was one of surpassing beauty and absolutely dazzling. The jewels worn by the ladies flashed and reflashed as they reflected the rays of the sunbeams that found their way through the transepts. The three tiers of galleries seated about 10,000 persons. The peers and peeresses were seated in the south transepts; the ambassadors and diplomatic corps right and left of the peers; members of the House of Commons in the north transepts, while the seats for members of the reigning families of Europe were within the communion rails. All the great learned societies and corporations were represented, whilst the notables of the law, science, art, agriculture, and workingmen representatives from all parts of the kingdom had seats duly allotted to them.

A GRAND AND THRILLING SERVICE.

The Queen's advent was arranged so that she entered the Abbey precisely at noon. Dr. Bridge, organist of the Abbey, who had for the occasion a specially trained choir of 250 voices, selected from the great choirs of London, and a number of eminent soloists, besides a large accompaniment of brass instruments and drums, gradually drew the immense congregation into silence to be prepared for the Queen's coming by rendering a number of selections in a manner that made every person within hearing of the great organ eager to catch the softest notes. When the Queen reached the Abbey, the State trumpeters in gold and crimson uniforms executed fanfares from the organ loft nearly in the centre of the building. When the clergy, at the head of the Royal procession, moved into the church the National Anthem was rendered on the organ—the music was thrilling. The audience rose as a unit and lent their ten thousand voices to accompany the choir. The effect was so grand, so profound, that many were moved to tears. At this moment the Queen appeared. Then the singing ceased and the "Processional March," by Handel, was given by the organ during the progress of the Queen and the Royal Family to the dais.

When they were seated, the Archbishop of Canterbury and the Dean of Westminster, who had taken their places within the sacrarium, began the services by asking God's blessing upon the Queen. The *Te Deum Laudamus* was then sung by the choir to the music composed by the Prince Consort, according to Her Majesty's request. The Lord's Prayer was then said, and the responses adapted to the occasion were intoned. Then three special prayers were offered up, after which the *Exaudiat te Dominus* was sung with organ and brass band accompaniment. The lesson for the day was then read by the Dean of Westminster, after which Dr. Bridge's special anthem selected by the Queen was rendered, followed by the choral *Gotha*, composed by the Prince Consort. In the rests the National Anthem was produced.

Two more special prayers for the defence of the Faith, the spiritual welfare of the kingdom, and for peace and love, followed, and were supplemented by the benediction which was pronounced by the Archbishop. When the benediction had been said, the Queen's sons knelt before her and kissed her hand. They arose, and Her Majesty kissed each upon the cheek. The princesses next advanced to the Queen and kissed her hand, and she kissed them all, favoring some twice, making unusual demonstrations over the Princess of Wales and Princess Beatrice; other relatives of the Queen then saluted, and she shook hands with some and kissed others, kissing the Crown Prince Frederick William of Germany twice, very heartily each time. At all this the congregation applauded warmly. Nothing in connection with the affair was more touching than these affectionate greetings extended to the Queen by her children in the presence of the throng that filled the Abbey. They spoke eloquently of the domestic love which has ever been characteristic of the Queen and her family.

LONDON AT NIGHT.

The illuminations were like the transformation scene in a pantomime. As the natural light faded, every window blazed and flashed, and as night darkened the whole city became a flood of light. Beautiful and elaborate designs in gas were to be seen everywhere, and in every pane. In the windows of private houses were to be seen old-time candles and colored oil lamps in clusters. Up to a late hour there seemed to be no diminution in the crowds which went singing, a living stream, good humored and enthusiastic.

The number of congratulatory telegrams to the Queen from public bodies and private individuals all over the world was so overwhelmingly large that it was impossible to answer them individually. The Queen was greatly touched by such expressions of loyalty and devotion from all classes of her subjects.

THE QUEEN'S JUBILEE GIFT.

The joint Jubilee Gift to the Queen from all her children and grandchildren is a gold and silver centrepiece for a table, adorned with precious stones. It comprises three parts resting on a common base, in the centre of which are the British Arms bearing the inscription, "Her Children and Grandchildren to our Beloved Mother and Grandmother." The middle portion consists of a vase adorned with the arms and the portraits of the donors. It has a solid gold lid surmounted by the Royal Crown. To the right and left respectively, are a lion and a unicorn.

PARIS.

A Jubilee Garden Party was given at the British Embassy. The guests numbered 1,000, and included the members of the Diplomatic Corps, the Cabinet Ministers, M. DeLesseps, M. Ferry, the Duc De Broglio, M. Floquet, and Marshal McMahon.

The *Journal des Debats* says: "We cordially envy Englishmen and would give a great deal could we ever be what they are to-day, a people mad with joy and happiness. This universal homage is ... d not only to the Queen, but to the woman who has given an example of two great virtues of royalty—gravity and dignity. Her influence has been great and salutary; and her great merit is, that in using her prerogative for the public weal she has never been tempted to strain its exercise."

NEW ZEALAND.

The celebration was commenced on the 20th, and was continued for three days throughout the country. The greatest enthusiasm prevailed, the natives joining heartily in the festivities. Thanksgiving services, balls, concerts and illuminations, were extensively indulged in, and the utmost loyalty was displayed.

RUSSIA.

The Russian press commenting on Queen Victoria's Jubilee says: "The British people's love for their Queen is merited by the internal reforms and improvements in the condition of the masses, which have been effected in England during the fifty years of Her Majesty's reign."

AUSTRIA.

The *Official Gazette* at Vienna says: "Millions of voices throughout the world-wide Empire extol the queenly and womanly virtues of Victoria. The day marks a long epoch in the political welfare of her realm. The whole world sympathises with the festival, for the fame of the Queen's blessed rule reaches every quarter of the globe. This sympathy is most cordially shared in by Austria's Sovereign."

AFRICA.

At Pietermaritzburg, Natal, on June 20th, thanksgiving services were held in honor of the Queen's Jubilee, after the Governor reviewed the troops. A number of children's festivals were held, and in the evening the town was illuminated. On the 22nd, 30,000 Kaffirs had a joy dance in the presence of the Governor. At Capetown the festivities included a grand military demonstration and the firing of 100 guns.

GIBRALTAR.

The Queen's Jubilee was celebrated by religious services in the Spanish Cathedral. The streets were beautifully decorated and the vessels at anchor were gay with bunting. There was a review of the garrison, and at night the promenades were all illuminated.

AUSTRALIA.

The Jubilee was celebrated in Melbourne, Australia, with great enthusiasm; also in New South Wales and Queensland.

CHILI.

Queen Victoria's Jubilee was celebrated at Valparaiso with great rejoicings.

GERMANY.

The Berlin *Post* says: "What makes Germany a sympathetic onlooker at the Jubilee is the plenitude of events which has crowded the last half century. This is a period of importance in the world's history, not only for Englishmen, but for the whole civilized world. The English people will feel that they have great reason for gratitude which cannot be better expressed than by more and more foresightedly and resolutely facing the great inevitable tasks of the future."

NEW YORK.

The flags of Great Britain and the United States were draped together in the vestibule of Trinity Church on the 19th of June, and several thousand persons attended the Jubilee Choral Services to celebrate the fiftieth anniversary of Her Majesty Queen Victoria. Each person received a programme of the services printed in red, blue and gold, with the Royal Arms emblazoned on the title page.

The few places mentioned, scattered over the five great divisions of the globe, are only given as representing the universality of the celebration, not only in the colonies and dependencies of Great Britain all over the world, but in foreign countries, nearly all of which were represented in London. In China, Japan, Turkey, Algeria, Italy, Servia, Bulgaria, Spain, Egypt, Norway, Sweden, Denmark, Holland, Switzerland, and in nearly every town in these countries the celebration was kept on a scale of great magnificence.

DOMINION OF CANADA.

From the Atlantic to the Pacific, in hamlet and village, city and town, whether the inhabitants were English, Irish, Scotch, French, German, Indian or Ethiopian, all united as Canadians to honor their Queen, and enjoy a hearty celebration of Her Majesty's Jubilee. If some solitary cynic, or false-hearted traitor may have nursed a feeling of disloyalty, either through ignorance or unmanly insolence, and by a threadbare recital of Ireland's wrongs for fifty years, or by the use of contemptuous epithets towards majesty itself, should have introduced a "rift within the lute" of the general harmony, or cause a blot on the fair escutcheon of Canada's fame, they are so insignificant as to only mar their own enjoyment of the universal Jubilee rejoicings.

It would have been the pride of the writer to have recorded the celebration of this glorious Jubilee in his native as in his adopted country, but, alas! that one element should still exist in Ireland which only reacts on their own natural instincts, and deprive themselves of the enjoyment of their innate noble and generous characteristics, so celebrated in prose and rhyme from time immemorial. Yet the fact must be acknowledged and deplored. Ireland, the sister of England and Scotland in peace and war, sharer of her glories and equal inheritor of her grand historic achievements and renown, has not done herself justice on this glorious occasion. Nor was this feeling confined to her own shores, but one or two self-constituted missionaries of agitation and discord, sought to introduce this same element amongst us in this fair land, by threats against the representative of Her Majesty in this Dominion, which, unfortunately for themselves and happily for Canada, only redounded to the honor and distinction of the noble Marquis of Lansdowne, and to their own utter shame and discomfiture. The names of these gentlemen are Mr. William O'Brien, M.P., and a Mr. Kilbride, who appeared as a representative "evicted tenant," living in a fine mansion with lawn, conservatory, avenue and gate-lodge, and yet would not pay his rent.

As landlords in Canada expect their tenants to pay their rent when due, Mr. Kilbride would not improve his position by emigrating to this country, as, to use a common Irish expression, he appears to have a "very good America at home." While these gentlemen were indulging in their rodomontade, the Marquis of Lansdowne and his lady were pursuing the "even tenor of their way," in receiving addresses and holding levees at Government House. Their visit of three weeks to Toronto called forth a display of spontaneous enthusiasm, such as was never accorded to any Governor-General in Canada. Their entry into the city on the 3rd May was one grand ovation from the railway station to Government House, and during their stay, on every occasion, whether in visiting public institutions or reviewing our volunteers, the affectionate devotion of the citizens was of the most marked character.

TORONTO.

The most enduring monument to commemorate the great event will be the erection of a new hospital for sick children, for which the citizens have voted the sum of $20,000.

The Jubilee celebrations were inaugurated by a Military Church Parade, on the 19th of June, when a Thanksgiving Service was held in St. James' Cathedral. The Bishop of Toronto and several leading clergymen officiated. The troops which marched to the church headed by their bands consisted of the Governor-General's Body Guard, Toronto Garrison Artillery, members and ex-members of the Queen's Own Rifles, Tenth Royal Grenadiers, and Army and Navy Pensioners. The service, which was most appropriate, was rendered unusually attractive by the addition of the services of the band of the "Queen's Own" to the musical programme. Major-General Sir Frederick Middleton and Colonel Gzowski, A.D.C., were present in the congregation. The sermon was preached by the Rev. Dr. O'Meara.

The Jubilee celebration was observed by religious services in the other churches on the same day, all of which were intensely interesting and fervent.

Jubilee Praise and Thanksgiving Services.

While no language could portray, or pen describe, the emotions which thrilled and vibrated in the hearts of the millions of Queen Victoria's subjects in all parts of the world, as in ode and anthem their voices joined in loud and harmonious acclaim in expressing the sentiments contained in "God Save the Queen," and with the swelling notes of the organ, now melted to tears and again lifted in rapture to the very gate of heaven, they gave expression to their feelings of gratitude and love for all the blessings enjoyed under the beneficent rule of our Empress Queen; yet if it were possible to collect and publish the sermons and addresses of ministers and laymen of all denominations, "distinct as the billows, yet one as the sea," who, in tens of thousands of churches in all parts of the world, on the 19th and 21st of June, 1887, expatiated on the theme of the Victorian age, comprehending all its vast and mighty interests, the personal goodness and virtues of the Queen, the purity of her court, the example of domestic love with its world-wide influence on society, the development of art, science, trade and commerce, the spread of civilization and education, the advance of literature, the origination of numberless benevolent and religious institutions, and the general advancement and present grandeur of the British Empire during the past fifty years, they would form a volume such as the world has never seen, and such a memento of the grand Jubilee as would eclipse all former histories of nations or monarchs since the world began.

The appointment of the 30th June and 1st July for the Jubilee celebration proved to be both appropriate and successful, combining the usual Dominion Day rejoicings with the anniversary of the Queen's accession. The principal feature of the first day's proceedings was a grand procession of nearly 12,000 children from the public schools, which was witnessed by immense crowds of the citizens, and was a sight of which any city the size of Toronto might well be proud. Nearly every child wore a jubilee medal or badge, while flags and banners were plentifully displayed.

Jubilee Service in the Metropolitan Church.

A grand united religious and musical service, in which all the Evangelical Churches were represented, was the crowning event of the 30th June. The magnificent edifice was crowded to overflowing, and was beautifully decorated with flags, plants and flowers. The musical portion of the service was the chief attraction, the selections being of the most appropriate and loyal character, and were quite as eloquent and even more inspiring than were the beautiful addresses delivered by the speakers. A large number of distinguished gentlemen occupied the platform, amongst whom were the Hon. Sir Alexander Campbell, the newly appointed Lieutenant-Governor of Ontario; Hon. O. Mowat, Premier; and W. H. Howland, Esq., Mayor also prominent clergymen of all denominations, while in the body of the church were members of the City Council, and representatives of the various National and Benevolent Societies, all moved by the same spirit of enthusiasm, and joining with the choir of nearly 200 voices in the music set apart for the audience, with "glad hearts and voices," to swell the general harmony.

The service commenced with Mr. Torrington's performance on the organ of Gounod's *March Cortege*, which was followed by the singing of "God Save the Queen" by the vast audience. The effect of this inspiring hymn, when joined in by thousands of voices, was most thrilling. The other selections were chiefly the same as given in Westminster Abbey, including Dr. Bridge's Jubilee Ode and Anthem. The addresses were practical, enthusiastic and eloquent, but above all breathed the spirit of true and genuine loyalty throughout.

The closing song and chorus were composed by Mr. F. H. Torrington, and were sung with great spirit and feeling:

> Old England calls upon her sons
> To honor England's Queen;
> Her sons respond, and daughters too,
> To keep her memory green.
> With loyal hearts and ready hands
> The Empire's children stand,
> Prepared to do, prepared to die!
> For Queen and native land.

> CHORUS.
> Victoria! Our Queen beloved,
> With loyal heart and hand,
> Thy colonies and fatherland
> United by thee stand.

> For fifty years our country's flag
> Hath borne, o'er earth and main,
> The name of Empress, Queen belov'd,
> With neither spot nor stain.
> Long may it bear Victoria's name,
> Long o'er us may she reign,
> And for our Empire broad and grand
> May she new honor gain.

> Upon our Queen, our Country, Flag,
>   God's blessing ever rest,
> With peace and plenty everywhere,
>   Her people's homes be blest.
> God save the Queen, her people pray,
>   From hearts sincere and free;
> God save our lov'd Victoria,
>   And crown her Jubilee.

AT THE SYNAGOGUE.

The services held by the Jewish residents were remarkable for their intense devotion to the person and character of Queen Victoria. The beautiful and appropriate prayers, the music and eloquent sermon by Rabbi Phillips, were all expressive of the reverence in which Her Majesty is held by the Jewish people throughout the world. He alluded in thrilling tones to the flag of England, which lent its protection to the Jew as well as the Gentile. The Jewish merchant kings had found guardianship beneath its folds, and Jewish legislators had found honored places in the Imperial courts. God had been gracious unto His chosen people and provided them with a protectress in their well-beloved Queen. At the conclusion of the discourse the ark was opened and prayers were offered for Her Majesty. The choir sang a number of Psalms in the original tongue, and the service concluded with the National Anthem in English.

Mr. Torrington's Amateur Orchestra.

In the evening a jubilee concert was given by the above organization, and was a splendid success. The appropriateness of the selections, and the excellent style in which they were rendered, elicited the enthusiasm of the audience. The feeling was one of mingled surprise and delight. To hear the performance of an orchestra of a year's existence, display such proficiency in time and brilliancy in execution must have surprised most of those present, and will, no doubt, have the same effect on those who still have the pleasure only in prospect. Toronto may now confidently look forward to being independent of foreign aid in producing the highest class of instrumental as well as vocal music by her own unaided talent. The orchestra numbers sixty performers, comprising sixteen first violins, ten second violins, four violas, five 'cellos, four double basses, five flutes, two piccolos, one oboe, one clarionette, three horns, two cornets, one trombone and tympani.

Dominion Day.

The grand event so long anticipated was one to be long remembered as perhaps the most remarkable and the most thoroughly delightful day in the history of Toronto. The clanging of bells all over the city at 11 a.m. announced to the 150,000 people of Toronto that the demonstration in honor of Her Majesty's Jubilee, in the shape of a procession, had started toward the Exhibition Grounds. The route was thronged with immense crowds of spectators, who cheered heartily as the various organizations appeared. The road was kept clear by a detachment of mounted police, after which came the Mayor and Aldermen in carriages; following them were the Trustees of the Public and Separate Schools, the Industrial Exhibition Trustees, and Board of the Public Library; then came the following societies, military corps and organizations in the order named, bands, banners and flags being interspersed in regular order:—Retired Officers, Army, Navy and Militia, in uniform; Veterans, Army and Navy; Veterans, Volunteers; Governor-General's Body Guard, Toronto Field Battery, Garrison Artillery, Queen's Own Rifles, Tenth Royal Grenadiers, Irish Protestant Benevolent Society, and Sons of Ireland, Sons of Canada, St. David's Society, Sons of England, St. George's Society, Young Men's Protestant Benevolent Association, Orangemen, Foresters, Knights of Pythias, Ancient Order of United Workmen, Manchester Unity (Oddfellows), Knights of the Maccabees, Peter Ogden Lodge (Oddfellows), Toronto Butchers' Association and the Toronto Fire Brigade.

The appearance of the procession was very fine, and took an hour to pass one point. Had the trades of the city joined in, the length would have been immensely extended, but they have reserved their procession for Exhibition week. At the grounds loyal and patriotic speeches were made by Mayor Howland,

Hon. O. Mowat, the Premier of Ontario, and others; altogether the arrangements for the full enjoyment of the day were most successfully carried out, and added another to the long list of the exhibitions of Toronto's loyalty.

Toronto in 1887.

Never in her history has Toronto made such rapid strides in all that constitutes progress and prosperity as during the past year. Houses, blocks, streets and avenues are still being built and opened up in every direction, and if any one should keep pace with the rapid improvements going on, he will have discovered the principle of "perpetual motion," as in no other way could track be kept of the marvellous growth of the city. Not only is the number of the buildings greater than in any previous year, but the style of private residences is more elegant, the surroundings more beautiful, and the expenditure of wealth more apparent than ever before. Warehouses have gone up in rapid succession, and the style of architecture, as well as the internal arrangements, are of the most modern and substantial character. As is usual in most large cities, the tendency is for each kind of wholesale trade to concentrate in one point. The dry goods trade, formerly confined to Yonge and Wellington Streets, has extended to Front and Bay, where whole blocks of warehouses have been erected, and what a short year ago was vacant land is now covered with magnificent buildings for the use of merchants and manufacturers.

As a specimen of this class of architecture we give a view of the new block on the corner of Bay and Wellington Streets, on the spot alluded to in our first edition as the historic residence of Mr. Mercer, where, in his small rough-cast cottage, he dispensed marriage licenses, and made shoes during his lifetime.

WYLD, GRASETT & DARLING.

This building of five stories is massive and striking, the style being an adaptation of the Romanesque. The basement is of large rough blocks of Credit Valley brown stone. Above this rises the ground story of Ohio grey stone. The walls above are

NEW WAREHOUSE OF WYLD, GRASETT & DARLING.

of red brick with stone dressings, and are surmounted at the corners with round stone conical-topped pinnacles. The entrance consists of two heavy dwarf arches at the corner of the two streets, with stone steps leading to a triangular porch in which is the main doorway. This consists of an interior arch supported upon red granite columns with carved capitals. The main and vestibule doors are of oak. Heavy columns of Bay of Fundy red granite, with carved capitals, separate the windows on the Bay Street front. The counting-room and offices are fitted in oak with polished pine ceilings. Elevators (of which there are three), speaking tubes and a dumb-waiter afford every facility for the despatch of business. The heating and ventilating arrangements are of the most complete character, as are also the fixtures for the display of goods; while the light admitted through plate-glass windows on the north, east and west affords every advantage to buyers. Mr. David B. Dick is the architect.

HOTEL ACCOMMODATION.

The interest connected with any institution contemporaneous with the reign of Her Majesty Queen Victoria, especially in a young city like Toronto, must be greatly enhanced on a Jubilee festival such as is now being celebrated. Amongst the institutions of Toronto as a commercial city none are more important than its hotels, as upon the accommodation they furnish will depend largely the inducements offered to visitors from all parts of the world to spend their time and money in studying the attractions and resources such a city may contain.

THE ROSSIN HOUSE

Is one of the few establishments that possess a history of half a century, although, as has been stated in the first edition of this work, it had not assumed its present name till 1853. The Rossin House has been under various forms identified with the history of Toronto for over fifty years.

In 1832, on this site, Mr. James G. Chewett erected the British Coffee House, which became a popular rendezvous of the leading citizens, being at the time the only place having the character of a "club house." In 1837 it was taken by the Government for military purposes. After its relinquishment by the Government it was conducted by Mrs. Eliah, as a hotel, and while under her management it became the club house of the Toronto Club. In this hotel the Hon. Colonel Bruce, Secretary and Aide-de-Camp to the Earl of Elgin, resided during his term of office.

From the time when Mr. Mark H. Irish, the present proprietor, assumed the management in 1876, the Rossin House has had a career of prosperity previously unknown. Having brought his well-known enterprise and ability, backed up by years of experience in the business, to bear upon the management, the hotel soon rose to a high character as possessing every characteristic of a first-class institution. Travellers from all parts of the world found their way to its precincts, and had their highest expectations fully realized in the comforts and conveniences it afforded. Distinguished visitors from Great Britain and the United States have here been entertained from time to time.

In 1860, His Royal Highness the Prince of Wales, with his suite, occupied apartments in the Rossin House. The same suite of rooms has been occupied by Prince Alfred (Duke of Edinburgh), and later by Prince Leopold, the late Duke of Albany. Lord Dufferin and party also occupied the same rooms, and amongst other distinguished guests have been many celebrated artists, including Mrs. Langtry and Madame Adelina Patti.

There are few hotels in Canada or the United States which equal the Rossin House for accommodation.

The number of its bedrooms is 187, all furnished in first-class style, while its drawing-rooms and boudoirs are perfectly sumptuous in their artistic decorations and furniture. Suites of apartments have been provided for families, with bathrooms and every convenience and comfort. The general arrangement of the house may be said to be complete in every detail. A handsome passenger elevator affords easy access to every floor, in addition to which are five stairways leading from the topmost story to the ground floor. At night, the heads of these points of egress are distinguished by red lamps, so that guests have only to approach one to find a way open to the street. For additional safety the staff remains on duty till midnight, when the hotel is surrendered to the care of four watchmen who tread the corridors, and make their regular rounds until four o'clock in the morning, when one section of the day staff commences its duties. The sanitary arrangements are perfect; the *cuisinerie* unexceptional, and the situation most central, commanding and convenient. The ventilation of the building is thorough and complete. The two dining halls when thrown into one will accommodate 450 guests, and the citizens of Toronto may well feel a pride in having a hotel, which, for fifty years, has held so conspicuous a place in her history.

Cathedral of St. Alban the Martyr.

The corner-stone of this building was laid on the 16th of June, 1887, by the Right Reverend Arthur Sweatman, D.D., Bishop of Toronto. The Cathedral Chapter was incorporated in 1883, and the Cathedral building was commenced in 1885.

The establishment of a Cathedral for the Diocese of Toronto has been under consideration for many years, the object being to have a Church and Episcopal residence altogether distinct from ordinary parochial organizations, and forming a central point in the diocese from which the Bishop, with the advice of his Chapter, may exercise the functions of his office and his oversight over the whole diocese. The Cathedral will be built in a central position as regards the city and suburbs, being a little north of Bloor Street, between Albany and Howland Avenues, and when completed will be an ornament to the city. The work will be of red Credit Valley stone, in the early English style, and the design is in every way worthy of a Cathedral of the Church of England. The architect is Mr. R. Windeyer.

After devotional exercises His Lordship laid the stone, using a handsome gold and silver trowel. Beneath the stone were deposited copies of the daily and Church papers, the current coins, with a memorial containing the date, the name of the building, the names of the Queen, Governor-General and Lieutenant-Governors, the Building Committee, Architect and Contractors. In his address His Lordship stated, that the property had increased in a few years from $4,000 to $58,000, and predicted that Bathurst Street, having a leading outlet to the north, would become a second Yonge Street. Houses are being built rapidly in the neighborhood and there is no doubt the erection

ST. ALBAN'S CATHEDRAL.

of this elegant building with a Chapter House and See, which will cost, when completed, $250,000, will enhance the value of property in the neighborhood and attract a superior class of residents.

Rev. Dr. Potts, President of the Methodist Conference, by special invitation made an appropriate address, expressing the hope that the Cathedral might be made a blessing, and that the Bishop might be long spared to preside over it.

DEAN.

The Right Reverend the Lord Bishop of Toronto.

CHAPTER.

The Ven. the Archdeacon of Peterboro'.	R. Snelling, Esq., LL.D., Q.C., *Registrar of the Diocese.*
The Ven. the Archdeacon of York.	
The Rev. Canon Brent, M.A.	The Hon. Geo. W. Allen, Senator.
The Rev. Canon Scadding, D.D.	His Honor Judge Benson.
The Rev. Canon Stennett, M.A.	Robert H. Bethune, Esq.
The Rev. Canon O'Meara, LL.D.	Edward M. Chadwick, Esq.
The Rev. Canon Dumoulin, M.A.	James Henderson, Esq.
The Rev. Canon Osler.	John Carter, Esq.
The Rev. Canon Tremayne, M.A.	John R. Cartwright, Esq.

Major Edward H. Foster.

Progress of Trade and Manufactures.

As the best evidence of the above a list of Importers and Manufacturers is given, not by way of a directory, nor at the request, or with the knowledge of any of those whose names are given, but to show the growth of the city during the past forty years, as will be seen by comparison with the list of business men in 1847. This list is by no means complete, as some names may be omitted and new business enterprises are constantly springing up in the city, either by removal from other places or directly by the investment of capital in manufactures through the confidence felt in the protection afforded by the present tariff. It will be borne in mind that the names of importers and manufacturers only are given, whereas all business houses in 1847-1850 are mentioned, a list of which in 1887 would far exceed our limits.

IMPORTERS.

BICYCLES.
Fane, T., & Co.
Robinson, Chas., & Co.

BUTTONS.
Edwards, E. W., & Co.
Flett, Lowndes & Co.

CARPETS.
Beatty, William, & Son.
Foster, T. G., & Co.
Kay, John.
Macdonald, John, & Co.
McMaster, Darling & Co.

CARRIAGE HARDWARE.
Brown, William.
Canada Carriage Parts Co.
Conboy, W. A, & Co.
Davidson, Charles, & Co.

COTTON THREAD.
Clark & Co.
Coates, J. & P.

CROCKERY.
Cross, W. H.
Drynan, J. S.
Edgar J., & Son.

CROCKERY.
Gowans, Kent & Co.
Harrison, Glover.
Lewers, R. S.
Patton & Co.
Tew, Richard & Co.

CYCLOSTYLES.
Oldham, W.

DENTISTS' SUPPLIES.
C. H. Hubbard.

DRY GOODS—WHOLESALE.
Boyd Bros. & Co.
Brock, W. R., & Co.
Bryce, McMurrich & Co.
Caldecott, Burton & Co.
Gale, J. W., & Co.
Gordon, McKay & Co.
Hughes Bros.
Macdonald, John & Co.
McMaster, Darling & Co.
McMaster, W. J., & Co.
Ogilvy, Alexander & Anderson.
Rooney, Nicholas.
Ross, Hilyard & Co.
Samson, Kennedy & Co.
Smith, G. B., & Partners.
Tait, Burch & Co.
Wyld, Grasett & Darling.

DRY GOODS—RETAIL.
Armson & Stone.
Botsford, C. S.
Catto, John, & Co.
Eaton, James, & Co.
Eaton, T., & Co.
Eastwood, John, & Son.
Fenner, E. C.
McKeown, Edward.
Murray, W. A., & Co.
Page & Page.
Perryman, Edward.
Petley & Petley.
Robb, Hugh.
Roche, Danford, & Co.
Scott, James.
Simpson, Robert.
Simpson & Simpson.
Thompson, Thos., & Son.
Walker, Robert, & Sons.
Woodhouse, Thomas.

DRUGGISTS' SUNDRIES.
Booth, George W.
Smith & McGlashan Co.

DRUGS.
Elliott & Co.
Evans, Son & Mason.

DRUGS.
Lowden & Co.
Pearce, James H., & Co.
Tallmadge, E. H., & Co.

FANCY GOODS.
Allen, C. & J.
Bleasdell, W H., & Co.
Foster & McCabe.
Kauffman, Carl.
Maycock, Edward.
Nelson, H. A., & Son.
Nerlich & Co.
Robertson, Frank C., & Co.
Russell, J. H.
Smith & Fudger.
Weese, G. A.

FANCY STATIONERY.
Bryce, William.
Taylor, C. M., & Co.

FIRE ARMS.
Cooper, W. M.
Stark, Charles.

FISHING TACKLE.
Allcock, Laight & Westwood.
Croft, Wm., & Son.
Leckie, John.

GAS FIXTURES.
Keith & Fitzsimmons.
Lear, R. H.
McGuire, J., & Co.

GENTS' FURNISHINGS.
Fisher & Fisher.
Sims, A. H., & Co.
Treble, J. M.

GROCERIES.
Davidson & Hay.
Dunbar, Richard.
Eby, Blain & Co.
Eckardt, Kyle & Co.
Forbes, McHardy & Co.
Fulton, Michie & Co.
Kieran, F., & Co.
Kinnear, T., & Co.
Lang, J. W., & Co.
Perkins, Ince & Co.
Sloan & Mason.
Smith, Frank & Co.
Smith & Keighley.
Warren Bros. & Boomer.

HARDWARE.
Aikenhead & Crombie.
Bertram & Co.
Bertram, J. & A.
Howland, H. S., & Son.

HARDWARE.
Lewis, Rice, & Son.
Risley & Kerrigan.
Samuel, M. & L., Benjamin & Co.
Thompson, Wm., & Co.

HATS, CAPS AND FURS.
Allan, A A , & Co.
Bastedo, C. N., & Co.
Dunnett, McPherson & Co.
Lugsdin, James.
McArthur, Gowanlock & Co.

LACE GOODS.
White, Joselin & Co.

LEATHER AND FINDINGS.
Alexander, D. M.
Belton, John.
Clarke, A. R., & Co.
Dowker, H. B.
Jacobi, Philip.
King Bros.
King, Joseph.
Knees, Charles.
McLean, D.
Parsons, C., & Co.
Pepler, James, & Son.
Proctor, Henry.

LINEN THREADS.
Davison, Samuel.

MEDITERRANEAN PRODUCE.
Bendelari, E., & Co.

MILLINERY.
Goulding, G., & Sons.
Ivey, John D., & Co.
McCall, D., & Co.
McKinnon, S. F., & Co.
May, Thomas, & Co.
Reid, Taylor & Bayne.

PAINTS AND OILS.
E. Harris Co.
Hovenden, Richard.
Sanderson & Pearcy.
Stewart & Wood.
Paton, J. W., & Co.

PLATE GLASS.
Cobban Manufacturing Co.
McCausland, J., & Son.
St. Helen's Glass Importing Co.
Toronto Plate Glass Importing Co.

PRINTERS' SUPPLIES.
Gwatkin & Son.
Miller & Richard.

SADDLERY HARDWARE.
Davidson, Charles, & Co.

SADDLERY HARDWARE.
Martin, G. W.
Spriggs & Buchanan.
Trees, Samuel.
Woodbridge, T. C.

SEWING MACHINES.
Empress Sewing Machine Co.
Singer Sewing Machine Co.
Wheeler & Wilson S. M. Co.

TAILORS' TRIMMINGS.
Edwards, E. W., & Co.
Mills & Hutchinson.

TEAS.
Cowan John W., & Co.
Mann, George, & Co.
Minto Bros.
Musson & Morrow.
Williamson & Lambe.

WATCHES, CLOCKS AND JEWELLERY.
Benham, H., & Co.
Ellis, James E., & Co.
Ellis, P. W., & Co.
Frenkel, Samuel.
Goldsmiths Co.
Gunther, E. & A.
Lee & Chillas.
Lowe & Anderson.
Robinson & Brother.
Rothschilds & Co.
Saunders, Max.
Scheuer, Edmund.
Segsworth, J. C.
Smith & Fudger.
Thayer & Co.
Windrum, S. B.

WOOL.
Frind, Paul.
Fisher, T. S., & Co.
Hallam, John.

WOOLLENS—WHOLESALE.
Alison, Thomas.
Darling, Cockshutt & Co.
Fisher, M , Sons & Co.
McKenzie & Hamilton.
Nichol, Sutherland & Co.
Ryan, John & Co.
Williamson, Dignam & Co.

WOOLLENS—RETAIL.
Bilton Bros.
Clark, P. M., & Co.
Saunders, Bernard.
Score, R., & Son.
Stovel & Armstrong.

YEAST.
Fleischman & Co.
Gillett, E. W.

MANUFACTURERS.

ACCOUNT BOOKS.
Brown Brothers.
Barber & Ellis Co.
Carson & Stewart.
Copp, Clark & Co.
Davis & Henderson.
Warwick & Son.

AGRICULTURAL IMPLEMENTS.
Abell, John.
Massey Manufacturing Co.

APPLE MACHINERY.
W. D. Moody & Co.

ARCHITECTURAL WOOD-CARVING.
Toronto Cabinet Co.

ART FURNITURE.
Ewing & Co.
Smith, W. P., & Co.

ARTIFICIAL LIMBS.
Authors & Cox.
Cluthe, Charles.
Swinburne, W. H.

AWNINGS AND TENTS.
Black, W. G.
Matthews, J. K.
National Manufacturing Co.
Pike, Duncan.

BAKING POWDER.
Clark & Co., J. P.
Collins, J. F.
Gillett, E. W.
Jardine, A., & Co.
Todhunter, Mitchell & Co.

BASKETS.
Ashdown, Richard.
Ehrensmann, A.
Moody, Edwin.
Moses, Andrew.
Theissen, John.

BELTING.
Canadian Rubber Co.
Dixon, F. E., & Co.
Gutta Percha & Rubber Man. Co.
Toronto Rubber Co.
Williams, A. R.

BELTS AND BRACES.
Morrison, Angus, & Co.

BILLIARD TABLES.
Samuel May & Co.

BISCUITS.
Christie, Brown & Co.
Hessin, William.

BLACKING AND GLUE.
Lamb, P. R., & Co.

BLACK LEAD.
Pugsley, Dingman & Co.

BLANKETS.
Standard Woollen Mills.

BOAT BUILDERS.
Akroyd & Son.
Bassett, Edward.
Cleudinning, J. A.
Evans, Alfred.
Forman, T. K.
Gunsell, C.
Heakes, S. R.
Hicks, S. L.
Hodson, Harry F.
Ibbotson, James.
Larsh, D. G.
Noverre, F. A.
Saulter, Thomas.
Warin, G. & J.

BOILERS.
Currie Boiler Works.
Doty, John, Engine Co.
Garton Boiler Manufacturing Co.
Inglis & Hunter.
Perkins, John.
Polson, Williams & Co.
Ramage, Alfred.
Williams, A. R.

BOLT AND NUT WORKS.
Ontario Bolt Co. (Limited).

BOOK BINDERS.
Barber & Ellis Co.
Blackhall, W. B.
Brown Brothers.
Canada Publishing Co.
Davis & Henderson.
Gage, W. J., & Co.
Hunter, Rose & Co.
Methodist Book and Pub. House.
Warwick & Sons.
Union Publishing House.

BOOTS AND SHOES.
Cooper & Smith.
Damer & Son.
Hamilton, H. F.

BOOTS AND SHOES.
Hamilton, W. B.
King, J. D., & Co.
Turner, Valiant & Co.
Weston, F. J., & Son.

BRASS FOUNDERS.
Arnott, A.
Dean, Thomas.
Earsman, A., & Son.
Fogg, John.
Lauder Bros.
Lauder & Thornton Manfg Co.
Meadows, Samuel.
Morrison, James.
Rabjohn, Richard.
Simpson & Whittaker.

BRIDGE BUILDERS.
Dominion Bridge Co.

BRUSHES AND BROOMS.
Barton, E. W.
Boeckh & Sons.
Cobb, William.
Nelson, H. A., & Sons.
Pearson, R. S.
Pullen, Joseph.
Richards, Thomas.
Rossiter, Aaron.
Sanderson & Pillow.
Smith, Robert.
Wilson, James.
Woods, Walter, & Co.

CANNERS AND PRESERVERS.
Richardson, C., & Co.
Snyder, William A., & Co.

CARRIAGES.
Briscoe, William.
Dixon, John.
Dixon, William.
Guy, Matthew.
Hutchinson & Son.
Symons & Lockhart.
Thompson Bros.

CARPETS.
Unser, George.

CHAINS.
Dominion Chain Works.

CHEMISTS, MANUFACTURING.
Evans' Sons & Mason.
Lyman Bros. & Co.
Toronto Chemical Works.

CIGARS.
Davis, S., & Sons.

CIGARS.
Dobson, W. E.
Eichhorn & Carpenter.
Fletcher, Michael.
O'Holloran, Denis.
Roberts, J. D.
Spilling Bros.
Taylor & Wilson.
Wood Brothers.

CIGAR BOXES.
Kidd, William, & Co.
Simmington, J., & Sons.

CLOTHING.
Lailey, Watson & Co.
Livingstone, Johnston & Co.

COCOA AND CHOCOLATE.
Todhunter, Mitchell & Co.

COFFEE AND SPICE MILLS.
Barton, Son & Co.
Dalton Brothers.
Ellis, Keighley & Co.
Watson, James.
Wilson, C., & Son.

CONFECTIONERY.
Beasley, William.
Craig, J. F.
Hessin, William.
Park, W. W., & Co.
Robertson Bros.
Watson, R. & T.

COMBS.
Elrick, C. G., & Co.

COPPERSMITHS.
American Copper Co.
Booth & Son.

CORKS AND BUNGS.
Auld, John.
Freysing & Co.

CORNICES AND GALVANIZED IRON.
Douglas Bros.

CORSETS.
Brush & Co.
Canniff, J. A.
Crompton Corset Co.
Gray & Harold Manufacturing Co.
Telfer Manufacturing Co.

DENTISTS' SUPPLIES.
Toronto Dental Manufacturing Co.

DIE MAKERS.
Banfield, A. H.

DOVETAIL AND JOINTED BOXES.
Wood, John, & Sons.
York Milling Co.

DRUGS.
Elliott & Co.
Lyman Bros. & Co.

ELECTRICAL APPARATUS.
Ball Electric Light Co.

ELECTRICIANS.
Frame & Co.
Norman, Addison.
Richardson, J. T.

ELECTROTYPERS AND STEREOTYPERS.
Diver, F., & Co.
Jones, J. L.
National Electro. and Stereo. Co.
Rolph, Smith & Co.

ELECTRO-PLATERS.
Dorion Plating and Manfg Co.
Paris Manufacturing Co.
Wells, W. W.

ELEVATORS.
Fensom Elevator Works.

ENGINES.
Doty, John.
Inglis & Hunter.
Northey & Co.
Perkins, John.
Polson, William, & Co.
Smith, Charles, & Co.
Williams, A. R.

FEATHER TRIMMINGS.
Woodcock, Edwin.

FEATHERS—OSTRICH.
Butler, J. W. A.
Dubois, Madame, & Fils.

FILES.
Graham File Works.

FIRE APPARATUS.
Fire Extinguishing Manfg Co.
Richardson, J. T.

FLOUR MILLS.
Barclay, Alexander.
Citizen Milling Co.
McLaughlin & Moore.

FURNACES AND RANGES.
Gurney, E. & C., Co.
Pease, J. F., Furnace Co.
Toronto Furnace Co.
Wheeler, Frank.

FURNITURE.
Allan Furniture Co.
Ewing & Co.
Hess Bros.
Jolliffe & Co.
Rogers, Chas., Sons & Co.
Samo, J. H.
Smith, W. T., & Co.
Spanner & Co.

FURRIERS.
Allan, A. A., & Co.
Baateclo, C. N., & Co.
Dineen, W. & D.
Gillespie, Ansley & Martin.
McPhail, Hewatt & Co.
Rogers, J. H.

GLASS STAINERS.
Dominion Stained Glass Co.
Elliott & Son.
Lyon, N. T.
McCausland & Son.

GOLD SILVER AND NICKLE PLATERS.
Millichamp, W. H.
Paris Manufacturing Co.
Welsh, A. H.
Wells, W. W.
Wyness Plating Co.

GRANITE WORKS.
Gullett, F. B.
Pearen, J. E.
McKay, George.

HARNESS.
Canadian Harness Co.
Lugsdin & Barnett.
Thompson, Thomas.
Toronto Winker and Saddle Co.

HATS.
American Felt Hat Manfg Co.
Gillespie, Ansley & Martin.
Langley, Neill & Co.
Rogers, J. H., & Co.

HOSIERY.
Toronto Knitting and Hosiery Co.
Universal Knitting Machine Co.
Winter, C. R.

HYDRANTS AND VALVES.
Smith, Charles, & Co.

INFANTS CARRIAGES.
Gendron Manufacturing Co.

IRON FENCING.
Toronto Hardware Manfg Co.

IRON FOUNDERS.
Boyle & Richardson.
Connor, Webb & Co.
Good, James.
Goodes & Hardie.
Medcalf, Alfred.
Munn, John.
Potts, S. W., & Son.
Rabjohn, Richard.
St. Lawrence Foundry Co.
Tomlinson, T., & Son.
Treloar, Blashford & Co.
Whitefield, John.

JEWELLERY.
Allport, E. H., & Co.
Bayley & Kerr.
Enfield, W. H.
Bomer & Gunning.
Butterworth, Henry.
Davis Bros.
Dewdney, A. H., & Bro.
Doherty & Co
Ellis, James E., & Co.
Ellis, P. W , & Co.
Goulden & Trovey.
Gunther, E. & A.
Hill, W. B.
Johnston, T. F.
Kent Brothers.
Lewis, William.
Morley, W. J.
Morrison, W. C.
Parkman, John.
Pearsall, Benjamin.
People's Watch and Jewellery Co.
Rice, G. F.
Trowern, E. M.
Ward, George.
Welsh, A. H
White, Samuel.
Windrum, S. B.
York, J. J.

JEWELLERS' BOXES.
Hemming Bros. & Co.

KNIT GOODS.
Lamb Knitting Machine Co.
New, J. H., & Co.

LADDERS.
McFarlane, George.

LADIES' FURNISHINGS.
Allan Manufacturing Co.
Page & Page.
Gray & Harold Manfg. Co.

LAMP FIXTURES.
Toronto Light King Lamp Co.

LINEN BAGS.
Dick, Ridout & Co.

LASTS.
Iredale, J. C , & Co.
Selway & London.

LEAD WORKS.
Ontario Lead and Barb Wire Co.
Robertson, James, & Co.

LETTER FILES.
Schlicht & Field Manfg. Co.

MANTLES—WOOD.
Ewing & Co.
Toronto Cabinet Co.
Wright, J., & Son.

MARBLE.
Gibson, J. G.
Gullett, F. B.
Heaslip, S. R.
Macintosh, D., & Son.
Oakley, George.
Pearen, J. E.
Powell & Parkinson.
Sheppard, R., & Son
Steiner, N. L.

MATTRASSES.
Cahill, D P.
Canada Wire Mattrass Co.
Chaney & Co.
Chapman, Charles.
Heppin, J. J.
Hewlett Manufacturing Co.
Savacool, N W.
Smith, H. J.
Thorne & Co.
Townshend, J. E.
VanSkiner, Samuel.
Wills, Mrs. E.
Whitworth & Restall.

METALLIC SHINGLES.
Metallic Roofing Co.

METALLURGISTS.
Dewar, J. D.

METAL STAMPS
Fell, J. C., & Co.
Kenyon, Tingley, Stewart & Co.

MILL MACHINERY.
Greey, Wm. & J. G.

MITTS AND GLOVES.
Clarke, A. R , & Co.

MOULDINGS.
Black, Andrew.
Cobban Manufacturing Co.
Harkins & Smyth.
McMahon & Woltz.
Matthews Bros & Co.
Threlkeld, J J., & Co.

NECKWEAR.
Levian, E. A., & Co.
Williamson, W. H., & Co.

OILS.
Crown Oil Co.
Empire Oil Co.
McColl Bros. & Co.
People's Oil Co.
Rex Oil Co.
Rogers, Samuel, & Co.
Sussman, Sons & Co. (Linseed).
Standard Lubricating Oil Co.
Star Oil Co.

OFFICE FURNITURE.
Bell, Wm. H., & Co.

ORGANS.
Bell, D., Son & Co.
Lye, Edward, & Son.
Warren, S. B., & Son.

ORGAN REEDS.
Newell, Augustus, & Co.

OVERALLS
Bradshaw, Alexander, & Son.
Friendly & Co.
Gray, R. H., & Co.
Latham & Lowe.

PACKING BOXES.
Barchard & Co.
Firstbrook Bros.
Powers, E. W.

PAINTS.
Peuchen, Collins & Co.
Toronto Lead and Color Co.

PAPER BAGS.
Brayley, Robert.
Howorth & Smith.
Kilgour Brothers.
Nimmo, John.

PAPER.
Buntin, Reid & Co.
Canada Paper Co.
Taylor Brothers.

PAPER BOXES.
Dominion Paper Box Co.
Hall, Samuel.
Harrison, J. H.

PIANOS.
Heintzman & Co.
Herr Piano Co.
Lansdowne Piano Co.
Mason & Risch.
Newcombe, Octavius, & Co.
Williams & Son.

PICKLES AND SAUCES.
Bryant, Gibson & Co.
Lundy & Co.
Park, W. W., & Co.
Richardson & Co.

PICTURE FRAMES.
Cobban Man. Co.
Cook & Bunker.
Ewing & Co.
Houston, W. J.
Matthews Bros. & Co.
Potts, Edwin.
Sproule, G. F.
Threlkeld, J. J., & Co.

PRINTING INK.
Canada Printing Ink Co.

PRINTING PRESSES.
Westman & Baker.
Vivian, J. H.

PUMPS.
Northey & Co.
Ontario Pump Co.
Plews, D. & C.
Smith, Chas., & Co.

RATTAN FURNITURE.
American Rattan Co.

REFRIGERATORS.
Bryce Bros.
Withrow & Hillock.

FES.
Taylor, .

SADDLERY HARDWARE.
Birmingham Manfg. Co.

SAILS.
Adams, James.
Pike, Duncan.

SAWS.
Robertson, James, & Co.

SCALES.
Warren, H. B., & Co.
White, J. G.
Wilson, C., & Son.

SEWING COTTONS.
Kerr & Co.

SHIRTS.
Williams, Greene & Rome.
Gale Manufacturing Co.

SHOW CASES.
Dominion Show Case Co.
Millichamp, W., & Co.

SILVERWARE.
Acme Silver Co.
Dorien Plating Co.
Hodges, Winans & Co.
Toronto Silver Plate Co.

SOAP.
Morse Soap Co.
Pugsley, Dingman & Co.
Toronto Soap Co.

SPRING BEDS.
Adams Manufacturing Co.
Hewlett Manufacturing Co.

STRAW GOODS.
Excelsior Straw Works.
Ontario Straw Goods Co.

STOVES.
Armstrong, J. R., & Co.
Gurney, E. & C. Co.
Harte & Smith Manfg. Co.
Toronto Stove Co.

SYRUP.
Toronto Syrup Co.

SUSPENDERS.
Loughrey, James.
McGregor, Archibald.
Morrison, Angus, & Co.

TANNERS.
Beardmore & Co.
Bickell & Wickett.
Clarke, A. R., & Co.
Guittard, Victor.
Heinrich George.
Marlatt & Armstrong.
Ontario Tanners' Supply Co.
Toronto Tanning Co.

TASSELS.
Silberstein, F., & Co.

TINNERS' SUPPLIES.
McDonald, Kemp & Co.
McDonald Manfg. Co.
McGolpin, W. J.

TRUNKS.
Clarke, H. E., & Co.

TWINES.
Taylor Brothers.

VARNISHES.
Mackenzie, Musson & Co.

VINEGAR.
Lytle, T. A., & Co.
Mathews Vinegar Manfg. Co.
Wilson, William.

WAGGONS.
Bethell, John.
Bilbrough, Charles.
Butt, Ephraim.
Elliott, G. R.
Fry, Richard.
Kearney, Patrick.
Mahaffey, W., & Son.
May, George.
McLatchie, John.
Morrison & Bolton.

WAGGONS.
Smith, William.
Sullivan, J. P.
Walker, John.

WALL PAPERS.
Staunton, M., & Co.

WASHING MACHINES.
Ferris & Co.
Walton, B. W.

WATCH CASES.
American Watch Case Co.

WHITE LEAD.
Ontario Lead Works.
Robertson, Jas., & Co.
Toronto Lead & Color Co.

WINDOW SHADES.
Canadian Window Shade Co.
Macfarlane, McKinley & Co.
Matthews, J. K.
Queen City Window Shade Co.

WIRE FENCING.
Toronto Picket Wire Fence Co.

WIRE MATS.
Steel Wire Mat Co.

WIRE WORKS.
Partridge, Frederick.
Ramsey, W. J.
Rowe & Teskey.
Toronto Wire Works.

WOOD TURNING.
Chandler, R. H.
Dinnis, Richard.
Firstbrook Bros.
Forbes, William.
Fox & Company.
Gall, George.
Hastings & Peterkin.
Kennedy & Co.
Madill & Co.
McCracken, R. A.
Moir & McColl.
Norton & Dinsmore.
Parkdale Lumber Man. & Bld. Co.
Powers, E. W.
Rathburn, George.
Scholey Bros.
Scott & Cross.
Simpson, William.
Smith, John B., & Son.
Wagner, J. P., & Co.
Withrow & Hillock.
Wood, John, & Son.
York Milling Co.

WOODEN WARE.
Brandon Manfg. Co.

WOOL MATS.
Robinson, J. W.

PERMANENT EXHIBITION OF MANUFACTURES.

The fact is now demonstrated in Toronto that the growth and prosperity of manufactures does not diminish the importation of British and foreign goods, but that the importation of goods which are not made in Canada goes on steadily side by side with home manufactures. And so the wise and judicious policy which has proved so successful, and has so immensely promoted the growth and prosperity of Toronto, has, at the same time, been equally beneficial to the farming interests by securing a large home market for all their productions.

The Permanent Exhibition of Manufactures.

Nothing in modern times has tended more to create competition, develop talent and promote the cultivation of art, science, trade and manufactures, than the exhibitions which have taken place during the past thirty-six years.

The idea of establishing a Permanent Exhibition of Manufactures in Toronto will be no exception to this rule, and the advantages to manufacturer and merchant in thus meeting for mutual exchange must be obvious. The exhibition of our domestic manufactures in a condensed form will save the merchant much trouble and expense, and promote the prosperity of both himself and the manufacturer. The building erected for the purpose is in every way suitable and convenient. The light, the arrangement of the goods, and the central position—being opposite the Queen's Hotel—will, no doubt, all tend to its success, which may already be said to be assured. Messrs. Nicholls and Howland deserve much credit for the conception and establishment of the Permanent Exhibition of Manufactures and Commercial Exchange in Toronto. Being free to the public, it will become a resort for visitors to the city.

Sherbourne Street Methodist Church.

This place of worship was opened on the 3rd of June, the services continuing for two weeks. Bishop Hurst, of Buffalo, Drs. Douglas and Carman, and Rev. E. A. Stafford officiated. The opening services were supplemented by an eloquent sermon preached on Sunday, the 26th of June, by the celebrated English Wesleyan divine and author, Rev. Mark Guy Pearse, who has thrilled and delighted large congregations by his sermons and lectures in Toronto and other cities in Canada during his late visit.

The building is in the Romanesque style of architecture, and is built of grey Credit Valley stone, with dressings of brown stone from the same quarries. The effect is harmonious and

SHERBOURNE STREET METHODIST CHURCH.

artistic, and the appearance is pleasing and attractive. The interior arrangements are excellent; the view of the platform being unobstructed, and the acoustic properties are good.

The gallery is of horse-shoe form, and has a light, ornamental appearance, having an iron front of rich design, decorated in bronzes. The windows are of stained glass. Folding chairs have been introduced instead of pews, and afford more room and equal comfort. The cost of the building will be about $50,000. Messrs. Langley & Burke are the architects.

Proposed Drives Round the City.

The proposed park system, by which a continuous drive round the city, by connecting the present parks, may be secured, is daily gaining favor, and is likely to be carried into effect before long. This scheme will, undoubtedly, tend more to make Toronto attractive than anything before attempted. When accomplished, the most romantic scenery, especially in the neighborhood of Rosedale, will be developed, and with the assistance of art, all the natural beauties enhanced to such an extent as to surprise and delight even those who have lived all their lifetime in the neighborhood, and present new features of beauty and interest to all visitors to the city.

In connection with the Don improvements now going on, the north-eastern portion of the city will shortly assume a position, as regards picturesque and romantic scenery, pleasure resorts, and sites for residences, equal to any around Toronto.

Trans-Pacific Steamers.

The most important event of the year for the Dominion in general, and Toronto in particular, has been the arrival of the steamship *Abyssinia* at Vancouver, from Yokohama, on the 14th of June, having made the passage in thirteen days fourteen hours, and being the first of the line. She had twenty-two cabin passengers for Liverpool, New York, and eastern points. Her cargo consisted of 2,830 tons of tea, silk and curios for Victoria, Winnipeg, St. Paul, Chicago, London, Hamilton, Toronto, Buffalo and New York.

Although the contract for carrying the mails to India *via* the Suez Canal has been renewed, the granting of a subsidy to a line of steamers between Vancouver and Hong Kong by the Imperial Government may now be considered *un fait accompli*, and it is reported that a British regiment is to be sent over the Canadian Pacific route to India within a short time; so that the prediction of a year ago is likely soon to be realized with regard to the prospects of Toronto on the line of this great highway.

Buildings Completed Last Year.

Bank of Montreal.
College of Pharmacy.
Manning's Arcade.
Orange Hall.
Young Men's Christian Association Building.
Quebec Bank.
New Fire Hall. Lombard Street.
Permanent Exhibition of Manufactures
Grant Lithographing Co's Build'g.
Sherbourne St. Methodist Church.
Avenue Road Methodist Church.
Episcopal Church of St. Barnabus.
Beverley Street Baptist Church.
R.C. Church of Our Lady of Lourdes.

Buildings in Course of Construction.

Parliament Buildings.
City Hall and Court House.
Canadian Bank of Commerce.
Medical Council Hall.
Cornell's New Block.
Barber & Ellis Co.'s Warehouse and Factory.
St. Alban's Cathedral.
St. Mary's R. C. Church.
Bloor Street Presbyterian Church.

Proposed Buildings and Churches.

O. Newcombe & Co.'s Piano Manufactory.
Herr & Co.'s Piano Manufactory.
Methodist College.
Drill Shed.
Canada Life Assurance Building.
Chalmer's Presbyterian Church.
St. Augustine's Episcopal Church.
St. Simon's Episcopal Church.
Richmond Street Methodist New Church.
Western Methodist Church.

Precious Metals in the World.

	1850	1886
Coined Gold	$1,025,000,000	$3,680,000,000
Uncoined	2,125,000,000	3,840,000,000
Total Gold	$3,150,000,000	$7,520,000,000
Coined Silver	$1,550,000,000	$2,600,000,000
Uncoined	5,200,000,000	5,150,000,000
Total Silver	$6,750,000,000	$7,750,000,000
Total Gold and Silver	$9,900,000,000	$15,270,000,000
Weight of Gold (tons)	4,550	10,700
Weight of Silver "	148,000	201,000
National debt, 1837		£788,000,000
National debt, 1887		746,000,000

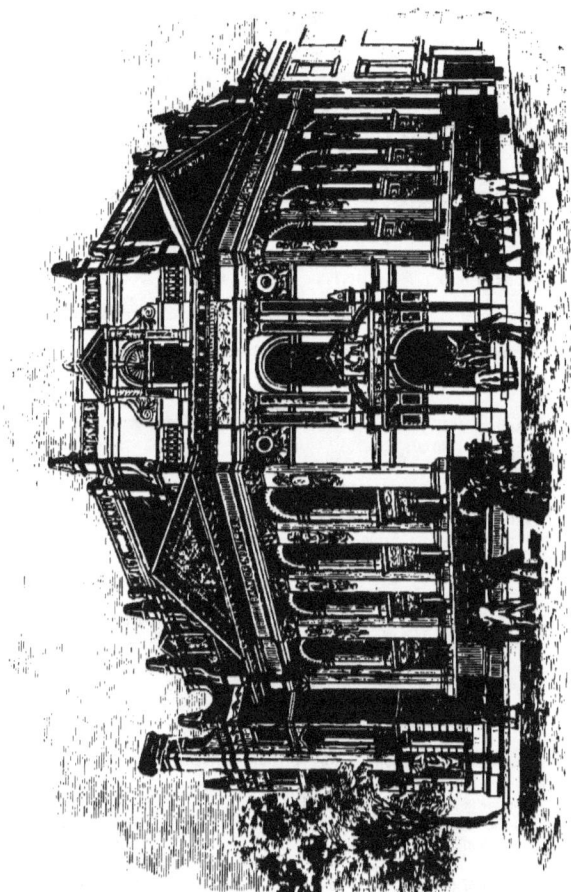

BANK OF MONTREAL, TORONTO.

New Lieutenant-Governor of Ontario.

Sir Alexander Campbell, K.C.M.G., was sworn in as Lieutenant-Governor on the 1st of June, 1887.

Customs, Assessment and Post Office Statistics.

TORONTO IMPORTS FOR YEAR ENDING 30TH JUNE, 1887.

Value in 1887.... $21,020,528	Duty in 1887.... $4,273,038
Value in 1886 ... 18,310,145	Duty in 1886.... 3,419,265
Increase $2,710,383	Increase $853,773

Exports for year ending 30th of June, 1887 .... $3,192,157

CITY ASSESSMENT.

Total for 1887 .... $82,837,400
Total for 1886 72,721,559

Increase $10,115,841

Estimated expenditure for 1887 .... $4,125,917

TORONTO POST-OFFICE STATISTICS FOR THE YEAR ENDING 31ST DECEMBER, 1886.

Amount of Money Orders issued $337,608 28
Amount of Money Orders paid 1,404,743 18

Number of Orders paid............................ 88,140

Amount deposited in the Post-Office Savings Bank . $553,648 00

Number of letters delivered by carriers, exclusive of
    box holders and general delivery.............. 9,776,400
Number of newspapers delivered................... 2,592,380
Number of letters posted 20,014,056
Number of cards posted.......................... 2,836,104

Amount of postage stamps sold $257,236 25

Steamers—A Comparison.

	LENGTH.	BREADTH.	TONNAGE.
Sirius, paddle, 1837	172 ft.	17 ft.	249
City of Rome, screw, 1887	500 ft.	52 ft.	8,144

The Railways of the United Kingdom.

In the year 1842 there were 1,857 miles of railways open, and in that year the trains carried 18,453,504 passengers, while the aggregate traffic receipts amounted to £3,820,122. At present the authorized capitals have an aggregate of £927,743,988 sterling, or about $4,600,000,000. Adopting the year 1843 to compare with that of 1885, the following results are disclosed:

	1843	1885
Miles of railway open	1,952	19,165
Total actual capital	£65,530,792	£818,858,058
Passengers	23,466,896	697,213,031

Canadian Railways.

In 1849, when the writer made his first journey to Montreal and Quebec, the only railroads in Canada were a few miles between Lachine and Montreal, and from Laprairie to St. John's, and were of the most primitive character, the rails being plain plates of iron fastened with iron spikes. The carriages were of English make and fashion, having doors at the sides only, and the compartments, consisting of six seats in each, were on the *vis-a-vis* principle. The Lachine road was utilized for the conveyance of the Upper Canada mails, and those passengers who preferred going through that way to Montreal rather than "shooting the rapids," or in case of the steamers not going through the same evening. In 1887 the principal railway statistics of the Dominion give the following figures:

Total mileage of railways completed	11,523
Amount of capital paid up	$653,759,944
Passengers carried	9,861,024
Tons of freight carried	15,670,400
Train mileage	30,481,088

Remarkable Features in the Royal Jubilee Procession.

Each section of the procession was preceded and followed by an escort of Life Guards, by heralds, and by grooms in gorgeous livery. The Life Guardsmen alone, with their magnificent horses, were a sight.

The staff of the Duke of Cambridge, the General commanding in chief, consisted of fifty generals—all of whom had been in battles, and nearly all of whom are distinguished soldiers—with their white plumes waving in the air, and their prancing steeds; the sight was one never to be forgotten, for who will again see half a hundred generals in procession? They were followed by native officers of the Indian Cavalry in gorgeous uniforms.

Every man of the picked troops which lined the streets, 10,000 on each side, was fully six feet in height.

Prince Frederick William, Crown Prince of Prussia, who is extremely popular in England, in his pure white uniform, shown off to perfection by his magnificent physique, out-topping all his Royal companions, was the "observed of all observers," and attracted more attention than even the Indian princes, although resplendent with diamonds and jewels.

Prince George of Greece, a splendid youth of seventeen, and six feet three inches in height, who is every inch a sailor, was much admired.

The decorations of the streets and houses along the route of the procession were most beautiful and elaborate.

The weather, which was essentially "Queen's weather," was perfect, and no single accident or unpleasantness occurred during the day to mar the enjoyment of the millions who witnessed the magnificent pageant.

The Children's Fete in Hyde Park.

No description of the Jubilee celebrations would be complete without some account of the children's *fete*. This was an assembly of an eminently domestic kind, one which appealed to all hearts and touched a sympathetic chord in every breast. The unnumbered thousands of spectators were all of one mind, and the happiness of the children was reflected in all faces present. The arrangements were perfect in every detail. The military bands, of which there were ten, were stationed at various parts of the ground and played at intervals throughout the day. In addition to a squadron of Life Guards, and a large number of the Foot Guards, there were 3,000 policemen, of whom 100 were mounted, co-operating with the military in keeping the ground clear. There were ten marquees, in which the food was distributed to the children, presided over by a number of the leading nobility, both ladies and gentlemen. The extent of the catering arrangements may be gathered from the fact that Messrs. Spiers & Pond supplied no fewer than 27,700 meat pies, as many cakes, as many oranges, 56,000 buns, and 9,000 gallons of lemonade and ginger ale.

As to the amusements, there was a small army of about 450 entertainers. Twenty Punch and Judy shows, eight marionnette theatres, eighty-six cosmoramic views and peepshows, nine troops of performing dogs, ponies, and monkeys, hundreds of Aunt Sallies and knock-'em-downs, a hundred large lucky dip barrels, a thousand skipping ropes with jubilee handles, 10,000 small balloons, and 42,000 toys, distributed at the centres of amusements, and to each child was given a Jubilee medal and mug.

The Prince and Princess of Wales, and their sons and daughters, accompanied by a large number of the Royal guests, visited the Park during the *fete*. The children rushed towards the Royal guests, when all etiquette vanished, and the princes and princesses, who seemed delighted at their position, mixed among the children with perfect freedom and pleasure. All at once the children began to sing " God Bless the Prince of Wales." When the Queen arrived, the children massed themselves along both sides of the road where Her Majesty passed, when the bands played the National Anthem and the children all sang with grand effect. When the Queen departed the whole assemblage sang " Rule Britannia."

This was a fitting and beautiful exhibition with which to close the public celebration of the grandest event in the history of any monarch of ancient or modern times.

Of the sixteen reigning sovereigns of the present time, leaving out the Queen herself, and including the President of the United States and Pope Leo, four were actually present, and all the others were represented on this glorious occasion. In the historic Abbey of Westminster, built by King Edward the Confessor, which, more than 800 years ago, Pope Nicholas II. ordained to be the place of enthronement for the monarchs of England, whose walls are hallowed by monuments to all whom England holds great—kings, statesmen, heroes, philanthropists and poets—the Queen, surrounded by her children, her grandchildren, and her great-grandchildren, returned thanks to the Almighty for her fifty years of reign. To witness this act of homage to the Divine power there came kings, princes, and potentates, and representatives from every nation in the world. Never in the history of England has so proud a sight been seen. There were Peers of the Realm, the Commons, High Officers of State; India furnished her princes, Canada and Australia and all the Colonies sent men who have sustained the dignity of the Crown in these distant lands. But hark! the benediction is pronounced, the choir sends up the final song of praise and triumph, its echoes die away in the groined roof of the Abbey; the great portals open, the brilliant procession files down the nave, issues forth, and wends its way back to the Palace. At this moment the lonely splendor of the crown vanishes. The reward of fifty years of beneficent reign has come. As the Queen passes the crown shines out in all its glory, but no longer alone, for it is illumined by the upturned faces of thousands and tens of thousands and millions of her grateful people, as they shout with one heart and one voice, "Long live the Queen."

Jubilee Choral Concert.

Dr. Mackenzie's "Ode," set to music by Mr. Bennett, was given at the Crystal Palace on the 24th of June, by 3,500 performers and celebrated soloists, before an immense audience, Madame Albani, an artiste of whom Canada may well feel proud, being the principal soprano singer, and was triumphantly successful. The "Ode" opens with a full chorus:

"For fifty years our Queen, Victoria, hail!"
  Wild clanging bells and thund'rous cannon
    Shook the air and made it quiver
  From Dee to Tamar, Thames to Shannon.

O Queen, the people of thine homelands greet thee,
  One in impulse, one in heart,
    Hushed are all discordant wranglings,
    Foemen stern now cease their janglings.
  Sword and shield are laid apart!
O Queen, in harmony thy lieges meet thee!

      Sons of the Dominion
        See, they lead the way!
      From where Atlantic surges,
        Pacific wavelets, play,
      From storied town and riverside,
        From mountain and from plain.
      An ancient throne their rallying-point,
        "God save the Queen!" their strain.

      Come now from Austral lands,
        Up from the under-world:
      Firm hearts and willing hands,
        Wide is their flag unfurled!
      Hark, their stentorian cheer,
        Heard once in deadly fight,
      Once when for cause held dear
      Brave souls that knew no fear
        Struck home for Britain's might.

      And India's dusky sons pass on
        In glittering array,
      The last and greatest tribute laid
        Before the throne this day.

  More than crown of monarch precious
  That which now thy people give thee.
  Flower-entwined, made of blossoms
  Gather'd in the beauteous garden
  Where forever bloom scent-laden
  Words and deeds of purest nature.
  Loving daughter, wife devoted,
  Tender parent, friend so faithful,

Ever with the stricken grieving,
Ever with the glad rejoicing,
Lo, on this great day we crown thee,
Queen of all our hearts, Victoria !

Lord of life and light and glory,
God of our world-empire's story,
Low we bow before Thy throne,
Praise is Thine, and Thine alone.
King of kings, protect this nation,
Lord of lords, be our salvation
 In the stress of trouble's day,
O Most High, on Thee relying,
Now and ever ill defying,
 We securely rest for aye !

Now in one heartfelt bond of love
For her who wields our Empire's power,
Now on this day of Jubilee.
Now in this glad and solemn hour
Let the prayerful anthem rise
High and higher to the skies.

As a climax, the author's new verse, which was added to the National Anthem, was given with all the force of choir, organ, orchestra, and the distant booming of cannon, which were fired by electricity from the conductor's desk.

The composer succeeded in infusing local coloring into each section represented in his composition. The arrival of the Canadians is indicated by the imitation of sleigh bells, and so with the other divisions of the Colonies, the music being adapted to each. The new verse added to the National Anthem is as follows:

For her we thank Thee, Lord,
And now, in glad accord,
 Thy goodness praise.
Strong thy defence and sure,
Keep her from harm secure,
So may thy love endure
 Through all her days.

www.ingramcontent.com/pod-product-compliance
Lightning Source LLC
Chambersburg PA
CBHW021233300426
44111CB00007B/532